Taboo Memories, Diasporic Voices

NEXT WAVE

New Directions in Women's Studies

A series edited by Inderpal Grewal, Caren Kaplan,

and Robyn Wiegman

Ella Shohat

TABOO MEMORIES, DIASPORIC VOICES

Duke University Press   Durham and London 2006

© 2006 Ella Shohat
Printed in the United States of America on acid-free paper ∞
Designed by C.H. Westmoreland
Typeset in Scala with Univers display by Keystone Typesetters, Inc.
Library of Congress Cataloging-in-Publication Data
appear on the last printed page of this book.
Title page art: "Land Mark (Foot Prints)," 2001–2002, from a series of
twenty-four color photographs by Jennifer Allora and Guillermo Calzadilla
*Acknowledgments for previously printed material and credits for
illustrations appear at the end of this book.*

para Robert, 'yuni

CONTENTS

ILLUSTRATIONS

PREFACE

It was sometime around the end of the last century that Ken Wissoker of Duke University Press approached me about doing a collection of my essays. Apart from the usual dilemmas about exactly which essays to "house" in this textual exhibition, it initially seemed a rather easy task to collate some pieces, known and not so known, from the 1980s and 1990s. While flipping through the wrinkled pages, however, I had a queasy feeling that displaying only "oldies" would constitute a kind of textual tomb, evoking for me the *geniza*—the Judaic storage or burial of paper bearing the scriptural traces of the name of the Divine. The whole process virtually begged for an ironic reflection on the academic correlatives of temples and disciples and sacred texts, and on the institutions that enshrine those texts. As a not-so-dead author, I sought to spare the reader, as far as possible, from participating in a quasi-necrophilic pilgrimage. The inclusion of more recent work, I believed, would facilitate a more vital back and forth shuttling between past and present.

Rather than speak to a frozen textual moment, then, *Taboo Memories,*

Diasporic Voices hopefully nourishes a fluid understanding of the "new" as always already a form of rewriting. The essays here are not gathered for purposes of archeological recovery; nor do they necessarily recapitulate my intellectual trajectory. They do, however, represent salient trends in my work. The act of selecting some essays became inevitably coupled with the casting out of other essays, some of which have enjoyed a symbolic afterlife in the form of the vociferous debates that they inspired, which can be read elsewhere.

Rather than aim for strict thematic coherence, the selection process was guided by the desire to give expression to a wide variety of theoretical concerns probed over a two-decade period. Some of the essays explicitly foreground postcolonial, diasporic, transnational, and feminist issues, while others embed those issues only as a quiet, subtextual presence. A minor theme within one essay, such as the racialized gendering of Cleopatra analyzed in "Gender and the Culture of Empire," may become a major theme in another essay—for example, in the allegorical reading of the heated contemporary debates about Cleopatra's origins, appearance, and belonging in "Disorienting Cleopatra: A Modern Trope of Identity." The reader of this collection will also encounter some perhaps surprising inclusions, such as " 'Lasers for Ladies': Endo Discourse and the Inscriptions of Science," which dissects both the medical gaze in particular and scientific discourses in general, issues pursued earlier in an essay not included here ("Imaging Terra Incognita: The Disciplinary Gaze of Empire," *Public Culture*, 3:2 [spring 1991]). Yet even these "unorthodox" texts fit into some of my larger concerns—in this case, with the ways in which visual culture shapes the (re)production of knowledge.

The book does not develop one single-minded "argument." Rather, the essays work out related concerns dispersed over various fields. Although on one level the essays stand alone, on another they orchestrate leitmotifs heard over and across the texts, creating a recombinant musical echo effect whereby the same themes emerge in very diverse contexts. Thus, the tropes of the "Promised Land" and "virgin land" are discussed in the essays concerning both Zionist discourse about Palestine and the Conquest imaginary about the Americas. The book reveals many other crossovers and echoes, however, at times popping up in apparently unlikely textual situations. The issue of anti-Semitism comes up not only in the obvious places, such as in the essays on Zionist discourse and Jewish historiography, but also in the essay on anticolonial writings, namely on Frantz Fanon. The debates over syncretism and hybridity surface not only in the quite predictable setting of the theorization of the "postcolonial" but also in relation to the question of Palestine and Arab-Jew, or in relation to the racial and cultural allegories triggered by the figure of Cleopatra, and epitomized by the archeological desire for a "pure" Mediterranean world. The issue of colonial power surfaces not only in the sound context of "Post-Third Worldist Culture," but also in the more improbable spot concerning the theory of cross-media translation ("The Cinema after Babel: Language, Difference, Power"). *Taboo Memories, Diasporic Voices* tries to place variegated theories into productive dialogue. The first essay, "Gendered Cartographies of Knowledge: Area Studies, Ethnic Studies, and Postcolonial Studies," provides a methodological overview that opens onto the various fields of inquiry developed in the subsequent essays. Calculatedly "undisciplined," the book generally betrays an unruliness toward disciplinary constraints. It engages such diverse fields as literary, media, and cultural theory; along with philosophy, historiography, sociology, anthropology, geography, archeology, and, to an extent, medicine and biology. The writing thus inhabits a kind of twilight zone, or no-(wo)man's-land, at the shifting frontiers of the diverse disciplines, where the reader may glimpse concepts that permeate a wide range of theories.

My work has always been preoccupied with speaking across usually segregated grids such as historical materialism, textual psychoanalysis, semiological narratology, and deconstructive poststructuralism. At the same time, the essays manifest a certain discomfort with all of these methodological tools, especially when exploring the elusive intersectionalities of social stratifications. Thus, I deploy these grids, but I also depart from them, in order to flesh out the critical perspectives associated with what has variously been called "postcolonial," "multicultural," and "transnational" feminism. These interwoven grids furnish a prism through which to view such issues as the narrating of geographies, the allegorization of ancient worlds, the ordering of historical memory, the imaging of imperial reason, the projection of utopias and distopias, the writing of the revolutionary nation, the poetics of diasporic displacement, and the mapping and remapping of knowledge. Some of the essays contain a metadiscursive dimension in that they probe the theoretical axioms and historical narratives implied by a given terminology—for example, in relation to the "postcolonial" ("Notes on the 'Post-Colonial'"), to "post-Zionism" ("The 'Postcolonial' in Translation"), and to the unstable naming of a place ("Taboo Memories, Diasporic Visions") or of a community ("Rupture and Return").

A number of the essays, notably "Gendered Cartographies of Knowledge: Area Studies, Ethnic Studies, and Postcolonial Studies," "Gender and the Culture of Empire," "Disorienting Cleopatra," "Post-Fanon and the Colonial," and "Post-Third Worldist Culture" tie together feminist analysis and the critique of colonialism and racism. Transcending the limited space allotted to culture in traditional base-superstructure Marxist analysis—where it is often regarded as but a mere epiphenomenal echo of the economic realm—my work has stressed a more fluid understanding of mutually imbricated and coterminous forces. Within this more diffuse notion of the politics of culture, I studied the construction of gender and race alongside the production of sexual and national identities as shaping, and as shaped by, diverse representational practices.

I was interested, more specifically, in critiquing at the same time (hetero)masculinist anticolonialist discourse from a gendered perspective and certain brands of feminism from an anticolonial perspective, advancing a feminist-analysis alert to heterogeneity and difference and attuned to historical and geographical positionality. Dominant feminist theory at that time tended to erase the question of national and racial affiliations, inadvertently endowing particular sexual identities with discursive universality. In contrast with single-axis feminist theory, the essays here pressure the question of gender relations without bypassing the contradictions arising from the unequal power configurations inherent in colonialism and neocolonialism, as well as in globalization and transnational capitalism. At the same time, I tried to show that Third Worldist thought often erased questions of gender and sexuality. Nationalist discourse elided the fact that colonialism subjugated men in ways different from women, resulting in the gendering of imperial as well as anti-imperial representations, seen in the "Algeria Unveiled" trope, in the homoeroticism of travel narratives, and in the rewriting of interracial desire. In sum, my work is situated along the seam lines of theoretical frameworks. While pursuing the tensions between feminist thought and anticolonial critique, the texts included here also simultaneously conjure up the possibilities of their cross-fertilization.

This book is written, above all, under the sign of the plural. Wandering through diverse spaces and times, it visits ancient Egypt, Greece, and Rome, the Bible and the Qur'an, the Reconquista and the Conquista, and old and new worlds, along with diverse terras incognitas, dark continents, harems, jungles, deserts, lost tribes, and promised lands. The essays look at how the past is translated and reinvented in function of diverse presents. Within a multichronotopic approach, this work also connects usually ghettoized geographies and histories, moving between the Americas and the Middle East, Africa and Europe. Some of the essays explore the cross-cultural translation of concepts and debates—for example, those concerning Eurocentrism and racism or feminism and post-nationalism. The essays "Gendered Cartographies of Knowledge" and "Post-Third Worldist Culture," for example, partly contest the narrating of the beginnings of "feminism," recontextualizing and reinvisioning gender-based resistance across multiple terrains. I try to shift the discussion of gender and sexuality, in other words, to take multiple histories and positionalities into account. (I further elaborated on the topic in the introduction to my *Talking Visions: Multicultural Feminism in a Transnational Age* [Cambridge, Mass.: MIT Press, 1998]).

The essay "The 'Postcolonial' in Translation: Reading Edward Said between English and Hebrew," meanwhile, focuses on the "travel" of the debates about Orientalism, postcolonialism, and post-Zionism between one institutional zone and political semantics and another, and specifically between the United States and Israel. Through a comparative historical counterpointing of these debates, I consider some key moments in the translation (in both literal and metaphorical senses) of Said's ideas into Hebrew. The essay engages the contradictory reception of Said's work, especially in left-liberal circles, where an eagerness to "go beyond" Said results in some ironic historical twists and boomerang effects. The issues examined include the nature of the "post" in the concepts of the "postcolonial" and "post-Zionism"; the problem of "hybridity" and "resistance" in the land of partitions and walls; and the mediation in Israel, via the Anglo-American academy, of the "subaltern" intellectual.

The tense Israel/Palestine debates are central not only to the Said essay but also to a number of other essays. Both "Taboo Memories, Diasporic Visions" and "Rupture and Return" treat the subject of Zionism and Palestine in conjunction with the issue of Arab-Jews, a subject first explored in my 1986 doctoral dissertation, "Israeli Cinema: East/West and the Politics of Representation," subsequently published by the University of Texas Press (1989). The essays included here elaborate and reconfigure formulations from essays published elsewhere—notably, "Master Narrative/Counter Readings" (in *Resisting Images: Essays on Cinema and History*, ed. by Robert Sklar and Charles Musser [Philadelphia: Temple University Press, 1990]), "Anomalies of the National" (in *Wide Angle*, 11:3 [July 1989]), and "Sephardim in Israel: Zionism from the Standpoint of Its Jewish Victims" (*Social Text*, 19/20 [fall 1988]). The last essay's title, a variation on

Said's well-known "Zionism from the Standpoint of Its Victims" (both essays were originally published in the journal *Social Text*) made the claim, at that time considered highly controversial, that Zionism, and the Jewish State, also had *Jewish* victims.

Although some metahistorians have argued that all nations are "invented," some nations, I would suggest, are more invented than others. Zionist historiography attempted mightily to normalize its very particular process of national invention. Since the early 1980s, I have been looking at Zionism not only in its actual historical unfolding but also through the prism of Zionism as a "master narrative" and a "discourse," one characterized by a simultaneously binarist and ambivalent projection of both "East" and "West." The essays scrutinize Zionism not only in its aspect as a national liberation movement but also as an ideology deeply embedded in (but not reducible to) a colonial matrix. Deconstructing Zionist and post-Zionist narratives of a homogeneous Jewish nation, the essays partially delve into the taboo-ridden issue of the intimate relationship between the question of Arab-Jews and the question of Palestine. Israeli national identity has too often been imagined as strictly European, in line with the Zionist idea of Israel as a Western outpost, pitting civilization against savagery and terror.

Reflecting on the polysemic concept of "return," my work investigates the close links between Zionist discourse and the production of scholarly knowledge about Israel/Palestine. An isolationist and compartmentalized approach to Jewish History, I argue, was the discursive byproduct of an anomalous project in which the state created the nation, not simply in the metaphorical sense of fabrication, but also in the literal sense of engineering the transplant of populations. My own biography, involving my family's hasty departure from Iraq via Cyprus to Israel, and then to the United States, is necessarily interwoven with this larger story of colonial partition, displacement, and multiple affiliations.

The title *Taboo Memories, Diasporic Voices* points to the book's dialectical movement between past and future, as well as between history and its rewriting. Many of the essays here deal with modes of representing collective memory—for example, in biblical and Qur'anic texts—and with the ways in which history is reshaped and reinvented through institutional discourse, scientific research, cultural practices, and the media and political activism. On the battlefield of history, rival chroniclers fight it out as diverse "narrators" claim copyrighted ownership over historical pain, or over the right to own, manufacture, and activate history. Memories that endanger the hegemonic narrative are forbidden, expelled, proscribed. Their marking as "taboo" ends up being internalized, even if only unconsciously, by the scarred bodies and souls who might have desired to tell history in a different way, from an alternative angle or perspective.

The word "taboo" in my title is meant to be multiply evocative. The taboo at times is literal, as in my discussion of the Second Commandment, the biblical proscription of "graven images" and the metaphorical prohibition on translating representation from one medium to another, in the essay "Sacred Word, Profane Image." The taboo is alluded to in my discussion of Fanon's revisionist psychiatry in "Post-Fanon and the Colonial," contrasted with Freud's approach in "Totem and Taboo." Some of the essays, moreover, transgressed a number of then (still?) regnant taboos: the taboo on critiquing Zionism, the taboo on the hyphen in the designation "Arab-Jew"; the taboo on bringing the colonial to bear on feminism, or gender and sexuality to bear on race and nation. More generally, the essays subvert taboos endemic to the canonical versions of disciplinary knowledge and to the single-ethnicity, single-nation, single-religion, or single-issue analytical framework. Passing through highly policed conceptual checkpoints, the essays in this collection strive to denaturalize doxa rooted in Eurocentric and phallocentric epistemologies, while also traversing the hierarchical ordering of disciplines and knowledge. (Some of these bad epistemic habits were unpacked more fully in *Unthinking Eurocentrism*, coauthored with Robert Stam [London: Routledge, 1994].)

Since my work has also touched on what later came to be called "visual culture," the reader may notice a recurrent effort to focus the readerly gaze on alternative forms of "texts." The visual field here includes not only films but also scientific illustrations, medical imagery, popular cartoons, documentary photographs, archival documents, postcards, maps, and posters—all used not merely for illustrative purposes but also as part of a larger argument concerning the discursive and ideological structuring of the visual. Thus, the set of essays that includes "The Cinema after Babel: Language, Difference, Power" (co-authored with Robert Stam) and "Sacred Word, Profane Image: Theologies of Adaptation" treat issues of visual culture and, more specifically, the theologically and philosophically fraught interface of word and image, the textual and the visual.

The primordial role of the visual is germane to my argument that science and popular culture have played a vital role in shaping historical, geographical, political, and cultural identities and identifications. As a product of science, the camera, for example, acquired an ethnographic aura, actively producing knowledge about non-European spaces. Providing anthropologists with testimonial evidence that legitimated their own professional mission, these silent images speak volumes about representation as violation. At the same time, these images supply the contemporary reader with a document of the culture of doumentation itself. I was especially keen to explore what happens when we reverse the conventional point of view to examine the gaze of the scientist, making it the object of critical analysis. The essays are less interested in the representation of exotic others than in the process of otherizing and exoticizing itself—interested, that is, in the production of alterity through discursive action and performance. Throughout, the essays address various enactments of the return of the gaze.

Although some of the essays in the volume—notably, "Sacred Word, Profane Image" and "Disorienting Cleopatra"—were published only recently, they were written intermittently over a long period and slowly elaborated as lectures over the years. The essay "Post-Fanon and the Colonial: A Situational Diagnosis," meanwhile, appears here for the first time. While my work has dialogued with Frantz Fanon since the early 1980s, this specific article was written over many years, based on a series of lectures given in diverse venues. Although devoted to the work of single intellectuals, both the essay on Fanon and the essay on Said hopefully avoid an author-centered approach, opting instead for a contextual, intertextual, and transdiscursive analysis. The most recent published essay, meanwhile, "The 'Postcolonial' in Translation: Reading Edward Said between English and Hebrew," was written at the invitation of the *Journal of Palestine Studies* for a special issue dedicated to Said's memory in the wake of his passing. The essay prolongs a few of the concerns initiated in one of my earlier essay about Said ("Antinomies of Exile: Said at the Frontiers of National Narrations" [Cambridge: Blackwell, 1993]),which is not included here but is available in the first Said "reader," edited by Michael Sprinker.

In most instances, the selected essays featured here appear basically as originally published. Some essays were supplemented with material that had originally been removed due to space limitations, while in other pieces paragraphs were eliminated to avoid overlap in this volume. Yet some slight overlapping between a few pieces published in disparate contexts is unavoidable, and at times the reader may encounter the same theme or argument repeated in several essays, although almost always in slightly altered form. It was virtually impossible to cleanse the essays of all repetition without sabotaging the train of thought particular to the individual essays. It also seems to me that such an imperfect aesthetics carries the traces of multiple temporal layers, allowing a kind of "present perfect" reading. My wish is that this book will be valuable both in providing a glimpse into some of the passionate debates around the politics of culture over the past three decades and, just as important, in vitally nourishing and feeding into current intellectual engagements.

Finally, I am grateful to Ken Wissoker for suggesting the idea of the book and for patiently waiting through the aforementioned century. I am also grateful to Caren Kaplan, Inderpal Grewal, and Robyn Wiegman for their unfailing support and for proposing to include this book in the Next Wave book series. At New York University, I am grateful to Dean Mary Schmidt-Campbell of New York University's Tisch School of the Arts and to Randy Martin at the Department of Art and Public Policy, as well as to my Middle Eastern and Islamic studies chairs, Michael Gilsenan and Zachary Lockman. Michele Zamora, Shaista Husain, Anjali Kamat, Leili Kashani, and Karim Tartoussieh offered invaluable help at different points. I am also indebted to Evelyn Alsultany, Ori Kleiner, Yvette Raby, Ivone Margulies, and especially to Yigal Nizri, who also suggested the cover image; and many thanks to Jennifer Allora and Guillermo Calzadilla for generously allowing me to use their Land Mark (Foot Prints) artwork. I am immensely appreciative of Richard Porton and, as always, of Robert Stam for close reading of the manuscript. My thanks to the Rockefeller Foundation for offering me residency at the Bellagio Center in Italy, where I worked on some of the essays included in this book. My final words are dedicated to my late friends George Custen and Dafne Depollo, as well as to Edward Said, whose solidarity and friendship over the past two decades I enormously miss.

GENDERED
CARTOGRAPHIES OF KNOWLEDGE

Area Studies, Ethnic Studies, and Postcolonial Studies

When gender is invoked outside of "Western" spaces, it is often subjected in the academy to a (inter)disciplinary order that anxiously and politely sends it "back" to the kingdom of area studies. There the designated savants of the day, it is assumed, will enlighten us about the plight of women; each outlandish geographical zone will be matched with an abused bodily part (bound feet, veiled faces, and excised clitorises). A doubly exclusionary logic (that which applies to women and to their geography) will quickly allot a discursive space for women as well as for gays/lesbians/bi/transgender from the diverse regions of the world. Even within multicultural feminist and queer cartographies of knowledge, the diverse regions are often presumed to exist in isolation from the "center" and from each other. Such approaches, I am afraid, have become a malady in women's studies programs, even those that have taken an important step toward multiculturalizing the curriculum.

Here I want to reflect on a relational understanding of feminism that assumes a provisional and conjunctural definition of feminism as a polysemic site of contradictory positionalities. Any dialogue about such fictive unities called "Middle Eastern women," or "Latin American gays/lesbians," for example—especially dialogues taking place within transnational frameworks—has to begin from the premise that genders, sexualities, races, classes, nations, and even continents exist not as hermetically sealed entities but, rather, as part of a permeable interwoven relationality. The interlinking of critical maps of knowledge is fundamental in a transnational age typified by the global "travel" of images, sounds, goods, and populations. A relational feminist project has therefore to analyze this new moment that requires rethinking identity designations, intellectual grids, and disciplinary boundaries. I believe we need to reflect on the relationships between the diverse interdisciplinary knowledges constituting multicultural/transnational feminist and queer inquiry: gender and sexuality studies, ethnic and race studies, area and postcolonial studies. Given that there is no single feminism, the question is: How do we orchestrate these conflictual perspectives in order to rearticulate the feminist terrains of struggle within this densely woven web?

In many institutions, multicultural feminists have faced criticism from feminist colleagues who perceive multiculturalism as somehow "bad for women."[1] Multiculturalism, in this view, is at best irrelevant and at worst divisive for the feminist cause. And while multicultural and transnational approaches are applauded, the production of knowledge still takes the form of an additive approach. In contrast, I hope to unpack the idea of the "Middle East" or "Latin America" as unified categories of analysis. The challenge, I think, is precisely to avoid a facile additive operation of merely piling up increasingly differentiated groups of women, men, or transgenders from different regions and ethnicities—all of whom are projected as presumably forming coherent, yet easily demarcated entities. The notion of a relational feminism, in contrast, goes beyond a mere description of the many cultures from which feminisms emerge; it transcends an additive approach that simply has women of the globe neatly neighbored and stocked, paraded in a United Nations–style "Family of Nations" pageant where each ethnically marked feminist speaks in her turn, dressed in national costume. To map resistant histories of gender and sexuality, we must place them in dialogical relation within, between, and among cultures, ethnicities, and nations

There is also a tendency in critical discourse to pit a rotating chain of marginalized communities against an unstated "white" or "Western" norm. This discourse assumes a neat binarism of black versus white and

Chicana versus Anglo or East versus West and North versus South—a binarism that ironically repositions whiteness and Westernness as normative. This conceptual binarism—as in black versus white or Eastern versus Western—puts on hold everyone else who does not fit in either category, sitting and awaiting their turn to speak. This "on hold" analytical method ends up producing gaps and silences. The relationships among the diverse "others" remain obscure. The challenge, therefore, is to produce knowledge within a kaleidoscopic framework of communities in relation without ever suggesting that all the positionings are identical. It is for this reason I dispute the clear and neat categorization of spaces allocated to each specific region. My work is more concerned with investigating multichronotopic links in the hope of creating an intellectual dialogue that bypasses the institutional scenario of (American) feminist/queer studies versus area studies. In the first, the logic and discourse of postmodernity is often invoked; in the second, that of modernization and development.

Ethnic studies tends to bracket areas outside the American experience. Highlighting national experiences within the British Commonwealth, postcolonial studies, meanwhile, often overlooks race in the United States. The diverse area studies, for their part, discount their connections to both postcolonial and ethnic studies, as well as the bonds between the various areas. Women's, gender, and sexuality curricula, meanwhile, often reproduce these same divisions. The single subject of women/gender/sexuality is apportioned out so that the West forms the norm, while the "rest" is relegated to the "backyards" of area studies and ethnic studies.[2] In sum, "single ethnicity," "single nation," and "single region" institutional thinking risks impeding critical feminist and queer scholars, political organizers, and cultural programmers who wish to collaborate in ways that go beyond a confining nation-state and regional-geographic imaginary.

Well-meaning curricula and cultural programs, meanwhile, applaud multiculturalism as the sum of the contributions of diverse ethnicities and races to the "development of the American Nation"—a formulation that incorporates a covert U.S. nationalist teleology. Women and gays and lesbians of color, meanwhile, have only intermittently critiqued the aporias of nationalist thinking in a transnational world. Race and sexuality within multiculturalism, feminism, and queer discourse tend to be framed as self-containedly American, oblivious not only to this country's colonizing history but also to its global presence. A corollary to this is the negative exceptionalism detectable in some work on American racism, which conveys a sense of the uniquely awful oppressiveness of the United States.

Ethnic nationalisms offer a negative variation on the conservatives' "melting pot" exceptionalism, emphasizing instead "racist" exceptionalism, i.e., a view of the United States as uniquely racist. This position elides the racialized colonial patterns shared by various colonial-settler nations, and thus diminishes the rich possibilities of a comparative approach.

While American studies is hardly acknowledged as an area studies, the traditional area studies, by its very conception, locates its object of investigation "elsewhere." Within these mutually exclusive frameworks, little institutional space remains for 1) the co-implicatedness of the United States and other regions whether politically or culturally; 2) diasporas living in between these worlds. American Women's studies programs tend to replicate these ghettoizations: Required courses focus on "pure" issues of gender and sexuality, while optional, "special topics" courses sweep through "women of color" and "Third World women." Within this approach, U.S. women of color are studied as sui generis, an entity unto themselves, while Third World women are seen as if living on another planet, in another time. Les/bi/gays in Africa, Asia, or Latin America tend to be further elided under the heterosexual frameworks of development studies, as well as under the binarist norms of heterosexuality. Multicultural courses focusing on women of color, meanwhile, tend to sever them from their colonial history, including that of the regions from which they came, with little interest in their multilayered postcolonial displacements. And when area studies begrudgingly makes room for women (not to speak of sexual minorities) of the geography in question, those groups too are severed from the cross-regional interconnectedness of histories and cultures.

American-based postcolonial theory, meanwhile, seldom dialogues with its U.S. context of production and reception. The innumerable postcolonial MLA papers elaborating abstract notions of "difference" and "alterity" rarely put these concepts into dialogue with "local" subalternities. The institutional embrace of a few Third World "postcolonials," largely by English and comparative literature departments, is partially a response to the U.S. civil rights and affirmative action struggles, yet the enthusiastic consumption of the theoretical aura of the "postcolonial" threatens to eclipse the less prestigious "ethnic studies" field.[3] Just as it is important to address the American national framework of "ethnic studies"—and specifically its impact on gender and sexuality studies—it is also urgent to address the tendency of postcolonial studies to ignore U.S. racial politics. Needless to say, the embrace of postcolonial theory and study is welcome, indeed overdue, but we also have to assess its institutional impact and politics of reception.

Given the token space granted critical work in general, institutional hierarchies end up generating a fighting-for-crumbs syndrome. Institutions tend to see people of color paradigmatically, as a series of substitutable others, indirectly disallowing a wider constellation of historical perspectives. Thus some selected academics speakers of poststructuralist-postcolonial discourses—even at times in spite of their radical politics—are seen as less threatening to university administrations than academics who are perceived as potentially linked to angry militant U.S. communities. Fundamentally conservative institutions, in this sense, get to do the "multiculti" thing without interrogating their own connection to contemporary U.S. racial politics. This is not to cast aspersion on specific intellectuals but rather to reflect on the ways in which postcolonial intellectuals, under the sign of "diversity," might be positioned as the "good academics" (much as the media construct "good ethnics"), as opposed to those "vulgar militants," so as to re-create subtle stratifications and hierarchies, even on the margins. The point is not to minimize the racism and subtle prejudice that "postcolonials" also face, nor is it to assume that postcolonials cannot also be activists. The point, rather, is that we be lucid not only about the differences among feminists of color but also about how institutional privileging of one discourse and field of inquiry at any particular historical moment might mean the blocking of other discourses and fields of inquiry, along with the sabotaging of possible alliances between the discursive fields and the communities mediated by them.

Although the face and drift of American studies have dramatically changed over the past two decades, affirmative action remains under attack, and the presence of African Americans, Chicanos/as, Puerto Ricans, and Native Americans in the academy remains disturbingly miniscule. Cultural and academic institutions may celebrate, and even produce, multicultural "stars," and may show an interest in the conceptual spaces opened up by postcolonial hybridity, but the marginalization both of U.S. "minorities" and of the non-English speaking world endures. The critique of Orientalist discourse initiated by Edward Said generated excitement in English and comparative literature faculties, but in its more fashion-conscious versions, including in some feminist scholarship, it has often focused on Orientalist discourse about "them," while "they" remain safely locked in area studies. (Orientalism with a vengeance!) The study of the postcolonial, one sometimes suspects, is relatively privileged in the United

States precisely because of its convenient remoteness from this country's racial matters, often relegated to other historical eras and other geographies, in ways that also ignore U.S. global "implicatedness." The vibrant space opened up by "cutting edge" postcolonial theory for critical scholarship is also contested, particularly since, as we have seen, some practitioners of ethnic studies feel displaced by it. Recognizing these tensions, and going beyond them, is crucial for dismantling the institutional barriers raised between postcolonial and ethnic studies.

The diverse interdisciplinary studies, furthermore, have different histories of institutional legitimization. Ethnic studies, women's studies, and gay/lesbian studies programs came about as a result of a 1960s bottom-up struggle among "minorities" to demand scholarly representation. The diverse area studies, in contrast, were instituted top-down by the U.S. defense department in the post–World War Two era. Governmental funding and university expansion of area studies initially formed part of cold war strategic cartographies of spheres-of-influence. Although the face and drift of area studies have dramatically changed over the years and many more voices have contributed to alternative scholarship, the dialogue between area studies and ethnic studies scholars further impacts gender and sexuality studies. For one reason, covert taboos restrict which women and gays and lesbians of color can move, as subjects of inquiry, from area to ethnic studies. For example, although immigration from North Africa and the Middle East dates back to the end of the nineteenth century, and although its flow has increased since the 1960s, Middle Easterners are seen as "forever foreign"; they are only seen as "from there." For some communities of color in the United States, the status of being "of color" is uncertain. Despite a history of imperialist, racist, and sexist attitudes toward the Middle East and North Africa, for example, and despite that region's participation in Third World nationalist struggles, "people of color" status has not usually been ascribed to Middle Easterners. The Middle Eastern diaspora at this conjuncture hardly forms a field consecrated within American studies or ethnic studies, or even within area studies.

Various veiled narcissisms still play a role in such formations. Even in more critical frameworks within U.S. academe, the production of knowledge tends to engender an implicit and barely perceptible U.S. nationalism. It undergirds certain versions of First World feminism, as well as certain versions of multiculturalism as articulated by women of color and queer discourses. Universities, unfortunately, erect disciplinary and conceptual boundaries that continue to quarantine interconnected fields of inquiry.

For example, the majority of women of the world are relegated to the margins of most curricula, fenced off within the Bantustans called "area studies"—such as Middle East studies—as though their lives are not also implicated by U.S. agendas and policies, and as though there is no Middle Eastern diaspora in the United States. Although nationalism is often seen as a specifically "Third World" malady, it is no less relevant to the labor, feminist, queer, and multicultural movements within the United States. In going over a substantial number of ethnic studies/women's studies/gender studies/queer studies curricula, it was not difficult to detect a submerged American nationalism that often permeates such practices and epistemologies, giving us a star-striped nationalism with a tan, a nationalism in drag, a rainbow nationalism. The "diversity committees" of educational institutions often glimpse multiculturalism and feminist/gay/lesbian perspectives through a largely unconscious national-exceptionalist lens. And while I have no quarrel with the idea of U.S. uniqueness, I do quarrel with the idea that uniqueness is unique to the United States. Every nation-state has a palimpsestic uniqueness all its own. And along with that shared uniqueness, historical parallels and global links exist between different national formations. The implicit nationalism of many multicultural, feminist, and queer curricula and agendas leads us to miss numerous opportunities for a relational analysis and for a cross-disciplinary and transnational connection.

Only a multiperspectival approach can capture the movement of feminist ideas across borders. We must worry about a globalist feminism that disseminates its programs internationally as the universal gospel, just as we have to be concerned about a localist feminism that surrenders all dialogue in the name of an overpowering relativism. One of the challenges facing multicultural/transnational feminism has to do with the translations of theories and actions from one context to another. In an Arab Muslim context, where feminism is often denounced as a Western import, and where Arab Muslim women articulate their version of what constitutes gender struggle, what would it mean to deploy a poststructuralist perspective that would critique the notions of experience, authenticity, and essentialism? What kind of relational maps of knowledge would help illuminate the negotiation of gender and sexuality as understood in diverse contexts, but with an emphasis on the linked historical experiences and discursive networks across borders? While one does not have to subscribe to any grand Theory with a capital "T," it would be foolish to deny that theorizing is an indispensable element in the envisioning of (any) social and political change. Such a project confronts the dilemmas resulting from, on the one hand, the difficulty of embracing fully an empiricist approach to experience—a method that implies the possibility of a direct access to a pre-discursive reality—and on the other, the difficulty of subscribing fully to a poststructuralism in which experience never seems to exist outside of the discourses that mediate them. The hope, in other words, is to transcend a referential verism (for example, that writing about experiences directly reflects the real) without falling into a hermeneutic nihilism whereby all texts become nothing more than a meaningless play of signification. Experience and knowledge within a multicultural/transnational feminist project, in this sense, have to be articulated as dialogical concepts, an interlocution situated in historical time and geographical space.

Some "Third World" women and U.S. "women of color" have at times denounced Theory itself as inherently Western and as an impediment to activism. They have critiqued white, Western—or, to be more precise, Eurocentric—theories for eliding experiences of "women of color." This indispensable critique, however, should not also allow us to forget a) the importance of looking critically at activist practices and of theorizing them as part of feminist agendas; b) the awareness that every practice is undergirded by some kind of theory, philosophy, worldview, or discursive grid— even when the practitioners claim not to have a theory; c) the fact that theorizing and theories are not a Western monopoly, a view that would inscribe in reverse a colonialist vision of the "West" as theoretical mind and the "non-West" as unreflecting body; d) that "Third World" women and "women of color" have themselves contributed to theorizing not only by writing theory per se, but also through their own, multi-axis thinking and activism, which has challenged multiple hegemonic discourses. In this sense, activism itself can be seen as a form of theorizing, a practical testing of ideas. Many activists have underestimated their own historical contribution to the West's questioning of totalizing narratives.

Other writers (such as Nelly Richards, Wahneema Lubiano, Inderpal Grewal, Caren Kaplan) have suggested that postmodernism, for example, is relevant to a feminist analysis of women of color and Third World women.[4] The various post-theories (poststructuralism, postmodernism, postcolonialism) are indeed useful, albeit problematic, tools for a critical feminist project. Here one may address this question from a different angle as well. The critique offered by anticolonial Third Worldist discourses was a crucial element in generating the critique of totalizing master narratives in the first place. Both structuralist semiotics and Third

Worldism had their long-term historical origins in a series of events that undermined the confidence in European modernity: the Holocaust (and in France, the Vichy collaboration with the Nazis), the postwar disintegration of the last European empires, and the "Third World" anticolonial revolution. Although the exalted term "theory" was rarely linked to anticolonial theorizing, Third Worldist thinking had an undeniable impact on First World "theory."[5] The structuralists codified, on some levels, arguments made by anticolonial thinkers. The critical work of "denaturalization" performed by what one might call the left wing of semiotics—for example Roland Barthes's dissection of the colonialist implications of a *Paris-Match* cover showing a black soldier saluting the French flag[6]—cannot be detached from the Third Worldist critique of European master narratives performed by such Francophone anticolonial writers as Aimé Césaire and Frantz Fanon.[7] Claude Lévi-Strauss's crucial turn from biological to linguistic models for a new anthropology was, to some extent, motivated by his visceral aversion to a biological anthropology deeply tainted by anti-Semitic and colonialist racism. Indeed, it was in the context of decolonization that the United Nations Educational, Scientific, and Cultural Organization (UNESCO) asked Lévi-Strauss to do the research that culminated in his *Race and History*, where the French anthropologist rejected any essentialist hierarchy of civilizations.[8]

The crisis of modernity is inseparable from Europe's loss of its privileged position as the model for the world. The discursive withdrawal from projecting Europe as a spokesperson on behalf of the Universal came into existence through and in relation to the critique of European humanism, explicitly addressed by Frantz Fanon in *The Wretched of the Earth*. The shared attempt by the feminist and the anticolonial movements to transform the "Other" from the object into the subject of history has to be understood in this historical conjuncture. It is hardly a coincidence that Simone de Beauvoir, in *The Second Sex*, charts the "The Birth of the Free Woman" in tropes redolent of the black struggle in the United States and anticolonial struggle in the "Third World."[9] Indeed, blacks and women in the United States, as numerous African-American feminists have suggested, began an uneasy yet fruitful dialogue about their parallel and intersecting battles for political representation over a century ago. What is at stake, however, is the nondialogical and unilateral historiography that narrates the emergence of feminism as a linear march from premodernity to modernity and postmodernity. As with the Eurocentrism that sees Europe as the unique source of meaning, as ontological "reality" to the rest of the world's shadow, monocultural feminism simply traces its formation back to a Western modernity unaffected by contemporaneous antiracist and anticolonial struggles. This narrative simplistically suggests that postmodernism—alone and unaided by any critical thought "outside" the imaginary space of the West—has opened up a space for diverse "others." The implied openness of this narrative, paradoxically, reveals its own closedness. While it is a commonplace in feminist studies to link modernity to the rise of feminism, it could be argued that the crisis of modernity in the wake of anticolonial and antiracist interrogation has also reshaped feminism itself, so that it has begun to shed the white man's and the white woman's burden of Enlightenment and its concomitant narrative of progress.

Feminist and queer thought often gets caught up in the tension between essentialist and antiessentialist discourses. While poststructuralist feminist, queer, and postcolonial theories reject essentialist articulations of identity, as well as biologistic and transhistorical determinations of gender, race, and sexual identity, a desire for political agency generates support for "affirmative action," implicitly premised on the very categories elsewhere rejected as essentialist, leading to a paradoxical situation in which theory deconstructs totalizing myths while activism nourishes them. Yet, essentialist discourse sometimes preempts analysis of power relations. One of the challenges for multicultural/transnational feminism, then, is to articulate its project in relation to gender essentialism, on the one hand, and cultural essentialism, on the other. Contrary to the "multiculturalism-is-bad-for-women" argument, the mediation of sexuality across cultural divides does not necessarily entail an endorsement of relativism.

The concept of *relationality* should not be confused with cultural *relativism*. Although the term *relationality* derives from structural linguistics, I use it here in a translinguistic sense. The translation of feminism across borders has to be situated historically as a set of contested practices, mediated by conflictual discourses, which themselves have repercussions and reverberations in the world. A cultural relativist approach would have the unfortunate effect of obliging the critic to regard cliterodectomy, for example, as simply representing a different cultural norm and therefore as a legitimate practice. (The echo of this argument within the U.S. legal system is the "cultural defense" of a variety of gender-based abuses such as wife battering within an immigrant community.) At the same time, it is necessary to steer clear of a universalist feminism premised on a Eurocentric discourse of modernity versus premodernity or developed versus underdeveloped—concepts grounded in a Promethean civilizing mission.

To articulate a complex critique of such practices as cliterodectomy, therefore, we would have to try to achieve the following: dissect the global media's tendency to fetishistically focus on rituals involving sexual organs and expose them as ambivalent sites of voyeuristic pleasure; avoid Eurocentric framing narratives that would transform a conjunctural praxis into cultural, national, or regional essences, whereby cliterodectomy, for example, comes to denote the very kernel of Egyptian, African, or Muslim culture; relate such oppressive practices to other practices of body mutilation and gendered pathologies in the "West," thereby avoiding the ascription of the cultural superiority to the "West" implicit in the double whammy of downplaying Western abuses while amplifying the abuses of others; dispute any idea of cultural traditions as coherent, static, and uninterrupted; compare the discourses about such practices associated with "tradition" with the technologically based practices—such as cosmetic surgery—associated with modernity and postmodernity; examine the active complicity of women in performing such oppressive practices rather than see them as passive victims of patriarchy; highlight the ways the practice is contested within the community itself, instead of producing the misleading image of a homogeneous group; interrogate Eurocentric versions of feminism that envision the elimination of such practices as entailing (even if only subliminally) a total cultural assimilation to the West; study the history of the practice in relation to the voices of dissent rather than manufacture narcissistic rescue narratives toward otherized cultures; examine such practices in the context of destructive globalization policies and International Monetary Fund–generated poverty whereby women's bodies become the symbolic site of "preserving tradition" (an issue often showcased by fundamentalist religious organizations but repressed by the state apparatus and transnational institutions); analyze critically the transnational asymmetries inherent in legislation around gender, immigration, and human rights in which support for gender- or sexuality-based asylum often recycles old colonial tropes of dark women or gay men trapped in brutal retrograde societies.

A relational analysis would thus have to address the operative terms and axes of stratification typical of specific contexts, along with the ways these terms and stratifications are translated and reinvoiced as they "travel" from one context to another. (For example, historically, the question of race is hardly central in the Middle East and North Africa, where one of the key concerns is religion.) Multicultural/transnational feminism in this sense is neither a universalist project nor a relativist project. The universalizing

Enlightenment discourse, the object of much postmodern critique, is a form of philosophical dogmatism; it excludes dialogue by making it impossible. Cultural relativism, meanwhile, also excludes dialogue by making it pointless, since within "I'm OK, you're OK" logic everything seems legitimate and therefore not debatable.

Eurocentric feminism sometimes has challenged gender-based essentialism while simultaneously inscribing notions of cultural essentialism. Third Worldist feminism, meanwhile, has emphasized cultural difference, and yet in some versions became associated with the idea of "Eastern" or African superiority over "Western" culture, virtually inverting Eurocentric hierarchical discourses. Arguments asserting cultural differences among women, in this sense, interrogate colonialist ideologies about difference, especially the superiority of Western culture but again do not necessarily interrogate the notion of cultural essence altogether. By tying together multiculturalism and feminism within a transnational frame, I hope to avoid replicating essentialist discourses about cultural differences among women. Therefore, the question of difference among women is not raised in order to suggest a fixed culturalist schism between Western and "Third World" women but, rather, to look at different positioning vis-à-vis histories of power, especially since the advent of colonialism. It is not a question of difference for the sake of difference but, rather of dialogical encounters of differences. My argument is not that "we're all different," a truism that forms the basis for cultural-relativist arguments, but rather that multicultural feminism is a situated practice within coimplicated and constitutively related histories and communities open to mutual illumination.

One can examine this question of mutual illumination in relation to feminist historiography. In this genre of writing, "Third World" women's involvement has often been deemed irrelevant for feminism. But I would propose to reread the history of "Third World" women, especially within anticolonial struggles, as a kind of subterranean, unrecognized form of feminism and as a legitimate part of feminist historiography, whether or not the activists themselves labeled their activities as feminist. The multicultural feminist project must disinter stories of survival from the rubble of the master narrative of progress. Historically, colonized women had been deeply involved in anticolonialist and antiracist movements, long before their dialogue with the "women's movement." It was their activism that often led to their political engagement in feminism. This type of antipatriarchal and even, at times, anti-heterosexist work within anti-colonial and antiracist struggles will remain marginal to the feminist canon as long as only one feminism retains the power of naming and narrativizing. The debate about what constitutes a legitimate feminist epistemology has long had to do with the privileging of single-issue feminism over a multi-axis analysis. Making visible these discrepant feminist histories is crucial for rearticulating what constitutes legitimate spaces, moments, and subject of feminist studies.

It seems imperative to make conceptual links between issues of gender and sexuality in the context of colonialism, imperialism, and Third World nationalism, on the one hand, and issues of race and ethnicity and multiculturalism, on the other. Many literary studies of culture and empire privilege the nineteenth century and twentieth century, but one could trace colonial discourses back to 1492, linking representations of "tradition" and globalization with contemporary discourses about, for example, modernity and postmodernity. The Columbus story, for example, allows us to trace Orientalism far back to the Reconquista in Spain—the expulsion of Jews and Muslims in 1492—and the Conquista of America in the same year. The historical discursive links between the Americas and the Orient thus predate the formation of contemporary geopolitics. Perhaps the first modern Orientalist was no other than Columbus, who after his arrival in the Caribbean continued to praise the war against both Muslims and Jews, baptizing the people of "India" on the island of Hispaniola. Reconquista discourses about Muslims, Jews, and (Asian) Indians crossed the Atlantic during Spain's Conquista. The colonial misrecognition inherent in the name "Indian" underlines the linked imaginaries of East and West Indies. Indeed, Columbus took to "India" (i.e., to the Americas) Conversos, fluent in Semitic languages, who were expected to speak to the Indians in their own language. (Was it with the help of such translators that Columbus wrote with great confidence and knowledge about the Carib and Arawak cultures?) American colonial discourse, in other words, did not simply take in Orientalist discourse, but was constituted by it. And later on, colonial discourse, which was itself shaped within the Americas, Sub-Saharan Africa, and East and South Asia, had an impact on the formation of specific Orientalist discourse directed at North Africa and West Asia—territories colonized quite late in the imperial game.

My point in making such links is to reimagine the study of regions in a way that transcends the ghettoization typical of traditional area studies. It is also a way to insist on the links that preceded the contemporary "global village." Globalization is not a completely new development; it must be seen as part of the much longer history of colonialism in which Europe attempted to submit the world to a single "universal" regime of truth and global institution of power. As Robert Stam and I argued in *Unthinking Eurocentrism*, the five-hundred-year colonial domination of indigenous peoples, the capitalist appropriation of resources, and the imperialist ordering of the world formed part of a massive world-historical globalizing movement that reached its apogee at the end of the twentieth century and the beginning of the twenty-first. Globalization theory in this sense has its roots in a diffusionist view of Europe's spreading its people, ideas, goods, and economic and political systems around the world. Thus, patriarchal colonial diffusionism has undergone a series of metamorphoses. It transmuted into modernization theory in the late 1940s and 1950s, embracing the idea that "Third World" nations would prosper economically by emulating the historical progress of the West, and it transmuted in the 1980s into globalization theory. Women of the "underdeveloped world," it was assumed, would have to be further modernized to "catch up."

Terms such as "underdeveloped" and "developing" project an infantilization trope on a global scale. These terms imply the political and economic immaturity of diverse Calibans suffering from a putative inbred dependence on the leadership of the modernizing forces. The in loco parentis discourse of paternalistic gradualism assumed the necessity of rescue narratives and the integration of peoples in the "far" corners of the "global village" into the vision of the "advanced" and "mature" nation-states. Liberal academic curricula and well-meaning human-rights programs thrive on a binarist demarcation of opposing twin concepts of modernity versus tradition and science versus religion. In this sense, modernization functions as the bridge between two opposite poles within a stagist narrative that paradoxically assumes the essential superiority of European hegemony while simultaneously generating programs to transform the underdeveloped community "into" modernity. Within this discourse, the "developing world" always seems to lag behind somehow—not simply economically, but also culturally—condemned to a perpetual game of catch-up in which it can only repeat on another register the history of the "advanced" world. When the "First World" reaches the stage of capitalism and postmodernism, the developing world hobbles along toward modernism and the beginnings of capitalism.

Like the sociology of modernization, the economics of development and the aesthetics of postmodernism, Eurocentric versions of transnationalism covertly assume a telos toward which "traditional" cultural practices are presumed to be evolving. Performed within the discursive framework of development and modernization, the study of "Third World" aesthetics tends to produce a Eurocentric narrative of "cultural development." Such a narrative also produces segregated notions of temporality and spatiality. A more adequate formulation of these transnational relationships would not see any world as either "ahead" or "behind." Instead, it would see all the "worlds" as coeval, living the same historical moment but under diverse modalities of subordination and hybridization. The spatiality and temporality of cultures as lived is scrambled, palimpsestic in all the worlds, with the premodern, the modern, and the postmodern coexisting and interlinked globally.

To place gender and sexuality studies, American and ethnic studies, and area and postcolonial studies in critical dialogue, in sum, would require a multichronotopic form of analysis, particularly in terms of the ways space is imagined and knowledge is mapped within academic institutional practices. It would ask us to place the often ghettoized histories, geographies, and discourses in politically and epistemologically synergetic relations. It would require showing how variegated pasts and presents, "locals" and "globals" parallel and intersect, overlap and contradict, while also analogizing and allegorizing one another.

NOTES

This text is based on a lecture given in conjunction with book-signing events for *Talking Visions: Multicultural Feminism in a Transnational Age* (New York: New Museum of Contemporary Art , Cambridge, Mass.: MIT Press, 1998). A shorter version appeared as "Area Studies, Transnationalism, and the Feminist Production of Knowledge," *Signs* 26, no. 4 (Summer 2001), a special issue on Globalization and Gender edited by A. Basu, Inderpal Grewal, Caren Kaplan, and L. Malkki.

1 See, for example, Susan Moller Okin, "Is Multiculturalism Bad for Women?" in *Is Multiculturalism Bad for Women?* ed. by Joshua Cohen, Matthew Howard, and Martha C. Nussbaum (Princeton: Princeton University Press, 1999).

2 My claims here about the diverse interdisciplinary programs are perhaps somewhat general, and certainly there are exceptions to the rule. I don't mean to be categorical here, but rather strategically reductive. I am basing these claims on my experience at diverse institutions, as well as on informal conversations with some colleagues. I have also examined numerous catalogues and course offerings of American universities.

3 Essays that address the relations between the "postcolonial" and the "multi-

cultural" include my "Notes on the Postcolonial," *Social Text* 31–32 (Spring 1992); Inderpal Grewal, "The Postcolonial, Ethnic Studies, and the Diaspora: the Contexts of Ethnic Immigrant/Migrant Cultural Studies in the U.S.," *Socialist Review* 24:4 (fall 1994), 45–74; and Ann DuCille, "Postcolonialism and Afrocentricity: Discourse and Dat Course," in the *Black Columbiad: Defining Moment in African-American Literature and Culture*, ed. by Werner Sollors and Maria Diedrich (Cambridge, Mass.: Harvard University Press, 1994).

4 See especially Inderpal Grewal's and Caren Kaplan's introduction to their co-edited volume *Scattered Hegemonies: Postmodernity and Transnational Feminist Practices*. (Minneapolis: University of Minnesota Press, 1996). See also the introduction to M. Jacqui Alexander and Chandra Talpade Mohanty, eds., *Feminist Genealogies, Colonial Legacies, Democratic Futures* (New York: Routledge, 1996).

5 See Ella Shohat and Robert Stam, *Unthinking Eurocentrism* (London: Routledge, 1994); Robert Stam, *Film Theory* (Oxford: Blackwell, 2000). For a related argument, see also Robert Young, *White Mythologies* (London: Routledge, 1990).

6 Roland Barthes, *Mythologies*, trans. by Annette Lavers (London: Jonathan Cape, 1972).

7 Aimé Césaire, *Discourse on Colonialism* (1955), trans. by Joan Pinkham (New York: New York University Press, 2000); Frantz Fanon, *The Wretched of the Earth*, trans. by Constance Farrington (New York: Grove Press, 1961).

8 Claude Lévi-Strauss, *Race and History* (Paris: UNESCO, 1952). For further discussion, see Stam, *Film Theory*.

9 Simone de Beauvoir, *The Second Sex* (New York: Vintage, 1949; reissued 1989).

GENDER AND
THE CULTURE OF EMPIRE

Toward a Feminist Ethnography of the Cinema

Although recent feminist film theory has acknowledged the issue of differences among women, there has been little attempt to explore and problematize the implications of these differences for the representation of gender relations within racially and culturally non-homogeneous textual environments.[1] While implicitly universalizing "womanhood," and without questioning the undergirding racial and national boundaries of its discourse, feminist film theory for the most part has not articulated its generally insightful analyses vis-à-vis the contradictions and asymmetries provoked by (post)colonial arrangements of power. This elision is especially striking since the beginnings of cinema coincided with the heights of imperialism between the late nineteenth century and World War One. Western cinema not only inherited and disseminated colonial discourse but also created a system of domination through monopolistic control of film distribution and exhibition in much of Asia, Africa, and Latin America. The critique of colonialism within cinema studies, meanwhile, has tended to downplay the significance of gender issues, thus eliding the fact

that (post)colonial discourse has impinged differently on the representation of men and women. Situated between these two major theoretical
frameworks, my essay attempts to synthesize feminist and (post)colonial
cultural critiques.

Here I explore Western cinema's geographical and historical constructs
as symptomatic of the colonialist imaginary generally but also more specifically as a product of a gendered Western gaze, an imbrication that reflects
the symbiotic relations between patriarchal and colonial articulations of
difference. I emphasize the role of sexual difference in the construction of
a number of superimposed oppositions—West-East, North-South—not
only on a narratological level but also on the level of the implicit structuring metaphors undergirding colonial discourse. While referring to some
resistant counternarratives, I also examine the structural analogies in the
colonialist positioning of different regions, particularly in sexual terms,
showing the extent to which Western representation of otherized territories serves diacritically to define "the West" itself.

GENDERED METAPHORS

Virgins, Adams, and the Prospero Complex

An examination of colonial discourse reveals the crucial role of gendered
metaphors in constructing the colonial "subaltern." Europe's "civilizing
mission" has often interwoven opposed yet linked narratives of Western
penetration of inviting virginal landscapes *and* of resisting libidinal nature.[2]
The early exaltation of the New World paradise, suggested, for example, by
Sir Walter Raleigh's report ("a country that hath yet her mayden head, never
sakt, turned, nor wrought")[3] and by Crèvecoeur's letters ("Here nature
opens her broad lap to receive the perpetual accession of new comers, and to
supply them with food")[4] gradually centered on the idealized figure of the
pioneer. Linked to nineteenth-century westward expansionism, the garden
symbol embraced metaphors related to growth, increase, cultivation, and
blissful agricultural labor.[5] At the same time, the discourse of Empire
suggests that "primitive" landscapes (deserts, jungles) are tamed; "shrew"
peoples (Native Americans, Africans, Arabs) are domesticated; and the
desert is made to bloom, all thanks to the infusion of Western dynamism
and enlightenment. Within this Promethean master narrative, subliminally gendered tropes such as "conquering the desolation" and "fecundat-
ing the wilderness" acquire heroic resonances of Western fertilization of
barren lands. The metaphoric portrayal of the (non-European) land as a

"virgin" coyly awaiting the touch of the colonizer implied that whole continents—Africa, America, Asia, and Australia—could only benefit from the emanation of colonial praxis. The revivification of a wasted soil evokes a quasidivine process of endowing life and meaning ex nihilo, of bringing order from chaos, plenitude from lack. Indeed, the West's "Prospero complex" is premised on an East/South portrayed as a Caliban's isle, the site of superimposed lacks calling for Western transformation of primeval matter. The engendering of "civilization," then, is clearly phallocentric, not unlike the mythical woman's birth from Adams rib.[6]

The American hero, as R. W. B. Lewis points out, has been celebrated as prelapsarian Adam, as a New Man emancipated from history (i.e., European history) before whom all the world and time lay available.[7] The American Adam archetype implied not only his status as a kind of creator, blessed with the divine prerogative of naming the elements of the scene about him, but also his fundamental innocence. Here colonial and patriarchal discourses are clearly interwoven. The biblical narration of Genesis recounts the creation of the world; the creation of Adam from earth (*adama* in Hebrew) in order for man to rule over nature. The power of creation is inextricably linked to the power of naming—God lends his naming authority to Adam as mark of his rule, and Eve is "called Woman because she was taken out of man." The question of naming played an important role not only in gender mythology but also in colonial narratives in which the "discoverer" gave names as a mark of possession ("America" as celebrating Amerigo Vespucci) or as bearers of a European global perspective ("Near East," "Middle East," "Far East"). Colonialism stripped "peripheral" places and their inhabitants of their "unpronounceable" indigenous names and outfitted them with names marking them as colonial property. The colonial explorer as depicted in *Robinson Crusoe* creates, demiurgelike, a whole civilization and has the power to name "his" islander "Friday," for he "saves" his life on that day. Friday, we recall, is the day God created Adam, further strengthening the analogy between the "self-sufficient" Crusoe and God (figure 1).

The notion of an American Adam elided a number of crucial facts—notably, that there were other civilizations in the New World; that the settlers were not creating "being from nothingness"; and that the settlers had scarcely jettisoned all their Old World cultural baggage, their deeply ingrained attitudes and discourses. Here the notion of "virginity," present, for example, in the etymology of Virginia, must be seen in diacritical relation to the metaphor of the (European) "motherland." A "virgin" land

1　The Promethean masternarrative: *Adventures of Robinson Crusoe* (1954)
(below) **2**　Between virginity and cannibalism: "America" (ca. 1600).
Engraving by Theodore Galle after a drawing by Jan Van der Straet (ca. 1575)

is implicitly available for defloration and fecundation. Assumed to lack owners, it therefore becomes the property of its "discoverers" and cultivators. The "purity" of the terminology masks the dispossession of the land and its resources. A land already fecund, already producing for the indigenous peoples, and thus a "mother" is metaphorically projected as virgin, "untouched nature" and therefore available and awaiting a master.

Colonial gendered metaphors are visibly rendered in Jan Van der Straet's pictorial representation of the discovery of America, focusing on the mythical figure of Amerigo Vespucci shown as bearing Europe's emblems of meaning (cross, armor, compass).[8] Behind him we see the vessels that will bring back to the Occident the treasures of the New World paradise. In front of him we see a welcoming naked woman, the Indian American (figure 2). If she is a harmonious extension of nature, he represents its scientific mastery.[9] Here, the conqueror, as Michel de Certeau puts it, "will write the body of the other and inscribe upon it his own history."[10]

In Nelson Pereira dos Santos's *Como Era Gostoso o Meu Francês* (How Tasty Was My Frenchman, 1970), the patriarchal discourse on the encounter between Europeans and indigenous Americans is subverted.[11] Partly based on a diary written by the German adventurer Hans Staden, the film concerns a Frenchman who is captured by the Tupinamba tribe and sentenced to death in response to previous massacres inflicted by Europeans on them (figure 3). Before his ritualized execution and cannibalization, however, he is given a wife, Sebiopepe (a widow of one of the Tupinamba massacred by the Europeans), and he is allowed to participate in the tribe's daily activities.[12] In the last shot, the camera zooms in on Sebiopepe's face as she casually and emotionlessly chews her Frenchman's flesh, despite her previous close relationship with him. This final image is followed by a citation from a report on genocide commited by Europeans, thus subverting the possibly disturbing nature of the last shot.[13]

If pictorial representations of the "discovery" tend to center on a nude indigenous American woman as a metaphor for the welcoming "new-found-land," in *How Tasty Was My Frenchman* the indigenous woman is far from being an object of European discourse. Presented as linked to her communal culture and history, she herself takes part in history. Her nudity is not contrasted with the discoverer's heavy clothing; rather, it is of a piece with a culture where nudity is encoded differently. Employing largely long shots in which characters appear nude as they perform their banal daily activities, the film undermines voyeurism and stands in contrast to the fetishistic Hollywood mode that tends to fragment the (female) body in

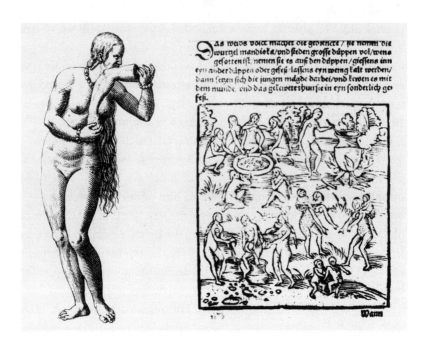

3 Counternarrative to "discovery discourse": *How Tasty Was My Frenchman* (1970)

close shots.[14] In her interaction with the Frenchman, Sebiopepe represents, above all, the voice of the indigenous American counternarrative.[15] In one scene, for example, a myth of origins prefigures the symbolic revolt of the Tupinamba. Sebiopepe begins to narrate in Tupi a Tupinamba Promethean myth concerning the god, Mair, who brought them knowledge. The Frenchman at one point takes over the narration and, in French, further recounts the deeds of the god, while we see him performing the divine deeds. The whitening of the Tupinamba God on the image track evokes the Promethean colonial discourse concerning the redemption of the "natives," but here that discourse is relativized, especially since the indigenous woman ends the myth in Tupi, recounting the rebellion of the people against the god while the image track shows the destruction of the Frenchman's work. Her voice then recounts the tale of the people who revolted, undercutting the masculinist myth of availability, submissiveness, and redemption.

Graphological Tropes

The inclination to project the non-Occident as feminine is seen even in the nineteenth-century Romantic depiction of the ancient Orient of Babylonia

4 The pornographic intertext of travel literature: Babylon in *Intolerance* (1916)

and Egypt, reproduced in films such as D. W. Griffith's *Intolerance* (1916) and Cecil B. DeMille's *Cleopatra* (1934). In *Intolerance*, Babylon signifies sexual excess, building on the Book of Revelation as "Babylon, the Great, the Mother of Harlots and of the Abominations of the Earth." DeMille's *Cleopatra* explicitly expresses this view by having the sexually manipulative Cleopatra addressed as Egypt and by presenting the Orient as exclusively the scene of carnal delights.[16] The ultimate subordination of Cleopatra and her country Egypt is not without contemporary colonial overtones. In a Roman court where the protagonists affect Anglo-aristocratic accents, and sarcastic jokes are made at the expense of a presumably black Cleopatra, it is asserted that Rome could never be turned into the Orient or ruled by an Egyptian. (A possibly dark Cleopatra is turned by Hollywood beauty conventions into a European-looking white woman, just as the iconography of Christ has gradually de-Semitized him.)[17] The visual infatuation with Babylon's and Egypt's material abundance, emphasized through a mise en scène of monumental architecture, domestic detail, and quasi-pornographic feasts, cannot be divorced from the intertext of colonial travel literature whose reports also obsessively recounted the details of Oriental sensual excesses (figure 4).

Cinema in this sense enacted a historiographical and anthropological role, writing (in light) the cultures of others. The early films' penchant for graphological signifiers such as hieroglyphs (in the different versions of *Cleopatra*), Hebrew script (*Intolerance*), and the image of an open book, as in "The Book of Intolerance" and the marginal "notes" accompanying the intertitles (which pedagogically supply the spectator with additional information), posits Hollywood as a kind of Western popular griot. By associating itself with writing, and particularly with "original" writing, early cinema lent a pedagogical, historical, and artistic aura to a medium still associated with circus-like entertainments. (It is not a coincidence, perhaps, that Siegfried Kracauer, for example, referred to films as "visible hieroglyphs.") And by linking a new apprentice art to ancient times and "exotic" places, cinema celebrated its ethnographic and quasi-archaeological powers to resuscitate forgotten and distant civilizations, a celebration implicit in the construction of pseudo-Egyptian movie palaces. The "birth" of cinema itself coincided with the imperialist moment, when diverse colonized civilizations were already shaping their conflicting identities vis-à-vis their colonizers. These films about the ancient world suggest, perhaps, a Romantic nostalgia for a "pure" civilization unsullied by Western "contamination." They also represent a Romantic search for the lost Eastern origins of Western civilizations, analogous to Heinrich Schlieman's excavations in Troy. It is within this context that we can understand the "structuring absence"—within the representations of Egypt, Babylonia, and the (biblical) Holy Land—of the contemporary colonized Arab Orient and its nationalist struggles.[18] Through a historiographical gesture, the films define the Orient as ancient and mysterious, participating in what Jacques Derrida in another context calls the "hieroglyphist prejudice." The cinematic Orient, then, is best epitomized by an iconography of papyruses, sphinxes, and mummies, whose existence and revival depend on the "look" and "reading" of the Westerner. This rescue of the past, in other words, suppresses the voice of the present and thus legitimates by default the availability of the space of the Orient for the geopolitical maneuvers of the Western powers.

The filmic mummified zone of ancient civilizations, then, is dialectically linked to the representation of the historical role of the West in the imperial age. Reproducing Western historiography, First World cinema narrates European penetration into the Third World through the figure of the "discoverer."[19] In most Western films about the colonies (such as *Bird of Paradise* [1932], *Wee Willie Winkie* [1937], *Black Narcissus* [1947], *The King and I* [1956], *Lawrence of Arabia* [1962], and even Buñuel's *Adventures of Robinson*

Crusoe [1954]), the spectator accompanies, quite literally, the explorer's perspective. A simple shift in focalization to that of the "natives," as occurs in the Australian Aboriginal film *Nice Coloured Girls* (1987),[20] or in the Brazilian film *How Tasty Was My Frenchman*, where the camera is placed on land with the "natives" rather than on a ship with the Europeans, reveals the illusory and intrusive nature of the "discovery." More usually, however, heroic status is attributed to the voyager (often a male scientist) come to master a new land and its treasures, the value of which the "primitive" residents had been unaware.[21] It is this construction of consciousness of "value" as pretext for (capitalist) ownership that legitimizes the colonizer's act of appropriation. The concept of "discovery," furthermore, carries gender overtones.[22] In this exploratory adventure, seen in such films as *Lawrence of Arabia* and the *Indiana Jones* series, the camera relays the hero's dynamic movement across a passive, static space, gradually stripping the land of its "enigma" as the spectator wins visual access to Oriental treasures through the eyes of the explorer protagonist. *Lawrence of Arabia* provides an example of Western historical representation whereby the individual Romantic "genius" leads the Arab national revolt, a dynamic phenomenon transformed into a passive entity awaiting T. E. Lawrence's inspiration. (Arab sources obviously have challenged this historical account.[23]) The unveiling of the mysteries of an unknown space becomes a *rite de passage* allegorizing the Western achievement of virile heroic stature.

Mapping Terra Incognita

The masculinist desire to master a new land is intimately linked to colonial history and even to its contemporary companion, philosophy, in which epistemology partially modeled itself on geography. The traditional discourse on nature as feminine—for example, Francis Bacon's idea that insofar as we learn the laws of nature through science, we become her master, as we are now in ignorance, in "her thralls"[24]—within the colonial context gains clear geopolitical implications. Bacon's search for expanding scientific knowledge is inseparable from the contemporaneous European geographical expansion, suggested by his language of analogies and metaphors: "As the immense regions of the West Indies had never been discovered, if the use of the compass had not first been known, it is no wonder that the discovery and advancement of arts hath made no greater progress, when the art of inventing and discovering of the sciences remains hitherto unknown."[25] And Bacon finds it "disgraceful [that] while the regions of the material globe . . . have been in our times laid widely open and revealed, the intellectual globe should remain shut up within the narrow limits of old discoveries."[26] Traveling into the indefiniteness of the ocean, the Faustian overreacher's voyage beyond the Pillars of Hercules aims at the possibility of a terra incognita on the other side of the ocean. Studying topography, systematizing the paths, as Hans Blumenberg points out, guarantees that the accidents of things coming to light ultimately lead to a universal acquaintance with the world. "So much had remained concealed from the human spirit throughout many centuries and was discovered neither by philosophy nor by the faculty of reason but rather by accident and favorable opportunity, because it was all too different and distant from what was familiar, so that no preconception *(praenotio aliqua)* could lead one to it."[27] The logic of explorers from Robinson Crusoe to Indiana Jones is, in this sense, based on the hope that "nature" conceals in its "womb" still more, outside the familiar paths of the power of imagination *(extra vias phantasiae)*. It is within this broader historical and intellectual context that we may understand the symptomatic image of penetration into a cave placed in a non-European land to discover that "Unknown," seen, for example, in the Rudyard Kipling–based *The Jungle Book* (1942), *Raiders of the Lost Ark* (1981), *Indiana Jones and the Temple of Doom* (1984), and in the E. M. Forster–based *A Passage to India* (1984).

At the heart of the imperial vision, the orgies of plunder were couched in the rhetoric of Reason. The aura of scientificity inscribed by images of maps and globes also helped legitimize colonial narratives about treasure islands. It was during the Renaissance, after all, that Europe's ability to map graphically intimated the Continent's potential domination all over the globe. The growing science of geography inspired numerous narratives about the mapping of new regions. European cartographic inscription, with the drawn compass serving as the imprimatur of scientific authority, determined the status and significance of places. The full tale of transforming the unknown into known is conveyed through titles and captions, as well as through drawings of places and characters. Artistic conventions of the time personify the world's continents as female, while individualizing them in stereotyped ways, with luxurious Asia sumptuously dressed, Africa either stylishly Moorish or barely clothed, and America as the naked savage.

A 1586 map of America labeled "Terra Septemtrionalis Incognita," cartographically "writes" the history of the "discovery" of 1492 (figure 5). There is a sailing ship, and at the bottom Columbus and his men encounter nude, largely female "natives." Below, we read a caption in Latin:

"America annos Dm 1492 a Christophoro Colombo nomine Regis Castello primum detecta." (Columbus who in the year 1492 was the first to have found America in the name of the King of Castille.) The left-right sequence takes us from the moment of "discovery" on the left to the realization of the map of America on the right. Cartography, in other words, is contextualized as the by-product of scientific discoveries and of heroic discoverers. The narrative of mastery is finally metaphorized through the denuded "native" body occupying the space behind Columbus.

Geography, then, was microcosmically reflected in the map-based adventures, which involved the drawing or deciphering of a map and its authentication through the physical contact with the "new" land. Western cinema, whether in anthropological films or in fictional films like *Morocco* (1930) and the *Indiana Jones* series, has relied on map imagery to plot the empire while simultaneously celebrating its own technological power—implicitly vis-à-vis the novel's reliance on words or static drawings and, later, still photographs—to illustrate vividly the topography. For example, venture-narrative films mark maps with moving arrows to signify the progress of the Westerner in his world navigation, a practice that characterizes even the recent *Raiders of the Lost Ark* and *Indiana Jones and the Temple of Doom*. By associating itself with the visual medium of maps, cinema represents itself scientifically as being a twentieth-century continuation of the discipline of geography.

Films often superimposed illustrative maps on shots of landscapes, subliminally imposing the map's "claim" over the land, virtually functioning as a legal document. *King Solomon's Mines* (1937, 1950, 1985; see figure 6), as Anne McClintock suggests in her discussion of the H. Rider Haggard work, explicitly genderizes the relation between the explorer and the topography.[28] Menahem Golan's version of *King Solomon's Mines*, for example, reveals in the second shot of the film a small nude female sculpture engraved with Canaanite signs, explained by the archaeologist to be a map leading to the twin mountains, the Breasts of Sheba, below which, in a cave, are hidden King Solomon's diamond mines. The camera voyeuristically tilts down on the female body/map, scrutinizing it from the excited perspective of the archaeologist and the antique dealer. The road to Utopia involves the deciphering of the map, of comprehending the female body; the legendary twin mountains and the cave metaphorize the desired telos of the hero's mission of plunder. The geology and topography of the land, then, are explicitly sexualized to resemble the physiology of a woman.

The recurrent image of the spinning globe similarly entitles the scientist

5 Terra Incognita or the power to name: A map of America (1586)

6 Map as a document of possession: *King Solomon's Mines* (1950)

to possess the world, since the globe, as the world's representation, allegorizes the relationship between creator and creation. Cinema's penchant for spinning-globe logos serves to celebrate the medium's kinetic possibilities as well as its global ubiquity, allowing spectators a cheap voyage while remaining in the metropolitan "centers." The Lumières brothers' fondness for location shooting at diverse Third World sites (India, Mexico, and Palestine) are symptomatic of this visual national-geographies mania. The spinning globe virtually became the trademark of the British Korda brothers' productions, many of whose films, such as *Sanders of the River* (1935), *The Drum* (1938), *The Four Feathers* (1939), and *The Jungle Book* concerned colonial themes.[29] The overarching global point of view sutures the spectator into a godlike cosmic perspective. Incorporating images of maps and globes, the Jules Verne–based film *Around the World in 80 Days* (1956), for example, begins with its omniscient narrator hailing the "shrinking of the world" as Verne was writing the book.[30] The "shrinking" relates the perspective of upper-class British men whose scientific confidence about circling the world in eighty days is materialized, thus linking the development of science to imperialist control: "Nothing is impossible. When science finally conquers the air it may be feasible to circle the globe in eighty hours," says David Niven's character (figure 7).

Science, knowledge, and technology can also be read allegorically as linked to imperial expansionism in the film's citation of George Méliès's film A *Trip to the Moon (Le Voyage dans la lune* [1902], based on Verne's *From the Earth to the Moon* [1865]), in which the "last frontier" explored is seen first in the imagistic phallic penetration of the rounded moon (figure 8).[31] This imagination of the "last frontier" as imperialism reached its heights, reproduces the historical discourse of the "first frontier." The narrative is structured similarly to the colonial captivity narrative in which the skeleton creatures carrying spears burst from the moon's simulacrum of a jungle but are defeated by the male explorers' umbrella-like guns, which magically eliminate the savage creatures. Such a film, not in any obvious sense "about" colonialism but produced in a period when most of the world was dominated by Europe, can thus be read as an analogue of imperial expansion.[32] Similarly, in recent science fiction films such as *Return of the Jedi* (1983), the conquest of outer space exists on a continuum with an imperial narrative in which the visualization of the planet provides the paradigm for the representation of Third World "underdevelopment" (deserts, jungles, and mountains). The Manichean relationship between the American hero and the new land and its natives involves exotic creatures,

7 Global ubiquity: *Around the World in 80 Days* (1956)

8 Penetrating the "last frontier": *A Trip to the Moon* (1902)

teddy bear–like Ewoks whose language remains a mystery throughout the film, who worship the technologically well-equipped hero, and who defend him against evil, ugly creatures possessing irrational motives. The American hero's physical and moral triumph legitimizes the destruction of the enemy, as does the paternal transformation of the friendly "elements" into servile objects, along with his assumed right to establish new outposts (and implicitly to hold on to old outposts, whether in Africa, Asia, or America).

The Dark Continent

The colonialist films are premised on initiating the Western spectator into an unknown culture. This is valid even for films set in "exotic" lands and ancient times that do *not* feature Western characters (for example, *Intolerance*,[33] *The Ten Commandments* [1923, 1956], *The Thief of Bagdad* [1924], and *Kismet* [1944]), yet whose Oriental heroes and heroines are played by Western stars. The spectator is subliminally invited to join an ethnographic tour of a celluloid-"preserved" culture, which implicitly celebrates the chronotopically magical aptitude of cinema for panoramic spectacle and temporal voyeurism, evoking André Bazin's formulation of cinema as possessing a "mummy complex."[34] Often, the spectator, identified with the gaze of the West (whether embodied by a Western male/female character or by a Western actor/actress masquerading as an Oriental), comes to master, in a remarkably telescoped period of time, the codes of a foreign culture shown, as Edward Said suggests, as simple, unselfconscious, and susceptible to facile apprehension. Any possibility of dialogic interaction and of a dialectical representation of the East–West relation is excluded from the outset. The films thus reproduce the colonialist mechanism by which the Orient, rendered devoid of any active historical or narrative role, becomes the object of study and spectacle.[35]

The portrayal of a Third World region as undeveloped, in the same vein, is reinforced by what can be called topographical reductionism—for example, the topographical reductionism of the Orient to desert and, metaphorically, to dreariness. The desert, a frequent reference in the dialogues and a visual motif throughout the Orientalist films, is presented as the essential unchanging decor of the history of the Orient. While the Arabs in such films as *Lawrence of Arabia*, *Exodus* (1960), and *Raiders of the Lost Ark* are associated with images of underdevelopment, the Westerner, as the antithesis of the Oriental desert, is associated with productive, creative pioneering, with the masculine redemption of the wilderness. A culturally overdetermined geographical-symbolic polarity, on a double East/West and South/North informs colonalist cinema. As if in a reversion to deterministic climate theories such as those of Madame de Staël or Hippolyte Taine, European cinema has shaped an East or South visual ecology of irrational primitivism and dangrous instincts. The barren land and the blazing sands, furthermore, metaphorize the exposed "hot" uncensored passions of the Orient, in short, the world of the out-of-control id.

The Orient as a metaphor for sexuality is encapsulated by the recurrent figure of the veiled woman. The inaccessibility of the veiled woman, mirroring the mystery of the Orient itself, requires a process of Western unveiling for comprehension. Veiled women in Orientalist paintings, photographs, and films expose flesh, ironically, more than they conceal it.[36] It is this process of exposing the female Other, of literally denuding her, that comes to allegorize the Western masculinist power of possession: that she, as a metaphor for her land, becomes available for Western penetration and knowledge. This intersection of the epistemological and the sexual in colonial discourse echoes Freud's metaphor of the "dark continent." Freud speaks of female sexuality in metaphors of darkness and obscurity often drawn from the realms of archaeology and exploration—the metaphor of the "dark continent," for example, echoing a book by the Victorian explorer Henry Morton Stanley, *In Darkest Africa*.[37] Seeing himself as explorer and discoverer of new worlds, Freud in *Studies on Hysteria* compared the role of the psychoanalyst to that of the archaeologist "clearing away the pathogenic psychical material layer by layer," which is analogous "with the technique of excavating a buried city."[38] The analogy, made in the context of examining a female patient, Fräulein Elisabeth Von R., calls attention to the role of the therapist in locating obscure trains of thought, followed by penetration, as Freud puts it in the first person: "I would penetrate into deeper layers of her memories at these points carrying out an investigation under hypnosis or by the use of some similar technique."[39]

Speaking generally of "penetrating deeply" into the "neurosis of women" thanks to a science that can give a "deeper and more coherent" insight into femininity,[40] Freud is perhaps unaware of the political overtones of his optical metaphor. Penetration, as Toril Moi suggests, is very much on Freud's mind as he approaches femininity,[41] including, one might add, the "dark continent of female sexuality." The notion of the necessary unveiling of the unconscious requires an obscure object to sustain the very desire to explore, penetrate, and master. David Macey's suggestion that psychoanalysis posits femininity as being in excess of its rationalist discourse, and then complains that it cannot explain it,[42] is equally applicable to the positioning of the Other in colonial discourse. Freud, furthermore, sometimes uses the language of violence—for example, "We force our way into the internal strata, overcoming resistances at all times."[43] (Symptomatically, Freud never elaborates on the lived reality of rape in his writngs.) Looking at the Eastern roots of "civilizations," Freud employs ancient myths and figures such as the Sphinx and Oedipus to draw parallels between the development of the civilization and that of the psyche. (Although Freud did not speculate at any great length on Egyptian mythology, over half of his private collection of antiquities reportedly consisted of ancient Egyptian sculptures and artifacts.[44]) The psychoanalyst who heals his patient from her suppressed past (most of Freud's studies of hysteria were conducted in relation to women) resembles the archaeologist who recovers the hidden past of civilization (most of which was "found" in colonized lands). As in archaeology, Freud's epistemology assumes the (white heterosexual) male as the bearer of knowledge who can penetrate woman and text while she, as a remote region, will let herself be explored till truth is uncovered.

The interweaving of archaeology and psychoanalysis touches on a nineteenth-century motif in which the voyage into the origins of the Orient becomes a voyage into the interior colonies of the "self." ("Un voyage en Orient [était] comme un grand acte de ma vie intèrieure," Alphonse de Lamartine wrote.[45]) The origins of archaeology, the search for the "roots of civilization" as a discipline, we know, are inextricably linked to imperial expansionism. In the cinema, the *Indiana Jones* series recycles exactly this colonial vision in which Western "knowledge" of ancient civilizations "rescues" the past from oblivion. It is this masculinist rescue in *Raiders of the Lost Ark* that legitimizes denuding the Egyptians of their heritage and confining it within Western metropolitan museums—an ideology implicit in the Orientalist *Intolerance, Cleopatra,* and the *Mummy* series. (These films, not surprisingly, tend to be programmed in museums that feature Egyptological exhibitions [figure 9].) *Raiders of the Lost Ark,* symptomatically, assumes a disjuncture between contemporary and ancient Egypt, since the space between the present and the past can "only" be bridged by the scientist. The full significance of the ancient archaeological objects within the Eurocentric vision of the Spielberg film is presumed to be understood only by the Western scientist, relegating the Egyptian people to the role of ignorant Arabs who happen to be sitting on a land full of historical treasures—much as they happen to "sit" on oil. Set in the mid-1930s

9 The West rescues the Egyptian past from oblivion: *The Mummy*, 1932 (top), and *Raiders of the Lost Ark*, 1981 (bottom)

when most of the world was still under colonial rule, the film regards the imperial presence in Egypt, furthermore, as completely natural, eliding a history of Arab nationalist revolts against foreign domination.

Often portrayed as a cowboy, the American hero transmutes into an archaeologist in an implicit search for the Eastern roots of Western civilization. Indiana Jones liberates the ancient Hebrew ark from illegal Egyptian possession, while also rescuing it from immoral Nazi control, subliminally reinforcing American and Jewish solidarity vis-à-vis the Nazis and their Arab assistants.[46] The geopolitical alignments here are as clear as in the inadvertent allegory of *The Ten Commandments*, where a WASPish Charlton Heston is made to incarnate Hebrew Moses struggling against the Egyptians, thus allegorizing in the context of the 1950s the contemporary struggle of the West (Israel and the United States) against Egyptians/Arabs.[47] That at the end of *Raiders of the Lost Ark* it is the U.S. Army that guards the "top secret" ark—with the active complicity of the ark itself—strengthens this evocation of geopolitical alliances.[48] *Raiders of the Lost Ark* significantly develops parallel linked plots in which the female protagonist, Marion, and the ark become the twin objects of the hero's search for harmony. The necklace that leads to the ark is first associated with Marion, who becomes herself the object of competing nationalist male desires. She is abducted by the Nazis and their Arab assistants much as the ark is hijacked by them, followed by Dr. Jones's rescue of Marion and the ark from the Nazis. The telos of the voyage into unknown regions—whether mental or geographical—then, is that the Westerner knows the Orient (in the epistemological and biblical senses) and at the same time brings it knowledge, rescuing it from its own obscurantism.

Egyptology and The Mummy

A different perspective on these issues is suggested in the Egyptian film *Al-Mumia* (The Mummy/The Night of Counting the Years, 1969), directed by Shadi Abdel Salam.[49] Based on the actual case of the discovery of pharaonic tombs in the Valley of the Kings in 1881, a year before the full British colonization of Egypt, the film opens with the French Egyptologist Gaston Maspero informing his colleagues about the black-market trade in antiquities coming from the reigns of pharaohs such as Ahmose,[50] Thutmose III,[51] and Ramses II.[52] The government's archaeological commission, under Maspero, delegates an expedition, headed by a young Egyptian archaeologist, to investigate the location of the tombs in Thebes to end the thefts. In Thebes, meanwhile, the headman of the Upper Egyptian

Horobbat tribe, which had been living off extracting artifacts from the pharaonic tombs, has just died, and his brother must initiate his two nephews into the secret of the mountain. Still in grief over their father's death, the sons are repelled by the dissection of the mummy merely to get at a gold necklace depicting the sacred "Eye of Horus." The protesting brothers must choose between two betrayals, both of them grave: the vulturelike looting of ancient kingdoms and the desecration of their mummies or the betrayal of their father's secret, with the consequence of cutting off their source of income and therefore their ability to feed hungry Horobbat mouths. Any revelation of the secret would mean ultimately destroying their family and tribe in the name of respect for "the dead," now viewed by the elders as nothing more than leathery mummies. The older brother is assassinated by the village elders when he refuses to sell the artifact on the black market, while the younger brother, Wannis, is torn between his guilt over owing his life to ancient Egyptian corpses ("How many bodies did my father violate in order to feed us?" he asks his mother) and the condemnation of his people. Wandering through the ruins of Thebes and Karnak—for him not simply mementoes of an older civilization but living reminders of his childhood playground—the long-take swirling camera movements render his ethical and even epistemological vertigo, the conflict between his responsibility to his Egyptian heritage and his immediate responsibility for present-day lives. After being reassured that the "effendi archaeologists" are trying to understand Egypt's past and not plunder it, he reveals the secret knowledge to Maspero's assistant. Before the village can prevent it, the expedition empties the graves and carries out the mummies, which are destined for the museum (figure 10).

Al-Mumia is set in the late nineteenth century, at the height of imperial Egyptology. By the time Britain occupied Egypt in 1882, the country was bereft of its archaeological treasures, which were exhibited in London and Paris as testimony of Western scientific progress. In the heroic, almost sanctimonious, language of the Egyptological mission, archaeological reports on the 1881 discovery describe the rescue of the ancient East's powerful kings from Arab clans in a way that associates the Westerner with emperors and royal dynasties. The simplistic positing of a rupture between present and past Egypt conveniently empowers the Western claim over Egypt's past,[53] thus naturalizing the presence of the Rosetta Stone, for example, in the British Museum. Abdel Salam's film implicitly challenges the archaeological master narrative by foregrounding the voices of those on the margins of Egyptological texts. If the film opens with an archaeological

10 Amplifying the voices on the margins of Egyptology: *Al-Mumia* (1969)

project and ends with its successful accomplishment, it also undermines that mission by focusing on the concrete dilemmas of living Egyptians in relation to their past. The nondiegetic musical motif based on Upper Egyptian popular music ("al-Arian"), and the slow rhythm evocative of the regional atmosphere, furthermore, convey cinematically the cultural force of their environment.[54] The film does not end, significantly, with the narrative closure of safe placement of the artifacts in a museum but, rather, with the slow vanishing of the boat carrying the Egyptologists and the mummies, all from the perspective of the devastated tribe. If *How Tasty Was My Frenchman* opens with the penetration of the Europeans seen from the perspective of the indigenous Americans, *Al-Mumia* ends with the emptiness left behind by European dispossession. Reportedly, the Egyptian women of the tribe mourned when the mummies were taken, yet Abdel Salam presents, in long shot and through de-psychologized editing, a unified communal silent gaze where the whistling wind becomes a voice of protest. Their gaze, far from conveying the triumphant conclusion of the archaeological narrative, unveils the disastrous rupture in their very lives, thus subverting the self-celebratory Egyptological definitions by unfolding a tale of dispossession and theft.[55]

Archaeological reports often inadvertently display metaphors that suggest capitalist values attached to their own profession. In his account of the

1881 discovery, the archaeologist Howard Carter, who worked on the discovery of Tutankhamen's tomb, writes: "Incredible as it may seem, the secret was kept for six years, and the family, with a banking account of forty or more dead pharaohs to draw upon, grew rich."[56] Abdel Salam's *Al-Mumia*, in contrast, emphasizes the ambivalent relationships between the tribe and the treasures, between the Egyptian people and their ancient heritage. The tribe lives on theft, yet its circumstances of hunger imply a critique of the imperial class system. The archaeological redemption, in other words, must be seen in its historical and cultural context as taking away the only power the tribe possesses while bringing nothing in return. It would be simplistic, however, to view *Al-Mumia* as a mere condemnation of Egyptology. The film illuminates class relations within a colonial dynamics that obliges the tribe to deal with the "small" black-market merchants, for the "effendies" from Cairo will not even pay the tribe and have them arrested. Class formations in Egyptian society, particularly within the imperial context, force the small village to regard the ancient artifacts as a means of survival, a system in which their secret becomes their only power. The effendies are viewed from the perspective of the tribe as strangers, cut off, in other words, from the national reality. In contrast with Western representations of Egypt, *Al-Mumia* does not stress the grandeur of ancient Egypt at the expense of contemporary Arab lives. Rather, it exposes the palimpsestic complexity of Egyptian identity.

An allegory of Egyptian identity, the film offers a meditation on the destiny of a national culture. "We have a national culture," says Shadi Abdel Salam, "but it lies buried at the bottom of the memory of the people who are not always aware of its great values."[57] Speaking in an improbably literary Arabic (rather than an existing dialect), the villagers embody both Arab culture heritage and continuity with the ancient past, emphasized, for example, through the ancient-Egyptian-style eye makeup worn by the actress Nadia Lutfi. In a symbolic, syncretic continuity of pharaonic and Arab Egypt, the film associates the ancient "Eye of Horus"—first shown in a close shot, as if looking at the brothers (directly at the spectator)—with the Arab sign of "khamsa," the hand extended against the evil eye, seen on the boat on which the older brother is murdered. Shots of a gigantic monumental fist similarly accompany a dialogue between Wannis and a migrant worker about a "hand holding a fate no one can read" and "what fate can you read in a stone hand?" suggesting the hazardous nature of reading fate at the hands of the monuments. The contemporary popular Middle Eastern culture of reading fate in the hands, in sum, is implicitly contrasted with the immortal grandeur but also the lifelessness of mere monu-ments.[58] A kind of visual dialogue of Arab Egypt with its past, furthermore, is rendered through montage—for example, when the image of the agoniz-ing Wannis, looking up at the gigantic monument, is juxtaposed with a high-angle shot of Wannis, this time presumably from the monument's point of view. The presentation of Egypt's national identity as an amalgam of histories and cultures evokes the formulations, for example, by the writers Taha Hussein and Tawfik al-Hakim of Egyptian identity as a syn-thesis of pharaonic past, Arabic language, and Islamic religion. The film's opening intertitle, drawn from *The Book of the Dead*, promises that the one who shall go shall also return, and the final intertitle, calling for the dead to "wake up,"[59] must also be seen within the context in which *Al-Mumia* was produced. During the period following the 1967 war, after Egypt's defeat by Israel, the regime of Gamal Abdel Nasser lost much of its allure, and the general mood of despair went hand in hand with a felt need for critical reassessments. In this sense, the ancient inscription of resurrection is also allegorically a call to Egypt of the late 1960s for national rebirth.

TEXTUAL/SEXUAL STRATEGIES

The Colonial Gaze

Still playing a significant role in post-colonial geopolitics, the predominant trope of "rescue" in colonial discourse forms the crucial site of the battle over representation. Not only has the Western imaginary metaphorically rendered the colonized land as a female to be saved from her environ/ mental disorder, it has also projected rather more literal narratives of rescue, specifically of Western and non-Western women—from African, Asian, Arab, or American-Indian men. The figure of the Arab assassin/ rapist, like that of the African cannibal, produces the narrative and ideolog-ical role of the Western liberator as integral to the colonial rescue fantasy. This projection, whose imagistic avatars include the polygamous Arab, the libidinous black buck, and the macho Latino, provides an indirect apologia for domination. In the case of the Orient, it carries with it religious/ theological overtones of the inferiority of the polygamous Islamic world to the Christian world as encapsulated by the monogamous couple. The justi-fication of Western expansion, then, becomes linked to issues of sexuality.

The intersection of colonial and gender discourses involves a shifting, contradictory subject positioning, whereby the Western woman can si-multaneously constitute "center" and "periphery," identity and alterity. A

I I   Sheltered in the tropics: Gender and ambivalence

Western female character, in these narratives, exists in a relation of subordination to her male counterpart and in a relation of domination toward
"non-Western" male and female characters. This textual relationality homologizes the historical positioning of colonial women who have played,
albeit with a difference, an oppressive role toward colonized people (both
men and women), at times actively perpetuating the legacy of empire
(figure 11).[60] This problematic role is anatomized in Ousmane Sembène's
La Noire de . . . (Black Girl, 1966) in the relationship between the Senegalese maid and her French employer, and to some extent by Mira Hamermesh's documentary on South Africa, *Maids and Madams* (1985). Such
narratives subvert the white-woman's-burden ideology of such films as *The
King and I* (1956), *Out of Africa* (1985), and *Gorillas in the Mist* (1989). In
colonialist narrative, however, white female characters become the instrument of the Eurocentric and phallocentric vision, and are thus granted a

gaze more powerful than that not only of non-Western women but also of non-Western men.

In the colonial context, given the shifting relational nature of power situations and representations, women can be granted an ephemeral "positional superiority" (Edward Said), a possibility exemplified in *The Sheik* (1921). Based on Edith Hull's novel, George Melford's *The Sheik* introduces the spectator to the Arab world first in the form of the "barbarous ritual" of the marriage market, depicted as a casino-lottery ritual from which Arab men select women to "serve as chattel slaves." At the same time, the Western female character, usually the object of the male gaze in Hollywood films, tends to be granted in the East an active (colonial) gaze, insofar as she now, temporarily within the narrative, becomes the sole delegate, as it were, of Western civilization. The "norms of the text" (Boris Uspensky) are represented by the Western male character, but in the moments of his absence, the white woman becomes the civilizing center of the film.[61] These racial and sexual hierarchies in the text are also clearly exemplified in Michael Powell's and Emeric Pressburger's *Black Narcissus*, where most of the narrative is focalized through the British nuns and their "civilizing mission" in India. But ultimately, the "norms of the text" are embodied by the British man, whose initial "prophecy" that the wild mountains of India are not suitable for and are beyond the control of the Christian missionaries is confirmed by the end of the narrative, with the virtual punishment of the nuns, as catastrophes and mental chaos penetrate their order. Yet in relation to the "natives" (both Indian men and women), the British female characters are privileged and form the "filter" and "center of consciousness" (Gèrard Genette) of the film.

The discourse on gender within a colonial context, in sum, suggests that Western women can occupy a relatively powerful position on the surface of the text, as the vehicles less for a sexual gaze than for a colonial gaze. In these friction-producing moments between sexual and national hierarchies, particularly as encapsulated through the relationship between Third World men and First World women, national identity (associated with the white female character) is relatively privileged over sexual identity (associated with the dark male character). The same ambivalence, meanwhile operates in relation to Third World men, whose punishment for interracial desire is simultaneously accompanied by spectatorial gratification for a male (hetero)sexual gaze as ephemerally relayed by a darker man. These contradictions between national and sexual hierarchies, embryonically present in early cinema, are accentuated in the recent liberal nostalgia-for-empire films featuring a venturesome female protagonist, and thus presumably appealing to feminist codes, while still reproducing colonialist narrative and cinematic power arrangements. The desexualization of the "good" African or Indian male (servant) in *Gorillas in the Mist*, *A Passage to India*, and *Out of Africa*, not unlike the desexualization of the black domestic servant, in *The Birth of a Nation* (1915) and *Gone With the Wind* (1939), is dialectically linked to the placement of the Western woman in the (white) "pater" paradigm vis-à-vis the "natives."

Rape and Rescue Fantasy

The chromatic sexual hierarchy in colonialist narrative, typical of Eurocentric racial conventions, has white women/men occupy the center of the narrative, with the white woman as the desired object of the male protagonists and antagonists. Marginalized within the narrative, Third World female characters—when not inscribed as metaphors for their virgin land, as in *Bird of Paradise*—appear largely as sexually hungry subalterns.[62] In one scene in *The Sheik*, Arab women—some of them black—fight quite literally over their Arab man. While the white woman has to be lured, made captive, and virtually raped to awaken her repressed desire, the Arab/black/Latin women are driven by a raging libido. Here one encounters some of the complementary contradictions in colonial discourse whereby a colonized land and its inhabitants are the object of the desire for chastity articulated in the virgin metaphors while also manifesting Victorian repression of sexuality, particularly female sexuality, through unleashing its pornographic impulse.[63]

The positing of female sexual enslavement by polygamous Third World men becomes especially ironic when we recall the subjection of African American women slaves on Southern plantations with the daily lived polygamy of white male slaveowners.[64] Images of black/Arab woman in "heat" versus "frigid" white woman also indirectly highlight the menacing figure of the black/Arab rapist and therefore mythically (Roland Barthes) elide the history of subordination of Third World women by First World men. The hot–frigid dichotomy, then, implies three interdependent axioms within the sexual politics of colonialist discourse: (1) the sexual interaction of black/Arab men and white women can *only* involve rape (since white women, within this perspective, cannot possibly desire black men); (2) the sexual interaction of white men and black/Arab women cannot involve rape (since black/Arab women are in perpetual heat and desire their white masters); and (3) the interaction of black/Arab men and black/

Arab women also cannot involve rape (since both are in perpetual heat). It was this racist combinatoire that generated the (largely unspoken) rationale for the castration and lynching of African American men, thought to be a threat to white women, and the immunity of white men to punishment for the rape of African American women. The denial of any erotic intercourse between Europeans and non-Europeans had the further advantage of maintaining the myth of the West's ethnic "purity."

It is within this logic that *The Birth of a Nation* obsessively links sexual and racial phobias. The animalistic "black," Gus, attempts to rape the virginal Flora, much as the "mulatto" Lynch tries to force Elsie into marriage, and the "mulatta" Lydia accuses an innocent white man of sexual abuse, while manipulating the unaware politician Stoneman through sexuality. The threat of African American political assertion is subliminally linked to black sexual potency. It is not surprising, therefore, that the only nonthreatening black figure, the "loyal" mammy, is portrayed as completely desexualized. The thematization of blacks' hypersexuality diacritically foils (white) masculinist acts of patriotism. It is the attempted rape of Flora that catalyzes the grand act of white "liberation." The opening intertitle, which states that the very presence of the African in America "planted the first seed of disunion," and the portrayal of idealized harmony between North and South (and between masters and slaves) before the abolition of slavery scapegoat libidinous blacks for destroying the nation. The rescue of Flora, of Elsie, and of the besieged Northerners and Southerners (who are now once again united "in common defense of their Aryan Birthright") operates as a didactic allegory whose telos is the Klansmen's vision of the "order of things" (figure 12). The closure of "mixed" marriage between North and South confirms national unity and establishes a certain sexual order in which the virginal, desired white woman is available only to white man. The superimposition of the Christ figure over the celebrating family/nation provides a religious benediction on the "birth." This abstract, metaphysical birth of the nation masks a more concrete notion of birth—no less relevant to the conception of the American nation—that of children from raped black women. Naming the mulatto "Lynch," similarly, crudely blames the victims of white-on-black violence. As a final twist, Griffith shows the white man as manifesting a latent rape desire toward innocent white women via a blackface surrogate, as if burnt cork were camouflaging the identity of the real perpetrator.

Even when not involving rape, the possibilities of erotic interaction in films prior to the 1960s were severely limited by apartheid-style ethnic and

12 National (white) fantasies about rape and rescue:
The Birth of a Nation (1915)

racial codes. The same Hollywood that at times could project mixed love
stories between Anglo-Americans and Latins or Arabs (especially if incarnated by white American actors and actresses such as Valentino in *The
Sheik*, Dorothy Lamour in *Road to Morocco* [1942], or Maureen O'Hara in
They Met in Argentina [1941]) was completely inhibited in relation to African, Asian, or Native American sexuality. This latent fear of blood tainting
in such melodramas as *Call Her Savage* (1932) and *Pinky* (1949) necessitates narratives where the "half-breed" ("Indian American" in *Call Her
Savage* and "black" in *Pinky*) female protagonists are prevented at the
closure of the films from participating in mixed marriage, ironically even
through the roles are played by "pure white" actresses. It is therefore the
generic space of melodrama that preoccupies itself with "interracial" romantic interaction. The "utopian" trajectory of constituting the couple in
the musical comedy, in contrast, could not allow for a racially "subaltern"
protagonist (figure 13).

The Production Code of the Motion Picture Producers and Distributors
of America, Inc., 1930–34, an even stricter version of the Hays Office
Codes of the 1920s, explicitly states: "Miscegenation (sex relations between the white and black races) is forbidden."[65] The delegitimizing of the
romantic union between "white" and "black" "races" is linked to a broader
exclusion of Africans, Asians, and Native Americans from participation in

13 The imperial path to the couple:
Road to Morocco (1942)

social institutions. Translating the obsession with "pure blood" into legal language, Southern miscegenation laws, as pointed out by African American feminists as early as the end of the nineteenth century,[66] were designed to maintain white (male) supremacy and to prevent a possible transfer of property to blacks in the post-abolition era. "Race" as a biological category, as Hazel Carby puts it, was subordinated to race as a political category.[67] It is within this context of an exclusionary ideology that we can understand the production code's universal censorship of sexual violence and brutality where the assumption is one of purely individual victimization, thus undermining a possible portrayal of the racially and sexually based violence toward African Americans and implicitly wiping out the memory of the rape, castration, and lynching from the American record.[68] The production code, in other words, eliminates a possible counternarrative by Third World people for whom sexual violence has often been at the kernel of their historical experience and identity.[69]

The Spectacle of Difference

An analysis of the history of First World cinema in racial and colonial terms uncovers a tendency toward national "allegory," in Fredric Jameson's sense, of texts that, even when narrating apparently private stories, manage to metaphorize the public sphere, where the microindividual is doubled by the macronation, and the personal and the political, the private and the historical, are inextricably linked.[70] The national and racial hierarchies of the cinema, in other words, allegorize extradiscursive social intercourse. In the period of the Good Neighbor Policy, Hollywood attempted to enlist Latin America for hemispheric unity against the Axis. As European film markets were reducing their film consumption due to the outbreak of World War Two, Hollywood, hoping for South American markets and pan-American political unity, flooded the screens with films featuring "Latin American" themes. Interestingly, the trope of "good neighbor" very rarely extended to winning family status through interracial or international marriage. Marginalized within the narrative, and often limited to roles as entertainers, the Latin American characters in *The Gang's All Here* (1943), *Too Many Girls* (1940), and *Weekend in Havana* (1941) at the finale tend to be left at the exact point from which they began, in contrast with the teleologically evolving status of the North American protagonists. Displaying exoticism, the musical numbers provided a spectacle of difference, performing the narrative function of uniting the North American couple vis-à-vis the South Americans.

Films such as *The Gang's All Here* demonstrate a generic performative division of labor. The solid, "serious," or romantic numbers such as "A Journey to a Star" tend to be performed by the North American protagonists Alice Faye and James Ellison, while the Latin American characters perform "unserious," "excessive" numbers involving swaying hips, exaggerated facial expressions, caricaturally sexy costumes, and "think-big" style props embodied by Carmen Miranda. Her figure in the number "The Lady with the Tutti-Frutti Hat" is dwarfed by gigantesque vegetative imagery (figure 14). The final idealized image of her as a virtual fertility goddess reverberates with the opening of the film where goods from the South are unloaded in the United States; the North here celebrates the South as the fecund feminine principle capable of giving birth to the goods the North consumes. The bananas in Miranda's number, furthermore, not only enact the agricultural reductionism of Latin America but also form phallic symbols, here raised by "voluptuous" Latinas over circular quasi-vaginal forms. (But the Latina, as the lyrics suggest, will take her hat off "only for Johnny Smith," just as the "Oriental" woman in films such as *Road to Morocco* would remove her veil only for the Anglo-American.) Similarly, Josephine Baker often wore skirts of jiggling bananas or colorful feathered costumes (figure 15). This construction of Latinness, or Africanness, or Orientalness as the locus of exoticism cannot be subsumed by hegemonic North American cultural codes. The South American characters therefore do not form part of any narrative development, and their presence is "tolerable" only on the folkloric level. Character interaction in this sense allegorizes the larger relation between the North and South (or West and East) and reflects an ambivalence of attraction–repulsion toward those on the "margins" of the Western empire.

Gender and colonial discurses intersect in Hollywood's exploitation of Asia, Africa, and Latin America as the pretexts for eroticized images, especially from 1934 through the mid-1950s when the restrictive production code forbade "scenes of passion" in all but the most puerile terms and required the upholding of the sanctity of the institution of marriage at all times. Miscegenation, nudity, sexually suggestive dances or costumes, and "excessive and lustful kissing" were prohibited, while adultery, illicit sex, seduction, or rape could never be more than suggested, and then only if absolutely essential to the plot and severely punished at the end. The Western obsession with the harem, for example, was not simply crucial for Hollywood's visualization of the Orient but also authorized the proliferation of sexual images projected onto an otherized elsewhere,

14 Fertility goddess: Carmen Miranda in *The Gang's All Here* (1943)

15 Erotic animalization: Josephine Baker in *Zou Zou* (1934)

much as the Orient, Africa, and Latin America played a similar role for Victorian culture.

Exoticizing and eroticizing the Third World allowed the imperial imaginary to play out its own fantasies of sexual domination. Already in the silent era, films often included eroticized dances, featuring a rather improbable mélange of Spanish and Indian choreographies, plus a touch of Middle Eastern belly dancing in *The Sheik*, and *Son of the Sheik* [1926]). These mélanges recall the frequent superimposition within Orientalist paintings of visual traces of civilizations as diverse as Arab, Persian, Chinese, and Indian into a single feature of the exotic Orient[71]—a painterly vision of the film's "mark of the plural" (Albert Memmi). Indeed, cinema invented a geographically incoherent Orient, where a simulacrum of coherence was produced through the repetition of visual leightmotifs. Even as cinema itself evolved and changed over a century, the Orient continued to be mechanically reproduced from film to film and from genre to genre.

Orientalism was also symptomatic of the intimate ties between popular culture and scientific expositions. American orientalism and Arab beginnings in the United States are intertwined with the exposition's spectacle-of-difference. Belly dance, for example, displayed Arab exotica alongside Filipino, Kenyan, and a multitude of other worldwide "authentic rituals." In the wake of its popularity in France, diverse American entrepreneurs imported the novelty to the 1876 Philadelphia Columbia Exposition that featured Tunisian dancers, and to the 1893 Chicago Century of Progress Exposition that imported an Algerian village from the Paris exposition. Coney Island dancer "Little Egypt" inspired a craze of imitators in Brooklyn but also enraged various puritan alarmists. The daring wiggling influenced the "hoochie-coochie" phenomenon, blending orientalism into the American burlesque and striptease shows. Captured by the newly invented cinematographic camera, the 1897 film *Fatima* documents the movements of a dark-haired woman, dressed in "exotic" costume, with her navel shockingly exposed. In a period before censorship was institutionalized, movie house owners and distributors faced local community pressures for decency, which threatened their profits, but also led at times to creative approaches. In the case of *Fatima*, an interposed see-through fence was painted on the celluloid, modestly covering the dancer's bosom and hip. Fatima's alluring dance was contained through fragmentation and concealment that simultaneously obscured and revealed. The oriental woman, now in the West, was veiled as it were, but only to tantalize the peeping viewer in the dark. The filming of the dancing Fatima extended the early movie camera's fascination with closely observed motion (galloping horses, arriving trains.) But it also prolonged the fixing of the gaze on a "deviant" movement—the serpentine dance.

A French coinage and a misnomer, the term "belly dance" (dance du ventre) itself linguistically fragments the body, calling attention to merely one element in a complex bodily balancing act. (In Arabic the dance is now called "raqs sharqi," or Eastern dance.) Belly dancers were not invited to display their performative-choreographic talents in European and American theaters and music halls, however; rather, they were themselves displayed as freakish specimens in colonial exhibitions where the non-European "world" was reconstructed for local consumption. The "authentic" Algerian villages and Cairo streets fabricated in Paris, London, or New York, with their detailed objects (killims, nargilas, diwans), offered a rich mise-en-scène for the rituals performed by their colorfully dressed "dwellers," who were brought all the way from Egypt and Algeria, and paraded before the West's bemused eyes. Drinking Turkish coffee, baking Berber bread, or dancing and singing were just a few of the "rituals" that went into the staging of the Orient. Fatima, in this sense, was not conjured up genie-like out of a bottle. A clear historical, cultural, and institutional context provided the ground for her appearance on the screen. Writing about his encounter with the Egyptian belly dancer Kuchuk Hanem, Flaubert, for example, established an important paradigm for representing the Orient. His Oriental travels inspired his fictional description of Salambo's mating dance with a snake and Salomé's luring dance in *Herodias*, a description that itself inspired a series of Orientalist imaging of dangerously seductive dancers with stripped navels and draped snakes. Meanwhile, travel narratives about camel riding, paintings of harems, photographs of labyrinthian bazaars, and postcards of veiled women with exposed breasts generated a greater appetite for flesh-and-blood Arab dancers.

An "Oriental" setting (most of the films on the Orient, Africa, and Latin America were studio shot) thus provided Hollywood filmmakers with a narrative license for exposing flesh without risking censorship; they could display the bare skin of Valentino, Douglas Fairbanks, and Johnny Weissmuller as well as that of scores of women, from Myrna Loy, Maureen O'Sullivan, and Marlene Dietrich dancing with her legs painted gold to Dolores Grey moving her hips with the "realistic" excuse of other, less civilized cultures. (The code that turned Jane's two-piece outfit into one piece in later films for the most part did not affect the nude breasts of African women in the background in the *Tarzan* series,[72] evoking *National Geographic Magazine*'s predilection for "native" nudity.) In the desert and the jungle, the traditional slow-paced process of courtship leading to marriage could be replaced with uninhibited fantasies of sexual domination and "freedom," and specifically with fantasies of polygamy and even rape of presumably repressed white women. The display of rape in a "natural" despotic context continues to the present, for example, in the several attempted rapes of Brooke Shields in *Sahara* (1983). The Orient, like Latin America and Africa, thus is posited as the locus of eroticism by a puritanical society, and a film industry, hemmed in by a moralistic code.

The Imaginary of the Harem

As with voyeuristic anthropological studies and moralistic travel literature concerning non-normative conceptions of sexuality, Western cinema diffused the anachronistic but still Victorian obsession with sexuality through the cinematic apparatus. The Western male's heroic desire finds an outlet in *Harum Scarum* (1965), a reflexive film featuring a carnival-like Orient reminiscent of Las Vegas, itself placed in the burning sands of the American desert of Nevada and offering haremlike nightclubs. The film opens with Elvis Presley—attired in an "Oriental" head wrap and vest—arriving on horseback in the desert (figure 16). On arrival, Presley leaps off his horse to free a woman from two evil Arabs who have tied her to a stake. The triumphant rescuer later sings:

> I'm gonna go where the desert sun is
> Go where I know the fun is
> Go where the harem girls dance
> Go where there's love and romance
>
> Out on the burning sands, in some caravan
> I'll find adventure, while I can
> To say the least, go on, go east, young man. . . .
>
> You'll feel like a sheik, so rich and grand
> With dancing girls at your command. . . .
>
> When paradise starts calling, into some tent I'm crawling. . . .
> I'll make love the way I planned. . . .
>
> Go east and drink and feast, go east young man.

16 Entering the inaccessible harem: *Harum Scarum* (1965)

Material abundance in Orientalist discourse, tied to a history of imperial enterprises, here functions as part of the generic utopia of the musical, constituting itself, in Jamesonian terms, as a projected fulfillment of what is desired and absent within the sociopolitical status quo. Yet the "absence" is explicitly within the masculinist imaginative terrain. The harem images offer an "open sesame" to an unknown, alluring, and tantalizingly forbidden world, posited as desirable to the instinctual primitive presumably inhabiting all men. In *Kismet* (1955), for example, the harem master entertains himself with a panopticonlike device that allows him to watch his many women without their knowledge. Authorizing a voyeuristic entrance into an inaccessible private space, the harem dream reflects a masculinist Utopia of (hetero)sexual omnipotence.[73]

The topos of the harem in contemporary popular culture draws, of course, on a long history of Orientalist fantasies. Western voyagers had no conceivable means of access to harems—indeed, the Arabic etymology of the word "harem," *ḥarim*, refers to something "forbidden." Yet Western texts delineate life in the harems with great assurance and apparent exactitude, rather like European Orientalist studio paintings—for example, the *Turkish Bath* (1862), which was painted without Ingres's ever visiting the Orient. The excursions to the Orient and on-location paintings by painters such as Ferdinand-Victor-Eugène Delacroix similarly served largely to authenticate an a priori vision. Inspired by the Arab popular tradition of fantastic tales, the travelers recounted the Orient to fellow Westerners according to the paradigms furnished by European translations of *Thousand and One Nights* (*Alf Laila wa-Laila*) tales, which were often translated quite loosely to satisfy the European taste for a passionately violent Orient.[74] This Orient was perhaps best encapsulated in the figure of Salomé, whose Semitic origins were highlighted by the nineteenth-century Orientalist ethnographic vogue (e.g., Hugo von Habermann, Otto Friedrich).

Largely an upper-class phenomenon, the historical harem was in fact most striking in its domesticity. Memoirs written by Egyptian and Turkish women depict the complex familial life and a strong network of female communality horizontally and vertically across class lines.[75] The isolated but relatively powerful harem women depended on working-class women, who were freer to move and therefore became an important connection to the outside world.[76] Despite their subordination, harem women, as Leila Ahmed points out, often owned and ran their property and could at times exercise crucial political power, thus revealing the harem as a site of contradictions.[77] Whereas Western discourse on the harem defined it simply as a male-dominated space, the accounts of the harem by Middle Eastern women testify to a system whereby a man's female relatives also shared the living space, allowing women access to other women, providing a protected space for the exchange of information and ideas safe from the eyes and the ears of men. (Contemporary Middle Eastern vestiges of this tradition are found in regular all-female gatherings at which women, as in the harems, carnivalize male power through jokes, stories, singing, and dancing.) In other words, the "harem," though patriarchal in nature, has been subjected to an ahistorical discourse whose Eurocentric assumptions left unquestioned the sexual oppression of the West. The Middle Eastern system of communal seclusion, then, must also be compared to the Western system of domestic "solitary confinement" for upper-middle-class women.[78]

European women constituted an enthusiastic audience for much of the nineteenth-century Orientalist poetry written by Beckford, Byron, and Moore, anticipating the spectatorial enthusiasm for exoticist films. As travelers, however, their discourse on the harems oscillates between Orientalist narratives and more dialogical testimonies. Western women participated in the Western colonial gaze; their writings often voyeuristically dwell on "Oriental" clothes, postures, and gestures, exoticizing the female Other.[79] If male narrators were intrigued by the harem as the locus of lesbian sexuality, female travelers, who as women enjoyed more access to female spaces, undermined the pornographic imagination of the harem. Interestingly, the detailed descriptions of Turkish women's bodies in Lady Mary Wortley Montagu's letters, particularly drawn from her visit to the *hammam* (baths), points to a subliminal erotic fascination with the female Other, a fascination masquerading, at times, as a male gaze:

> I perceiv'd that the Ladys with the finest skins and most delicate shapes had the greatest share of my admiration, th'o their faces were sometimes less beautiful than those of their companions. To tell you the truth, I had the wickedness enough to wish secretly that Mr. Gervase had been there invisible. I fancy it would have very much improv'd his art to see so many fine Women naked in different postures.[80]

Female travelers, furthermore, were compelled to situate their own oppression vis-à-vis that of "Oriental" women. Lady Mary Wortley Montagu often measures the freedom endowed to English vis-à-vis Turkish women, suggesting the paradoxes of harems and veils:

> 'Tis very easy to see that they have more liberty than we have, no woman of what rank soever being permitted to go in the streets without two muslins, one that covers her face all but her eyes and another that hides the whole dress. . . . You may guess how effectually this disguises them, that there is no distinguishing the great lady from her slave, and 'tis impossible for the most jealous husband to know his wife when he meets her, and no man dare either touch or follow a women in the streets. . . . The perpetual masquerade gives them entire liberty of following their inclinations without danger of discovery.[81]

In fact, Lady Mary Wortley Montagu implicitly suggests an awareness, on the part of Turkish women, not simply of their oppression but also of that of European women. Recounting the day she was undressed in the bathhouse *hamman* by the lady of the house, who was struck at the sight of the stays, she quoted the lady's remark that "the Husbands in England were much worse than in the East; for they ty'd up their wives in boxes, of the shape of their bodies."[82]

The popular image making of the Orient internalized, in other words, the codes of male-oriented travel narratives. The continuities between the representation of the native body and the female body are obvious when we compare Hollywood's ethnography with Hollywood's pornography. Ironically, we find a latent inscription of harems and despots even in texts not set in the Orient. What might be called "harem structures," in fact, permeate Western mass-mediated culture. Busby Berkeley's musical numbers, for example, project a haremlike structure reminiscent of Hollywood's mythical Orient. Like the harem, his musical numbers involve a multitude of women who, as Lucy Fischer suggests, serve as signifiers of male power over infinitely substitutable females.[83] The mise en scène of both harem scenes and musical numbers is organized around the scopic privilege of the master and his limitless pleasure in an exclusive place inaccessible to other men. Berkeley's panopticonlike camera links visual pleasure with a kind of surveillance of manipulated female movement. The camera's omnipresent and mobile gaze, its magic carpet–like airborne prowling along confined females embodies the overarching look of the absent/present master—that is, of both the director/producer and vicariously of the spectator. The production numbers tend to exclude the male presence but allow for the fantasies of the spectator, positioning his or her gaze as that of a despot entertained by a plurality of females. Rendered virtually identical, the women in Berkeley's numbers evoke the analogy between the musical show and the harem not only as a textual construct but also as a studio practice whose patriarchal structure of casting is conceived as a kind of beauty contest (a "Judgment of Paris"). Speaking of his casting methods, Berkeley himself recounted a day in which he interviewed 723 women to select only three: "My sixteen regular girls were sitting on the side waiting; so after I picked the three girls I put them next to my special sixteen and they matched just like pearls."[84]

The Desert Odyssey

The exoticist films allow for subliminally transsexual tropes. The phantasm of the Orient gives an outlet for a carnivalesque play with national and, at times, gender identities. Isabelle Adjani in *Ishtar* is disguised as an Arab male rebel and Brooke Shields as an American male racer in the Sahara desert, while Rudolph Valentino (*The Sheik* and *Son of the Sheik*), Douglas Fairbanks (*The Thief of Bagdad*), Elvis Presley (*Harum Scarum*), Peter O'Toole (*Lawrence of Arabia*), and Warren Beatty and Dustin Hoffman (*Ishtar*) wear Arab disguise. Masquerading manifests a latent desire to transgress fixed national and gender identities. In *The Sheik*, the Agnes Ayres character, assisted by Arab women, wears an Arab woman's dress to penetrate the Oriental "marriage market," assuming the "inferior" position of the Arab women in order, paradoxically, to empower herself with a gaze on Oriental despotism. The gender switching in more recent films such as *Sahara* and *Ishtar* also allows for harmless transgressions of the coded "feminine" body language. In counternarratives such as *La Battaglia di Algeri* (*The Battle of Algiers*, 1966), however, gender and national disguises take on different signification.[85] Women of the Algerian National Liberation Front (FLN) wear Western "modern" dress, dye their hair blond, and even act coquettishly with French soldiers.[86] Here it is the Third World that masquerades as the West, not as an act of self-effacing mimicry, but as a way of sabotaging the colonial regime of assimilation.

Since clothing over the last few centuries, as a result of what J. C. Flugel calls "the Great Masculine Renunciation,"[87] has been limited to austere, uncolorful, and unplayful costumes, the projection to the phantasmic locus of the Orient allows the imagination to go exuberantly "native." Historically, the widely disseminated popular image in newspapers and newsreels of T. E. Lawrence in flowing Arab costume has partially inspired films such as *The Sheik* and *Son of The Sheik*, whose bisexual appeal can be located in their closet construction of Western man as "feminine."[88] The coded "feminine" look, therefore, is played out within the safe space of the Orient, through the "realistic" embodiment of the Other. David Lean's Lawrence, despite his classical association with norms of heroic manliness, is also bathed in a homoerotic light. When accepted by the Arab tribe, he is dressed all in white and at one point is set on a horse, moving delicately, virtually captured like a bride. Drawing a sword from his sheath, Peter O'Toole's character shifts the gendered signification of the phallic symbol by using it as a mirror to look at his own newly acquired "feminine" oriental image. More generally, the relationship between Lawrence and Omar Sharif's character gradually modulates from initial male rivalry to an implied erotic attraction, in which Sharif is associated with female imagery, best encapsulated in the scene where he is seen empathazing in misty-eyed close-up with the tormented Lawrence (figure 17). The interracial homoerotic subtext in *Lawrence of Arabia* forms part of a long tradition of colonial narratives from novels such as *Robinson Crusoe* (Crusoe and Friday) and *The Adventures of Huckleberry Finn* (Huck and Jim) to filmic adaptations such as *Around the World in 80 Days* (Phileas Fogg and his dark servant Passepartout).[89] Most texts about empire, from the Western genre to recent nostalgia-for-empire films such as *Mountains of the Moon* (1989), however, are pervaded by white homoeroticism; male explorers, deprived of women, are "forced" into physical intimacy, weave bonds of affection and desire in the course of travails in unknown, hostile lands. Homoeroticism, then, can simultaneously permeate homophobic colonialist texts.

Within this symptomatic dialectic we may also understand the textual displacement of white heterosexual desires onto African, Arab, and Latino men who play the id to the Western masculinist superego. In *The Sheik*, for example, Valentino, as long as he is known to the spectator only as Arab, acts as the id, but when he is revealed to be the son of Europeans, he is transformed into a superego figure who nobly risks his life to rescue the Englishwoman from "real" Arab rapists.[90] And the Englishwoman overcomes her sexual repression only in the desert, after being sexually provoked repeatedly by the sheik. Valentino, the "Latin lover," is here projected into another "exotic" space where he can act out sexual fantasies unthinkable in a contemporaneous American or European setting. The desert, in this sense, functions narratively as the site of moral liminality (figure 18). Orientalist films often begin in the city—where European civilization has already tamed the East—but withhold the most dramatic conflicts for the desert; where women are defenseless, and white women, more specifically, can easily become the captives of romantic sheiks or evil Arabs. The positioning of a rapeable white woman by a lustful male in an isolated desert locale gives displaced expression to a masculinist fantasy of despotic control over the Western woman "close to home," suspending any intervening protective code of morality. Puritanical Hollywood thus claims to censure women's adventurousness and the male tyranny of harems and rapes—but only, paradoxically, as a way of gratifying Western interracial sexual desires.

The male rescue fantasy and the chastening of female rebellion also undergird the narrative of a more recent reworking of *The Sheik* and *Son of the Sheik*, Menahem Golan's *Sahara*. In *Sahara*, the central figure, Dale (Brooke Shields), a feisty race-car driver and only daughter of a 1920s car manufacturer, is presented as reckless, daring, and assertive for entering the male domain of the Oriental desert and for entering the "men only" race. She also literally disguises herself as a man and adopts his profession and his mastery of the desert land through technology (figure 19). Captured by desert tribesmen, she becomes a commodity fought over within the tribe and between tribes; the camera's fetishization of her body, however, is the ironic reminder of the Western projection of stars' bodies as commodity. Scenes of Shields wrestling with her captors not only suture the Western spectator to a national rescue operation but also invite the

17 The interracial homoerotic subtext: *Lawrence of Arabia* (1962)

18 The desert as the site of the sexual imaginary: *The Sheik* (1921)

19 Gender transgressions in the Oriental desert:
Brooke Shields in *Sahara* (1982)

implied spectator into an orgiastic voyeurism. The desire for the Western woman and the fear of losing control over her are manifested in her punishment through several attempted rapes by Arabs. But at the end, the courageous winner of the race decides "on her own" to return to the noble light-skinned sheik who had rescued her from cruel Arabs at the risk of his own life. The woman, who could have won independence, still "voluntarily" prefers the ancient ways of gender hierarchies.

At times, it is implied that women, while offended by Arab and Muslim rapists, actually *prefer* masterful men like Valentino.[91] Following the screening of *The Sheik*, newspaper columnists were asking, "Do women like masterful men?" To this Valentino replied: "Yes. All women like a little cave-man stuff. No matter whether they are feminists, suffragettes or so-called new women, they like to have a masterful man who makes them do things he asserts."[92] Edith Hull expressed similar opinions: "There can be only one head in a house. Despite modern desire for equality of sexes I still believe that physically and morally it is better that the head should be the man."[93] Hull's novel and Monic Katterjohn's adaptation gratify, to some extent, a projected Western female desire for an "exotic" lover, for a romantic, sensual, passionate, but non-lethal, play with the *Liebestod*, a release of the id for the (segregated) upper-middle-class Occidental woman.[94] (The author of the source novel claimed to have written the book for relaxation when her husband was in the war and she was alone in India. She decided to visit Algeria, where she was impressed with the fine work the French government was doing.) In this sense the phantasm of the Orient can be incorporated by Western women as part of a broader colonial discourse on the "exotic" while simultaneously constituting an imaginary locus for suppressed sexual desires.

When literalized through the rescue of a woman from a lascivious Arab, the rescue fantasy not only allegorizes the rescue of the Orient from its own instinctual destructiveness but also addresses a didactic *bildungsroman* to women at home, perpetuating by contrast the myth of the sexual egalitarianism of the West. The exoticist narratives delegitimize Third World national identities and give voice to antifeminist backlash, responding to the threat to institutionalized patriarchal power presented by the woman's suffrage movements and the nascent feminist struggle. In this sense, the narrative of Western women in the Third World can be read as a projected didactic allegory insinuating the dangerous nature of the "uncivilized man" and, by implication, lauding the freedom presumably enjoyed by Western women. In *The Sheik* and *Sahara*, the English female character directly rebels against the "civilized tradition" of marriage at the beginning of the film, calling it "captivity," only to later become literally captive of lusting dark men. Transgressing male space (penetrating the marriage market by masquerading as an Arab woman in *The Sheik*, masquerading as a male race-car driver in *Sahara*), the female protagonists' hubris, their failure to appreciate Western males who protect them against desert Arabs, leads to a "fall" and the "pedagogical" chastening of attempted rapes. The telos—or, quite literally, "homecoming"—of this desert odyssey is the disciplinary punishment of female desire for liberation and renewed spectatorial appreciation for the existing sexual, racial, and national-imperial order.

My discussion of colonial constructions of gender has aimed to analyze the crucial role of sexual difference for the culture of empire. Western popular culture in this sense has operated on the same Eurocentric discursive continuum as such disciplines as philosophy, Egyptology, anthropology, historiography, and geography. From the erotic projections of *The Sheik* to the spectacular historiography of *Lawrence of Arabia*, or from the fantastic storytelling of *The Mummy* (1932) to the Egyptological mission of *Raiders of the Lost Ark*, my reading has tried to suggest that, despite some differences having to do with disparate historical moments, hegemonic Western representation has been locked into a series of Eurocentric articulations of power. Although a feminist reading of (post)colonial discourse must take into account the national and historical specificities of that discourse, it is equally important to chart the broader structural analogies in the representation of diverse colonized spaces. Challenged as we have seen by resistant counternarratives (such as *How Tasty Was My Frenchman, Nice Coloured Girls,* and *Al-Mumia*), imperial narratives are organized around metaphors of rape, fantasies of rescue, and eroticized geographies.

NOTES

1 Different sections of this essay were presented at several conferences: Third World Film Institute, New York University, New York, 1984; Middle East Studies Association, Los Angeles, 1988; Humanities Council Faculty Seminar on Race and Gender, New York University, New York, 1988; Society for Cinema Studies, University of Iowa, Iowa City, 1989; Gender and Colonialism, University of California, Berkeley, 1989; Rewriting the (Post)Modern: (Post)Colonialism/Feminism/Late Capitalism, University of Utah, Humanities Center, Salt Lake City, 1990.

2 Some of my discussion is indebted to Said's notion of the "femininization" of the Orient: Edward Said, *Orientalism* (New York: Vintage, 1979). See also Francis Barker et al., eds. *Europe and Its Others,* vols. 1–2 (Colchester: University of Essex, 1985), esp. Peter Hulme, "Polytropic Man: Tropes of Sexuality and Mobility in Early Colonial Discourse," vol. 2, and Jose Rabasa, "Allegories of the Atlas," vol. 2. Some of my discussion on gendered metaphors appears in Ella Shohat, "Imagining Terra Incognita: The Disciplinary Gaze of Empire," *Public Culture* 3, no. 2 (1991): 41–70.

3 Sir Walter Raleigh, "Discovery of Guiana," as cited in Susan Griffin, *Woman and Nature: The Roaring Inside Her* (New York: Harper and Row, 1978), 47.

4 J. Hector St. John de Crevecoeur, *Letters from an American Farmer, 1782,* as cited in Henry Nash Smith, *Virgin Land: The American West as Symbol and Myth* (Cambridge, Mass.: Harvard University Press, 1950), 121.

5 See Smith, *Virgin Land.* For nineteenth-century North American expansionist ideology, see Richard Slotkin, *The Fatal Environment: The Myth of the Frontier in the Age of Industrialization, 1880–1890* (Middletown, Conn.: Wesleyan University Press, 1985).

6 For an examination of the representation of the American frontiers and gender issues, see Annette Kolodny, *The Lay of the Land: Metaphors as Experience and History in American Life and Letters* (Chapel Hill: University of North Carolina Press, 1975); idem, *The Land before Her: Fantasy and Experience of the American Frontiers, 1630–1860* (Chapel Hill: University of North Carolina Press, 1984).

7 R. W. B. Lewis, *The American Adam: Innocence, Tragedy, and Tradition in the Nineteenth Century* (Chicago: University of Chicago Press, 1959). Hans Blumen-

berg interestingly points out in relation to Francis Bacon that the resituation of paradise, as the goal of history, was supposed to promise magical facility. The knowledge of nature for him is connected to his definition of the paradisiac condition as mastery by means of the word: Hans Blumenberg, *The Legitimacy of the Modern Age*, trans. by Robert Wallace (Cambridge, Mass.: MIT Press, 1983).

8 Jan Van der Straet's representation of America has been cited by several scholars: Michel de Certeau, "Avant propos," in *L'Ecriture de l'histoire* (Paris: Gallimard, 1975); Olivier Richon, "Representation, the Despot, and the Harem: Some Questions around an Academic Orientalist Painting by Lecomte-du-Nouy" (1885) in Barker et al., *Europe and Its Others*, vol. 1.

9 The gendering of colonial encounters between a "feminine" nature and "masculine" scientist draws on a preexisting discourse that has genderized the encounter between "Man and Nature" in the West itself. For a full discussion, see, for example, Griffin, *Woman and Nature*.

10 De Certeau, "Avant propos."

11 The film was distributed in the United States as *How Tasty Was My Little Frenchman*.

12 For a close analysis of *How Tasty Was My Frenchman*, see Richard Peña, "How Tasty Was My Little Frenchman," in *Brazilian Cinema*, ed. by Randal Johnson and Robert Stam, reprint. ed. (Austin: University of Texas Press, 1985 [1982]).

13 The report concerns another tribe, the Tupiniquim, who were massacred by their "allies," the Portuguese. It confirms the indigenous American stance, mediated in the film through the Tupinamba tribe, that despite tactical alliances, the Europeans, whether French or Portuguese, have similar desires in relation to the indigenous American land.

14 Shot in Parati (Brazil), the film mimicked indigenous American attitudes toward nudity by having the actors remain nude throughout the duration of the shooting. This production method is, of course, different from the industrial approach to shooting scenes of nudity. *How Tasty Was My Frenchman* can also be seen as part of a counterculture of the late 1960s and its general interest in non-Western societies as alternative possibilities.

15 *How Tasty Was My Frenchman* does not criticize patriarchal structures within indigenous American societies.

16 Although Cleopatra was addressed as "Egypt" in *Antony and Cleopatra*, Shakespeare there and in *The Tempest* offers a complex dialectic between the West and "its Others."

17 Colonialist representations have their roots in what Martin Bernal calls the "Aryan model," a model that projects a presumably clear and monolithic historical trajectory leading from classical Greece (constructed as "pure," "Western," and "democratic") to imperial Rome and then to the metropolitan capitals of Europe and the United States. See Martin Bernal, *Black Athena: The Afroasiatic Roots of Classical Civilization, Volume 1: The Fabrication of Ancient Greece, 1785–1985* (New Brunswick, N.J.: Rutgers University Press, 1987). "History" is made to seem synonymous with a linear notion of European "progress." This Eurocentric view is premised on crucial exclusions of internal and external Others: the African and

Semitic cultures that strongly inflected the culture of classical Greece; the Islamic and Arabic-Sephardic culture that played an invaluable cultural role during the so-called Dark and Middle Ages; and the diverse indigenous peoples whose land and natural resources were violently appropriated and whose cultures were constructed as "savage" and "irrational."

18 Egyptology's mania for a mere ancient Egypt, for example, is ironic in an Arab context where Egypt is often perceived as *the* model of an Arab country.

19 This is true even for those films produced after the great wave of national liberation movements in the Third World.

20 Tracey Moffatt's *Nice Coloured Girls* (1987) explores the relocations established between white settlers and Aboriginal women over the past two hundred years, juxtaposing the "first encounter" with present-day urban encounters. Conveying the perspective of Aboriginal women, the film situates their oppression within a historical context in which voices and images from the past play a crucial role.

21 Female voyagers very rarely occupy the center of the narrative. In contrast to scientist heroes, they tend to occupy the "feminine" actantial slot of the "helping professions"—educators and nurses (*The King and I, Black Narcissus*).

22 The passive–active division is, of course, based on stereotypically sexist imagery.

23 See, for example, Suleiman Mousa, *T. E. Lawrence: An Arab View*, trans. by Albert Butros (New York: Oxford University Press, 1966).

24 See Francis Bacon, *Advancement of Learning* and *Novum Organum* (New York: Colonial Press, 1899).

25 Ibid., 135.

26 Idem, *Novum Organum*, in *The Works of Francis Bacon*, ed. by James Spedding et al. (London: Longmans, 1870), 82.

27 Blumenberg, *The Legitimacy of the Modern Age*, 389.

28 For an illuminating reading of Haggard's *King Solomon's Mines*, see Anne McClintock, "Maidens, Maps, and Mines: The Reinvention of Patriarchy in Colonial South Africa," *South Atlantic Quarterly* 87, no. 1 (1988).

29 Television has incorporated this penchant for spinning-globe logos especially in news programs, displaying its authority over the world.

30 *Around the World in 80 Days* feminizes national maps by placing images of "native" women on the backs of maps of specific countries. The balloon used by the protagonist is referred to as "she" and called "La Coquette."

31 The feminine designation of "the moon" in French, *la lune*, is reproduced by the "feminine" iconography of the moon.

32 George Mèliés's filmography includes a relatively great number of films related to colonial exploration and Orientalist fantasies, such as *Le Fakir-Mystère Indien* (1896), *Vente d'esclaves au Harem* (1897), *Cleopatre* (1899), *La Vengeance de Bouddah* (1901), *Les Aventures de Robinson Crusoe* (1902), and *Le Palais des milles et une nuits* (1905). Interestingly, Mèliés's early fascination with spectacles dates back to his visits to the Egyptian Hall shows, directed by Maskelyne and Cooke and devoted to fantastic spectacles.

33 Here I am referring especially to the Babylon section.

34 Bazin's Malraux-inspired statement in the opening of "The Ontology of the Photographic Image" suggests that "at the origin of painting and sculpture there lies a mummy complex": André Bazin, *What Is Cinema?* trans. by Hugh Gray (Berkeley: University of California Press, 1967), 9. The ritual of cinema, in this sense, is not unlike the Egyptian religious rituals, which provided "a defence against the passage of time," thus satisfying "a basic psychological need in man, for death is but the victory of time." In this interesting analogy, Bazin, it seems to me, offers an existentialist interpretation of the mummy that at the same time undermines Egyptian religion itself, since the ancient Egyptians above all axiomatically assumed the reality of life after death—toward which the mummy was no more than a means.

35 In this essay, I refer to some of the various subgenres of Hollywood Orientalist film, of which I have identified seven: (1) stories concerning contemporary Westerners in the Orient (*The Sheik* [1921], *Road to Morocco* [1942], *Casablanca* [1942], *The Man Who Knew Too Much* [1956], *Raiders of the Lost Ark* [1981], *Sahara* [1983], *Ishtar* [1987]); (2) films concerning "Orientals" in the First World (*Black Sunday* [1977], *Back to the Future* [1985]); (3) films based on ancient history, such as the diverse versions of *Cleopatra;* (4) films based on contemporary history (*Exodus* [1960], *Lawrence of Arabia* [1962]; (5) films based on the Bible (*Judith of Bethulia* [1913], *Samson and Delilah* [1949], *The Ten Commandments* [1956]); (6) films based on *The Arabian Nights* (*The Thief of Bagdad* [1924], *Oriental Dream* [1944], *Kismet* [1955]); and (7) films in which ancient Egypt and its mythologized enigmas serve as pretext for contemporary horror mystery and romance (the *Mummy* series). I view these films partially in the light of Edward Said's indispensable contribution to anticolonial discourse—that is, his genealogical critique of Orientalism as the discursive formation by which European culture was able to manage, and even produce, the Orient during the post-Enlightenment period.

36 Malek Alloula examines this issue in French postcards of Algeria. See Alloula, *The Colonial Harem*, trans. by Myrna Godzich and Wlad Godzich (Minneapolis: University of Minnesota Press, 1986).

37 Freud associates Africa and femininity in *The Interpretation of Dreams* when he speaks of Haggard's *She* as "a strange book, but full of hidden meaning, . . . the eternal feminine. . . . *She* describes an adventurous road that had scarcely even been trodden before, leading into an undiscovered region": James Strachey, ed., *The Standard Edition of the Complete Psychological Works of Sigmund Freud* (London: Hogarth Press, 1953–74), vols. 4–5, 453–54.

38 Joseph Breuer and Sigmund Freud, *Studies in Hysteria*, trans. by James Strachey and Anna Freud (New York: Basic Books, 1957), 139.

39 Ibid., 193.

40 Sigmund Freud, "On Transformations of Instinct as Exemplified in Anal Erotism," in Strachey, *The Standard Edition of the Complete Psychological Works of Sigmund Freud*, 17:129, 135.

41 Toril Moi, "Representation of Patriarchy: Sexuality and Epistemology in

Freud's Dora," in *In Dora's Case: Freud, Hysteria, Feminism*, ed. by Charles Bren-heimer and Claire Kahane (London: Virago, 1985), 198.

42 David Macey, *Lacan in Contexts* (London: Verso, 1988), 178–80.

43 Breuer and Freud, *Studies in Hysteria*, 292.

44 Stephan Salisbury, "In Dr. Freud's Collection, Objects of Desire," *New York Times*, 3 September 1989.

45 "My voyage to the Orient was like a grand act of my interior life."

46 Linking Jews to the history, politics, and culture of the West must be seen as continuous with Zionist discourse, which has elided the largely Third World Arab history and culture of Middle Eastern Sephardic Jews. For a full discussion of the problematics generated by Zionist discourse, see Ella Shohat, "Sephardim in Israel: Zionism from the Standpoint of Its Jewish Victims," *Social Text* 19–20 (Fall 1988). This debate was partially continued in *Critical Inquiry* 15, no. 3 (1989), in the section "An Exchange on Edward Said and Difference." See esp. Edward Said, "Response," *Critical Inquiry* 15, no. 3 (1989): 634–46.

47 *The Ten Commandments*, partially shot on location in Egypt, was banned by the Egyptian government.

48 On another level, we might discern a hidden Jewish substratum undergird-ing the film. In the ancient past, Egypt dispossessed the Hebrews of their ark, and in the present (the 1930s), the Nazis have done so. But in a time tunnel, Harrison Ford is sent to fight the Nazis in the name of a Jewish shrine (the word "Jewish" is, of course, never mentioned in the film), and in the course of events the rescuer is rescued by the rescuee. A fantasy of liberation from a history of victimization is played out by Steven Spielberg, using biblical myths of wonders worked against ancient Egyptians, this time redeployed against the Nazis—miracles absent during the Holocaust. The Hebrew ark itself performs miracles and dissolves the Nazis, saving Dr. Jones and his girlfriend, Marion, from the Germans, who, unlike the Americans, do not respect the divine law of never looking at the Holy of Holies. The Jewish religious prohibition of looking at God's image and the prohibition of graven images (with the consequent cultural deemphasis on visual arts) is trium-phant over the Christian predilection for religious visualization. The film, in the typical paradox of cinematic voyeurism, punishes the hubris of the "Christian" who looks at divine beauty, while at the same time nourishing the spectator's visual pleasure.

49 *Al-Mumia* (The Mummy) was screened in the United States under the title *The Night of Counting the Years*.

50 Ahmose freed Egypt from the Hyksos invaders and ushered in the "New Empire" period of ancient Egyptian history.

51 Thutmose III, Egypt's greatest warrior pharaoh, conquered Palestine and Syria.

52 Ramses II is the reputed pharaoh of the Exodus.

53 Howard Carter's and A. C. Mace's narrative of their predecessor's 1881 discovery, for example, links the Egyptologists' rescue of mummies to the ancient Egyptian priests' protection of their kings. "There, huddled together in a shallow, ill-cut grave, lay the most powerful monarchs of the ancient East, kings whose names were familiar to the whole world, whom no one in his wildest moments had ever dreamed of seeing. There they had remained, where the priests in secrecy had hurriedly brought them that dark night three thousand years ago; and on their coffins and mummies, neatly docketed, were the records of their journeyings from one hiding place to another. Some had been wrapped, and two or three in the course of their many wanderings had been moved to other coffins. In forty-eight hours—we don't do things quite so hastily nowadays—the tomb was cleared; the kings were embarked upon the museum barge": Shirley Glubok, ed., *Discovering Tut-ankh-Amen's Tomb* (abridged and adapted from Howard Carter and A. C. Mace, *The Tomb of Tut-ankh-Amen*) (New York: Macmillan, 1968), 15.

54 In a relatively recent interview following the screening of *Al-Mumia* on Egyptian television, Shadi Abdel Salam was slightly criticized for relying on a Western musician when Egypt has its own musicians. Abdel Salam insisted that the Italian musician was chosen for his technical knowledge, and that his role was basically to arrange a preexisting popular Egyptian music: Hassan Aawara, "*Al-Mumia,*" *al-Anba*, 30 October 1983 (in Arabic).

55 In addition to Edward Said's pioneering critical writings on Orientalist discourse, and specifically on Egypt, see Timothy Mitchell, *Colonising Egypt* (Cambridge: Cambridge University Press, 1988).

56 Glubok, *Discovering Tut-ankh-Amen's Tomb*, 15.

57 Guy Hennebelle, "Chadi Abdel Salam Prix Georges Sadoul 1970: La momie est uno reflexion sur le destin d'une culture nationale," *Lettres Françoises* 1366 (30 December 1977): 17.

58 "They were the mightiest Pharaohs. What became of them?"—a meditation in the film that is reminiscent in some ways of Shelly's poem "Ozymandias."

59 See E. A. Wallis Budge, ed., *The Book of the Dead* (London: Arkana, 1989).

60 See, for example, Cynthia Enloe, *Bananas, Beaches, and Bases: Making Feminist Sense of International Politics* (Berkeley: University of California Press, 1989), 19–41.

61 See Boris Uspensky, *A Poetics of Composition* (Berkeley: University of California Press, 1973).

62 For a critical discussion of the representation of black female sexuality in the cinema, see Jane Gaines, "White Privilege and Looking Relations—Race and Gender in Feminist Film Theory," *Screen* 29, no. 4 (1988). On black spectatorship and reception of dominant films, see, for example, Jacqueline Bobo, "*The Color Purple*: Black Women as Cultural Readers," in *Female Spectators: Looking at Films and Television*, ed. by Diedre Pridram (New York: Verso, 1988); Manthia Diawara, "Black Spectatorship: Problems of Identification and Resistance," *Screen* 29, no. 4 (1988).

63 The mystery in the *Mummy* films, which often involves a kind *of Liebestod*, or haunting heterosexual attraction—for example, *The Mummy* (1932), *The Mummy's Hand* (1940), *The Mummy's Curse*—can be seen in this sense as allegorizing the mysteries of sexuality itself.

64 In her striking autobiography, Harriet Jacobs recounts the history of her family, focusing especially on the degradation of slavery and the sexual oppression she suffered as a slave woman. Her daily struggle against racial and sexual abuse is well illustrated in the cases of her master, who was determined to turn her into his concubine; his jealous wife, who added her own versions of harassment; and the future congressman who, after fathering her children, did not keep his promise to set them free: Fagan Yellin, ed., *Incidents in the Life of a Slave Girl Written by Herself* (Cambridge, Mass.: Harvard University Press, 1987).

65 Citations from the Production Code of the Motion Picture Producers and Distributors of America, Inc., 1930–34, are taken from Garth Jowett, *Film: The Democratic Art* (Boston: Little Brown, 1976).

66 I am thinking especially of Anna Julia Cooper and Ida B. Wells.

67 Hazel V. Carby, "Lynching, Empire, and Sexuality," *Critical Inquiry* 12, no. 1 (1985).

68 For a discussion of rape and racial violence, see, for example, Jacquelyn Dowd Hall, " 'The Mind That Burns in Each Body': Women, Rape, and Racial Violence," in *Powers of Desire*, ed. by Ann Snitow et al. (New York: Monthly Review Press, 1983).

69 Haile Gerima's *Bush Mama* anatomizes contemporary American power structures in which rape performed by a white policeman is subjectivized through the helpless young black woman.

70 Fredric Jameson, "Third World Literature in the Era of Multinational Capitalism," *Social Text* 15 (Fall 1986). Although Jameson speaks of allegory in a Third World context, I found the category germane for the First World, increasingly characterized by "Othernesses" and "differences" within itself.

71 For example, Ferdinand-Victor-Eugène Delacoix, as Lawrence Michalak points out, borrowed Indian clothing from a set designer for his models, threw in some "Assyrian" motifs from travel books and Persian miniatures, and invented the rest of the Maghreb from his imagination: Lawrence Michalak, "Popular French Perspectives on the Maghreb: Orientalist Painting of the Late 19th and Early 20th Centuries," in *Connaissances du Maghreb: Sciences sociales et colonisation*, ed. by Jean-Claude Vatin (Paris: Editions du Centre National de la Recherche Scientifique, 1984).

72 Images of nude breasts of African women in the *Tarzan* series relied on travelogues. In the film *Reassemblage* (1982), Trinh T. Minh-ha attempts to question the focus on breasts in ethnological cinema. For her broader critique of anthropology, see *Women, Native, Other* (Bloomington: Indiana University Press, 1989), 47–76.

73 Federico Fellini's *8½*, meanwhile, self-mockingly exposes this pornographic imagination of the King Solomon–style harem as merely amplifying the protagonist's actual lived polygamy.

74 For the Orientalist ideology undergirding the translations of *Thousand and One Nights* to European languages, see Rana Kabbani, *Europe's Myths of Orient* (Bloomington: Indiana University Press, 1986).

75 See, for example, Huda Shaarawi, *Harem Years: The Memoirs of an Egyptian Feminist (1879–1924)*, trans. by Margot Badran (New York: Feminist Press at City University of New York, 1987).

76 See Lois Beck and Nikki Keddie, eds., *Women in the Muslim World* (Cambridge, Mass.: Harvard University Press, 1978); Mervat Hatem, "The Politics of Sexuality and Gender in Segregated Patriarchal Systems: The Case of the Eighteenth- and Nineteenth-Century Egypt," *Feminist Studies* 12, no. 2 (1986).

77 For a critique of Eurocentric representations of the harem, see Leila Ahmed, "Western Ethnocentrism and Perceptions of the Harem," *Feminist Studies* 8, no. 3 (1982).

78 The artistic representation of the solitary confinement of upper-middle-class Western women within the household is fascinatingly researched and analyzed in Bram Dijkstra, *Idols of Perversity* (New York: Oxford University Press, 1986).

79 Protofeminist Western women such as Hubertine Auclert, Françoise Correze, Mathea Gaudry, and Germaine Tillion, as Marnia Lazreg suggests, reproduced Orientalist discourse in their writings. For a critique of Western feminism and colonial discourse, see, for example, Marnia Lazreg, "Feminism and Difference: The Perils of Writing as a Woman on Women in Algeria," *Feminist Studies* 14, no. 3 (1988); Chandra Talpade Mohanty, "Under Western Eyes: Feminist Scholarship and Colonial Discourses," *boundary 2* 12 (1984); Gayatri Chakravorty Spivak, "French Feminism in an International Frame," *Yale French Studies* 62 (1981); idem, *In Other Worlds: Essays in Cultural Politics* (New York: Methuen, 1987), chap. 3.

80 Robert Halsband, ed., *The Complete Letters of Lady Mary Wortley Montagu*, vol. 1 (London: Oxford University Press, 1965), 314.

81 Idem, *The Selected Letters of Lady Mary Wortley Montagu* (New York: St. Martin's Press, 1970), 96–97.

82 Idem, *The Complete Letters of Lady Mary Wortley Montagu*, 314–15.

83 For an analysis of the "mechanical reproduction" of women in Busby Berkeley's films, see Lucy Fischer, "The Image of Woman as Image: The Optical Politics of *Dames*," in *Sexual Stratagems: The World of Women in Film*, ed. by Patricia Erens (New York: Horizon Press, 1979).

84 As quoted ibid., 44.

85 For a detailed analysis of *The Battle of Algiers*, see Robert Stam, "Three Women, Three Bombs: *The Battle of Algiers* Notes and Analysis," in *Film Study Extract* (New York: Macmillan, 1975). See also Barbara Harlow's introduction in Alloula, *The Colonial Harem*, ix–xxii.

86 In *Battle of Algiers*, Algerian men of the FLN at one point wear Arab women's dress, a disguise whose ultimate goal is to assert Algerian national identity. This ephemeral change of gender identities within anticolonial texts requires a more elaborate analysis of the Third World masculine rescue operation of Third World women from the violation of First World men. Such feminist criticism directed at the works of Frantz Fanon and Malek Alloula within the Algerian–French context has also been addressed, in the black–white North American context, to Malcolm X and the Black Panthers.

87 See J. C. Flugel, *The Psychology of Clothes* (London: Hogarth Press, 1930). For an extended discussion of Flugel's writing on fashion, see Kaja Silverman, "The Fragments of a Fashionable Discourse," in *Studies in Entertainment: Critical Approaches to Mass Culture*, ed. by Tania Modleski (Bloomington: Indiana University Press, 1986); idem, *The Acoustic Mirror: The Female Voice in Psychoanalysis and Cinema* (Bloomington: Indiana University Press, 1988), 24–27.

88 The American journalist Lowell Thomas was instrumental in popularizing T. E. Lawrence in the West. His show, which consisted of lectures and footage he shot from the Middle Eastern front, after a short time was moved to Madison Square Garden. See John E. Mack, *A Prince of Our Disorder: The Life of T. E. Lawrence* (Boston: Little Brown, 1976).

89 Leslie Fiedler argues that homoerotic friendship between white men and black or indigenous men is at the core of the classical American novel. See Leslie Fiedler, *Love and Death in the American Novel* (New York: Criterion Books, 1960).

90 Interestingly, Fiedler's *The Inadvertent Epic* comments on another white female novelist, Margaret Mitchell, whose *Gone With the Wind* is structured according to scenarios of interethnic rapes.

91 For an analysis of Valentino and female spectatorship, see Miriam Hansen, "Pleasure, Ambivalence, Identification: Valentino and Female Spectatorship." *Cinema Journal* 25, no. 4 (1986).

92 *Movie Weekly*, 19 November 1921.

93 Ibid.

94 Denis de Rougemont partially traces the *Liebestod* motif to Arabic poetry. See Denis de Rougemont, *Love in the Western World*, trans. by Montgomery Belgion (New York: Harper and Row, 1974).

SACRED WORD, PROFANE IMAGE

Theologies of Adaptation

Poststructuralist discourses about translation challenge the idiom of "fidelity" and "betrayal" that assumes an innocent correspondence or symmetry between two textual worlds. Rather than a transparent and coherent presentation of an already existing source, or a process of mimicking an originary text, translation always involves acts of mediation, constructedness, and representation. At the same time, these mediations do not escape the gravitational pull of geography and history; they are shaped and produced within specific cultural contexts that imply a "take" on the very act of translation. As a mode of translation, the adaptation of words into images, or novels into film, has often been seen as an aesthetic challenge involving the movement across two differing, even clashing, media. Yet the displacement of written text onto a cinematic space, I suggest, cannot be appreciated solely in its formal dimension. Rather, it must be seen within a larger, millennial movement across philosophical traditions and cultural spaces.

Given that the status of words and images varies widely within and across cultures, how can we speak of adaptation without addressing the veristic substratum haunting both novel and film? What happens, for example, in the movement from word to image within aesthetic traditions where verism has *not* occupied center stage and where the very act of visual representation has been enmeshed in taboos and prohibitions? Here I want to explore both the multifaceted relations between texts and images, especially as shaped within a Judeo-Islamic space and the implications of these relations for film as a medium and adaptation as a practice. In fact, the tenuous and problematic dichotomy of image versus word was itself produced within a specific moment of monotheist rupture from polytheism. Yet over millennia, the word–image clash has never resulted in "pure" religious practices, as is evident from certain syncretisms found even within monotheism. Such syncretism is due, perhaps, to the impossibility of an isolationist approach to the senses. Any negation of the very interdependence of the senses becomes to an extent a futile philosophical endeavor. Since the Enlightenment, the separation of the senses, each endowed with essential qualities and placed within a hierarchy, has acquired a significant scientific meaning—that is, the privileging of the abstract over the concrete and of mind over body. Kant's preference for the sublime of pure reason, for example, secularized the monotheist investment in the disembodied God.[1]

The novel's veristic procedures, one might argue, came into existence in an era pressured by two related and diacritical forces: on the one hand, the grounding of modern science in visuality, in the objective gaze—for example, in a Cartesian perspectivalism that supposes an observing standpoint "outside," and on the other, the growing philosophical importance of a certain aniconism culminating in the twentieth-century privileging of "language" and linguistics.[2] Yet unlike figurative representations, the novel as a medium retained an a priori affinity with the religion of the word and scripture. Might the denigration of the cinema and adaptation be linked partly to the biblical phobia toward the apparatuses of visual representation? Can some of the hostility to filmic adaptations of novels, one wonders, be traced in some subliminal and mediated way to this biblical injunction against the fetish of the image, the cult of star worship, and the fabrication of false gods? In what ways has faith in the sacred word provoked contemporary iconoclastic anxiety, perceiving adaptation as an inherently idolatrous betrayal?[3] And how do we begin to account for adaptation when it is not of a book but, rather, of *The Book*, and one that virtually decrees that it *not* be adapted?

Born in a kind of righteous rage against the fetish of the image, monotheism explicitly prohibited the practice of "graven images" as part of the Ten Commandments, the first "contractual" agreement, or covenant, between God and the People of Israel as mediated by Moses. The First Commandment, "Thou shalt have no other Gods before Me (*Lo yihie lekha elohim aherim 'al panai*)," is immediately followed by the Second Commandment, "Thou shalt not make unto thee any graven image, or any likeness of any thing that is in heaven above, or that is in the earth beneath, or that is in the water under the earth (*lo ta'ase lekha pesel ve-kol tmuna asher ba-shamayim mi-ma'al va-asher ba-aretz mi-tahat va-asher ba-mayim mi-tahat la-aretz*)" (Exodus 20: 3–4). Yet Deuteronomy's verbal mediation in the expression of the taboo on visual representation paradoxically elicits in the reader's mind the very image of what is prohibited:

> Lest ye corrupt yourselves, and make you a graven image, the similitude of any figure, the likeness of male or female, the likeness of any beast that is on the earth, the likeness of any winged fowl that flieth in the air, the likeness of any thing that creepeth on the ground, the likeness of any fish that is in the waters beneath the earth: and lest thou lift up thine eyes unto heaven, and when thou seest the sun, and the moon, and the stars, even all the host of heaven, shouldest be driven to worship them, and serve them, which the LORD thy God hath divided unto all nations under the whole heaven. (Deuteronomy 4: 16–19)

The passage that stipulates the interdiction of visual representation contains its own violation. The description elicits mental moving images of, for example, flying birds and swimming fish while at the same time asking the reader to negate the very visuality elicited.

The concept of a god who is at once One and indivisible is imbricated from the outset in the admonition both against worshiping other gods and against the very medium used in worshiping them—to wit, any medium generating visual representations. Here, then, we find one of the ancestral sources of the demonization of visual media. The biblical prohibition of graven images furthermore comes with a positive corollary: the affirmation of the Holy Word. In fact, Judaic culture is thoroughly predicated on concepts having to do with the "word" and "hearing." Central to the "covenant" (*brith* in Hebrew) between God and his Jewish people, for example, is the duty of male circumcision—a ritual of purity and loyalty to God—known as *brith mila*, where, interestingly, "circumcision" shares the same etymology as "word," i.e., " mila." While designating the action committed on the newly born male body, the term can also be seen as evoking language as signifying the relationship to God. The linguistic genealogy of the Ten Commandments, or *'aseret ha-dibrot*, similarly, derives from the root "d.b.r," signifying "speak," while the Torah expression of fidelity *"na'ase ve-nishma'* (we shall do and listen)," along with the daily prayer *"Shma' Israel adonai alohenu adonai eḥad* (Listen Israel, adonai our God, one God)," places words, written and spoken, at the center of the believer's act. In contrast to the ancient Egyptian and Greek visual representations of gods, which often attached a human head to animals' bodies—for example, sphinxes or centaurs—the Jewish God could neither be represented in animal form nor be miscegenated as a cross between the human and the animal. With the Hebrew, as with the Arabic alphabet, an aesthetic of abstraction informs even the theological conception of a nonrepresentational alphabet, a feature contrasting with Egyptian hieroglyphs based on resemblance, where the relation between signifier and signified was as much iconic as symbolic.

Within the monotheistic tradition all souls are equally created in the image of God. But the biblical formulations, which on one level seem democratizing via-à-vis polytheism, also embed a series of hierarchies: man over woman (whose existence derives from Adam's rib), humans over animals, and animate over inanimate. God endows Adam—whom He created from "Adama," or earth in Hebrew—with the power of the word, the power to name, and thus granted him a verbal dominion over a world entrusted to him by his creator. Although man constitutes an imagistic representation of God, the divine itself was not to be represented in imagistic form. The very origins of monotheism are rooted in the idea not only of the indivisibility of God but also of his invisibility, whence the prohibition of visual representation—that is, the censure on making any representation of an eternal God from perishable materials fashioned by mortal human beings. The original prohibition of "graven images" is motivated by a double hostility, first to idolatry (the worship of idols) and second to polytheism (the worship of many gods). The words articulating the prohibition are also significant. One common biblical phrase in Hebrew to designate the practice of graven images is *'avodah zarah* (literally, "alien," "foreign," or "strange" work, but figuratively "false worship"). The other phrase is *'akum*, an abbreviation for *'ovdei kokhavim u-mazalot*—that is, workers/worshipers of stars and constellations (a phrasing oddly reminiscent of the Hollywood Dream Factory and its worship of stars and love of astrology). Within Abrahamic–Mosaic theology,[4] truth thus lies in the worship of the invisible, where believing is *not* seeing, and where not seeing *is* believing.

A favorite within biblical filmic adaptations precisely because of its spectacularity, the Torah story of the golden calf (*'egel ha-zahav*) bears on these issues. In that story, the People of Israel, soon after their exodus from Egypt, wait for Moses to bring his message from God, but his extended absence triggers their skepticism about the novel idea of a single invisible God. They erect a golden calf, thereby provoking Moses's outrage, culminating in his violent act of smashing the idol. A foundational narrative for the iconoclastic tradition, the story of the golden calf has initiated generations of Jews and other monotheists into the theological anomaly constituted by monotheism vis-à-vis polytheism. Moses leads *Benei Israel* forty years in the desert to cleanse them of their Egyptian habits, ensuring the death of "*dor ha-midbar* (the desert generation)" *prior* to entering Canaan, a land to be filled with a new generation that "did not know Egypt."

Idolatry was prohibited in Christianity, too, as expressed in St. Paul's cautioning against the *speculum obscurum*—the glass through which we see only darkly—or in the iconoclastic controversy of the eighth-century Byzantine church. Often the church accommodated the "pagan" penchant for animal symbolism by figuring Christ as lamb or fish. The iconoclasm of Protestantism, with its repugnance for crucifixes, saints' statues, and ecclesiastical artifice, in a sense constitutes a partial re-Judaization of Christianity.[5] Islam, for its part, also reinforced iconoclasm, highlighted through descriptions of the Prophet Muhammad's battle against the idolaters in the Ka'aba, while also recounting the smashing of idols by Abraham, the father of monotheism (Qur'an, sura 21:53/52–70). Arab history before the revelation of Islam is defined negatively as "*al-Jahiliyah*," the early period of worshiping idols (*ansab*), only to be transcended by the ensuing prohibition of iconic representation, for no object (*sanam*) can be venerated next to God.[6] Although the wall-painting decorations of palaces could portray the rulers' battles, hunts, drinking, and dancing, figural representations of living creatures were to be avoided within designated spaces of worship. Some Persian manuscripts, however, did contain winged figures accompanying Muhammad's ascension to Paradise, and in some cases the Shi'ites produced pictorial representations of diverse holy figures.[7] The Qur'an does not explicitly state that the representation of living creatures is forbidden, yet most Muslim legal scholars viewed it as a violation, since it entailed an usurpation of the uniquely creative power attributed solely to God.[8]

The prohibition of graven images condenses a number of theological arguments having to do with interrelated anxieties circling around God's image: (1) the fear of substituting the image itself for God and thus committing idolatry—worshiping the object "standing in" for God rather than God; (2) the fear of portraying God inaccurately in a kind of failed mimesis or wrongful representation; (3) the fear of embodying an infinite God in finite materials; (4) the fear of portraying God in shapes and forms made by finite humans; (5) the fear of giving "flesh" to God; and, ultimately, (6) the fear of representing the unrepresentable, that which is above and beyond representation.[9] The prohibition of graven images, furthermore, linked the religious condemnation of representing deity with the assertion of the epistemological impossibility of actually knowing the deity. How can the unknown and the transcendent be represented visually? Although man is created in God's image, this same supposedly God-like man, paradoxically, cannot know God. The knowledge is unilateral and nonreciprocal. Any attempt at representation thus amounts to a sacrilege precisely because it would force God's invisible abstractness to "descend" into the "bad neighborhood" of the visible and the earthly.

While visual representation is the main object of the taboo, *verbal* representations of God are not regarded as entirely innocent, either. The Sephardic philosopher Maimonides (Ibn Maimun), in his Arabic treatise *The Guide for the Perplexed* (*Dalalat al-ḥa'irin*), concludes, after a thorough investigation, that representing God in words can also be a sacrilege, if figurative biblical language is understood literally.[10] Maimonides's blurring of the distinction between the visual and language is rich in its implications for adaptation practices, for aesthetic theory, and for word–image relations. Extrapolating Maimonides's argument, as we shall see, would place most of cinema's five tracks under a cloud of suspicion: the visual track most obviously, but also the phonetic speech and written materials track. The very act of representation, of translating, as it were, from the verbal to the visual, entails an anxiety, for to represent God is to contain and diminish him. Maimonides censured verbal descriptions of God because they might elicit images in the responding human mind. God could be spoken about only in the negative—that which He was not. Within this theology of the negation, it is noteworthy that both Hebrew and Arabic lack any exact equivalent for the word "representation," which by definition has something "stand for" something else. Yet the very act of semiotic substitution is at the core of monotheistic anxiety. The concept of *representation* also suggests something that is both present and absent. The prefix "re" in the word "representation" implies presence through absence, since "representation" by definition is not direct—that is, present. It entails invocation of absence through an act of repetition, of presenting anew that which is not present. Yet when God's existence is addressed only in the negative, how can repetition take place? An absent presence, in other words, does not lend itself to re-presentation.

Within Judeo-Islamic theology, the importance of the word is predicated on its paradigmatic substitution for the visual. The desire for the visual and for a translation of the sacred into the perceptible is sublimated and displaced, as it were, onto other objects, images, and senses. Within these objects, the word reigns, whether in the form of the *mezuzah* (a small case nailed to the doorframe containing a scroll of parchment inscribed with the words of *"shma' Israel,"* along with the words of a companion passage from Deuteronomy), or in the *tefillin* (phylacteries—a leather case also containing a scroll designed for Jewish men to bind words to their hands and between their eyes during prayer), or in *aron ha-kodesh* (the sacred space in the synagogue containing the biblical scrolls). Judaic culture's enthusiastic embrace of textuality as a generative (and regenerative) matrix founded a way of life. It cultivated the mystique and even the erotics of the text in its physicality: the touch of the *tefillin* on the male body, the kissing of the *mezuzah* at the threshold, and the dance around the Torah scroll. Allegorical expressions are often linked to the idea of a sacred language— the language of the Bible delivered by God—involving various degrees of concealment, especially the Torah as a fragmentary discourse, virtually soliciting the hermeneutic deciphering that typifies, for example, the Talmudic commentaries. The historical narrative of the Jewish people has been deeply imprinted and "engraved" by texts. The messianic verses of the Sephardic poet Edmond Jabès describe Judaism as preeminently a passion for writing. For the homeless Jew, Jabès argues, the book is the fatherland and home is Holy Writ. Jabès anticipates, in this sense, not only George Steiner's idea of a textual homeland but also the glorification of the text and writing in the work of Jacques Derrida. In his essay on Jabès, Derrida speaks of the "pure and founding exchange" between the Jew and writing: The Jew chooses the scripture (writing, *écriture*), and Scripture chooses the Jew.[11]

In both Judaism and Islam, letters themselves become signs of the sublime as well as a site of visual pleasure, developed particularly within the art of calligraphy. In Islam, writing is crucial, since God communicated and revealed himself through his Word, in the Arabic language—itself a subject for a major theological debate about whether the divine language is *khaliq* (creator) or *makhluq* (created). The genealogy of the word "Qur'an" derives from "q.r.a," the linguistic root of the word "read." "Read," says the Qur'an (96: 3–5), "And thy Lord is the Most Bounteous, Who teacheth by the pen, Teacheth man that which he knows not." At the same time, the Qur'an (92) states: "O believers, wine and games of chance and statues and (divining) arrows are an abomination of Satan's handiwork; then avoid it!"

Whereas the art of writing was revered, the art of figurative images was more controversial. The visual artist could in a sense be viewed as usurping God's prerogative as the sole "author" of life. The production of the visual, as with Judaism, was often displaced onto other mediated forms. The surfaces of mosques and public buildings, for example, were covered with Arabic writing shaped in forms that would enhance the architectural design of a building. Calligraphy turned letters into a sensual visual medium, designing myriad geometric or vegetal forms created out of words, either through repetition or through sentences, often highlighting the greatness of God, His eternity and glory. Calligraphy gradually became the most important Islamic art form, deployed even in nonreligious contexts, adorning coins, textiles, and pottery. The Judaic and Islamic censure of "graven images" and the preference for abstract geometric designs, known as arabesques, cast theological suspicion on directly figurative representation and thus in a sense on the ontology of the mimetic arts. While Roman Catholicism shared the Judaic prohibition of substituting an image of God for God, it also accommodated the desire for a visual, for the visible God. Brilliant paintings and frescos representing sacred scenes, including those of individual saints and even some pictorial adumbrations of the deity, adorn churches. Within the Judeo-Islamic ethos, a visible carnal divinity, such as that shown in Michelangelo's painting on the ceiling of the Sistine Chapel featuring a bearded male God in the process of creating Adam, would be virtually unimaginable.

Marking the beginning of the so-called modern encounter between Europe and the Muslim world, the arrival of French forces in Ottoman Alexandria in 1798, along with the nineteenth- and twentieth-century imperial domination of North Africa and West Asia, triggered a complex aesthetic dialogue revolving around issues of mimesis and verism.[12] Initiated both by individuals and institutions, a growing movement of translations of European literature (largely French and English) had an impact on the production of modern Arabic literature (the realist novel, in particular) as a syncretic site, mingling diverse Arabic literary traditions with veristic "Western" procedures. On one level, the idea of mimetic art, as we have seen, would seem almost inherently alien to the monotheistic tradition and to Judeo-Muslim aesthetic regimes. Within this perspective, Judeo-Muslim culture, partial to the abstract, would seem to be essentially antithetical to the diverse techniques and movement of reproducing the real: the Renaissance perspective in the arts, the nineteenth-century rise of realism and naturalism as literary "dominants," and the ever more refined technologies of verism—specifically, the still and cinematographic cameras with their built-in Renaissance perspective.

Verism did indeed pose an interesting challenge to cultures where mimesis had not constituted the norm. At the same time, however, Judeo-Muslim civilizational space cannot be reduced to the taboo on graven images, or viewed as completely disallowing the representation of living creatures, or as devoid of all mimetic practices. The Umayyad mosque in Damascus, for example, utilized mosaics that portray houses and the natural world within a relatively realistic fashion. In palaces, as suggested earlier, the visual taboo was not fully respected; whence, the decoration of walls in tiles, wood, or stucco, as well as wall painting, depicting human beings engaged in parties, wars, or hunting. Offering its own mimetic form, miniature art invited sensual pleasure. Illustrative images drawn in manuscripts—for example, the stories of *Kalila wa-Dimna* from the twelfth and thirteenth centuries—contained pictures of birds and animals.[13] Furthermore, the Eurocentric narrative that emplots artistic history, like history in general, in a linear trajectory leading from the Bible and *The Odyssey* to literary realism and artistic modernism, raises the question of whether such foundational texts, like their cultural geography, can be defined simply as Western.[14] Telling the history of the novel as emerging solely from "Europe"—defined as completely apart from the cultural spaces of North Africa and West Asia—and then "spreading" to Africa and Asia constitutes a problematic diffusionist narrative. The emergence of the novel, within another perspective, could be narrated as coming into existence within the syncretic worlds of the Mediterranean.[15] Even the canonical European novel *Don Quixote* has the narrator refer to translation from an Arabic manuscript, a cultural intertext marginalized by canonical literary history.[16] A more dialogic view of the relationship between the so-called East and West would allow for spaces of syncretism, such as the uncovering of the traces of Arabic literature and art within Iberian culture and, through it, within the European Renaissance.

The cultural dialogue between the "West" and the "rest" is not of recent date, nor is it unidirectional, whereby the rest simply follow the West. The

high points of Western history—Greece, Rome, Renaissance, Enlightenment, Modernism—can be said to have been moments of cultural fusion,
moments when Europe became traversed by currents from elsewhere.
Western art has been at least partly indebted to and transformed by non-
Western art.[17] The movement of aesthetic ideas, then, has always been (at
least) two-way—whence, the Moorish influence on the poetry of courtly
love, the African influence on modernist painting, the impact of Asian
forms (Kabuki, Noh drama, Balinese theatre, ideographic writing) on
Western theater and film, and the influence of Arab and Africanized dance
forms on such choreographers as Ruth St. Denis, Martha Graham, and
George Balanchine.[18] Artistic modernism traditionally has been defined
in contradistinction to realism as the dominant norm in representation.
Within most cultural geographies, however, realism was rarely the dominant aesthetic mode. Modernist reflexivity as a reaction against realism, in
other words, could scarcely wield the same power of scandal and provocation. Modernism in this sense can be seen as a rather provincial, local
rebellion. Vast regions of the world, and long periods of artistic history,
have shown little allegiance to, or even interest in, realism. In India, a two-
thousand-year tradition of narrative circles back to classical Sanskrit drama
and epics, which tell the myths of Hindu culture through an aesthetic
based less on coherent character and linear plot than on the subtle modu-
lations of mood and feeling (*rasa*).[19] While a Euro-diffusionist narrative
makes Europe a perpetual fountain of artistic innovation, one could argue
for a multidirectional flow of aesthetic ideas, with crisscrossing ripples and
eddies of influence.

At the same time, in the wake of the colonial reencounter between Europe and the Arab world, verism nonetheless entered a new geopolitical semantics. Coming to occupy a central role in Arab aesthetic practices, verism
was genealogically linked to the discourse of modernization—a discourse
shared by both imperialist and nationalist ideologies. As appendages to the
modernization project, art schools were founded in cities like Istanbul,
Alexandria, and Beirut. Artists of the "Orient" were learning to "disorient"
regional aesthetics by mimicking Western styles of mimesis. Figurative art
signaled a world in transition, in contrast to the largely abstract art of Islam,
now rendered "traditional," an obsolescent practice that inevitably would
have to be abandoned in favor of the forces of progress. Within this
melioristic metanarrative, mimesis conveyed not merely learning a mode
of artistic technique, but also the process of becoming conversant with the
aesthetic and cultural norms of so-called Western modernity.

A photograph in the January 1939 issue of *National Geographic* magazine inadvertently captures some of the paradoxes resulting from the intertwined arrival of verism and nationalist modernization in Muslim spaces. The photograph documents mostly female students drawing a nude female model in a "life class" at the Academy of Art in Istanbul (figure 20). Although the photo does not show the nude model, the reader/viewer receives a glimpse of her image(s) through the various canvases. In a kind of *mise en abyme*, this photograph records not only the process of making realistic images; it also makes the viewer aware of the very process of viewing via the photographic lens, since the viewer's ability to see is inscribed in the mechanics of the camera itself as the scientific reincarnation of Renaissance perspective and of the mimesis of three-dimensionality. Verism as artistic practice was gaining importance in the same place and around the same time that Erich Auerbach wrote his magnum opus *Mimesis* concerning the Western tradition of realistic representation. Notably, it was in Turkey, a site of syncretism between Greek mimesis and Islamic arabesque, that Auerbach, a German Jewish refugee, contrasted the Hebrew Bible and Hellenic mythology, whose central figures had lived in the same region millennia earlier. Indeed, *Mimesis* itself was premised on a dichotomy between Hebraism, associated with ethics, depth, equality, and the word, and Hellenism, associated with aesthetics, superficiality, hierarchy, and the image.[20]

Several hundred years after the introduction of Renaissance perspective, and almost a century after the introduction of the camera, there should be nothing unusual about the photo of the art school. Yet the novelty of a life class in a Muslim space merits the *National Geographic* gaze. The photo celebrates the apprenticeship of the young Turkish women in the creation of figurative art while also signaling that a world in transition is unfolding in front of the reader/viewer's eyes. The largely abstract art of Islam is implicitly rendered "traditional," replaced by the new of the modern movement. The photo's caption—"From Veiled Women to Life Classes with Nude Models"—explicitly links changing conventions in aesthetics to transformations in conceptions of gender. Wearing white gowns and standing in front of their canvases, the modern Turkish women—symbolic daughters of the new father of the nation, Atatürk—abandon Muslim aesthetics, associated with the fallen Ottoman Empire, along with the veil. Mimesis here conveys the process within a telos of becoming "like" and "repeating" the aesthetic and cultural norms of "Western modernity."

In this strange rendezvous between "East" and "West," realistic aes-

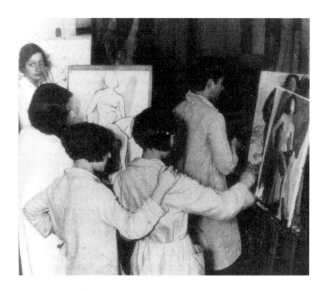

20 Imitating mimesis in Istanbul: *National Geographic* magazine
(January 1939)

thetics signified modernity, while non-figurative art was implicitly cast as past times. Yet such an encounter generates some fascinating paradoxes. During the same period that the "Orient" was learning realism, the "Occident," partly inspired by the non-West, was unlearning it. The ideology of political and economic modernization found its aesthetic corollary not in avant-garde modernism but, rather, in realism and in modernizing through the mastery of up-to-date veristic techniques. In the same period that the modernist avant-garde was rebelling against mimesis, opting for new modes of abstract, geometric, and minimalist representation, Muslim aesthetic practices, then, were prodded toward mimetic realism as an integral part of modernity. Yet, discourses about aesthetic modernization have been detached from the East's contemporaneous experimentation with the modernist languages of futurism, surrealism, and cubism. The so-called non-West, in this sense, has been often cast out of the metanarrative of art history, always seeming to lag behind the West's aesthetic advancement.

The spread of modernization ideology into the Middle East had the effect of promoting realism as the embodiment of modernity rather than that of the avant-garde modernism. A product of modernity, the cinema registered and reinforced this aesthetic tendency. It was not the nonspatial painting of the miniature and the geometrical composition of the arabesque that were "translated" to the screen but, rather, the mimetic qualities of the novel. In some ways, the novel's verism seemed more appropriate to a technology whose "essence" seemed to be equated with the "real." The penchant for adapting novels reached a kind of paroxysm in the 1950s, as the work of celebrated Egyptian writers such as Ihsan Abd al-Quddous, Tawfik al-Hakim, and Youssef al-Seba'i was brought to the screen. Well-known French, English, and Russian novels were also adapted by French-educated filmmakers, such as Togo Mizrahi, Youssef Wahbi, Henri Barakat, and Hassan al-Imam, who Egyptianized the non-Egyptian novels and remade films already adapted to the screen in France or Hollywood. Among such readapted novels were Emile Zola's *Thérèse Raquin*, Anatole France's *Thais*, Dostoevsky's *Crime and Punishment* and *The Brothers Karamazov*, and Tolstoy's *Resurrection* and *Anna Karenina*. At least fifteen French novels were adapted numerous times, including Victor Hugo's *Les Misérables*; Balzac's *Le père Goriot*; Dumas's *The Count of Monte Cristo*, actually adapted seven times; and Pagnol's *The Trilogy*, adapted four times.[21] Verism was propelled to center stage, signifying the double-edged sword of modernity: assimilation to hegemonic Western culture as well as resistance to its aesthetic regime.

Representations of living creatures within the diverse technologies of verism were becoming a virtual lingua franca within a modernizing aesthetic trend in Arab Muslim cultural practices. Photographic and cinematographic images, significantly, were not categorically prohibited. Based on theological interpretations of the *ḥadith*, or the Prophet's sayings—"Angels do not enter a house where an image is stored unless it is a sign on fabric (*ina al-mala'ika la tadkhulu baytan fih suratun illa raqamun fi thawbin*)"— photography was considered not a creation but a sign produced in a pattern or a formula.[22] Photography and the cinema were defined not as creating souls in the likeness of God but, instead, as presenting God's creation and thus reinforcing his power rather than competing with Him.[23] Yet treating holy matters within the profane space of novels and films did provoke tensions, themselves allegorizing the diverse force fields shaping contemporary identities in Arab Muslim spaces. The question of the novel as a "modern" literary form, adapting religious subjects within veristic fiction, became itself a contested terrain. And in the colonial and neocolonial context of the negative portrayal of Muslim religion, the adaptation of the Holy Text for the screen triggered clashes. Thus, even apart from the problem of cinematic adaptation, novels already formed a conflictual space. To take a recent example, *The Satanic Verses* did not have to wait for screen adaptation to provoke an Islamicist fatwa against the author Salman Rushdie.

In the Middle East, the colonial clash has also left its imprint on the image–word debate. From its outset, Egyptian cinema was the site of cultural tensions, especially when European companies attempted to produce films touching on Islamic themes. The film *Al-Zouhour al-Qatela* (Fatal Flowers, 1918), for example, offended the Islamic community by garbling several phrases from the Qur'an, thus provoking the first case of censorship.[24] A more severe case occurred in 1926 around the anticipated production of a film about the grandeur of the early days of Islam. The Turkish writer Wedad Orfi, who initiated the idea, approached the Egyptian director and actor Youssef Wahbi to play the role of the Prophet Muhammad in a film to be financed by the Turkish government and a major German producer. Within a modernizing vision that characterized the new Turkish nation, it is not surprising that Atatürk, as well as the Istanbul council of *ulama* (scholars of religious law), gave their approval. Upon learning of the plan, the Islamic Al-Azhar University in Cairo alerted Egyptian public opinion, and published a juridical decision, stipulating that Islam categorically forbids the representation of the Prophet and his Companions on the screen. King Fouad sent a severe warning to Wahbi, threatening to exile him and strip him of his Egyptian nationality.[25] The protests resulted in the abandoning of the adaptation of the Qur'an, for while the representations of living creatures within the framework of the relatively profane could be tolerated, such representations within the realm of the sacred were unacceptable.

These protests triggered the 1930 prohibition against portraying the Prophet and the four righteous caliphs, while, later, the 1976 censorship law explicitly stated that "heavenly religions [i.e., the monotheistic religions, known in Arabic as *ahl al-kitab*, or the People of the Book] should not be criticized. Heresy and magic should not be positively portrayed."[26] Suspicion of the cinema led some religious scholars in Saudi Arabia to oppose even the building of movie theaters, although films have been watched within the private sphere. With the growing power of Islamicists in Egypt, in 1986 the prohibition was expanded to include all the biblical holy figures and prophets—for example, Abraham, Moses, Jesus—mentioned in the Qur'an.[27] And more recently, Youssef Chahine's film *Al-Muhajir* (The Emigrant, 1994), a loose adaptation of Joseph's story, angered the Islamicists due to the representation of one of the Qur'an's holy figures, obliging the director (of Catholic background) to defend his cinematic reading of the biblical story in court. Although its presumed "dubious morality" as a social institution has stirred much apprehension, the cinema's intrinsic capacity to violate a deeply ingrained taboo, in sum, has also contributed to its guilty status.

The spread of veristic-mimetic practices has not, for the most part, interrupted the millennial aesthetic code governing sacred spaces, which has continued to resolve the problem of visual pleasure and the censure of graven images through a complex mode of aesthetic abstraction. If in the past two centuries images of living creatures have inundated Arab Muslim visual culture, this limited verism could exist mostly because it was reserved for the realm of the mundane and thus did not interfere with the more deeply ingrained taboo. Arab novelists and filmmakers have often respected the spatial division between the sacred and the profane, drawing the contours of the realist novel and film to exclude religiously prohibited visual representations. In contrast, film history in Christian-dominated societies has frequently presented prominent religious figures such as Christ. Since the inception of cinema, missionaries in Africa and Asia used screenings of such films as *From the Manger to the Cross* (1912) to convert and spread the word of Christ. It was not the mere act of representing Christ or Christian figures that provoked official Catholic wrath against Luis Buñuel's work but, rather, the films' satirical stance toward Christianity.

Mel Brooks's satirical adaptation of the Bible's tale of the Tablets of the Covenant (*Luḥot ha-Brith*) on Mount Sinai in *History of the World, Part I* (1981; figure 21) was also at odds with the Orthodox Jewish perspective. The Brooks film has Moses, who receives three rather than two tablets, reduce the number of the commandments after he drops one of the tablets, thus calling attention to the arbitrariness of the Torah's number ten. In a reflexive moment, the film also calls attention to its own transgression of the commandment condemning *any* visual representation of the sacred. In Israel, meanwhile, despite the political marginalization of religious parties during the decades of Labor Party rule, satires of the Bible in the public sphere were usually met by political pressures for censorship. A mid-1970s TV program, *Nikui Rosh* (Head Cleaning), re-enacted the biblical story of the deliverance of the Torah, casting a funny-looking comedian (Dubby Gal) as Moses. Barefoot on the hot desert sand, as God delivers an interminable message, Moses hops from foot to foot, his suffering exacerbated by the heat of the burning bush. Shown on the state-owned TV

21 Breaking the Ten Commandments: *History of the World, Part I* (1981)

station, the scene provoked the protests of the religious parties for having subsidized offensive images. Apart from the carnivalesque parody of the grand monotheistic moment, *Nikui Rosh* transgressed another taboo by endowing Moses with an image. Not only does Jewish culture barely display any archive of representations of Moses, but even Moses's tomb was intended to remain unknown. Unlike Hollywood's "map of the stars" that guides the vision of pilgrims in search of local deities, Judaic tradition reinforces the importance of the biblical obscuring of Moses's burial place, precisely in order to prevent this iconoclast leader from becoming himself the object of idolatrous worship.

In the case of Judeo-Muslim tradition, even a respectful visual representation of prophets and of God comes under suspicion, and the act of mimetic visualization itself is subjected to surveillance. Interpreting the prohibition on graven images strictly, members of the Jewish Ashkenazi faction of Naturei Karta, for example, for the most part have resisted the camera, shielding their faces with hats or hands to ward off photographers. Given this context of a deeply ingrained taboo, it is no coincidence that the screens of both Israel and the Muslim/Arab states have not proliferated in adaptations of the Bible or the Qur'an. In Egypt, most films about Islam were produced in the wake of Gamal Abdel Nasser's revolution during the 1950s and 1960s and constituted a vehicle for promoting and staging national cohesion.[28] Most narratives were set in the early days of Islam, such as *Bilal, Mu'adhin al-Rasul* (Bilal, The Prophet's Muezzin, 1953)[29] by Ahmad al-Tukhi, who also directed *Intisar al-Islam* (The Victory of Islam, 1952) and *Bayt Allah al-Haram* (The House of God, 1957) while only a few were produced about latter-day Arab Muslim figures, such as Salah al-Din (1961), who fought against the crusaders, or about mystic figures such as al-Sayed Ahmed al-Badawi (1953, by Baha Eddine Charaf) who spread Islam in the thirteenth century in Egypt.[30]

At the same time, the largely veristic procedures of Arab, Israeli, Turkish, and Iranian cinemas have performed a certain rupture with the non-veristic visual tradition, tending instead to adhere to the rules of mimetic realism. Thus, within a film culture that has largely departed from the Islamic principles of visual representation, a faithful adaptation of the Qur'anic narrative has posed serious aesthetic challenges.[31] While the Qur'an can be said to possess narrative qualities that the historical realist genre can easily accommodate, the scriptural taboo places obstacles to its "translation" into the cinema. Arab films that sought the historical genre to tell of Islam resolved the problem of representing holy figures by avoiding it, even while the narrative unfolds all in the name of God and His prophet.

Mustafa Akkad's film *Al-Risala* (The Message, 1976), however, represents a rare mode of adaptation of the Qur'anic narrative concerning the Prophet's life.[32] The script received the theological imprimatur of Al-Azhar University, partly due to the filmmaker's innovative approach to evoking the sacred without actually visually representing it. Never represented in the film, the Prophet Muhammad's presence is only implied. The film's images show what is relatively unsacred, acknowledging, as it were, the inferiority of the visual and its fallibility in the face of the holy. As announced at the film's opening, *The Message* was submitted to the scholars and historians of Islam at Al-Azhar University in Cairo and the High Islamic Congress of the Shi'ites in Lebanon, who approved the "accuracy and fidelity of this film." After a short prelude, the intertitles inform us that:

> THE MAKERS OF THIS FILM HONOUR THE ISLAMIC TRADITION
> WHICH HOLDS THAT THE IMPERSONATION OF THE PROPHET
> OFFENDS AGAINST THE SPIRITUALITY OF HIS MESSAGE.
> THEREFORE, THE PERSON OF MOHAMMAD
> WILL NOT BE SHOWN.

Written in capital letters and in bold to emphasize this crucial piece of information, the warning addresses various publics, especially those fearful of blasphemy as well as those expecting a spectacular epic film in the Hollywood biblical tradition. On the one hand, the film's grand scale, its high production values, its "location" shooting—with Morocco and Libya standing in for the holy cities of Saudi Arabia (Mecca and Medina)—its international crew, its wide-screen cinematography, its ostentatious commentative music, and its larger-than-life heroes would all seem to point to a multiple generic affiliation with a number of spectacular genres: the biblical epic, the historical film, and the war film. The story of God's revelation to Muhammad and Islam's triumph over the idolaters of Mecca would seem to offer the celebrated hero as a vehicle for spectatorial identification. While traditional identification is facilitated via recognized stars, especially Anthony Quinn in the role of Hamza, Muhammad's uncle and close follower, the truly central hero remains incognito. The film's introductory intertitles undercut any possible desire or anxiety concerning the visual representation of the hero of both religion and film. Against the grain of the spectacular epic tradition, the intertitles announce a conspicuous lack—that of the visual (and aural) pleasure of getting to know our hero and star, the Prophet Muhammad himself. In this sense, religious fidelity—to the text and to religious values—paradoxically entails *in*fidelity to certain fundamental features of the film medium. The intertitles seem to promise nothing but frustration of the scopophilic cinematic experience.

In the context of adaptation, the word "fidelity" is often associated with the expectation of an exact correlation between the "original" literary text and its filmic representation, with the word "infidelity" suggesting a betrayal of the canonical text. In the context of adapting the Qur'an, "infidelity," however, takes on serious overtones, as it involves a betrayal of God's word in the most literal sense, since the Qur'an, like the Bible, is believed to be an unmediated delivery of the sacred word. The burden of fidelity in the case of Qur'anic screen adaptation is multifold. First, within the theological stricture concerning visual representation, the film's capacity to represent is not equated with the act of interpretation; the filmmaker is expected to play a "neutral" role and cannot presume to offer or "add" interpretations, an act reserved for the scholars of the Qur'an. Yet the very permission given for making *The Message* inadvertently does imply some form of interpretation, since the Qur'an, as we have seen, is ambiguous on the subject of making images.

Second, the filmmaker is expected to abide by the tradition of avoiding imaging the Prophet, never using the cinematic space to represent the nonvisualizable. Even if little is revealed about his appearance, Muhammad acts, speaks, and is talked about in the Qur'an. In the film, third-person speech about the Prophet does not pose a theological problem, since it does not involve his immediate presence on the screen. However, although Muhammad is an absent presence in the film, on a number of occasions he is addressed in the second person, as "you." In a few rare instances, the spectator is even placed within the subjective point of view of Muhammad himself. In one early sequence set against the backdrop of Ka'aba, for example, we witness myriad idolatrous practices. A few of the leading pagans suddenly turn their gaze in the direction of the camera/spectator, their faces manifesting awe and anxiety, underlined by a gentle murmur of wind on the sound track. The idolaters briefly suspend their activities, followed by a visitor's question: "Who is that man who looked into my soul?" The visual, the sound, and the dialogue tracks are all orchestrated to imply a holy presence, which we infer to be that of Muhammad himself. The Prophet's observation of the sinful activities constitutes the film's first deployment of a disembodied gaze. The ensuing dialogue proceeds to orient the spectator, affirming that *The Message* employs an unconventional language to signify the screen presence of an invisible presence.

The Message negotiates this dialectics of presence-absence through a highly unusual deployment of point-of-view shots, over-the-shoulder shots, and shot/counter-shots, all unconnected, as it were, to any "visible" subject who might "anchor" these shots within a specific body and face. While the film *Lady in the Lake* (1947) sutured the spectator into a total viewpoint of an unseen subject, *The Message*'s new twist on cinematic language entails a positioning of the spectator within multiple modes of address. In one instance, we hear a dialogue to the effect that Muhammad is now on a mountain, followed by an aerial shot that carries us to the mountain and into the darkness of a cave, as well as to what we assume to be Muhammad's presence, all accompanied by the now familiar sound of rushing wind. The black screen is reigned over by an acousmatic voice enunciating: "Muhammad, Read! In the name of thy Lord who created Man from a sensitive drop of blood, who teaches Man what he knows not. . . . Read!" An image of a flame, slowly moving up from the bottom to the center of the screen, conjures up what literally becomes light out of darkness. We have not seen Muhammad or heard his voice, but we did hear *a* voice, implied to represent the words of the angel Gabriel. Is this voice an enactment of Gabriel's voice or does it merely relay quotations excerpted from the Qur'an and read by the film's sporadic voiceover? *The Message*'s codified language tempts the spectator into inferring that the voice could not possibly be diegetic, since that would denote an explicit reenactment of Gabriel, when the film never even provides the mortal prophet with a literal voice. Such denotation would amount to an acoustic corollary to the re-presentation in flesh of a divine figure. The very act of an actor lending his voice to a prophet, or to an angel—not to mention to God—would be construed as sacrilege. However, despite the spectator's initiation into the film's governing theological logic and aesthetic code of effacing holy figures, the cinematic status of Gabriel's voice remains ambiguous. Even if we feign that the film's narrator is not performing the voice of an angel, his acousmatic presence ironically places him at the apex of the sound track's vocal hierarchy. His deep and sanctimonious male voice, as well as his non-diegetic position, elevates him to the privileged slot of the omniscient narrator with a radiating, God-like authority.

Placing us within the Prophet's subjectivity, some sequences, as we have seen, suture the spectator into a static, literal point of view. Others, meanwhile, engage the viewer in Muhammad's dynamic movement across space as well as in his interaction with diverse interlocutors. When Muhammad escapes the idolatrous Meccans into a cave, for example, the film cuts from the searching Meccans riding in the wide, open desert to the claustrophobic darkness of a cave, as "Muhammad" glances through the unbroken spider's web at the approaching enemies (figure 22). The film deploys an over-the-shoulder, low-angle shot, as if looking from Muhammad's sitting position inside the cave at the standing Meccans who wonder over his whereabouts. In this over-the-shoulder shot, however, the spectator is deprived of a literal shoulder over which he or she could "lean" his or her cinematic gaze. Yet since the spectator is cognitively already accustomed to the film's coded language, he or she makes the visual leap and "fills in" the gap. The Meccans at the cave's entrance, illuminated by the bright sun, are seen within Muhammad's point of view; the spectator's senses, perceptions, and knowledge are confined to the trapped hero's "eyes" and "ears." The overlapping between primary identification (i.e., with the camera and with the spectator's own perception) and secondary identification (with characters and the diegesis) enhances the increasing suspense, happily resolved through an additional thrill of a "firsthand" experience of a deus ex machina intervention: the unbroken web convinces the persecutors to leave, since Muhammad could not possibly be hiding inside the cave. Human logic fails the antagonists, and, allegorically, the *kafir*, the infidel or unbelieving spectator, for God's hand possesses different rational, dictating scenarios written from above (*maktub*).

22 The Prophet Muhammad's disembodied gaze: *The Message* (1976)

In other sequences, characters speak to Muhammad, or more precisely to the camera from diverse angles, furnishing the spectator with a sense of the Prophet's corporeality and bodily kinesis: sitting, standing, getting off a camel, building a mosque, or walking away from an offensive enemy. In these sequences, the deployment of the conventional shot/counter-shot only highlights the unequal status of the two interlocutors vis-à-vis the camera: the seen/heard and the unseen/unheard. In contrast to Christian theological acrobatics to explicate the Holy Trinity, Jesus in Muslim tradition is revered not as a deity but only as a prophet who, like Muhammad, is thought of as a mortal figure, with the difference that the latter is said to be the *last* prophet. Yet despite the film's endorsement of Muslim theology, its formal procedures for rendering the Prophet as a visual absence ironically only endow him with God's own attributes as the invisible deity. At the same time, in spite of Muhammad's concealment, the film offers the spectator another inadvertent blasphemous experience: the vicarious power of "being" the Prophet. The diverse characters approaching Muhammad address the camera directly, having the effect of conflating the Prophet with the viewer. As a result, the spectator is converted *into* Muhammad—a cinematic act that paradoxically would seem even more sacrilegious than simply revealing a corporeal Prophet on the screen. To put it differently, while such aesthetic paradigms observe the prohibition, they also betray tensions rooted in the challenge of translating across differing media.

Unlike the cinema in the Muslim world, where adaptation was bound to frustrate any desire to gaze at God and his prophets, Hollywood's biblical films emerged from a long history of Christian visual representation of divine figures, even if some of the producers were of Jewish descent. Often happily endorsed by Christian denominations, biblical films represented holy figures such as Moses or Christ in a way that gave an additional twist to the phrase "larger than life." At the same time, in Hollywood, too, biblical narratives were subjected to a surveillance regime. The Hays Office Code and the Production Code of 1934 explicitly forbade the negative depiction of religious figures. For the church, adaptation—as in the case of Arab cinema—was judged in terms of its faithfulness to the original text. Quite in contrast to a poststructuralist stance concerning the ubiquity of mediation, the theological expectations about biblical and Qur'anic adaptation for the screen have tended to be dominated by a nonreflexive discourse in which an adaptation does not form a mode of "reading" and "writing." The filmmaker is conceived as faithful "follower" or disciple who offers no exegesis on the holy text.

Often deploying the spectacular epic, biblical adaptations, however, were inevitably mediated by narrative and generic codes, located within the space of both the fantastic and the testimonial. The cinema's apparatus of the "real," of nurturing the illusion of facticity, absorbed the biblical story into the aura of the moving image, where the history of God and his people was reincarnated, unfolding before the spectator's eye in a kind of a ghastly repetition of time past. The Christian concept of the Holy Trinity opened the way for visually representing the divinity, for God always already comes re-presented, reincarnated through his Son, dressing himself in flesh to reveal himself to his flock. (Could Jesus be thought of as a filial form of adaptation?) Rather than a violation of God's decree, the artistic procedure of endowing God with an image is accepted as homage, a mimesis of God's own descent to earth in perceptible human form.

God himself made his debut in silent cinema, and his presence over the next century of film has been felt in diverse genres, including the spectacular epic, the quotidian drama, and the satirical comedy. Although according to the Bible God made man in his own image, a few films have projected God in man's image, making casting an unusually difficult task. Carl Reiner's film *Oh God!* (1977), adapted by Larry Gelbart from Avery Corman's novel, has George Burns play a sympathetic eighty-year-old man/God who chooses a supermarket manager (John Denver) to spread the Word to the rest of the world. Vittorio de Sica enacts the role of God in the fantastic Italian comedy *Ballerina e buon dio* (Ballerina and the Good

God, 1958), directed by Antonio Leonviola. In Yvan Le Moine's and Frédéeric Fonteyne's Belgian comedy *Les sept péchés capitaux* (Seven Deadly Sins, 1992), Robert Mitchum reincarnates an American God who smokes cigars and speaks English. In the animated N B C series *God, the Devil, and Bob* (2000), James Garner gives voice to a laid-back, aging hippie God clashing with the Devil, speaking in the slick, British-accented voice of Alan Cumming. Antônio Fagundes performs an exhausted, down-to-earth God resting from his labors in the northeast of Brazil in Carlos Dieguess's *Deus é Brasileiro* (God Is Brazilian, 2003). Playing God constitutes a rare challenge for actors. How would a method actor prepare for the role? Since omnipotence and omniscience are not available to be accessed in the form of "sense memories," what feelings does the actor draw on to re-create the sensation of creating the universe?

Although God's color, like his shape, is not described in the Bible, God has largely been cast as white. One of the few exceptions is Marc Connelly's and William Keighley's *The Green Pastures* (1936), in which African American actors, using black English vernacular, perform Old Testament characters, including Moses and God, against the backdrop of a Southern-style heaven. "De Lawd," played by Rex Ingram (figure 23), loves mankind but is also frustrated with its wicked ways. Potentially threatening to white spectators, the image of a black God is "balanced" by the segregated filmic space as well as by the stereotypicality of the representation. The written prelude, furthermore, acts as a virtual disclaimer:

> God appears in many forms to those who believe in him. Thousands of Negroes in the Deep South visualize God and Heaven in terms of people and things they know in their everyday life. *The Green Pastures* is an attempt to portray that humble, reverent conception.

Betraying anxiety about whites' reception, the film authorizes itself to project a black God image through a narrative of God-is-created-in-the-believer's-image, qualified by an implicitly patronizing view that these believers have no access to the true (white) God. Yet the portrayal of a black God is nonetheless remarkable in light of the historical whitening of the figure of Christ. More recently, Morgan Freeman played God in Tom Shadyac's *Bruce Almighty* (2003), about a man (Jim Carrey) who complains about God until Freeman as God appears and endows him with extraordinary powers for a twenty-four-hour period. Such recent casting in a racially mixed filmic space also stands in contrast to earlier all-black-cast biblical films. At the same time, even films that portray a black God remain faithful

23 Casting a black God: "De Lawd" in *The Green Pastures* (1936)

to the biblical gendered rhetoric about God. It is rare to find a cinematic portrayal of God as a woman. One such anomaly is Kevin Smith's unorthodox satirical film *Dogma* (1999), which has Alanis Morissette appear as God/woman at the end, although she does not exactly become a truly personified god. And Lars van Trier's *Breaking the Waves* (1996) has the protagonist speak to God and also for God or perhaps even as God, in a dialogue in which the same voice—even if enacted through different intonations—ironically impersonates both the Creator and the created, the woman.

God's cinematic incarnation requires concrete choices involving complexion, facial features, and figure. Unlike in novels, in the cinema appearance and description are grounded in the concrete and the specific. Phrases such as "sad face," "seductive eyes," or "God's hands" have to be translated into the shape, color, and features of a particular performer. The visual adaptation of oral and written narratives, including biblical ones about God, forces the painter, photographer, or filmmaker to take a stance. Cinematic production necessitates a selection of actors and a casting process that inevitably locates face and body in concepts of gender and race. In Western iconography, for example, Christ was gradually de-Semitized; his appearance was remodeled as Aryan, which was deemed more appropriate for a supreme being within a white normative ethos. This image of Christ has persisted in contemporary visual culture, including in Hollywood, in the cinemas of the Americas and in European film. In Franco Zeffirelli's epic *Jesus of Nazareth* (1977), the blue-eyed Robert Powell was cast in the role of Jesus, and Olivia Hussey was cast in the role of Mary, who was also spared any overly Semitic appearance.

Whether in respectful films such as Ferdinand Zecca's *La vie et la passion de Jesus-Christ* (The Life and the Passion of Jesus Christ, 1905), Sidney Olcott's *From the Manger to the Cross* (1912; figure 24),[33] and Mel Gibson's *The Passion of the Christ* (2004); or in revisionist interpretations such as Pier Paolo Pasolini's Marxist *Il Vangelo secondo Matteo* (The Gospel According to Matthew, 1964); or in irreverent narratives such as Louis Buñuel's *L'âge d'or* (The Golden Age, 1930), Terry Jones's *Monty Python's Life of Brian* (1979), Jean-Luc Godard's *Hail Mary* (1985), and, to an extent, Martin Scorsese's *The Last Temptation of Christ* (1988), many filmic adaptations of the New Testament have featured Christ on the screen, portraying him in the flesh. Adaptations based on the "Old Testament" (i.e., the Jewish Bible), meanwhile, have tended to focus on the signs and symptoms of God's works without attributing an actual face and body. Thus, in a sense these films remain "faithful" to the biblical narrative that eschews any description of God's corporeality as well as to the prohibition against visualizing God. Given that the classical narrative film places its hero at the center as a vehicle for spectatorial identification, the biblical film was faced with an unusual challenge. Even if mediated via one of His messengers, such as Moses, the absence of the main protagonist—the usual raison d'être of the story and its teleology—the force behind Moses, remains invisible throughout such films. One might understand the affinity of the biblical film with the spectacular epic genre as a form of compensation for the absence of the One in whose name the narrative unfolds. The excessive visuality of the spectacular in most Hollywood biblical films thus displaces two "lacks"—the verbal nature of the Book and a central character devoid of visual traits. Generally, filmic adaptations draw on the novel's descriptions of characters, translating the visuality of the verbal into film language. In the case of biblical adaptations, however, the written word of the source text itself denies access to the visuality of the protagonist, believed to be the very creator of the word.

While Hollywood's biblical adaptations can be said to remain faithful to this de-visualization of God, they can simultaneously be seen as subverting it by reversing the biblical hierarchy of word over image. The "ontologically" kinetic status of the filmic image, as well as its widely perceived status as a technology of truth (i.e., its "reality effect") lends cinema a certain supremacy over the written word. Cinema lent indexical credibility to the Bible, authenticating and arming it with visual evidence, as it were.

24 Christ on location: *From the Manger to the Cross* (1912)

At the same time, cinema implicitly celebrated its own technological superiority over the Bible's "mere" verbality. In a kind of ironic reversal, it was now the Word that depended on a totemic image. Moses's name and words have exercised their awe for millennia, but now millions, when they hear the name, conjure up the figure of Charlton Heston. As a modern fetish, cinema has provided a secular form of star-worship cults while substituting its storytelling for the traditional narrator mesmerizing his or her tribe around the fire in the dark of night. The ability of cinema to chart the world like the cartographer, to chronicle events like the historiographer, to "dig" into the distant past like the archeologist, to anatomize "exotic" customs like the anthropologist—all have propelled it to the role of a powerful, popular storyteller. Manifesting its cultural legitimacy, cinema borrowed the Bible's aura through the act of adaptation but simultaneously staged its own preeminence through an extravagant visuality.

Even though their forms and themes constitute a major break with both the literary canon and popular narrative traditions, novels written in Arabic and Hebrew have possessed a certain prestige by virtue of working with and through the sacred languages of the Bible and the Qur'an. The unfolding of nationalist modernization teleologies in the Arabic and Hebrew realist novel, and specifically their role in the larger project of language standardization, could not erase the historical traces of the sacred inscribed in the Word. The twin product of science and entertainment, cinema, meanwhile, had to struggle for its seventh-art status within various cultural geographies. Early on, cinema enacted a historiographical and anthropological role, writing (in light) national and religious narratives. The penchant of Hollywood's silent films for graphological signifiers, such as hieroglyphs and Hebrew script or simply images of an open book, illuminates cinema's potential as an archivist and historiographer. Through the visual cornucopia of text, and especially of the "original" sacred text, early cinema granted an aura of civilizational depth to an infant medium still associated with lowbrow entertainment.

Early film theory was also concerned with the relationship between the image and the word, the visual and the written. Film theorists like Sergei Eisenstein saw both Egyptian hieroglyphs and Japanese ideograms as anticipatory of the cinema. Eisenstein's view seems to bring us full circle: Cinema prolongs the visual conceptual logic of the ideogram or the hieroglyph, in which writing is motivated in that it mimics its referents. Unlike language, which inhabits the realm of the abstract and arbitrary word, cinema exists within the realm of the concrete and of visible resemblance. The very phrase "graven images," at the same time, conjures up the ideas of André Bazin, for whom the cinema registers or "engraves" images, which for him guarantees film's capacity for revelation. Certain notions within postwar film theory—for example, the ideas of *auteurism*, camera-stylo, and film-writing, or *écriture*—meanwhile gesture toward restoring the sacred aura of the word.

The transformation of the sacred word into the realm of the visual has generated paradoxes in Hollywood cinema, as well. Although not explicitly an adaptation of a biblical narrative, Steven Spielberg's *Raiders of the Lost Ark* (1981) can be seen as an anachronistic staging of the clash between the monotheist Moses and pagan Egyptians, as well as between Jewish and Christian readings of the Bible. *Raiders of the Lost Ark* reveals a hidden Jewish substratum, even in the absence of Jewish characters and even though the word "Jewish" remains unuttered throughout the narrative. Indiana Jones liberates the ancient Hebrew ark from illegitimate Egyptian Arab possession and Nazi sequestration. Biblical myths of wonders wrought against ancient Egyptians are now redeployed against the Nazis. The Hebrew ark miraculously dissolves the Nazis, who, unlike the American hero, ignore the divine injunction against looking at the Holy of Holies. The censure of "graven images," and specifically the Jewish prohibition against looking at the sacred, triumph over the Christian predilection for religious visualization. Instantiating the typical paradox of cinematic voyeurism, the film punishes the Christian German for his hubris of daring gaze at the divine beauty while simultaneously generating spectacular visual pleasure for the viewer, who is able, thanks to the cinema's magic, to possess a Godlike power to see even what the hero himself cannot see.

While the imaging of God's body was censured in the Judeo-Islamic tradition, in both the Bible and the Qur'an God does speak, and His voice is heard, although it is never described. Yet in the cinema, in contrast to a written text, the voice raises the problem of embodiment. The voice, not unlike body and face, is inevitably specific: It is gendered and accented, and sometime classed and raced; it has a grain, an accent, an intonation, a timbre, a pronunciation, and even a vocal mannerism, all of which may remain "inaudible" in a text. While silent biblical films could simply cite Christ's or God's words in the form of intertitles, talking films, when not relying on written materials, were compelled to relay the specificity of the audible voice. Adaptations for the screen entail descriptive attributes, necessitating an audible embodiment of God's voice. The voice, furthermore, has to be mediated via a specific language. In biblical spectaculars, the ancient Egyptians and the Israelites all speak English, as, for that matter, does God. All have as their lingua franca the English of Southern California, with a touch of a British accent to convey greater prestige. (In fact, the English of God and of the ancient Hebrews does not in itself constitute a sacrilege to traditional or Orthodox Judaism that maintains Hebrew's sacredness, a language to be retained solely for holy rituals.) In biblical films, God's voice—deep, masculine, serious, resonant—delivers a kind of authority conventionally associated with the documentary off-screen narration and symptomatically called "Voice of God" narration.

The aura of the disembodied voice can be traced genealogically to the biblical paradox of the invisibility of the omnipresent. Playing on a primordial monotheist awe of the unseen Creator, dystopian science fiction and suspense films have often deployed an omniscient incorporeal voice. In the opening of each episode of the TV series *Mission Impossible* (CBS, 1966–73), a prerecorded message outlines the latest top-secret assignment for the Cold War warriors, the Impossible Mission Force. The taped words (performed by the actor Bob Johnson) always concluded with the same warning: "This tape will self-destruct in five seconds." Framing the narrative, the all-knowing voice appears and disappears at the beginning of each program, but the unfolding action dutifully reenacts his word. The viewers, identifying with the heroes' intricate and virtually impossible mission, are left in the dark as to the actual face of the authority figure who, thanks to miraculous technology, has all the traces of his own voice—the recorded tape—vanish in a cloud of smoke.

Critical literary discourse refers to the "omniscient narrator" or to the "invisible narrator," imperceptible like God, to the point, as Flaubert suggested, of being "refined out of existence." The special kind of authority exerted by the unseen voice has not gone unnoticed in film theory, as when Michel Chion speaks of the acousmatic voice as the voice that is heard but whose source cannot be detected in the shot, as in the case of the off-screen narrator in *The Wizard of Oz* (1939).[34] Biblical films, more specifically, endow cinema itself with an aura of the miraculous, for cinema can magically reproduce the voice of the all-seeing omnipotent deity. Here the cinematic soundtrack possesses a capacity that the Bible itself did not have: the capacity to give voice back to God. While the divine voice in the Bible is mediated by the written word, in the cinema the voice is conveyed literally, as real sound. It is as if the cinema had the Godlike ability to reincarnate the voice of God, returning the biblical word to its original spoken mode. Although God remains intangible on the screen, his voice, at least, is susceptible to mimesis, re-presenting in the flesh the scriptural "spoken" words. Within traditional Judeo-Muslim space, meanwhile, the enacting of God's voice or His vocalization provokes anxieties similar in nature to those provoked by His visualization, since even the disembodied voice is considered to be corporeal. The film *The Message*, as we have seen, responded to this anxiety by avoiding any direct enactment of the voice of God or of his prophet, Muhammad. The film intermittently uses a male voiceover narrator, who recites scenes and sayings from the Qur'an that do evoke the presence of an authority beyond the spectator's perceptible senses. At other instances, God's "spoken" words are "heard" via the visual—that is, through the representation of written material quoted from the Qur'an.

The epic-spectacular generic space, meanwhile, cannot be seen as the antithesis of the biblical representation, since the Bible itself constitutes a mélange of genres.[35] Indeed, the Bible proliferates in spectacular scenes on an epic scale: "And all the people saw the thunderings, and the lightnings, and the noise of the trumpet, and the mountain smoking: and when the people saw it, they removed and stood afar off" (Exodus 20:18). God's visuality is absent, but the visual symptoms of his power are omnipresent and grand in scope, virtually constituting a visual language. It would be misleading, in other words, to contrast the cinema as a purely visual medium with the Bible as a purely verbal medium. The features of a biblical spectacular film—astounding miracles, horrendous plagues, parted seas, burning bushes—are already present in the Ur-text prior to adaptation. Spectacular moments in biblical passages offer nature's sublime disturbances, such as lightning and floods, as signs of the divinity behind them, while God himself remains obscure and unintelligible. His "appearance" through cloud and fire has traditionally been interpreted as a manifestation created by God for the purpose of revelation, rather than as a display of God himself or even of something resembling him.[36] Deuteronomy describes the Israelites' experience on Mount Sinai as a matter of hearing the voice of God without perceiving any shape (Deuteronomy 4:12). The God who decreed the prohibition of graven images, the biblical text suggests, does not reveal himself to his chosen people. The adaptation of biblical stories, even by Hollywood's image-making machine, then, is itself constrained by a source text, the Bible, which obscures God's image. The adaptation theology guiding most biblical films betrays an ambivalent relationship to the source text's anti-visual injunction. It renders God's words and his audio-visual manifestations as a spectacle, yet leaves the precise nature of his image an unresolved enigma.

The aniconism typical of monotheism has been echoed in discourses about the cinema, which, especially since the introduction of semiology, Marxism, and psychoanalysis, have been concerned with obsessive mimesis, fetishistic voyeurism, the fixating gaze, star worship, and idolatrous iconicity. The powerful apparatus of cinema was said to produce reality effects that delude the spectator into believing in the three-dimensionality of the moving image. Spellbound and transfixed in the dark, the spectator was paradigmatically imagined as somnambulating in a shrine, a hypnotized believer in a false god. The pseudo-ancient Egyptian and Greek architectural designs of the movie palace only intensified the association of cinema with ritual and pilgrimage. As in the Mosaic rejection of graven images, apparatus theory inclined to view cinema as an iconic space that entraps the spectator in an illusionistic primal error—substituting a representation of an object for the actual object. Echoes of monotheist anxiety about the substitution error are detectable in what I call the "literarist" ambivalence toward filmic adaptation. From this perspective, while the act of adaptation might seem, on the one hand, to affirm the desirability of the word, on the other hand, the actual adaptation is despised as merely a surrogate icon incapable of surpassing the true god, the supreme textual being. Films based on novels are regarded as doubly iconic both in relation to a preexisting reality and vis-à-vis the novel. Within this literarist theology, film incarnates an earthly embodied object inferior to heavenly words, while the practice of adaptation remains always already an act of inauthenticity and deviance.

Literarist adaptation discourse has also been haunted by creationist and originary theologies. In the beginning was God who created Adam in his image, but Adam is constitutionally incapable of seeing the all-perceiving creator, who, in any case, warns against even thinking of creating his image. Imitation of God and a reproduction of his image, to evoke Walter Benjamin, would diminish His aura, premised on uniqueness and inaccessibility. Seen as mere repetition of the authentic word, film, in literarist adaptation discourse, is often assigned the actantial slot of the corporeal body vis-à-vis the novel's "faceless" abstractness. If in the beginning there was always the word and the novel, film is then bound within this logic to reenact the novel as divine creation to be refashioned in the creator's image. Defined as a lack, cinema becomes a mere speculum that registers a copy of the originary word, just as man is God's fallible reflection and just as all creators ultimately mimic, on a smaller scale, the Creator. Rather than another mode of mediation, cinema's visual facility is reduced to an iconic object deemed to forever orbit around the holy text. Novels, furthermore, enjoy a certain aura derived from the very seniority of the medium of the word, through which God and monotheism are said to bring order out of chaos. Literarist discourse about the novel/film inscribes the creator−created dualism, in which the author of the wor(l)d always remains the primeval and primordial source from which everything else emanates and back toward which everything refers. But within another perspective, the adapted novel can be seen as the creature of the film, just as God can be seen as the copy of (wo)man. In sum, monotheism's conception of God and His representation in a sense homologizes the intricate relationship between novel and film.

The aniconism of literarist adaptation discourse is premised on numerous misconceptions about the complex nature of cinema. Adaptation conventionally has been viewed as a transition from what is wrongly understood to be a uniquely verbal medium (the novel) to what is understood, again wrongly, to be a uniquely visual medium (film). The visual and the written remain locked within a rigid discursive dichotomy that obscures the "languagedness" of the image and the visuality of the word, whether literally through its graphic image or through the images it elicits in the reader and the viewer. Although the word−image dichotomy is inscribed at the very beginnings of monotheism, even the biblical hermeneutic tradition itself, as we have seen, has at times acknowledged that images and words are not easily separable. Words may elicit images, while narrative offers the unfolding of a movement in verbal time and space, which triggers imagery in the mind of the reader (and the viewer). God's own scriptural name, commonly pronounced "*yehova*," constitutes the Bible's most sacred word. Yet His name also inscribes the very prohibition on its utterance, thus paradoxically producing God's textual presence as a merely visual mark, discernible only to the eye that sees. Images, for their part, may elicit words in the mind of the viewer, whether in the form of proverbs, metaphors, or concepts.

The monotheist locus classicus of the prohibition on graven images left its residue in the valorization of the text and in the view of filmic adaptation as an act of infidelity, a kind of denigration. Symptomatic of a certain logophilia and iconophobia, the rejection of adaptation manifests a deep investment in the word as a privileged medium of signification offering privileged access to a higher truth. An imprecise and reductive discourse about cinema as merely a visual medium, then, underestimates the potential of film language to transform "The Book" into multiple realms in which the word, images, sounds, dialogue, music, and written materials all constitute, together, the complex space called the cinema. Transcending such false dichotomies as the "visual" and the "verbal" is crucial for criticizing the orthodoxy of literarist adaptation theologies. To write complexly about the "translation" of "The Book" for the screen thus requires moving beyond an iconophobia rooted in the adoration of the word and beyond a logophobia rooted in the fetishism of the image. Theological anxiety concerning the adaptation of sacred texts thus allegorizes the very discourses about adaptation: the anxiety of moving from the sacred and the canonical to the flesh-and-blood incarnation, grounded in the concrete and the specific—and, inevitably, the profane.

NOTES

I   "Perhaps the most sublime passage in the Jewish Law," writes Kant, "is the commandment: Thou shall not make unto thee any graven image. . . . This commandment alone can explain the enthusiasm that the Jewish people in its civilized era felt for its religion when it compared itself with other peoples, or can explain the pride that Islam inspires. The same holds also for our presentation of the moral law, and for the disposition within us for morality": Immanuel Kant, *Critique of Judgment*, trans. by Werner S. Pluhar (Indianapolis: Hackett, 1987), 135.

2 For an account of the visualist inclination of Western modern science, see Walter J. Ong, *The Presence of the Word* (New Haven, Conn.: Yale University Press, 1967). On anti-ocularism, see Martin Jay, *Downcast Eyes: The Denigration of Vision in Twentieth-Century French Thought* (Berkeley: University of California Press, 1993).

3 For more on the literary prejudices toward cinema, see Robert Stam, "Introduction: The Theory and Practice of Adaptation," in *Literature and Film: A Guide to the Theory and Practice of Film Adaptation*, ed. by Robert Stam and Alessandra Raengo (Oxford: Blackwell, 2005), 1–52.

4 The hyphen placed between Abrahamic and Mosaic tradition is meant also to evoke Mesopotamia as monotheism's cultural geography, since the discussion of monotheism's origins usually centers on ancient Egypt. Extending studies from the fields of archaeology and myth into psychoanalysis, Sigmund Freud's *Moses and Monotheism*, for example, wrestles with the European and non-European geographies of Jewish identity, highlighting monotheism's beginnings in the realm of the Egyptian—that is, that both Moses, the founder of Jewish identity, and Akhenaton, the founder of monotheism, were Egyptian.

5 On Protestant iconoclasm, see, for example, Carlos M. N. Eire, *War against the Idols: The Reformation of Worship from Erasmus to Calvin* (Cambridge: Cambridge University Press, 1986).

6 On Islam's iconoclasm, see, for example, G. R. Hawting, *The Idea of Idolatry and the Emergence of Islam: From Polemic to History*, Cambridge Studies in Islamic Civilization (Cambridge: Cambridge University Press, 1999).

7 Similarly, when 'Ala al-Din Kay-Qubad (1219–36) built the walls around his city Konia in Asia Minor, he set up on each side of one of the great gates a winged figure: Thomas W. Arnold, *Painting in Islam: A Study of the Place of Pictorial Art in Muslim Culture* (New York: Dover, 1965), 24.

8 For a more complete discussion, see Bishr Fares, "Philosophie et jurisprudence illustrées par les Arabes: La querelle des images en Islam," (Damascus: Institut de Damas, Melanges Louis Massignon, 1957); Ahmad Muhammad, "Muslims and Taswir," *Muslim World* 45, no. 3 (July 1995): 250–68.

9 For elaborate discussions of the theological and philosophical dimensions of this debate, see especially Moshe Halbertal and Avishai Margalit, *Idolatry*, trans. by Naomi Goldblum (Cambridge, Mass.: Harvard University Press, 1992); Jan Assmann, *Moses the Egyptian: The Memory of Egypt in Western Monotheism* (Cambridge, Mass.: Harvard University Press, 1997).

10 Moses Maimonides (Ibn Maimun), *The Guide of the Perplexed*, trans. by Shlomo Pines, 2 vols (Chicago: University of Chicago Press, 1963).

11 See Jacques Derrida, "Edmond Jabès and the Question of the Book," in idem, *Writing and Difference*, trans. by Alan Bass (Chicago: University of Chicago Press, 1978), 64–78. See also George Steiner, "Our Homeland the Text," *Salmagundi* 66 (Winter–Spring 1985): 4–25. Here one may want to note the intersection between the twentieth-century "linguistic turn" and the revalorization of Judaism as the religion of the word.

12 On the "modern" beginnings of the movement of translation into Arabic, see Ibrahim Abu-Lughod, *Arab Rediscovery of Europe: A Study in Cultural Encounters* (Princeton, N.J.: Princeton University Press, 1963).

13 On these elements of mimesis in the history of Arab art, see Albert Hourani, *A History of the Arab Peoples* (New York: Warner Books, 1991).

14 Robert Stam and I elaborate a critique of the Eurocentric narrative of "History" and "Geography" in *Unthinking Eurocentrism* (New York: Routledge, 1994).

15 The novel, according to Margaret Ann Doody, did not begin in the Renaissance. Rather, it forms part of a continuous history of about 2,000 years of contact between southern Europe, western Asia, and northern Africa. Papyrus fragments of novels suggest that novel reading was popular among Egyptians in the second century A.D., while the title of Heliodorus's *Aithiopika*, the longest of the surviving Greek novels, means "Ethiopian Story": Margaret Ann Doody, *The True Story of the Novel* (New Brunswick, N.J.: Rutgers University Press, 1996), 18.

16 A Renaissance Italian writer like Boccaccio, as Robert Stam suggests, found it normal to draw on the Eastern repertoire of the fables of Bidpai and Sindbad the Philosopher, while writers like Cervantes and Fielding were quite aware of and influenced by such texts. In *Don Quixote*, the narrator has a Castilian-speaking Morisco translate a parchment book in Arabic, and he mentions that a translator for a "more ancient language" (i.e., Hebrew) would not be difficult to find: Robert Stam, *Literature through Film: Realism, Magic, and the Art of Adaptation* (Oxford: Blackwell, 2005).

17 The debt of the European avant-garde to the arts of Africa, Asia, and indigenous America has been extensively documented. Fenand Leger, Blaise Cendrars, and Darius Milhaud based their staging of "La Creation du Monde" on African cosmology. Georges Bataille, who wrote about pre-Columbian art and the avant-garde generally, cultivated the mystique of Vodun and of African art.

18 Ruth St. Denis's Oriental mélange, I would argue, must be seen within the context of the coming to America of Arab belly dancers via the diverse expositions, which staged the Orient in the late nineteenth century and early twentieth century. Documented on film (Fatima, 1897), belly dance inspired the hoochie-coochie craze, blending the Orientalism of "exotic" dances into the American burlesque. See Ella Shohat, "Coming To America: Reflections on Hair and Memory Loss," in *Going Global: The Transnational Reception of Third World Women Writers*, ed. by Lisa Suhair Majaj and Amal Amireh (New York: Garland, 2000), 284–300.

19 On a critique of the metanarrative of art history, see Ella Shohat and Robert Stam, "Narrativizing Visual Culture: Towards a Polycentric Aesthetics," in *The Visual Culture Reader*, ed. by Nicholas Mirzoeff (London: Routledge, 1998), 27–49.

20 Auerbach, in fact, registered an intellectual debate that began in the nineteenth century, in which Jewish German intellectuals such as Heinrich Heine, Hermann Cohen, Heinrich Graetz, and Frantz Rosenzweig have responded to a diverse anti-Semitic denigration of Hebraism and the veneration of Hellenism, the latter for possessing visual art and the former for lacking it. See Erich Auerbach, *Mimesis: The Representation of Reality in Western Literature*, trans. by Willard R. Trask (Princeton: Princeton University Press, 1953); Kalman P. Bland, "Anti-Semitism and Aniconism: The Germanophone Requiem for Jewish Visual

Art," in *Jewish Identity in Modern Art History*, ed. by Catherine M. Soussloff (Berkeley: University of California Press, 1999).

21 Mahmoud Kassem, "Adaptation, égyptianisation et 'remake,'" in *Egypte: 100 ans de cinéma*, ed. by Magda Wassef (Paris: Editions Plume, Institut du Monde Arabe, 1995), 238, 241.

22 For a discussion of the aesthetic concerns raised by the Islamic prohibition on graven images, see Allen Terry, "Aniconism and Figural Representation in Islamic Art," in idem, *Five Essays on Islamic Art* (Sebastopol, Calif.: Solipsist Press, 1988), 17–37; Barbara Brend, *Islamic Art* (Cambridge, Mass.: Harvard University Press, 1991); Oleg Grabar, *The Mediation of the Ornament* (Princeton, N.J.: Princeton University Press, 1992); Viola Shafik, *Arab Cinema: History and Cultural Identity* (Cairo: American University of Cairo Press, 1998); Hamid Dabashi, "In the Absence of the Face," *Social Research* 67, no. 1 (2000): 127–85.

23 Shafik, *Arab Cinema*, 49.

24 Samir Farid, "La censure mode d'emploi," in Wassef, *Egypte*, 102–17.

25 Ibid., 102.

26 Shafik, *Arab Cinema*, 34.

27 Ibid., 49, 221. For further discussion of the history of censorship in Arab cinema, see Viola Shafik, "Egyptian Cinema," in *Companion Encyclopedia of Middle Eastern and North African Film*, ed. by Oliver Leaman (London: Routledge, 2001), 23–129.

28 Shafik, *Arab Cinema*, 170–72. Shafik also points out that the production of Muslim religious feature films shifted at the end of the Nasser era to television.

29 While "Bilal, The Prophet's Muezzin" is the correct translation of the Arabic title, the film was distributed in English-speaking countries under the title *Bilal, the Prophet's Call to Prayer*.

30 See Ahmed Rafaat Bahgat, "Cinéma et histoire: Du Baiser dans le désert à l'Émigré," in Wassef, *Egypte*, 176.

31 On the Qur'anic narrative, see, for example, Mustansir Mir, "Qur'ān as Literature," *Religion and Literature* 20, no. 1 (Spring 1988): 49–66. I thank Ahmad Dallal for his insightful comments on this issue.

32 In the United States, the film can be purchased in most shops or on websites that sell Islamic religious artifacts.

33 Produced by major film companies—Pathe and Kalem—*La vie e la passion de Jesus-Christ* and *From Manger to the Cross* were profitable. *From Manger to the Cross* is considered the first moving picture to be shot on location in the land where Christ lived and died rather than against painted backdrops. Despite the help of its Palestinian "faithful guide," Ameen Zaroun, the crew encountered difficulties, resulting in the relocation of some of the filming to Egypt. Recounting the filming in Jerusalem's Via Dolorosa, Gene Gauntier, the film's scenarist who also played the Virgin Mary, described the crew's fear for their life as a "mob of angry Arabs and Turks . . . muttered threats" and "demanded Baksheesh." Conjuring up images of encirclement, her narrative virtually evokes the crucifixion story. The "greedy" Arabs and Turks, ironically, stood in for the Jews in the film. With the endorsement of Christian organizations, missionaries screened the New Testa-

ment films across Africa and Asia for non-Christian—or recently converted—viewers, some of whom encountered Christ's image for the first time via the cinema. Although *From Manger to the Cross* was influenced by the famous biblical woodcuts of Gustave Doré (1866), it also helped shape a cinematic iconography of Jesus, played by the English actor Robert Henderson-Bland. Interestingly, Guantier raised doubts about making a religious picture with "the Man of God" portrayed in the flesh instead as a light or a shadow.

34 Michel Chion, *Audio-Vision*, ed. and trans. by Claudia Gorbman (New York: Columbia University Press, 1993).

35 On genres of the Bible, see Robert Alter, *The Art of Biblical Narrative* (New York: Basic Books, 1981).

36 Onkelos, the Bible translator and commentator, interpreted God's "appearance" as merely a manifestation of His presence that was not to be confused with God.

THE CINEMA AFTER BABEL

Language, Difference, Power

With Robert Stam

The reality of language difference, the worldwide babble of mutually in-comprehensible tongues and idioms, entails consequences for the cinema that have yet to be explored. While contemporary theoretical work has concerned itself with film as language, little attention has been directed to the role of language and language difference *within* film. Working out of the tradition of Saussure-derived linguistics, cine-semioticians have exam-ined the analogies and disanalogies between "natural language" and film as a discursive practice, but they have not delineated the impact on the cinema of the prodigality of tongues in which it is produced, spoken, and received. Our purpose will be to explore, in a necessarily speculative fash-ion, the myriad ways in which the sheer fact of linguistic diversity im-pinges on film as a signifying practice and on the cinema as an "encratic" institution that is deeply embedded in multiform relations of power.

When we say "language," we refer, first of all, to the clearly distinct idioms—English, French, Russian, Arabic—recognized as linguistic unities by grammars and lexicons. We refer, as well, however, to the multiple "languages" that inhabit a single culture or a single speech community—at least insofar as these intralinguistic differences bear on questions of intercultural film reception. We follow the thought of Mikhail Bakhtin, for whom the "crude" boundaries separating natural languages ("polyglossia") represent only one extreme on a continuum. For Bakhtin, every apparently unified linguistic community is also characterized by "heteroglossia," or "many-languagedness," in which the idioms of different generations, classes, races, genders, and locales compete for ascendancy. For Bakhtin, language is the arena for the clash of differently oriented social accents; each word is subjected to conflicting pronunciations, intonations, and allusions. Every language is a set of languages, and every speaking subject opens onto a multiplicity of languages. All communication entails an apprenticeship in the language of the other, a kind of translation or coming to terms with meaning on the boundaries of one's own set of languages and those of another. Thus, interlinguistic translation has as its counterpart the *intra*linguistic "translation" required for dialogue between diverse individuals and between diverse communities.[1]

Contemporary thought has been haunted by the idea of language. Central to the project of thinkers as diverse as Bertrand Russell, Ludwig Wittgenstein, Ernst Cassirer, Martin Heidegger, Maurice Merleau-Ponty, and even Jacques Derrida is the idea that language so completely structures our grasp of the world that "reality" can be seen as an effect of linguistic convention. According to the Sapir-Whorf hypothesis, language *is* culture, and those who "inhabit" different languages might be said to inhabit different worlds. The grammatical and semantic fields of a language—indeed, its entire conceptual framework—install speakers in habitual grooves of perception and expression that predispose them to experience the world in culturally specific ways. This linguistic "relativity principle" has as its corollary the view of all languages as fundamentally equal. For contemporary linguistics, languages do not exist in a hierarchy of value. The notion of "primitive" languages, rooted in the evolutionary assumption that the complex develops from the simple, here lacks pertinence, since every language is perfectly suited to the cultural needs and cultural reality of its speakers.

But if all languages are created equal, some are made "more equal than others." Inscribed within the play of power, languages are caught up in artificial hierarchies rooted in cultural hegemonies and political oppression. English, for example, as a function of its colonizing status, became the linguistic vehicle for the projection of Anglo-American power, technology, and finance. Hollywood especially came to incarnate a linguistic hubris bred of empire. Presuming to speak for others in *its* native idiom, Hollywood proposed to tell the story of other nations not only to Americans, but also for the other nations themselves, and always in English. In Cecil B. DeMille epics, both the ancient Egyptians and the Israelites spoke English, and so, for that matter, did God. In Hollywood, the Greeks of *The Odyssey*, the Romans of *Ben Hur*, Cleopatra of Egypt, Madame Bovary of France, Count Vronsky of Russia, Helen of Troy, and Jesus of Nazareth all had as their lingua franca the English of Southern California. Hollywood both profited from and promoted the universalization of the English language as *the* idiom of speaking subjects, thus contributing indirectly to the subtle erosion of the linguistic autonomy of other cultures. By virtue of its global diffusion, Hollywood became an agent in the dissemination of Anglo-American cultural hegemony.[2]

THEORETICAL PREAMBLE: LANGUAGE IN THE CINEMA

Before exploring the question of language difference and power, we must first examine the theoretical basis of our discussion. That we can consider the role of language difference in film at all is made possible by the fact that language itself variably penetrates the diverse "tracks" of the cinema. At what points, then, does language, and therefore language difference, "enter" the cinema? In *Language and Cinema*, Christian Metz stresses the linguistic character of two of the five tracks—recorded phonetic sound and writing in the image.[3] (These two, we might add, can exchange places, with written material substituting for phonetic dialogue, as in the celebrated "dialogue of the book covers" in Jean-Luc Godard's *Une femme est une femme* [A Woman Is a Woman]; figure 25). Language—at least, potentially—however, pervades *all* the filmic tracks. The music and noise tracks, for example, can embrace linguistic elements. Recorded music is often accompanied by lyrics, and even when it is not so accompanied, it can evoke lyrics. The purely instrumental version of "Melancholy Baby" in Fritz Lang's *Scarlet Street* (1945) elicits in the spectator the mental presence of the words of that song. In *Dr. Strangelove* (1964), Stanley Kubrick exploits this evocation of remembered lyrics to ironic effect when he superimposes the well-known melody of "Try a Little Tenderness" on images of nuclear bombers. Even apart from lyrics, the allegedly abstract art of music is permeated with semantic values. The musicologist Jean-Jacques Nattiez, for example, sees music as deeply embedded in social discourses, includ-

25 The "dialogue of the book covers": *A Woman Is a Woman* (1963)

ing verbal discourses.[4] Nor are recorded noises necessarily "innocent" of language. Setting aside the question of the cultural relativity of the boundaries separating noise from music from language—one culture's "noise" may be another culture's "language," as in the case of African talking drums—we discover the frequent imbrication of noise and language in countless films. The stylized murmur of conversing voices in classical Hollywood restaurant sequences renders human speech as background noise, while Jacques Tati films give voice to an international esperanto of aural effects—vacuum cleaners that wheeze and vinyl seats that go "pooof"—characteristic of the postmodernist environment.

But the linguistic presence cannot be confined to the soundtrack or to written materials within the image. The image track itself is infiltrated by the ubiquitous agency of language. This infiltration of the iconic by the symbolic, to borrow Peircean terminology, takes many forms, ranging from the perceptual-lexical to the more diffusely anthropological. Perception itself is oriented by the linguistic. The codes of iconic recognition and designation, as Metz points out in "The Perceived and the Named," structure the very vision of the spectator who thus brings language, as it were, to the image.[5] So tyrannical is the hold of linguistic form on our visual orientation that we perceive even lines and shapes as "straight" or "curved" or "zigzag" according to the classificatory suggestiveness of the linguistic terms themselves. Our language provides us with orienting metaphors having to do with the conceptualization of space (having power is to be "at the top") and the spatialization of emotion (happy is "up"). Verbal discourse structures the very formation of images. Boris Eikhenbaum, viewing film metaphor as parasitic on verbal metaphor, speaks of image translations of linguistic tropes.[6] Spectators understand visual metaphors only when a corresponding metaphoric expression exists in their own language; otherwise, the metaphor goes unperceived. In a still broader sense, the anthropological figures generated by a language or culture, such as the structural metaphor linking light and intelligence in classical Greek, or the association of darkness with obscurity and the sinister (as in Freud's "dark continent of female sexuality," with its suggestive linking of Africa and woman), shape our vision and thinking in ways yet to be charted.

The verbal–visual nexus has suggestive ramifications for film practice. Camera angles can literalize specific locutions such as "look up to" or "oversee" or "look down on." In such "literalisms," as Stephen Heath points out, the visual impact derives from strict fidelity to a linguistic metaphor.[7] Vandamm's coded threat to Eve Kendall in *North by Northwest* (1959)—"This matter is best disposed of from a great height"—is made literal by Hitchcock's abrupt self-referential shift to a high angle. Hitchcock's films, in fact, constantly highlight the interface of word and image. At times, whole sequences and even entire films are structured by linguistic formulations. *The Wrong Man* (1957) is informed in its entirety by the quibbling sentence, "Manny plays the bass." He plays the bass, quite literally, in the Stork Club, but he also plays the role of the *base* when he is falsely accused and forced to mimic the actions of the real thief. The overture sequence of *Strangers on a Train* (1951) similarly orchestrates an elaborate verbal and visual play on the expressions "crisscross" and "double-cross" (crossed railroad tracks, crossed legs, crossed tennis racquets, tennis doubles, double scotches, alternating montage as double, lap-dissolve as a "crisscross" of images, and so forth).[8] Hitchcock's cameo appearance significantly shows him carrying a double bass, in a film featuring two doppelgänger characters, each, in his way, "base." At times, the interplay of verbal–visual puns and equivalences becomes at once subliminal and pervasive. The first post-credit shots of *Psycho*, for example, subtly prefigure that film's obsession with avian imagery by literalizing the notion of a "bird's-eye view" of a city appropriately named Phoenix, while the airborne crane shots visually mimic the soaring movements of a bird through the air (figure 26).[9]

At times, language enters the cinematic experience in ways that are only obliquely related to the five tracks of the film text. Within the apparatus itself, in certain locales and at certain historical moments, intermediary speaking figures have been employed to negotiate, as it were, between text and audience. Noël Burch has emphasized the silent-period lecturer whose role was to construct continuity and comment on the action and

26 Figures of speech: The "bird's-eye view" in *Psycho* (1960)

thus orient audience response. In *To the Distant Observer*, he speaks of the lecturer's Japanese cousins, the Benshi who read and interpreted filmic images for their narrative content, avatars of an institution that persisted into the late 1930s.[10] We might also speak in this context of those films that create a space for dialogue with the spectator. Radicalizing Bela Balazs's call, in the '30s, for post-screening political discussions, the Argentinian filmmakers Fernando Solanas and Octavio Getino in *La hora de los hornos* (The Hour of the Furnaces, 1968) incorporate into the text programmed interruptions of the projections to allow for debate concerning the central political issues raised by the film. Thus, the cinematic apparatus, which generally favors only deferred communication, opens itself up to person-to-person dialogue in a provocative amalgam of cinema/theater/political rally. The passive and silent cinematic experience, that *rendezvous manqué* between exhibitionist and voyeur, is transformed into a "theatrical" and linguistic encounter between human beings present in the flesh.

Along with such programmed linguistic interventions, language enters the cinematic experience in other, more extemporaneous ways. Dialogue, already present in the film and metaphorically evoked in the "dialogue" between film and spectator, at times becomes literal through the impromptu verbal participation of the audience. This participation can take a multiplicity of forms. Boisterous talk sometimes disturbs the reverential silence of the art theaters, behavior that is quickly shushed or reprimanded, as if a religious rite were being desecrated.[11] (The ideal in the cinema, Eikhenbaum points out, is not to sense the presence of the other spectators, but to be alone with the film, to become deaf and dumb to the rest of the world.)[12] In some communities, conventions of spectating are such that the "naive" audience is encouraged to address verbal warnings or approval to the actors/characters on the screen (the rest of us, Metz suggests, confine such thoughts to the privacy of our minds)—thus the collectivity celebrates its own existence. At times, a full-scale dialogue can break out among the spectators themselves in the form of repartee or argument; the film in such cases loses its diegetic hold over the audience as the spectacle is displaced from screen to audience, producing a form of distantiation generated not by the text but by its receivers. A similar distantiation takes place when paralinguistic expressions such as feminist hisses question and relativize the macho wisdom of a paternalistic "hero." In all of these cases, the presence of language within the movie theater substantially modifies the experience of the film.

This linguistic assertiveness on the part of the audience takes extreme forms within the cult-film phenomenon. In the 1960s, audiences at Humphrey Bogart retrospectives began to deliver Bogart's lines in unison, verbally reinforcing the text and at times anticipating specific words and gestures (punctuating Bogart's climactic pistol shots in *Key Largo*, for example, with rhythmic chants of "More! More! More!"). This trend reached its apotheosis with the U.S. cult of *The Rocky Horror Picture Show*, in which an audience of repeat viewers elaborated a dynamically evolving parallel parody text, combining the synched repetition of songs and lines from the film with interpolated phrases that "play off" and mock the official dialogue in a kind of subversive pop-culture equivalent to the traditional school memorization of classical texts.

Even when verbal language is absent from both film and movie theater, semantic processes take place in the mind of the spectator through what the Russian formalists called "inner speech." Inner speech in this sense refers to the intrapsychic signification, the pulse of thought that is implicated in language. Film viewing, according to Eikhenbaum, is "accompanied by a constant process of internal speech," whereby images and sounds are projected onto a kind of verbal screen that functions as a constant ground for meaning.[13] Inner speech, which we address to ourselves, provides the discursive "glue" between shots and sequences. Our purpose here is not to summarize the theoretical work performed on inner speech by Lev Vygotsky, Valentin Voloshinov, Sergei Eisenstein, Stephen Heath, and Paul Willemen, but only to speculate on its relevance to the question of language difference in the cinema.[14]

If all film experience involves a kind of translation—from the images and sounds of the text into the internalized discourse of the spectator—interlingual cinematic experiences entail specific and more complicated mechanisms. In the case of the subtitled film, we hear the more or less alien sounds of another tongue. If the language neighbors our own, we may recognize a substantial proportion of words and phrases. If it is more distant, we may find ourselves adrift on an alien sea of undecipherable phonic substance. Specific sound combinations might remind us of locutions in our own language, but we cannot be certain they are not phonetic *faux amis*. The intertitles and subtitles of foreign films, meanwhile, trigger a process of what linguists call "endophony"—that is, the soundless mental enunciation of words, the calling to mind of the phonetic signifier. But the interlingual film experience is perceptually bifurcated: We hear another's language while we read our own. As spectators, we forge a synthetic unity that transcends the heteroglot source material. The processes of hearing and reading, furthermore, are not identical. Each sets in motion a distinct form of inner speech. Reading is relatively cerebral, while hearing prompts associative processes more deeply rooted in our psychic past. We must also distinguish between the experience of the silent versus that of the sound film. While the lecturers, choral accompaniments, and titles of "silent" cinema hardly suggest a wordless Bazinian freedom of the imagination, sound dialogue may inflect inner speech in a more overdetermined manner. Theoreticians of the film experience, in any case, have not adequately explored the nuances of the presence of language and language difference, the subtle ways in which an inaudible but nonetheless real aggregate of discursive privacies, the accumulative pressure of inner speech, quietly alters the film experience.

THE VAGARIES OF TRANSLATION: FILM TITLES

We have yet to examine the implications of language *difference* for film. What are the practical, analytical, and theoretical consequences of the intersection of film and natural language? The import of such questions becomes evident already with the translator of titles, intertitles, and subtitles. Title translations, for example, often involve serious miscalculations due to haste, laziness, or insufficient mastery of source or target language. (While publishers would never engage a hack translator for *A la recherche du temps perdu*, film distributors, perhaps out of vestigial scorn for a low-status medium, regularly engage incompetents.) A Romanian bureaucrat, for example, misled by the phonetic resemblance between Italian *moderate* (quiet) and Romanian *moderat* (cautious) and between *cantabile* (book-keeper) and *comtabil* (accountant), construed *Moderate Cantabile*, the Peter Brook adaptation of the Duras novel, as *The Quiet Accountant*. But the question of film translation is more complex than such an egregious error would suggest. Perfect translation is in the best of circumstances a virtual impossibility. Languages are not ossified nomenclatures, parallel lexical lists from which one need merely choose matching items on the basis of a one-to-one correspondence. Even an untranslated title can subtly change by virtue of acquiring a new linguistic and cultural environment. Proper names, for example, may shift pronunciation or connotation in a new context. Even a technically correct translation entails subtle modifications. The English *Day for Night* correctly renders the cinematographic procedure known in French as *La nuit américaine*, but a nuance is lost with the disappearance of *américaine*, pointing, as it does in the Truffaut film, to the nostalgic memory of the classic Hollywood film.

A truly perfect translation, George Steiner points out, would offer an interpretation so exhaustive as to leave no single unit in the source text—phonetic, grammatical, semantic, contextual—out of account yet at the same time would add nothing in the way of paraphrase or explication.[15] Since interlingual translation merely intensifies the usual slippages and detours of all communication, since all language is caught up in the unending spiral of *différance*, and since all discourse is intensely conventionalized and embedded in cultural particularity, no absolute transparency is possible; there remains always a core of mutual incommensurability. Our emphasis here will not be on the "loss" of an original purity—a notion traceable to the traditional belief that no sacred text or divine expression can be transcribed without forfeit—but rather on a dynamic process of cultural recoding, a change in the form of linguistic energy rather than a fall from Edenic purity.

The translator who wishes to be "faithful" to an original film title is confronted with myriad choices. To what, first of all, is one to be faithful—to the literal denotation, to the attendant connotations, or to the tone and stylistic form? Since each word exists at the crossroads of multiple semes, any translation arrests in a knot a process of infinite association, of constantly shifting undertones and overtones. Puns and wordplay in this sense constitute a paradigmatic instance of the challenges posed by verbal polysemy. The "pieces" in the film *Five Easy Pieces*, for example, are at once musical, filmic, and sexual. Another language is hardly likely to feature the same relation between the phonemic and the semantic (what linguists call paranomasia) and thus be able to orchestrate the same constellation of meanings. The Hebrew rendering *Resisei ha-Haim* (Shards of Life), for example, diminishes the rich resonances of the English title. The "wave" in Michael Snow's *Wavelength* similarly condenses multiple significations—sea waves, sine waves, sound waves, new wave—and anticipates the film's structuring play on "sea" and "see," all of which would be virtually impossible to convey in another language. Given the challenge of an unattainable adequation, the translator, in "principled despair," must settle for a semantic and affective approximation.

The title, as that sequence of signs that circulates in the world in the form of advertisement or announcement prior even to the film's screening, constitutes an especially privileged locus in the discursive chain of film. As hermeneutic pointers, titles promise, prefigure, orient. Titles are generally assumed to bear an indexical relation to the signified of the narrative events. Even when they are reflexive (*A Movie*) or perversely nonindexical (*Un Chien Andalou*), titles still point to some feature of the text in question. When original titles seem insufficiently indexical, translators are sometimes tempted to "improve" them. But if a change is to be made, which narrative events should be evoked and in what manner? Since titles posit enigmas and nudge the audience in the direction of a specific reading, to change the title is to change, however subtly, the reading. The Brazilian rendering of Hitchcock's *Vertigo* (1958) as *Um Corpo Que Cai* (A Body That Falls) provides a teasing clue, not present in the original, and anticipates events that occur far into the narrative. Some translations virtually destroy the hermeneutic mechanism at the center of the film's diegesis. The shock of the climactic revelation of *Psycho* (1960), for example, is severely compromised when the film is entitled, as it was in Portugal, *O Homen Que Era Mae* (The Man Who Was His Mother).

Even the flagrant ineptitude of this last example still would not authorize us to posit a norm of total adequacy in translation. First, we naively assume that the original title is somehow "correct," involving a motivated, necessary, and natural relation between signifier and signified. But the original title also might have been different: *Un Chien Andalou*, we now know, almost became *It Is Dangerous to Lean Inside*, and *L'Age d'Or* was almost titled *The Icy Waters of Selfish Calculation*. Every title represents an arbitrary freezing of a Heraclitean swirl of possibilities. There can be no unproblematic return to origins; the process of translation simply reopens a question arbitrarily foreclosed at an earlier point. Given this arbitrariness, some translators, not surprisingly, take liberties with the original by making strong gestures of interpretation.[16] Three distinct renderings of Woody Allen's *Annie Hall* (1977) show the nature of this process. The German rendering as *Der Stadt Neurotiker* (The City Neurotic) operates at least two transformations: It elides the feminine proper name in favor of a presumably masculine functional substantive, and it implies a causal relation between the city and the protagonist's neurosis. The Brazilian *Noivo Neurotico, Noiva Nervosa* (Neurotic Boyfriend, Nervous Girlfriend) also elides the feminine proper name, this time in favor of quadruple alliteration and a farcically judgmental title strongly reminiscent of the Italian erotic comedies then popular in Brazil. The Israeli *ha-Roman Sheli 'im Annie* (My Romance with Annie), finally, retains mention of Annie but specifies genre—romance—while shifting focalization to the male hero, seen as the author of the romance and titular proprietor of the female protagonist.

Discourse is always shaped by an audience, by what Tzvetan Todorov calls the *allocutaire*—those to whom the discourse is addressed—whose potential reaction must be taken into account. A film title is one turn taken in a kind of dialogue, forming part of an ongoing interlocution between film and spectator. Torn from its normal linguistic environment, the title in translation enters an alien field of what Bakhtin calls "prior speakings." The English phrase "horse's mouth," for example, enters a paradigm of proverbial expressions such as "straight from the horse's mouth" and "don't look a gift horse in the mouth," a fact lost on the Polish translator who literally construed the Ronald Neame film *The Horse's Mouth* (1958) as *Konsky Pysk* (Mouth of the Horse). Since the figurative expression "straight from the horse's mouth" does not exist in Polish, the title became inadvertently non-indexical and surrealist, leading frustrated viewers to expect a horse that never materializes. Commercial considerations, meanwhile, lead to "parasitical" translations that strive to exploit a previous film's box-office success. Israeli distributors, hoping to capitalize on the success of Mel Brooks's *Blazing Saddles* (1974), rereleased Brooks's earlier *Twelve Chairs* as *Kis'ot Lohatim* (Blazing Chairs). The commercial intertext also motivates the gratuitous eroticization of titles. In a particularly grotesque example, Bergman's *Persona* became in Brazil *Quando as Mulheres Pecam* (When Women Sin); thus, the rich resonances of the original title—at once psychoanalytic, theatrical, and philosophical—yield to the calculated sexism of a title whose puritanical lasciviousness led local spectators to expect a film in the tradition of the Brazilian *pornochanchadas*.

The heavy or tragic tonalities of an original title at times modulate in translation into a more cheerful or even comic mode. The explosively oxymoronic title, linking love and death, of Alain Resnais's *Hiroshima mon amour* is defused, ironically, in Japan, the scene of the original necropolis, to become a subdued *Nijúyokikan no jóji* (Twenty-Four Hour Affair). F. W. Murnau's *Der Letzte Mann* (The Last Man, 1924), by a similar process, becomes in English *The Last Laugh*, thus deflecting attention away from the tragic thrust of the core story to the comic resolution of the happy end. In the case of New German cinema, titles have undergone analogous metamorphoses: Margarethe von Trotta's *Der Bleierne Zeit* (The Leaden Time, 1981) becomes a more innocuous *Marianne and Julianne*, suggesting a tale of female friendship in which the assonance of the two names performs a variation on the alliteration of *Jules and Jim*. The rendering of Wim Wenders's *Im Lauf der Zeit* (In the Course of Time, 1976), with its philosophical and cinematic resonances, as a playful *Kings of the Road*, with its echo of the Roger Miller song, similarly turns it into just another road movie. In such cases, the reflective angst associated with many New German films, seen by the filmmakers themselves as part of a political duty to keep the spirit of negation alive in the post-Nazi years, has been kidnapped by an alien optimism.

At times, the political and ideological subtext of such connotative shifts is closer to the surface. Krzysztof Kieslowski's *Amator* (Amateur), a reflexive film about a Polish worker-cinéaste, was rendered in English as *Camera Buff*, which highlights the protagonist's fascination with filmmaking but elides another connotation operative in the Polish title—namely, that the hero's amateurism is not only cinematic but also political, whence his difficulties with the authorities who quietly scuttle his career. Many translated titles perform this kind of subtle depoliticization. The English rendering of *Salvatore Giuliano* as *Bandit's Revenge* transforms a highly politicized film into what sounds like a revenge western. (The Japanese rendering as *Shishirino Kusoi Kuri* [Black Fog in Sicily], in contrast, politicizes the title, since "black fog" in Japanese can connote governmental corruption.) Ousmane Sembene's *La Noire de . . .* (The Black Woman from . . .) rendered as *Black Girl* sheds both the ambiguity of *noire* as "woman/girl" and the ellipses implying that the protagonist might have come from any number of African countries. Luis Buñuel's titles have especially suffered from a process of sentimentalization and depoliticization. The masculine subject pronoun of *El* (He, 1952) suggests a broad critique of patriarchy. Translated as *This Strange Passion*, the new title emphasizes the schizophrenic comportment of a pathologically jealous madman rather than the "normal" pathology *of* machismo. *Los Olvidados* (The Forgotten Ones, 1950) similarly became in English the more melodramatically enticing *The Young and the Damned*. While the original title implicitly indicts the bourgeois audience—it is they who have forgotten the slum dwellers—the English title promises a kind of lurid youth picture, offering more conventional satisfactions for the spectator. In French, *Los Olvidados* became a lachrymose *Pitié pour eux* (Pity for Them), exemplifying exactly the kind of condescending charity excoriated by the film.

SOUND AND LANGUAGE DIFFERENCE: SUBTITLES

The challenge of translation took on special complexity with the advent of sound. Major film industries experimented with diverse approaches. Initially, dubbing, subtitles, and native-language translators were tried. In 1929, MGM embarked on an expensive program to replicate all its feature films in three different linguistic versions, and in 1930, Paramount established a studio near Paris to create foreign films in five languages. The British, French, and German industries, meanwhile, followed Hollywood's lead in multiple versions, albeit on a smaller scale.[17] In Czechoslovakia, Josef Slechta invented a "sound camera" that sharply reduced dependence on German and American sound equipment. Eastern European audiences flocked to the movie theaters to hear local stars speak and sing in their native language. In Latin America, similarly, local industries were encouraged by the arrival of sound. Hoping to break North American domination of their markets, filmmakers developed the popular carnival-based *chanchada* in Brazil and the tango film in Argentina, while Mexico competed with Argentina in supplying Latin America with Spanish-speaking films. Despite earlier European resistance to Hollywood domination, it was only with the coming of sound, ironically, that many Latin American film critics and spectators began to complain about the "foreignness" of North American films. Silence had had the effect of masking the national origins of the films. Thanks to the "visual esperanto" of silent film, which includes many cross-cultural codes, spectators not only read the intertitles in their own language but also imagined dialogue in their own language. Cinema was retroactively perceived as foreign and colonialist precisely because other-languaged dialogue destroyed the masking effect of silence.[18]

With sound, the transition from an imagined universality into nationality and language difference modified the relationship between spectator and film. Despite the sensation of plenitude engendered by the addition of sound, the change also brought certain psychic losses. With silent cinema, the desiring spectators dreamed phantasmatic voices to match the faces of their favorite stars. With sound, spectators were obliged to confront particular voices speaking particular languages that were not necessarily identifiable with their own. Greta Garbo, it turned out, had an "attractive" Swedish accent, but John Gilbert's voice was "reedy" and "unpleasant." "Charlot" wasn't French after all—although, of course, French spectators *knew* that Charlie Chaplin was Anglo-American. We speak here of the psychic regime of "*je sais, mais quand-meme*" (I know, but still). The effect of loss was analogous, in some respects, to that experienced by lovers of a novel when dreamed characters are incarnated in a film by specific actors with specific voices and physiognomies. At the same time, silent cinema was retroactively perceived as mute or silent, its "lack" revealed by the encroaching presence of sound. Silent-film intertitles, Mary Ann Doane has pointed out, had the effect of separating an actor's speech from the image of his or her body.[19] The terms proposed to designate the redefined cinematic entity, not surprisingly, celebrate the reuniting of voice and body by emphasizing the dialogue track: "the talkies," *le cinéma parlant, cinema falado* ("spoken cinema," in Portuguese). Other designations, less vococentric, were more inclusive in their perception of the role of sound: "sound cinema," *cinema sonore*, and perhaps the most adequate to a medium of images and sounds, the Hebrew *kolnoa* (sound-voice/movement).

Once it became obvious that the production of multiple foreign-language versions of films was not a viable option, producers, distributors, and exhibitors were left with the fundamental choice of either subtitles (dominant in such countries as France and the United States) or post-synchronization (the standard practice in Italy and Germany). In the case of subtitles, all of the processes characteristic of title translation—filtration of meaning through ideological and cultural grids, the mediation of a social superego—operate with equal force. For those familiar with both source and target language, subtitles offer the pretext for a linguistic game of "spot the error."[20] There would be little point in cataloguing such errors; our intention is only to plot the trajectory of their slippage, the direction of their drift. That the English version of Godard's *Masculin, Féminin* (1965) translates *brûler à napalm* (burning with napalm) as "burning Nepal" is not, finally,

crucial. More significant is the tendency, with New Wave films, to bowdler-
ize the French dialogue. (Censorship, for Freud, we are reminded, was a
kind of "translation.") The English subtitles of *Breathless*, for example,
consistently play down the aggressive *grossièreté* of the original. Belmondo's
opening "*Je suis con*" becomes an inoffensive "I'm stupid," and his "*Va te
faire foutre!*" addressed directly to the camera/audience is rendered as a
desexualized "Go hang yourself."[21] The tendency to shy away from sexually
connoted words reflects, perhaps, a higher coefficient of puritanism within
a society—or, at least, among its translators. Repressive regimes, meanwhile, have exploited subtitling and dubbing as a mechanism for censorship. To avoid any hint of adultery between Ava Gardner and Clark Gable in
Mogambo, the censor-translators of Franco's Spain reportedly transformed
the pair into brother and sister, thus arousing audiences with the even
spicier theme of incest.[22]

Some films are striking in their *omission* of subtitles. Film translators
tend to be vococentric, concentrating on spoken dialogue while ignoring
other linguistic messages such as background conversation, radio announcements, and television commercials, not to mention written materials such as posters, marquees, billboards, and newspapers. Thus, the
spectator unfamiliar with the source language misses certain ironies and
nuances.[23] The non-French speaker, for example, misses the play between
text and image generated by the written materials pervading *Deux ou trois
choses que je sais d'elle* (Two or Three Things I Know about Her, 1966), a
film that might be seen as a gloss on Roland Barthes's dictum that "we are
still, more than ever, a civilization of writing"[24] (figure 27). The omission of
nonvocal linguistic messages can also compromise a film's political tendency, since it is often precisely through such messages that a story gains
its social or historical context. Radio allusions to the war in Algeria in
Agnes Varda's *Cléo de 5 à 7* (Cleo from 5 to 7, 1962) scandalized the
partisans of L'Algerie Française but went untranslated in the English version. At times, the linguistic strategies of a film compromise its political
thrust. In Costa-Gavras's *Hanna K* (1983), presumably a pro-Palestinian
film, Arabic dialogue is left unsubtitled, while English masquerades as
Hebrew, thus affirming an Israel-U.S. cultural link while downplaying any
specific Jewish Israeli identity. Subtitles, finally, can inject revolutionary
messages into nonrevolutionary films. In the late 1960s and '70s, French
leftists reportedly "kidnapped" kung fu films, giving them revolutionary
titles such as *La dialectique peut-elle casser des briques?* (Can the Dialectic
Break Bricks?) and incendiary subtitles. A sequence of devastating karate

27 Text-image interplay: *Two or Three Things I Know about Her* (1967)

blows would be subtitled, "Down with the bourgeoisie!" thus providing a leftist political "anchorage" for what were essentially exploitation films.

The linguistic mediation of subtitles dramatically affects the film experience. For audiences in countries where imported films predominate, subtitles are a normal, taken-for-granted part of the film experience. Literalizing the semiotic textual metaphor, spectators actually *read* films as much as they see and hear them, and the energy devoted to reading subtitles inevitably detracts from close attention to images and sounds. In many Third World countries, in fact, the penetration of subtitled foreign films has indirectly led to the physical neglect of the sound systems in the theaters, exhibitors being guided by the spurious logic that spectators occupied in reading subtitles will not be overly concerned with the quality of sound.[25] In countries such as India and Israel, the spectator is at times confronted with vertical tiers of multilingual subtitles. In cases where the films themselves are multilingual, subtitles have an effect of homogenization for the foreign spectator. The exuberant polyglossia of such films as Moshe Mizrahi's *Ha-Bait be-Rhov Shlush* (The House on Chelouche Street, 1973), which features Hebrew, Arabic, Yiddish, Ladino, Spanish, and Russian, or Youssef Chahine's *Iskandereiya . . . leh?* (Alexandria Why? 1978), which deploys the diverse languages spoken in the cosmopolitan Alexandria of the '40s, is "leveled" by monolingual subtitles when shown abroad.

SOUND AND LANGUAGE DIFFERENCE: POST-SYNCHRONIZATION

The choice of post-synchronization as opposed to subtitling has significant consequences. Post-synchronization, or "dubbing," can be defined for our purposes as the technical procedure by which a voice, whether of the original performer or of another, is "glued" to a visible speaking figure in the image. With dubbing, the original and adopted texts are homogeneous in their material of expression: what was phonetic in the original remains phonetic in the translation, unlike subtitles, where the phonetic original becomes graphological in the translation. With subtitles, the difference in material of expression allows for the juxtaposition of two parallel texts, one aural and the other written, and thus for the possibility of comparison. Errors become potentially "visible" not only to privileged spectators familiar with the languages in question, but also to the general viewer conscious of small inconsistencies: a disproportion in duration between spoken utterance and written translation, for example, or the failure of subtitles to register obvious linguistic disturbances such as a lisp or a stutter. The single-track nature of dubbing, in contrast, makes comparison impossible. Without the original script or version, there is simply nothing with which to compare the dubbed rendition.[26] Given our desire to believe that the heard voices actually emanate from the actors/characters on the screen, we repress all awareness of the possibility of an incorrect translation. In fact, we forget that there has been any translation at all.

While subtitling resembles a kind of summary prose translation, dubbing is more comparable to the complex juggling of sense, rhythm, and technical prosody involved in poetic translation. Subtitles can concentrate meaning, transforming redundant into more efficient language, or they might (although this possibility is rarely explored) explicate a punning reference or offer contextual footnotes. With dubbing, in contrast, each visible sign of speech activity must be somehow rendered; words or sounds must be fitted to the moving mouth. Dubbing in this sense poses immense *technical* as well as *linguistic* challenges. Interlingual dubbing substitutes a separate and new sound recording in a second language for the original text. The newly recorded dialogue, separated from the noise and music tracks, must be carefully matched with the articulatory movements, and the audible speech results in what István Fodor calls, on the analogy of "phoneme" and "morpheme," a "dischroneme"—that is, the minimal unit of non-coincidence of speech and movement—in contrast with the "synchroneme," or successful matching of dubbed voice and articulatory movement.[27] This matching is diversely articulated with specific cinematic codes such as angle, scale, lighting, and so forth, with exigencies varying according to whether a shot is close-up or *plan américain*, profile or frontal, well or dimly lit. Direct address at close camera range—the extreme close-up of Kane's "Rosebud" or the disembodied lips mouthing the lyrics of the initial song in *The Rocky Horror Picture Show*—poses the greatest challenge because it amplifies attention to speech movement. A long or darkly lit shot, meanwhile, can blur the distinctive visual features of speech production, and the noise and music tracks can divert attention from the speech organs. Even screen format affects our experience of synchronous matching. Wide-screen splays out the speech organs and thus poses more difficult challenges than standard format.

Along with phonetic synchrony, dubbers also strive for what Fodor calls "character synchrony"—that is, the skillful match between the timber, volume, tempo, and style of the speech of the acoustic personifier (the dubber) and the physical gestures and facial expressions of the screen actor. As with any translation, the rendering can never be fully "faithful"; the chameleonism of dubbing is always partial. While words are socially shared and therefore more or less translatable, voices are as irreducibly individual as fingerprints. The same word pronounced by a Marlene Dietrich, a Woody Allen, or an Orson Welles is in a sense no longer the same word; each voice imprints a special resonance and coloring. The practice of dubbing can lead to a number of anomalous situations. When the target audience is aware, from other films, of the voice and acting style of a given player, the dubbed voice is often an irritant. Those familiar with Jean-Pierre Léaud, for example, are likely to be annoyed by the dubbed English version of Truffaut's *Day for Night*. The memory of the "real" voice provokes a kind of resistance to the substitute. In international co-productions, meanwhile, a multilingual player might dub himself or herself into a second or even a third language for foreign versions, so that each linguistic situation results in a new dubbing configuration. At times, the dubbers themselves achieve a certain status and notoriety. In the '30s in Germany, according to Jay Leyda, dubbers earned salaries in proportion to the stars they were dubbing (since audiences insisted on hearing the same voice), resulting in a kind of parasitic star system. In India, meanwhile, stardom is "bifurcated," as imaged stars share popularity with the unseen "playback singers" whose voices they borrow.

The Italian situation as regards dubbing calls for special comment. Post-synchronization has been a feature of Italian cinema since fascism, but it forms part of a process of cultural leveling that dates back to the unification of Italy. Since most Italian actors speak "dialect" rather than the "official" Tuscan, they are made to speak an artificial language uttered in studios by a specialized corps of dubbers. While well-known actors (Vittorio Gassman, Marcello Mastroianni, Monica Vitti) dub themselves, many less-well-known actors have never been heard in their own voice. The dubbing of foreign films, meanwhile, results in Italians' seeing bastardized versions in which cultural specificities are flattened. Within the specialized linguistic code developed for translating the western, for example, as Geoffrey Nowell-Smith points out, the Union and the Confederacy are rendered as *"nordista"* and *"sudista,"* geographical terms with precise connotations in Italy (evoking the tension between "feudal" south and developing capitalist north), so that the Civil War is read in "terms of the Risorgimento." Such abuses led in 1967 to an angry manifesto, signed by Michelangelo Antonioni, Marco Bellocchio, Bernardo Bertolucci, Pier Paolo Pasolini, Francesco Rosi, and others denouncing obligatory post-synchronization: "Contemporary developments in theoretical studies on the sound film imply the need to take up a position at the outset against the systematic abuse of dubbing, which consistently compromises the expressive values of the film." Post-synchronization and the dubbing translation of foreign films, the authors conclude, "are the two equally absurd and unacceptable sides of one and the same problem."[28]

Post-synchronization exploits our naive faith in cinematic reality, our belief that the temporal coincidence of moving lips with phonetic sounds points to a causal and existential connection. Buñuel subverts this faith in *Cet obscur objet du désir* (That Obsure Object of Desire, 1977) by having two actresses, dubbed by a third voice, play the same role (figure 28). Split in the image, the character regains a semblance of unity through the soundtrack. Post-synchronization also forms part of the film's elaboration of the themes of Frenchness and Spanishness: a film by a Spaniard who has lived in France, adopting a French novel about Spain (*La femme et le pantin*) whose Spanish protagonist is transformed by Buñuel into a Frenchman but is played by a Spaniard (Fernando Rey) and dubbed by a well-known French actor (Michel Piccoli). Other filmmakers deploy more explicitly disruptive strategies to highlight the factitious nature of post-synchronization. Godard in *Tout va bien* (1972) and Marcel Hanoun in *Une simple histoire* deliberately misdub to sabotage the fictive unity of voice and image. A Brazilian film, significantly entitled *Voz do Brasil* (Voice of Brazil) after a widely detested official radio news broadcast, shows an American film being dubbed in a

Brazilian sound studio. As the film loop of an emotionally charged sequence passes on the screen, the dubbing technicians do their work and exchange trivialities. We are struck by the disjunction between the passionate drama on the screen and the apparent boredom in the studio, as well as by the contrast between the glamorous star and the ordinary-looking woman lending her voice. Film dubbers usually remain, to borrow Pierre Schaeffer's term, *acousmatique*: Their voices are heard, but the real source of the enunciation remains invisible. The provocation of *Voz do Brasil* is to reveal the hidden face of these normally acousmatic dubbers and thus render visible the effaced labor of a particular cinematic process.

The marriage of convenience that weds a voice from one language and culture to an imaged speaker coming from another often triggers a kind of battle of linguistic and cultural codes. Linguistic communication is multitrack; every language carries with it a constellation of corollary features having to do with oral articulation, facial expression, and bodily movement. Certain locutions are regularly accompanied, often without the speaker's awareness, by codified gestures and automatic motions. The norms of physical expressiveness, moreover, sharply vary from culture to culture. Extroverted peoples accompany their words with a livelier play of gesticulations than more introverted peoples. Michael Anderson's *Around the World in Eighty Days* contrasts the expressive codes of the phlegmatic Englishman Phineas Fogg with those of the vehemently gesticulating Frenchman Passepartout. In *Trouble in Paradise* (1932), Ernst Lubitsch humorously counterpoints the speech manners of southern and northern Europeans. Recounting a robbery to the Italian police, the Edward Everett Horton character speaks in English (posited as putative French) while the Italian interpreter ferries his words over to the police. Horton's speech is unemotional, efficient, and gestureless, while the interpreter's is flamboyant and animated, with lively facial expressions and emphatic Italianate gestures. In a single long take, Lubitsch recurrently pans with the shuttling translator, alternately placing with Horton or the police but never *with* the police, further underlining the linguistic and cultural gulf between them.

To graft one language, with its own system of linking sound and gesture, onto the visible behavior associated with another, then, is to foster a kind of cultural violence and dislocation. Relatively slight when the languages and cultures closely neighbor, this dislocation becomes major when they are more distant, resulting in a clash of cultural repertoires. Brazilian television, like many broadcasting outlets in the Third World, for example,

28 One character, two actresses, and a voice: *That Obscure Object of Desire* (1997)

constantly programs American films and television series in which American media stars speak fluent dubbed Portuguese. The match of the moving mouths of Kojak, Colombo, and Starsky and Hutch with the sounds of Brazilian Portuguese, however, results in a kind of monstrosity, a collision between the cultural codes associated with Brazilian Portuguese (strong affectivity, a tendency toward hyperbole, lively gestural accompaniment of spoken discourse) and those associated with police-detective English (minimal affectivity, understatement, controlled gestures, a cool, hard, tough demeanor). A Brazilian avant-garde film, Wilson Coutinho's *Cildo Meireles* (1981), exploits this gap to satiric effect by matching the image of John Wayne on horseback to incongruous discourse in Portuguese. Wayne's moving lips, in this case, are made to articulate contemporary theories of *différance* and deconstruction. When his antagonists resist his intellectual claims, our hero guns the logocentric heretics down.

LANGUAGE AND POWER

Although languages as abstract entities do not exist in hierarchies of value, languages as lived operate within hierarchies of power. Language and power intersect not only in obvious conflicts concerning official tongues, but also wherever the question of language difference becomes involved with asymmetrical political arrangements. As a potent symbol of collective identity, language is the focus of fierce loyalties that exist at the razor edge of national difference. In South Africa, blacks protest the imposition of Afrikaans as the official language of education; in the United States, Latinos struggle for bilingual education and examinations. What are the implications of this language–power intersection for the cinema? What is the linguistic dimension of an emerging cinema within a situation of "unstable bilingualism" such as that of Quebec? How many of the estimated 5,000 languages currently in use are actually spoken in the cinema? Are there major languages completely lacking in cinematic representation? How many appear briefly in an ethnographic film and as quickly disappear? How many films are never subtitled due to insufficient funds and therefore never distributed internationally? What about anticolonialist films (Gillo Pontecorvo's *Burn!*) artificially made to speak a hegemonic language to guarantee geographic distribution and economic survival?

The penetration of a hegemonic language often helps clear the path for cinematic domination. In the aftermath of World War Two, English became what George Steiner has called the "vulgate" of Anglo-American power. Countless films in the postwar period, as a consequence, reflect the prestige and projection of English and the axiomatic self-confidence of its speakers. The producer Prokosch, in Godard's *Contempt*, embodies the self-importance and linguistic arrogance of the industrial managers of American cinema. While he is more or less monolingual, his European collaborators move easily from language to language. In *Der Amerikanische Freund* (The American Friend, 1977), Wim Wenders calls attention to the lack of linguistic reciprocity between American and European. The major non-American characters all speak English along with their native language, while the American friend Tom, the "cowboy in Hamburg," speaks only English. Jonathan's last sentence to the Swiss doctor—"It hurts in any language"—echoes another filmic demonstration of linguistic non-reciprocity: Miguel/Michael's response in *Touch of Evil* to Quinlan's insistence that he speak English and not Spanish: "I think it will be unpleasant in any language." Like many New German films, *The American Friend* critically foregrounds the widespread dissemination of English and of American popular culture, thus illustrating the ways that "the Yanks," as another Wenders character puts it in *Kings of the Road*, "have colonized our subconscious."[29]

One could speak, as well, in this context of any number of metaphorical "colonizations" having to do with region, class, race, and gender. Human beings do not enter simply into language as a master code. They participate in it as socially constituted subjects. Where there is no true communality of interest, power relations determine the conditions of social meeting and linguistic exchange. Even monolingual societies are characterized by heteroglossia; they englobe multiple "languages" or "dialects" that both reveal and produce social position, each existing in a distinct relation to the hegemonic language. The "word," in Bakhtin's sense, is a sensitive barometer of social pressure and dynamics. In many British New Wave films, upper-class English is worn like a coat of arms, an instrument of exclusion, while working-class speech is carried like a stigmata. A cynical reincarnation of Eliza Doolittle, the protagonist of Clive Donner's *Nothing but the Best* (1964) gradually sheds his working-class speech in favor of Oxbridge English to scale the social heights. In Perry Henzell's *The Harder They Come* (1973), similarly, the singer-protagonist's lower-class status is marked by his speaking Jamaican "dialect" while the upper-class figures more closely approximate "standard" English, thus positing a homology between class and linguistic hegemony. (A dialect, it has been said, is only a "language without an army"—or, we might add, without economic or political power.)[30] Issues of race also intersect with questions of language, power, and social stratification. Black English in the United States was often called "bad" English because linguists failed to take into account the specific historical African roots and imminent logical structure of black speech. Not unlike women, blacks developed internal codes of communication and defense, a coded language of resistance.[31] One of the innovations of Melvin Van Peebles's *Sweet Sweetback's Baad Asssss Song* (1971)—whose very title resonates with black intonations—was to abandon Sidney Poitier, just-like-white-people, middle-class diction to get down and talk black.

The interest of Sembene's *Black Girl* lies in having the film's female protagonist stand at the point of convergence of multiple oppressions—as maid, as black, as woman, as African—and in conveying her oppression specifically through language. Diouana, who the spectator knows to be fluent in French, overhears her employer say of her, "She understands French . . . by instinct . . . like an animal." The colonialist, who according to Fanon cannot speak of the colonized without resorting to the bestiary, here transforms the most defining human characteristic—the capacity for language—into a sign of animality. The gap of knowledge between the spectator, aware of Diouana's fluency, and her unknowing French employers serves to expose the colonialist habit of linguistic nonreciprocity. This typically colonialist asymmetry (Diouana knows their language, but they do not know hers) distinguishes colonial bilingualism from ordinary linguistic dualism. For the colonizer, as Memmi points out, the language and culture of the colonized are degraded and unworthy of interest, while for the colonized mastery of the colonizer's tongue is both a means of survival and a daily humiliation. The colonized language exercises no power and enjoys no prestige in everyday life; it is not used in government offices or the court system, and even street signs make the native feel foreign in his or her own land. Possession of two languages is not a matter of having two tools. Rather, it entails participation in two conflicting psychic and cultural realms. Through a long apprenticeship in unequal dialogue, the colonized becomes simultaneously self and other. The mother tongue, which holds emotional impact and in which tenderness and wonder are expressed, is precisely the one least valued.[32]

For the colonizer, to be human is to speak *his* language. In countless films, linguistic discrimination goes hand in hand with condescending characterization and distorted social portraiture. The Native Americans of Hollywood westerns, denuded of their own idiom, mouth pidgin English, a mark of their inability to master the "civilized" language. In many films set in the Third World, the language of the colonized is reduced to a jumble of background noises while the "native" characters are obliged to meet the colonizer on his or her linguistic turf. In films set in North Africa, Arabic exists as an indecipherable murmur, while the "real" language is the French of Jean Gabin in *Pépé le Moko* or the English of Bogart and Bergman in *Casablanca*. Even in David Lean's *Lawrence of Arabia* (1962), which is pretentiously, even ostentatiously, sympathetic to the Arabs, we hear almost no Arabic. Instead, English is spoken in a motley of accents, almost all of which (Omar Sharif's being the exception) have little to do with Arabic. The Arabs' paralinguistic war cries, meanwhile, recall the "barbaric yawp" of the "Indians" of countless westerns. The caricatural representation of Arabic in the cinema prolongs the Eurocentric "Oriental-ist" tradition in both linguistics and literature. Ernst Renan invented the contrast, flattering to Europe's self-image, between the "organic" and "dynamic" Indo-European languages and the "inorganic" Semitic lan-guages—"arrested, totally ossified, incapable of self-regeneration."[33] For romantics such as Alphonse de Lamartine, Gerard de Nerval, and Gustave Flaubert, meanwhile, the Orient served as a mirror for their Western nar-cissism, when it was not a backdrop for the pageant of their sensibilities. Lamartine saw his trip to the Orient as "*un grand acte de ma vie intérieure* (a great act in my interior life)" and discoursed with supreme confidence on the subject of Arabic poetry, despite his total ignorance of the language.[34] Twentieth-century filmmakers in certain respects have inherited the atti-tudes of the nineteenth-century philological tradition (so ably anatomized by Edward Said), pointing out "defects, virtues, barbarisms, and shortcom-ings in the language, the people and the civilization."[35]

Colonizing cinema, meanwhile, committed its own "barbarisms" in re-lation to the languages of the colonized. One of the early cases of censor-ship in Egypt emanates from a Western source. The film *Al-Zouhour al-Qatela* (Fatal Flowers, 1918) outraged the Islamic community by garbling well-known phrases from the Qur'an. A similarly cavalier attitude toward linguistic sensitivities led to the misattribution of major languages. Mer-vyn LeRoy's *Latin Lovers* (1953), for example, mistakenly suggests that the national language of Brazil is Spanish. Although Carmen Miranda was called the "Brazilian bombshell," the names given her characters (such as Rosita Cochellas in *A Date with Judy*, 1948), were more Hispanic than Brazilian.[36] Although she reportedly spoke excellent English, Miranda was prodded to speak in her distinctive caricatural manner (the linguistic correlative of her Tutti-Frutti hat), thus reflecting one of many ways that Latins were ridiculed by Hollywood cinema. The dubbed version of Marcel Camus's *Orfeu Negro* (Black Orpheus, 1959), finally, substitutes a variety of Caribbean accents in English for the Brazilian Portuguese of the original, thus placing diverse Third World communities under what Memmi calls "the mark of the plural"—that is, "They are all the same."

The existing global distribution of power makes the First World nations of the West cultural "transmitters" while it reduces Third World nations to "receivers." Given this unidirectional flow of sounds, images, and information, Third World countries are constantly inundated with North American cultural products—from television series and Hollywood films to bestsellers and top-forty hits. The omnipresence of English phrases in Brazil, for example, can be seen as a linguistic symptom of neocolonialism. A carnival samba penned shortly after the arrival of American sound films already lamented the widespread currency of English phrases: "Goodbye, goodbye boy/Quit your mania for speaking English/It doesn't become you." One stanza explicitly links the dissemination of English to the economic power of the Anglo-American electricity monopoly "Light": "It's no longer *Boa Noite* or *Bom Dia*/Now it's Good Morning and Good Night/And in the *favelas* they scorn the kerosene lamp/and only use the light from Light." Hollywood, meanwhile, became the beacon toward which the Third World looked, the model of "true" cinema. The linguistic corollary of domination was the assumption that some languages were inherently more "cinematic" than others. The English "I love you," Brazilian critics argued in the '20s, was infinitely more beautiful and cinematic than the Portuguese "*Eu te amo.*" The focus on the phrase "I love you" is in this case highly overdetermined, reflecting not only the lure of a romantic model of cinema projecting glamor and beautiful stars, but also an intuitive sense of the erotics of linguistic colonialism—that is, that the colonizing language exercises a kind of phallic power. Behind the preference, as well, was the notion that there are "beautiful" and "ugly" languages, a notion that came to pervade countries with a colonized complex of inferiority.[37] It was in the face of this prejudice that the Brazilian filmmaker Arnaldo Jabor defiantly entitled his film *Eu Te Amo* (1981) and insisted that the title remain in Portuguese even when distributed abroad.

It is against this same backdrop that we must understand the linguistic duality of Carlos Diegues's *Bye Bye Brazil* (figure 29). Precisely because of the widespread dissemination of English, the film was titled in English even in Brazil. The theme song by Chico Buarque features English

29 Colonial ambivalence: Cultural duality in *Bye Bye Brazil* (1979)

30 Egyptian perspective on Hollywood: *Alexandria Why?* (1979)

expressions like "bye bye" and "night and day" and " OK " as an index of the Americanization (and multinationalization) of a world in which tribal chiefs wear designer jeans and backwoods rock groups sound like the Bee Gees. Even the name of the traveling entertainment troupe, "Caravana Rolidei"—a phonetic transcription of the Brazilian pronunciation of the English "holiday"—reflects this linguistic colonization. A typical colonial ambivalence operates here: on the one hand, sincere affection for an alien tongue, and on the other, the penchant for parody and creative distortion, the refusal to "get it straight."

Many Third World films ring the changes on the subject of linguistic colonialism. Chahine's *Alexandria Why?* a reflexive film about an aspiring Egyptian filmmaker who entertains Hollywood dreams, explores the linguistic palimpsest that was Egypt at the time of World War II. Chahine offers an Egyptian perspective on Western cultural products and political conflicts (figure 30). From the protagonist's point of view, we watch his adored American musical comedies, subtitled in Arabic, and European newsreels with Arabic voiceover. (At certain points, in a linguistic Chinese box effect, the Arabic subtitles of the American film-within-the-film are enclosed within the English subtitles of *Alexandria Why?* itself.) In another sequence, an Egyptian theater production pokes fun at the occupying powers. Each European power is reduced to a stereotypical cultural emblem: Hitler's moustache, Churchill's cigar, a French chef, an Italian pizza. In a reversal of traditional representation, it is now the colonized who consciously caricature the colonizer. As representatives of the Allied and Axis powers chaotically pursue each other across the stage, mumbling in their own idioms, the Egyptian characters remain seated, spectators of an alien war on their land. Irrationality, a feature insistently projected by the West onto Arabs and their language, here boomerangs against the Europeans.

Language is a social battleground, the place where political struggles are engaged both comprehensively and intimately. In *Xala* (1975), Sembene again inter-articulates questions of language, culture, and power. The protagonist, El Hadji, a polygamous Senegalese businessman who becomes afflicted with *xala*—a religiously sanctioned curse of impotence—embodies neocolonized attitudes of the African elite so vehemently denounced by Fanon. Sembene structures the film around the opposition of Wolof and French as the focal point of conflict. While the elite make public speeches in Wolof and wear African dress, they speak French among themselves and reveal European suits beneath their African garb. Many of the characterizations revolve around the question of language. El Hadji's first wife, Adja, representing a precolonial African woman, speaks Wolof and wears traditional clothes. The second wife, Oumi, representing the colonized imitator of European fashions, speaks French and wears wigs, sunglasses, and low-cut dresses. El Hadji's daughter, Rama, finally, represents a progressive synthesis of Africa and Europe; she knows French but insists on speaking Wolof to her Francophile father. Here again conflicts involving language are made to carry a strong charge of social and cultural tension.

The title of Glauber Rocha's *Der Leone have sept cabeças* (The Lion Has Seven Heads) subverts the linguistic positioning of the spectator by mingling the languages of five of Africa's colonizers. Rocha's Brechtian fable animates emblematic figures representing the diverse colonizers, further suggesting an identity of roles among them by having an Italian speaker play the role of the American, a Frenchman play the German, and so forth. Another polyglot fable, Raoul Ruiz's *Het Dak van de Walvis* (The Top of the Whale, 1981) also focuses on the linguistic aspect of oppression. The point of departure for the film, according to Ruiz, was his discovery that certain tribes in Chile, due to their traumatizing memory of genocide, spoke their own language only among themselves and never in front of a European.[38] The resulting tale, about a French anthropologist's visit to the last surviving members of an Indian tribe whose language has defied all attempts at interpretation, is turned by Ruiz into a sardonic demystification of the colonialist undergirdings of anthropology.

The intonation of the same word, Bakhtin argues, differs profoundly between inimical social groups. "You taught me language," Caliban tells Prospero in *The Tempest*, "and my profit on it is, I know how to curse. The red plague rid you for learning me your language." In the social life of the utterance as a concrete social act, we began by saying, each word is subject to rival pronunciations, intonations, and allusions. While the discourse of power strives to make a single language official, one dialect among many, into *the* language, language is in fact the site of heteroglossia, open to historical process. There is no political struggle, according to Bakhtin, that does not also pass through the word. Languages can serve to oppress and alienate but also to liberate. We have tried to question the presumption of the masters of language. The "system" of language so dear to the Saussureans, we have implicitly suggested, is subject to what Bakhtin calls centripetal and centrifugal forces; it is always susceptible to subversion. By shifting attention from the abstract system of *langue* to the concrete heterogeneity of *parole*, we have tried to stress the dialogic nature of language in the cinema and its constantly changing relationship to power, and thus to point to the possibility of reappropriating its dynamism in the world.

NOTES

We thank Jay Leyda, Richard Porton, and James Stam for their generous suggestions. We also thank the following for proposing noteworthy examples of inaccurate title translation: Wilson de Barros, Kyoko Hirano, Lynne Jackson, Joel Kanoff, Daniel Kazamiersky, Ivone Margulies, Margaret Pennar, Peter Rado, Jerzy Rosenberg, Susan Ryan, Bill Simon, Harald Stadler, and João Luiz Vieira.

1 For Bakhtin's ideas concerning language, see *Problems of Dostoevski's Poetics* (Ann Arbor, Mich.: Ardis, 1973); idem, *Rabelais and His World* (Cambridge, Mass.: MIT Press, 1968); and idem, *The Dialogic Imagination* (Austin: University of Texas Press, 1981). See also V. N. Volosinov, *Marxism and the Philosophy of Language* (New York: Seminar Press, 1973). The authorship of *Marxism and the Philosophy of Language* is disputed. There is considerable evidence that Bakhtin wrote substantial portions of it or, at least, worked in extremely close collaboration with Volosinov. See also "Forum on Mikhail Bakhtin," *Critical Inquiry* 10, no. 2 (December 1983), a special issue devoted to Bakhtin, as well as the *Revue de l'Universite d'Ottawa/University of Ottawa Review* 53, no. 1 (January–March 1983).

2 One might easily posit an analogy here between English as the international language and dominant cinema as the film language, with alternative idioms being reduced to the status of "dialects."

3 See Christian Metz, *Language and Cinema* (The Hague: Mouton, 1974). One element not emphasised by Metz is the interarticulation of written materials in the image with the specifically cinematic codes. The diverse directionality of the scripts of different languages—the fact that Hebrew and Arabic are read "horizontally" from right to left, for example, or that Chinese is read in vertical columns—can inflect camera movements over script. Wayne Wang's *Chan Is Missing* (1982), for example, repeatedly pans down vertically over Chinese written materials.

4 See Jean-Jacques Nattiez, *Fondements d'une sémiologie de la musique* (Paris: Union Générale d'Editions, 1975).

5 See Christian Metz, "The Perceived and the Named," *Visual Communication* 6, no. 3 (1980): 56–68, originally published as "Le perçu et le nommé," in *Pour une esthétique sans entrave—Mélanges Mikel Dufrenne* (Paris: Editions 10/18, 1975), and reprinted in *Essais Sémiotiques* (Paris: Klincksieck, 1977). The concluding section of the essay is translated as "Aural Objects" in "Cinema/Sound," special issue, *Yale French Studies*, no. 60 (1980).

6 See Boris Eikhenbaum, "Problems of Film Stylistics," *Screen*, vol. 15, no. 3, Fall 1974, 7–32.

7 See Stephen Heath, "Language, Sight and Sound," in *Cinema and Language*, ed. by Stephen Heath and Patricia Mellencamp (Frederick, Md.: University Publications of America, 1983).

8 A number of critics have commented on the patterned doubling of this

opening sequence. See, for example, Ronald Christ, "Strangers on a Train: The Pattern of Encounter," in *Focus on Hitchcock*, ed. by Albert J. La Valley (Englewood Cliffs, N.J.: Prentice-Hall, 1972).

9 Hitchcock further develops the trope of the "bird's-eye view" in *The Birds*, this time in both aural and visual terms. For more on verbally informed structures in both Hitchcock and Buñuel, see Robert Stam, "Hitchcock and Buñuel: Desire and the Law," *Studies in the Literary Imagination* (Fall 1983).

10 See Noël Burch, *To the Distant Observer: Form and Meaning in the Japanese Cinema* (Berkeley: University of California Press, 1979). See also idem, "Approaching Japanese Film," in Heath and Mellencamp, *Cinema and Language*, for brief speculations on the role of language in constructing what Burch calls the "profound otherness" of classical Japanese cinema.

11 Some New York theaters have institutionalized silence with pre-feature intertitles: "Talking during the Projection of the Film Disturbs Others: Please Be Considerate." (Apparently, the cinematic institution has links not only to the theater and religion, but also to the library.)

12 See Eikhenbaum, "Problems of Film Stylistics."

13 See ibid., 34.

14 See L. S. Vygotsky, *Thought and Language* (Cambridge, Mass.: MIT Press, 1962); S. M. Eisenstein, *Film Form* (New York: Harcourt Brace and World, 1949); Volosinov, *Marxism and the Philosophy of Language*; Stephen Heath, "Language, Sight and Sound," in idem, *Questions of Cinema* (London: Macmillan, 1980); Paul Willemen, "Reflections on Eikhenbaum's Concept of Internal Speech in the Cinema," *Screen*, vol. 15, no. 4, Winter 1974–75; idem, "Notes on Subjectivity," *Screen*, vol. 19, no. 1, Spring 1978; idem, "Cinematic Discourse: The Problem of Inner Speech," *Screen*, vol. 22, no. 3 (1981). The notion of inner speech has philosophical antecedents in such thinkers as Herder, Humboldt, Thomas Aquinas, and even Plato. See James Stam, *Inquiries into the Origin of Language* (New York: Harper and Row, 1976).

15 See George Steiner, *After Babel: Aspects of Language and Translation* (New York: Oxford University Press, 1975).

16 Godard's descriptive *A Bout de Souffle* (Breathless) became in Japanese an imperative exhortation (perhaps reflecting a distant observer's caricatural view of French existentialism), *Katie ni Shiyagare* (Do Whatever You Like!).

17 For a discussion of the transition to sound in Europe, see Douglas Gomery, "Economic Struggle and Hollywood Imperialism; Europe Converts to Sound," *Yale French Studies* no. 60 (1980).

18 For more discussion of Brazilian critics' response to sound, see Ismail Xavier, *Sétima arte: Um culto moderno* (São Paulo: Editora Perspectiva, 1978). See also see Jean-Claude Bernardet and Maria Rita Galvao, *O nacional e o popular na cultura brasileira* (São Paulo: Brasiliense/Embrafiime, 1983), 230–31.

19 See Mary Ann Doane, "The Voice in the Cinema: The Articulation of Body and Space," *Yale French Studies*, no. 60 (1980).

20 Multilingual films such as *Le Mépris* (Contempt, 1963) require some subtitles wherever they are screened. In *Contempt*, they form an integral part of the signification of a film that is deeply concerned with diverse "translations" within the polyglot atmosphere of international co-productions. Italian post-synchronization eliminated the role of the interpreter, leading Godard to dissociate himself from the Italian version of the film.

21 The Brazilian subtitles of Woody Allen's *Everything You Always Wanted to Know about Sex*, in anticipation not only of Brazilian censors but also of an audience not always attuned to the cultural ramifications of Jewishness, elided all that was explicitly sexual or specifically Jewish.

22 See *New York Times*, 7 November 1983.

23 It should be pointed out that titles can also operate in the opposite direction. Certain English subtitles for Godard's *Sauve qui peut (la vie)* render readable what was barely audible, even for native French speakers, in the original.

24 See Roland Barthes, "Rhetoric of the Image," in idem, *Image–Music–Text*, ed. by Stephen Heath (New York: Hill and Wang, 1977).

25 In Israel, films spoken in Hebrew have at times been subtitled in Hebrew due to lack of confidence in the sound systems of the movie theaters.

26 A partial exception to this rule occurs in the case of the hybrid form, common in documentaries and in newscasts, that combines the dubbed voice of a translator simultaneously with the original voices, at low volume, in the background.

27 See István Fodor, *Film Dubbing: Phonetic, Semiotic, Esthetic and Psychological Aspects* (Hamburg: Buske Verlag, 1976). Fodor's book is thorough and useful but limited by an underlying assumption of the ultimate possibility of a virtually total adequation between original and dubbed version. The book also limits itself to European languages.

28 See Geoffrey Nowell-Smith, "Italy Sotto Voce," *Sight and Sound*, vol. 37, no. 3, Summer 1968, 145–47.

29 The wide dissemination of American cultural forms accounts for the frequent nontranslation into German of American film titles: *Easy Rider, American Graffiti, Taxi Driver, Hair, Apocalypse Now*, and *Reds* were all left untranslated for German exhibition. In other cases, titles are changed into different English titles: *Being There* became *Welcome, Mr. Chance*. Or an original English title is supplemented by a German addition: *The Fog* became *The Fog: Der Nebel des Grauen* (The Fog of Horror).

30 The use of the term "dialect" apparently dates back to the early colonial era, when it was assumed that verbal communication systems unaccompanied by extensive written literature were somehow unworthy of the term "language." Thus, Europe speaks languages, while Africa, for example, speaks "dialects." In fact, a country like Nigeria speaks hundreds of languages—that is, fully developed linguistic systems that, unlike dialects, are not mutually intelligible.

31 A study of the relation between sexual difference and language difference in the cinema would necessarily touch on the play of gender in films whose diegesis features multiple languages (e.g., the association of Catherine in *Jules and Jim* with the German neuter and androgyny) and the implications for film of the fact that different languages "see" gender differently.

32 For Memmi on colonial bilingualism, see Albert Memmi, *The Colonizer and the Colonized* (Boston: Beacon Press, 1967).

33 See Edward Said, *Orientalism* (New York: Pantheon, 1978), 142.

34 Ibid., 177–78.

35 Ibid., 142.

36 Stanley Donen's *Blame It on Rio* continues this tradition of Hispanicizing Brazilian names.

37 Israel, interestingly, offers a similar phenomenon. Many members of the film milieu considered Hebrew intrinsically non-cinematic and an "obstacle" to "good" dialogue, implicitly suggesting a kind of shame about speaking a Semitic rather than a European language. The protagonist of a '70s TV series *Hedva ve Ani* (Hedva and I) complained that it is impossible to say the Hebrew "*Ani ohev otach*" because, unlike "I love you" or "*je t'aime*," it is "ugly."

38 See "Entretien avec Raoul Ruiz," *Cahiers du Cinéma*, March 1983.

"LASERS FOR LADIES"

Endo Discourse and the Inscriptions of Science

Feminist theory has produced an impressive corpus of texts on the imaging of the female body in the arts, photography, cinema, and the media.[1] This discussion of the visual has privileged the surface body, while the notion of the gaze has been premised on desire and pleasure. But what happens when feminist cultural critics delve into the taboo territory of studying the imaging of the pathological interior body? How do we then speak of text and reader, of representation and spectatorship, of producers and consumers of images? In an era when x-ray, ultrasound, and video laparoscopy have thoroughly charted the terra incognita of bones, chromosomes, and reproductive organs, feminist critique cannot afford to surrender the interior body to the curtained authority of the medical office. Unlearning the censorship of the living body's visualized organs—particularly in a context where women critics can be *subjects* of these imaging technologies—is a prerequisite for reclaiming the body from the monopoly of scientific disciplining and for democratizing access to the medicalized body.

As part of my argument for a cultural-studies intervention in medical discourses of the interior body, I will focus on a generally nonlethal female disease, endometriosis, as a site of tension between the hegemonic scientific inscription of the female body and a critical feminist voicing of women's agency. Precisely because of its gendered character and public invisibility, endometriosis illuminates the coexistence of an up-to-date endoscopic panopticon (laparoscopy, laser laparoscopy, video laparoscopy) with an old, myopic discourse concerning femaleness. My discussion here of "endo discourse" forms part of an ongoing, resistant postmodernist argument for a possible dialogue between, on the one hand, scientific research and medical technologies, and, on the other, feminist critique and community-based empowerment.[2] Equally stressing discourse, institution, text, spectatorship, and reception, this chapter interweaves an investigation into a range of writings and practices around endometriosis—from academic scientific journals and mass-media health magazines to self-help newsletters and alternative publications—with almost a decade of conversations carried out with women participating in endo support groups, with some emphasis placed on the implications of video-laparoscopic spectatorship.

A QUESTION OF ENIGMA AND THE DISCOURSE OF HYSTERIA

Familiarly referred to as "endo" among its bearers, endometriosis is a chronic women's disease characterized by the presence of functioning endometrial tissue—the tissue of the uterine lining—in places where it is not usually found.[3] In the case of endometriosis, the endometrium—often described as the support system of a "wasted," potential embryo, for which it regularly builds up, then sheds each month in the absence of an embryo to use it—migrates to other parts of the body and begins to grow in the form of scar tissue, cysts, and benign tumors, mostly in reproductive sites (ovaries, cul-de-sac, fallopian tubes), gastrointestinal sites (rectosigmoid colon, rectum, small bowel), urinary-tract sites (bladder, ureter, kidney), and lower genital sites (cervix, vagina, vulva).[4] These "islands" of tissue remain responsive to the body's monthly releases of reproductive hormones, which can exact from them an excruciatingly painful inflammatory response during menstruation and intercourse. They may also cause infertility, ruptured endometrioma, and ectopic pregnancy. Other symptoms include vomiting, fatigue, low back pain, rectal pain, blood in the stool, blood in the urine, fever, and tenderness around the kidneys.

Endometriosis was not recognized as a disease for a long time. It was first described in the medical literature in 1896,[5] but it was not named until 1925 by Dr. John Sampson. A submerged presence of endometriosis can be detected in a nineteenth-century ad for Lydia E. Pinkham's Vegetable Compound: Below an image of a sick white woman in bed, surrounded by feminine cushions and flowers, appear the words "Nervous Breakdown." The testimonials that follow describe "female trouble," and are clearly symptomatic of endometriosis, but the convoluted language of "nervous, ailing women" inscribe a hysterical female figure.[6] Almost a century later, the ad for the Endometriosis Association used the image of a sick woman to promote endo consciousness by clearly asserting the materiality of a disease: a woman in bed, who has just rushed home from work—the shoes and the briefcase are still by her bedside—holding a bottle of hot water on her abdomen. In marked contrast to the dreamy look of Lydia Pinkham's woman, the facial expression of pain in the Endometriosis Association woman, or in that of an 1987 Krames Communications booklet, "A Guide to Managing Endometriosis," illustrate the everyday experience of illness. The texts, meanwhile, call attention to symptoms such as severe menstrual pain and heavy menstrual flow as signs of physical pathology, rather than of female (ab)normality, showing women of diverse racial backgrounds taking charge of their bodies despite endometriosis.

An estimated 5 million to 10 million women in the United States today suffer pain and disability from endometriosis, yet little is known about the causes of what is still referred to in medical circles as "the female plague."[7] The enigma around the disease is accompanied by frequent ignorance and misdiagnosis in medical clinics, where women are prescribed tranquilizers to cure what doctors commonly describe as "a problem in the head." Women's pain, particularly in the area of their reproductive organs, tends to be attributed to fantasy, to signs of a neurotic personality, or just to the melancholy fate of being a woman. As Nancy Peterson, the director of the Endometriosis Treatment Program in Bend, Oregon, ironically comments: "If a man had a disease that causes him to be unable to father a child, to have unbearable pain during sex and unbearable pain during bowel movements, [which was] treated by feminizing hormones and surgery, endo would be declared a national emergency in this country."[8]

As part of the struggle to empower endo women, Mary Lou Ballweg, co-founder and president of the U.S.–Canada Endometriosis Association, has produced a series of cartoons, "Joe with Endo," in collaboration with the artist Meri Lan, in which a reversal of gender roles points to the role of institutional power in rendering endometriosis as female hysteria. In one cartoon, a female gynecologist paternalistically tells her ailing patient: "Well, Joe, I told you last time . . . this problem is really a mental thing. All men have some tension with sex once in a while. . . . You'll adjust." And when Joe argues that he has never had this problem before, suggesting that it may actually be a physiological problem rather than psychological, she replies, "Look, Joe, let's be honest. We both know you're the high-strung type. Let's try some valium and see if it helps, O.K.?"[9]

The frequency of words like "enigma," "conundrum," "unknown," "perplexing," "mystery," and "puzzling" in endo medical texts clearly recalls the discursive history that links female anatomy, sexuality, and psyche to the uncanny.[10] Indeed, the medical investigation of endometriosis perpetuates the "gendering" scientific ritual of measuring the unruly body against the norms of the observing scientist. Medical writing has theorized endometriosis in terms of disorderly female biology, behavior, and personality, at times measuring women's reproductive physiology against a primate model. As Dr. Joe Vincent Meigs wrote in 1940: "The monkey mates as soon as she becomes of age, and has offspring until she can no longer have any or until she dies. Menstruation in this animal must be rare. As women have the same physiology it must be wrong to put off childbearing until 14 to 20 years of menstrual life have passed."[11]

Such passages erect primate behavior as a model for women's choices. Social expectations of women as mothers, furthermore, are still haunted by the masculinist mythology of the bleeding woman.[12] Menstruation is perceived as abnormal; its presence must be minimized. If the female cycle is extolled "as a productive enterprise," Emily Martin points out, "menstruation must necessarily be viewed as a failure."[13] Considering the theory that endometriosis is caused by a retrograde menstruation,[14] Meigs argued that "nature certainly did not intend that refluxed bleeding should be responsible for the growth of invasive tissue in the pelvis. Menstruation itself may be a kind of abnormality, for it occurs only infrequently in monkeys in their natural habitat."[15] Beneath such attempts to suppress "female blood" lies the suggestion that female physiology is a priori unnatural, even prior to the a posteriori deviance of delaying pregnancy. The submerged anxiety over the menstruating woman historically inscribed in masculinist popular culture—and, notably, in medical writing—is exacerbated in the case of menstrual "endo women," whose blood tends to be "thicker" and flows "excessively."

The biological "abnormalities" of 1940s medical discourse have now, to some extent, given way to other terms, focusing on psychological disorders. A recent study of chronic pelvic pain, however, found no association between affective disorder and endometriosis.[16] Nevertheless, most studies since the 1950s have attempted to establish such links. In the 1980s, in academic publications such as the *American Journal of Psychiatry* and the *Western Journal of Medicine*, scientists argued for the relationship between endometriosis and "bipolar mood disorder," "affective disorder," and other mental illnesses. By positing a necessary "interaction of body type and psychic demeanor," these scientists associate endometriosis with a deviant personality: "The main characteristics involve being mesomorphic but underweight, having above-average intelligence, a higher than normal anxiety level, egocentrism, and a need for perfection."[17] These scholarly articles argue that endometriosis and bipolar mood disorders are "two poorly understood clinical syndromes," and since "hormonal fluctuations have been studied in relation to both, there could be a possible relationship."[18] The logic behind such studies, it seems, is that the addition of one female enigma to another may lead to an unveiling of the mysteries of the female organism. However, it is precisely the unresolved status of endometriosis that allows for this explanation of one enigma by another, ultimately positing femininity as overflowing the boundaries of rationalist discourse.[19]

RACE, CLASS, AND THE "CAREER WOMAN'S DISEASE"

The attempt to establish links between women's behavior and endometriosis is imbricated in the social construction of gender. In his 1940 article in *Annals of Surgery*, Meigs writes:

> In August, 1938, in an editorial, attention was drawn to the fact that endometriosis was increasing in frequency and that there was probably some reason for it. It was felt that the increase might be due to delayed marriages and the lack of early and frequent child-bearing, and suggested that the economic difficulties of the day were responsible for the increased frequency. . . . The real reason for the frequency [of endometriosis] is that endometriomata are not tumors but represent abnormal physiology due to the late marriage and delayed and infrequent child-bearing. The latter is due to the economic times we live in, and my plea is that patients with apparent infertility, evidences of underdevelopment, and older girls about to be married, be taught how to become pregnant and not how to avoid pregnancy, even though their finances are limited.[20]

Medical texts have often attributed endo-related infertility to lack of reproductivity. "If girls would learn to follow nature and have children early," doctors have warned, "neither endometriosis nor the resulting infertility would exist."[21] The anxiety that medical texts manifest around the non(re)productive vessel is sometimes displayed in a rhetoric that weaves the scientific and the metaphysical in a way unusual for the post-Enlightenment. As Dr. Roger Scott and Dr. Richard Te Linde write in "External Endometriosis: The Scourge of the Private Patient," their 1950s article in *Annals of Surgery*, "A large number of women must accept this childless state as God's will or fate's bidding until the element of pain presents itself."[22] Their study reverberates with quasi-biblical castigation, implying that women who postpone or forgo childbearing betray the telos of their natural role. But women's misguided conduct, it is suggested, can be redeemed if they redirect themselves toward a blessed heterosexual union, which will put an end to endo— hence, the article's focus on "behavioral changes." Implicit in this perspective is the suggestion that medical research into the etiology of endometriosis is almost unnecessary, for the disease is clearly an unfortunate consequence of a woman's deviant lifestyle.

During the 1940s, the principal hypothesis concerning the origins of endometriosis had revolved around late marriage and childbearing. Since the post–World War Two era, as "earlier marriages and childbearing have been the rule,"[23] medical texts, meanwhile, faced a different challenge. The new theorizing of endometriosis argued that, "possibly, more than a passing consideration should be given to the dietary habits or the emotional and environmental changes incidental to the larger pocketbook."[24] The shift into a skewed version of class analysis within the brief period of one decade parallels the transition of the North American middle class into the relatively prosperous 1950s. In this context of obsessive popular images of the "American family"—male provider in gray flannel suit coming home to playful son, daughter, dog, and beaming blonde wife, who, with perfect timing, delivers a roast turkey straight from a shining oven—scientific discourse delivered its own vision of the gendered division of labor. Lurking behind the desire to detect endometriosis in the "larger pocketbook" is an ideological subtext of benevolent equilibrium and fair exchange: In an era of multiplying magical household gadgets born of the wedding of science and capitalism, women, presumably with more "free time" to spend in leisurely consumption, must pay back with female labor, producing new human beings out of the (female) reproductive machine.

Since the 1960s, in the context of the feminist movement, endometriosis has often been referred to as the "career woman's disease" because of its enduring association with the choice not to bear children. A few recent studies, however, have shown endometriosis to be an "equal opportunity disease," striking women of all socioeconomic, racial, and age groups,[25] but doctors are still inclined to diagnose it largely in white professionals. In December 1980, in the *Houston Chronicle*, Dr. Veasy Buttram described "the typical patient with endometriosis as an ambitious woman who delays marriage until completion of college and postpones childbearing until financial security has been attained."[26] The rhetoric of earlier decades— "modern economic trends are responsible for delayed marriage," "youth is the proper time to have children and it is right that [women] be urged to do so"[27]—echoes in contemporary medical texts. Doctors still prescribe pregnancy as a cure for endometriosis, eliding the typical scenario of the endo woman who does get pregnant, but then simply becomes a mother with endometriosis.

Despite variations having to do with different historical moments, most endo theories share a structural positioning of women as the generators of their own disease. Writing from their specific sexual, class, racial, and national context, scientists have systematically closed their eyes to the startling fact that the disease has been diagnosed in girls in their early teens as well as in women who have given birth to over ten children—a contradiction of the hegemonic endo theory that "prolonged cyclic menstruation not interrupted by pregnancy constitutes a major risk factor for the disease."[28] Science's rush to search for the origins of endo in the fertile area of female deviation recalls AIDS discourses in relation to gay men: The victims are blamed for bringing the disease upon themselves. Relegated to the realm of the metaphysical, endometriosis is seen as the inevitable conclusion to the hubris of "going against nature." Just as AIDS is deemed God's revenge on "unnatural" homosexual conduct, endometriosis is deemed God's revenge on the unnatural conduct of preternaturally ambitious professional women.

Furthermore, much of the 1980s research into the condition has been dedicated to the assumed relationship between endometriosis and infertility. The authors of diverse classifications of endometriosis—for example, Buttram's—are fond of the peritoneal/ovarian/tubal/cul-de-sac division. Concerned only with forms of endometriosis related to infertility, they consider other forms so insignificant as hardly to merit classification. Endometriosis of the ureter or appendix, let alone of the lungs, the muscles of the arms or legs, or the pelvic lymph nodes, is shrugged off, since endometrial symptoms in these areas "have not yet been related to infertility," and therefore "a separate classification seems impractical."[29]

Medical writings tend to categorize endometriosis patients and prescribe remedies according to a woman's reproductive age and her desire for fertility. Ovaries are not removed if a woman's ability to bear children can be preserved, but "patients in whom childbearing is complicated or not desired" are met with "definitive treatment by surgical excision of the endometriotic tissue and the pelvic organs."[30] The "hysterectomy treatment" is the standard prescription for women disinclined to bear children and for those who have already performed their reproductive duty. In medical texts on endometriosis, however, the consequences of hysterectomy for women, such as osteoporosis and heart disease—not to mention emotional trauma—are relegated to marginalia. One of the "Joe with Endo" cartoons again deploys the carnivalesque strategy of gender inversion to criticize physicians' automatic decision to use hysterectomy to "solve" endo: A female doctor casually misinforms Joe that "the definitive cure is the removal of the testicles. Then there'll be no hormones to feed this endometriosis." Shocked and alarmed by the idea of castration, Joe receives the blasé response that "We don't usually use that word . . . too frightening." And to Joe's proposal that "there *must* be something else!" the doctor answers patronizingly: "You men. You get so attached to your organs. Besides, if we remove them you'll never worry about cancer."[31]

The notion of curing endometriosis through the two extreme approaches of sterilization and childbearing is thoroughly mythologized. Similarly, other "treatments"—conservative surgery and hormonal therapy—are meant to enable reproduction in the future. Since endometriosis is often defined in terms of women's reproductive capacities, some gynecological clinics are reluctant to treat endo patients unless they demonstrate a desire to conceive. Women with endometriosis may also be pressured into having babies as therapy, even when they are ambivalent about or clearly uninterested in the prospect of motherhood. The walls of expensive clinics are often decorated with the doctors' triumphant trophies: photographs of the scores of babies issuing from treatment, signed, as it were, with the doctors' authorial monogram.[32] The medical apparatus nurtures the female organs (for women who can afford it) toward the victorious resolution of reproduction. Endometriosis is treated seriously only when it interferes with conception, displacing a more conventional medical narrative of healing bodies, no matter what. Thus, it is difficult to imagine less reproductively oriented photos in a gynecological clinic, showing women performing other activities made possible by endo treatment, for example, dancing, or having sex without pain. Endo discourse suggests that science has made it possible to correct nature's "fuck-ups," but in the "natural" way: by helping to strengthen the traditional heterosexual family.

It is not women's desire for heterosexual marriage and children that is being criticized here but, rather, the medical establishment's representation of endometriosis as merely an obstacle to the normal trajectory of motherhood.[33] In fact, the fertility approach to endometriosis often introduces a Catch-22 situation: Pregnancy is recommended as the cure for endo, but endo that affects fertility makes pregnancy impossible. To superimpose a teleological narrative of birth, motherhood, and heterosexual parenthood on endometriosis only hinders a serious investigation into the cure for the disease. Babies do not cure endometriosis, and fertility clinics do not cater to endo women's health needs. What about the women with endometriosis who *can* conceive children? What about the woman who already has both children and endometriosis? Or the woman who continues to have endometriosis even after hysterectomy? While the in/fertile female constitutes the desired object of the scientific gaze, the endo female looms in the background as an object yet to be deciphered—a split that renders both subjectivities invisible.[34]

The erasure of women's agency in medical discourse is deeply ingrained in class and racial discourses, grounding the racialized female body differently, and even in opposite ways. In most medical studies, white upper-middle-class professional women are considered the primary risk group for pelvic endometriosis.[35] At times, class analysis of endometriosis overrides race considerations. Dr. F. P. Lloyd wrote in a 1964 issue of the *American Journal of Obstetrics and Gynecology* that the occurrence of pelvic endometriosis in blacks approaches that of whites as blacks achieve a higher socioeconomic status and standard of living.[36] It seems that African American women cannot move up the social ladder without risking a white professional women's disease—a revealing sign that both groups of women "moved out of their place." (One wonders at exactly which step of the tax bracket the disease is likely to strike.)

Race, however, remains a major paradigm for medical researchers at pains to prove that women of color and Third World women are endo-free.[37] Many medical scholars who have "researched" Third World women have reached the astonishing conclusions that "in the Middle East and in India our colleagues seldom encounter endometriosis," that "through personal observations endometriosis is almost nonexistent among peasant women of South Vietnam and Afghanistan," and that "endometriosis was comparatively infrequent in Mexican Indian women."[38] Scientific studies that racialize endometriosis lead to the misdiagnosis of women of color, whose endo symptoms may have other causes, such as pelvic inflammatory disease.

Inflammatory ailments carry sexual overtones of redness and heat. While upper-middle-class white women are diagnosed with a career-related disease, black women are diagnosed with a sexually connoted one.[39] In a recent series of 190 laparoscopies performed on black women, however, Dr. Donald L. Chatman noted that 21 percent of his subjects, previously diagnosed as having pelvic inflammatory disease, in fact had endometriosis.[40] The real question, then, is not why endometriosis strikes the white-skinned woman, but what is at stake in the massive medical literature that persists in racially codifying a disease associated with the reproductive organs. The relationship between race and the diagnosis of endo might be better explained by differential access to medical care and health information.[41] Yet, what, then, are the implications of positing a low rate of endometriosis for women of color and Third World women? Medical discourse implicitly, it seems, makes the argument (for white women to hear) that Asian or African women's low rate of endometriosis and high birthrate prove that the postponement of pregnancy adds to the risk of developing the disease. "Paradoxically, white middle-class women," Rayna Rapp points out, "are both better served by reproductive medicine, and also more controlled by it, than women of less privileged groups."[42]

Women of color and Third World women are subjected to what one might call a dis-reproductive medical apparatus: By avoiding diagnosis of endometriosis—a disease publicly linked to infertility—in women of color, the medical system excludes them from the reproduction track of presumed cure. Physicians may be more likely to diagnose pelvic inflammatory disease in women of color where the "cure" is often sterilization. The selective approach that tends to apply the hysterectomy solution to white endo women according to age and the desire to have children takes on an entirely different accent in the case of women of color for whom hysterectomy is seen to be the one and only cure. It is difficult to avoid the conclusion of what Stuart Hall calls "inferential racism" in the treatment, knowledge, and approach to endometriosis. If white women's delayed childbearing is presented as disorderly conduct, women of color's precipitous fertility is seen as disorderly for the opposite reasons. And while one type of disorderly conduct requires coaxing into fertility as a cure, the other requires reinforcement of infertility.

That pro-lifers choose to remain willfully ignorant of the policies of sterilization imposed, for example, in Bolivia and Puerto Rico—and documented, respectively, in films like Jorge Sanjinés's and the Grupo Ukamau's *Yawar mallku* (Blood of the Condor, 1969) and Ana Maria Garcia's *La Operación* (The Operation, 1981)—shows the hypocrisy and contradiction of their lack of concern for *these* women's bodies. With U.S complicity, and without a single pro-life silent scream, Bolivian indigenous women have been forcibly sterilized at the same time that the former regime of Hugo Banzer, as Angela Gilliam points out, agreed to resettle 30,000 white South Africans to help the "racial imbalance" of a country that still has an indigenous majority.[43] The U.S. government legalized sterilization in Puerto Rico in 1937 to manage the menace of what was called "excess population."[44] Federal strategies of modernization, as Maria Milagros Lopez points out, have included population control through a massive program of public sterilization "services."[45] Since the 1950s, 35 percent of Puerto Rican women in their reproductive years have been sterilized, at times pressured by doctors' "modern" advice, and at others waking up to a reality of "tied tubes" performed without their prior knowledge or consent.

If in Puerto Rico women were the guinea pigs for contraceptive experimentation, in the United States, as Angela Davis points out, women's bodies have been the site of a historical overlapping between the movement for birth control and the ideology of eugenics.[46] And as Cheryl Johnson-Odim argues, the "fact that surgical sterilization remains free and that federal funding for abortions has been disallowed means that it is poor women to whom the *choice* to abort is denied, and their ranks are disproportionately populated by women of color."[47] This history of discriminatory sterilization policies and the medical establishment's unfounded racialization of the female body discursively imbues the endo body with a hidden demographic agenda.

KEYHOLE SURGERY AND LASER ILLUMINATIONS

A key therapy for endometriosis requires "hormonal suppression of the production of estrogen by the ovaries."[48] Given the fertility dogma, articles have proliferated in medical journals on methods of hormone suppression. Strangely echoing the figure of the menstruating body as aberrant, the endo body undergoes a hormonal mimicry of either menopause or pregnancy in what amounts to a postmodern virtual de-menstrualization of the bleeding female. Hormones (Danazol and Lupron, for example) have deleterious side effects that are obscured by the triumphant narrative of hormonal progress. They produce pseudomenopause, forcing a young woman to proleptically experience a kind of flash-forward. In her early twenties, she is turned into a simulacrum of youth with the physiology of a woman in her forties or fifties trapped inside her; she may experience hot flashes, osteoporosis, and decreased sexual drive. Pseudomenopause, then, is a painful preview of aging and mortality.[49] This virtual menopausal hybrid woman transgresses conventional concepts of pre- and postmenopausal women: She is an "in-between" woman, occupying two temporalities. (An exploration of this pre/post-hybrid might have added an interesting dimension to the discussion of female spectatorship in Yvonne Rainer's 1990 film *Privilege*, which considers the politics of aging and menopause.) Both chemically and hormonally induced pseudomenopause and pseudopregnancy may lessen the symptoms of endometriosis, but they do little to heal endo women and much to undermine their health. Yet, recent studies of the links between endometriosis and the immune system propose a female body that ought to remain open and ready for any kind of hormonal (mis)treatment to maximize its procreativity.[50]

Surgery as a "cure" for endometriosis encompasses a variety of procedures, from traditional laparotomy to video (laser) laparoscopy. But given the degree of specialization and practice required to use laser laparoscopy, most doctors still choose the traditional laparotomy operation. Often performed on an outpatient basis, and under general anesthesia, laparoscopy involves the insertion of a lighted periscopelike instrument through a small incision near the navel, enabling the surgeon to inspect the organs in the abdomen. Laparoscopy has been combined with laser technologies, first medically employed for eye surgery and used in gynecology only since 1980.[51] More precise than electrocautery or cryosurgery, the powerful combination of the laser and the laparoscope reduces blood loss as well as the risk of infection from external viruses. As Dr. Camran Nezhat, the director of the Fertility and Endocrinology Center in Atlanta and an adviser to the Endometriosis Association, points out, the laser can be concentrated and its energy focused to a pinpoint, allowing the vaporization of small endometrial implants without destroying surrounding tissue. Moreover, the laser beam can reach sites that would be difficult to reach with the scalpel. Laser surgery can also be done more quickly than conventional laparotomy, so that the patient can be anesthetized for less time; it also reduces the possibility of scar formation. With the CO_2 laser beam, surgeons can vaporize or make an incision as small as a millimeter without touching the tissue. The energy of the carbon-dioxide laser beam is absorbed almost completely at a depth of a millimeter from the tissue. It can therefore be used over vital organs without damaging underlying structures.[52]

Gradually, more surgeons are combining a video camera, video recorder, and high-resolution video monitor with laser laparoscopy. Here a view of the operating field (what the surgeon sees through the laparoscope) is projected onto the video monitor and videotaped for future reference. The surgeon views the monitor during the procedure, rather than looking through the laparoscope.[53] The technology allows the surgeon to work in a comfortable, upright posture (watching the video monitor) rather than bent over the laparoscope. Fatigue is lessened, and precision is enhanced. The technology also provides a permanent video record of the procedure for verification, insurance, and follow-up purposes.[54]

These meaningful advances in medical technology have substantially improved endo women's quality of life. Like hormones, however, laser surgery removes the symptoms of endometriosis only temporarily. Laser laparoscopy is generally followed by hormone treatments that suppress the disease but often leave the woman susceptible to a "return of the repressed" in the form of myriad future side effects. Thus, while the advent of relatively noninvasive procedures such as laser laparoscopy used in tandem with video augers a technical/medical advance, the continued medical resistance to more collaborative models of treatment and healing remain a problem. I am not, in other words, proposing that there is something inherently wrong with the technologies or the doctors that use them. Rather, my concern is with a discursive tradition that has consistently dismissed the voices of endo women and refused any dialogue with self-help organizations that have been in the forefront of facilitating the circulation of information on endo. For example, a *Newsweek* article, "Conquering Endometriosis: Lasers Battle the 'Career Woman's Disease'" (1986), presents lasers as a panacea, offering a triumphal narrative of science coming to women's rescue.[55] Similarly, a *Science News* article (1981), "Lasers versus Female Complaints," sets up a classical gendered opposition, casting women as hysterical whiners and associating lasers with the male scientists who use technology to take care of "female complaints."[56]

Positing science as masculine and nature as feminine, as some of these articles implicitly do, effectively requires a narrative of heroic mastery in which women have no investigatory role toward their own bodies. This medical discourse not only excludes the voices of women scientists and patients; it paradoxically hails the advances of the technology—which is a treatment but not necessarily a cure—while simultaneously undermining the reality of the disease. It is no surprise, then, that the images accompanying such articles typically feature male doctors holding the video laparoscope, while women are represented as framed body parts. A 1983 illustration in *Health* magazine, accompanying an article titled "Lasers for Ladies," shows a video camera shooting a phallic laser ray that penetrates the lower abdomen of a reclining (headless) female in a bathing suit, creating a prominent hole (figure 31).[57] Without any apparent irony, this visualization of penetration transmutes medical scrutiny into an erotic gaze.

The erotic component of the (masculine) gaze of knowledge/power produces on its female object has been the subject of much feminist investigation. In fact, a number of feminist artists have addressed this pattern in the mass-media representations of medical technologies and female patients. In a recent collage titled *Love at First Site* (1990), Sherry Millner juxtaposes 1950s magazine images of three male gynecologists hovering over a female patient, each facing a strategic part of her body: Two have their heads in close proximity to her breasts, and the third holds a camera at her vagina. The "patient" is in fact a mannequin wearing a 1950s bathing suit, thus placing the artificially constructed woman of the fashion industry on a continuum with the woman as constructed by the medical gaze.

In sharp contrast to the feminist publications of the Endometriosis Association, articles in scientific journals and mass-media magazines, as well as their accompanying visuals, suppress women's narratives and their struggle for democratic access to new technologies and to research on alternative healing. In other words, scientific and mass-media endo discourse surgically removes women's voices from the discussion of their own bodies. While the hormone-treatment discourse focuses on the suppression of the disorderly body, the representation of laser-video gyno-technology privileges an exploratory voyeurism into an anesthetized body, and it is this form of voyeurism that subtly underpins the ways in which video laser laparoscopy lends itself to a master narrative of penetration, exploration, and cleansing of an always already polluted female body. (Laparoscopy's nickname, significantly, is "keyhole surgery."[58]) Video lapa-

LASERS FOR LADIES
... ladies with gynecological warts and other problems

Bob Hiemstra

31 "Lasers for Ladies": *Health* magazine

roscopy narrates the very act of transformation from the inside out. In physiological cinema, the camera, as Lisa Cartwright points out, was "incorporated as an instrument within the life of the body under study."[59] In video laparoscopy, the camera not only observes and documents the surgery; it also performs it. Thus, it becomes an agent "acting not only on the body but in and through it."[60]

In hegemonic endo discourse, the video camera renders the interior body accessible while also transforming the doctor into the author of a videotape of a newly fashioned body. The combination of video and laser laparoscopy can also record the surgical procedure; the doctor becomes filmmaker, or, more precisely, videomaker. The hand that wields the scalpel triggers the camera. Although this transformation of the act of looking into the act of visual recording results in the patient having access to a video-laparoscopic record of the surgery and the interior of her own body, the medical discourse exclusively focuses on the surgeon as the videotape auteur.

Along with the language of voyeurism and auteurship, one also finds in this discourse a rhetoric of pollution and purity. Indeed, in some gynecological clinics, the term "cleanup" is casually used to refer to the laser-surgery cleansing of the body. Video laparoscopy is used not only to document endometriosis but also to (temporarily) cleanse the body: The silvery tube of the laser is seen cutting, burning, and separating out the malignant tissues, shooting water to rinse away the blood, and finally vacuuming away the unwanted matter. Abnormal tissue and tubal obstructions are vaporized; the smoke is suctioned out. Although the rhetoric of "clean up" pervades all surgical discourse, and is in no way restricted to women and their reproductive organs, it has special resonance and irony when applied to women, given the medical-discursive legacy that figures the female body as a walking pathological laboratory. Thus, in medical texts one often encounters a subliminal image of a filth-producing female body foiled by science's laser-eye machines, which probe the interior and spit out a cleansing fire. Video images of blood, smoke, and water on the screen depict the viscera as a kind of abstract action-painting battle zone. It is an apocalyptic imagery of cleansing the landscape through fire and flood. But in spite of all the thrilling special effects of the endo surgery, only the symptoms have been eradicated; the "evil" is left to fester—the endometriosis has not been cured and can always return.

Although medical and mass-media texts show a near-fetishistic fascination with each new gyno-technological invention, most remain silent about the stagnation in endometriosis research. Endometriosis activists, however, are often much more ambivalent about novel uterus-imaging technologies. When video laparoscopy, for example, is hailed for conquering the farthest reaches of the interior, it is not the effectiveness of this technology that is in question. Rather, it is the scientific community's unwillingness to address endo etiology—its origins as well as its prevention and cure—that is in question.

This privileging of industrial gyno-technological discoveries fails to acknowledge the perspective of the "object" under investigation. In the case of video laparoscopy, the notion of scientific discovery is grafted onto a discourse of technological expansion into the "virgin land" of the female body, hitherto untouched by such a penetrating gaze. This implicit link between the technological and the epistemological dates back to Francis Bacon's analogy between scientific and geographic discoveries. ("And as the immense regions of the West Indies had never been discovered, if the use of the compass had not first been known, it is no wonder that the discovery and the advancement of arts hath made no greater progress, when the art of inventing and discovering of the sciences remains hitherto unknown.")[61] It also evokes Sigmund Freud's analogy between psychoanalytic and archaeological excavations: He compares "clearing away the pathogenic psychical material layer by layer" with "the technique of excavating a buried city."[62] An enigmatic space, the endo female body requires the "pioneering work" of voyages into unknown "dark continents," its terra incognita.[63] The visual lay of the body, spread out for exploration, promotes sonogram and video laparoscopy as the postmodern cartography of the female interior. And it is thus the language of "exploration" and "conquest" that shapes these ultrasound and video-laparoscopic visuals. With x-ray as a black-and-white photograph, and video laparoscopy as a color documentary film, the surgeon is positioned as a traveling image maker of the female body, whose organs he or she explores, documents, and rearranges.

In other words, video laparoscopy is more than a means of observing and recording pathological organs. It literally reconfigures the body. Whereas access to the invisible interior was formerly possible only by dissecting cadavers in autopsies and cutting the body open in surgery, recent imaging technologies permit that access with only a minimal incision. Through the camera-and-monitor apparatus, the surgeon can remove an ovarian cyst without having to remove the ovary, helping the patient to maintain an externally more aesthetic body, with fewer scars. Video laparoscopy, like cosmetic surgery, even allows for a "before" and "after" image. Yet the tendency of endometriosis to recur means there can never be a perfect cosmetic reconstruction. The laser's costume designing of the body is not permanent, and there may be many "befores" and many "afters."

Institutionalized endo discourse tends not to acknowledge this limitation and celebrates instead the "revolution"[64] of laser laparoscopy as a new weapon in science's video war against a self-destructive uterus. The laser, Prometheus-like, brings light into the body's dark corners. The once opaque womb is stripped of its mystery, and the light of scientific knowledge shines on the dark inner sanctum. Tropes of light and darkness, informed by Enlightenment ideas, are projected onto an out-of-control (female) nature. Superimposed on the language of exploration in endo discourse, in a sense, is a quasi-military language of projectiles fired with precision at the target "by going into the uterus through the vagina."[65] As constructed in scientific discourse (Bacon, Freud), the enigma often requires uncovering, unveiling, and penetration. Video laparoscopy, in a sense, only literalizes the metaphor.

While the language of infiltration is appropriate on one level, since there is an actual penetration in such surgery, on another level it occludes women's voices and historically has been premised on a colonizing model of exploration. Medical technologies, furthermore, could be conceived alternatively as a collaborative project in which women participate in scientific investigation and technological healing. Within this perspective, scientific enigmas are not detached from women's bodies but are studied and remapped through a dialogical process.

This other story is already beginning to be enacted by the few scientists who have worked with self-help organizations. In his foreword to Mary Lou Ballweg's and the Endometriosis Association's *Overcoming Endometriosis*, Dr. Camran Nezhat, for example, speaks in language rooted in community ("sharing," "partnership," "working together"). The only time the word "conquering" is evoked, it is used to suggest a notion of community, of "conquering together" the disease. Doctors working closely with the Endometriosis Association conceive of making the "doctor–patient relationship truly a partnership,"[66] reframing in a sense science's institutional authority. These few pockets of disruption evoke the possibility of altering the power-knowledge relationship in the direction of a more dialogical scientific practice.

Medical texts' celebration of laser surgery often displaces the issue of research into endometriosis—research not profitable to the multimillion-dollar medical-technology industry. Part of the new endo story being told, meanwhile, involves accepting endometriosis as a disease worthy of research and funding. Critical endo discourse, in other words, promotes the aim of raising awareness about preventive and holistic care and funding research over and beyond the special effects of gyno-technology.

SELF-SPECTATORSHIP AND THE HEALING GAZE

In the fertility clinic, where the surgeon tends to be represented as both a scientist and a videomaker documenting "science's war against nature," video laparoscopy becomes a tool to plumb the "inherent" mysteries of the female body and female sexuality (figure 32). Although a surgical procedure, video laparoscopy must also be understood as a form of cinematic representation of the female body, taking into account the complex relations between looks, spectatorship, and gendered and racialized identities. The ways that endo women view video-laparoscopic images pose a challenge to models of spectatorship premised on desire and pleasure. For example, the eroticism associated with the scientific gaze, as vividly illustrated in the lasers-for-ladies image, is radically undermined in video laparoscopy by the endo spectacle itself. The interior inscribed on the

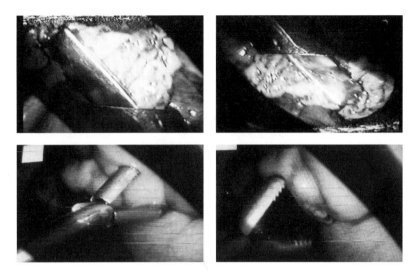

32 Video laparoscopy: Suctioning out a cyst. Photograph by Lynne Jackson.

video screen is more emetic than erotic: pinkish, reddish, and brownish organs and viscera, which recall those of poultry,[67] confront most viewers with a sense of dizzying mortality, only heightened by the fact that these images give visual form to the fighting of a disease. In this model of spectatorship—one not yet addressed in film theory—endo women are agents in a healing gaze.

Insofar as the video screen is transmuted into a specular image of the interior body, which cannot ordinarily be reflected in the mirror, binaries of beautiful–ugly and black–white are temporarily erased. Going beyond the epidermis appears to erase the markers of racial difference. Video laparoscopy allows one not only to look into a previously invisible interior of the body but also to create a narrative of bodily transformation and healing. Video laparoscopy, then, raises questions about narrative structure and spectatorial identification, specifically bringing up the issue of what one might call *self-spectatorship*. How can feminist cultural criticism address the particular experiences of women watching their own surgery post facto? And what is the nature of identification for a female spectator watching the inside of a body on the screen that happens to be her own?

Conversations with endo women who have watched their own video laparoscopy tapes reveal certain spectatorial tendencies,[68] ranging from an anxious refusal to watch something that brings back a traumatic moment to a more confident hope that watching these images will contribute to healing through the process of "getting back in touch with our bodies."[69] The refusal to watch is not limited to women who experienced unsuccessful surgeries. Post-video-laparoscopic spectatorship is ambivalently implicated in unconscious body memory. In this rendezvous between conscious spectator and unconscious patient, who happen to be one and the same person, video-laparoscopic images may trigger a relived memory of past pain, along with a prosthetic experience of the removed cyst in the form of renewed endo pain. An inevitable anxiety emerges when confronting a cinematic depiction of one's own bodily fragility, along with a fear of reexperiencing consciously what one formerly experienced unconsciously: the penetration of camera-tube, laser, vaporizer, and the action of cutting, burning, and suctioning, seen in a kind of a retroactive mirror image. Watching one's own video laparoscopy tape may provoke a visceral, physical reaction, of intuitively touching the previously or currently sensitive organs, particularly those in the lower abdomen. The patient/spectator who cannot bear the sight is divided between fear and the temptation to look at the video screen.

The knowledge of whether the surgery was a success or a failure affects how the endo spectator responds to the images. In a "happy ending" video laparoscopy, the patient/spectator may identify with the slow efforts of tweezers grabbing scar tissue, or the vaporizer suctioning out a cyst, particularly when that woman feels that she has been "invaded by a sneaky unstable alien."[70] In instances of unsuccessful video laparoscopy, when the surgeon was unable to excise a cyst and had to revert to traditional laparotomy, fewer women wanted to play their videotapes. Some gave them to their endo support groups to watch and study in their absence as part of a follow-up discussion. In all cases, the desire to master the details of the medical procedure, whether through viewing the tapes or discussing them in a group, is bound up in the wish to be an agent of one's own healing.

The strange reflexivity of these images, in some ways, makes them difficult to view. Just as videotaped laser eye surgery suggests, à la Buñuel, the slicing of an open eye, video laparoscopy evokes the camera obscura of the cinematic apparatus. The metaphors of cinema as dream, of regress to the womb, are here made literal by a spectator who peers into the uterus, although one that is well lit and in living color. However, the living color of dissected organs subverts the subject effect: Here there can be no regression to protective darkness. And in any case, what does it mean for the self-spectating woman to "escape" to her own ailing womb?

Microscopic video enlargement makes the visuals strikingly dramatic by providing a magnified look at the organs and the machinery. In endo self-spectatorship—or, better, in vicarious self-spectatorship—identification with one's own organs, temporarily injured by the invasive burning/cutting machine, is inevitable, even if one often has to look away from the screen. But this identificatory impulse can be accompanied by another identification with the camera itself. Sharing the point of view of the camera, the self-spectator looks at her own body through the camera's penetrating eye that preceded her into herself. If there is a kind of anxiety at the sight of the burning laser and the vaporizer taking out chunks of her body, there is also an identification—particularly after the first viewing—with the lasers and vaporizers themselves as the machines that battle the invasive tissues. In this sense, it is also the surgeon's perspective that the spectator internalizes, thus allowing the endo woman to transform vicariously herself into a surgeon, an agent of her own healing. Video laparoscopy can realize what a member of the Endometriosis Association expressed: "I wish I could perform the 'lap' myself so I could see the 'enemy' for myself."[71]

Viewing these silent moving images, intended to enable the scientist to monitor the surgery, can become a kind of epistemological boomerang in which the gazed upon can return the gaze. Despite the lasers-for-ladies representation of laparoscopic technologies, these techniques cannot and should not be reduced to or equated with a voyeuristic/militarist apparatus, since they also contain a returned gaze, and may contribute to a dialogical interaction between endo women and scientific research. Thus, video laparoscopy offers the possibility not just of a "black box" documentation of a gynecological voyage of dissection and suture, but also a collaborative study of endometriosis, where the interior arena is not restricted to the eyes of the surgeon. If pathological and anatomical dissections are premised on an immobile corpse, at the service of medical and legal institutions, in video laparoscopy the "dead" object (usually) returns to life, able to watch, critique, and participate in the ongoing struggle for healing. Thus, her surgical immobility assumes her future mobility—her ability to look back and talk back.[72]

Video-laparoscopic viewing, I should point out, does not usually form part of endo self-help meetings, which are more devoted to sharing information and support. In fact, endo women more commonly first watch the Endometriosis Association production *You're Not Alone . . . Understanding Endometriosis* (1988). A conventional documentary about the disease, the film features experts in the field as well as voices of the association chapters' members who speak of their experiences—from prediagnostic loneliness to postoperative participation—in self-help groups. When women in the self-help groups view such videos, they do so in a context of ongoing support and a certain shared intimacy. The group often becomes a site where a range of intense emotions are expressed, including tears, frustration, and even a carnivalesque laughter at the grotesque nature of the body caught up in chronic disease and its own mortality.

If women are to become active participants in a multidimensional project to heal women's diseases, collective viewing of medical procedures such as video laparoscopy may serve to counter the ceding of the female body to medical institutions and to shape healing-oriented spectatorship. Although a few self-help endo groups come close to video-laparoscopy activism, the use of camera and monitor in video laparoscopy cannot be compared with media activism around AIDS, for example,[73] since the subject of the videos is a strictly surgical procedure, and their producer is not exactly the endo patient. Video-laparoscopic tapes are owned by a selective group of endometriosis patients who have had access to this kind of still relatively uncommon surgery, and who asked for the tape from (or were given the tape by) the surgeon. However, one might imagine an endo media activism that would include self-spectating women narrating their experiences and receptions of video laparoscopy. These images could also be deployed in the mass media to gain political visibility for endometriosis. As a strategy for empowerment, collective self-spectatorship allows nonprofessionals to study diverse surgical performances outside the disciplinary boundaries of the medical establishment. Procedures such as video laparoscopy can play a significant role in democratizing access to our bodies, potentially turning patients, their families, and their communities into knowledgeable participants in scientific research and medical technologies.

NOTES

I thank the Endometriosis Association, and particularly Mary Lou Ballweg, its co-founder and president, for its invaluable information and courageous work over the years, and Cecily Marcus for her enthusiastic assistance in my research into medical discourses about endometriosis. I am especially grateful to Robert Stam for his generous support, whether through our conversations or through his comments on the essay. I am also indebted to the supportive discussions and suggestions I have received from Lisa Cartwright, Faye Ginsburg, Lynne Jackson, Caren Kaplan, Smadar Lavie, Mary Lawler, Ivone Margulies, Constance Penley, Eric Smoodin, and Paula Treichler. Special thanks to Lisa Cartwright and Ann

Kaplan for encouraging me to present sections of this article at the Pembroke Center at Brown University and at the Humanities Institute at State University of New York at Stony Brook. Finally, I acknowledge the Society for the Humanities at Cornell University for awarding me time during 1991–92 to begin writing on a topic I had contemplated for years but until then had never dared broach.

1 The title "Lasers for Ladies" is borrowed from a short article (of the same title) by Michelle Bekey that appeared in *Health*, vol. 15, May 1983, 16.

2 I will use the phrase "endo discourse" to encompass a whole textual body produced around endometriosis that refers both to hegemonic medical and alternative discourses. Although physicians use the official name "endometriosis," the disease is at times referred to as "endo" in self-help groups.

3 The etymology of endometrium derives from the Greek "endo," the mucous membrane lining, and "metra," uterus, which itself derives from "metr," mother. The endometrium tissue that lines the inside of the uterus builds up and sheds each month in the menstrual cycle.

4 For a full account of sites, symptoms, and complications, see Mary Lou Ballweg and the Endometriosis Association, *Overcoming Endometriosis: New Help from the Endometriosis Association* (New York: Congdon and Weed, 1987); Kate Weinstein, *Living with Endometriosis: How to Cope with the Physical and Emotional Challenges* (Reading, Mass.: Addison-Wesley, 1987).

5 George B. Haydon, "A Study of 569 Cases of Endometriosis," *American Journal of Obstetrics and Gynecology* 43 (1942): 704.

6 The ad is reproduced in Ballweg and the Endometriosis Association, *Overcoming Endometriosis*, 19.

7 The phrase is taken from J. H. Bellina of Louisiana State University School of Medicine, as cited in Dietrick E. Thomsen, "Lasers versus Female Complaints," *Science News*, vol. 9, no. 6, 7 February 1981, 91.

8 As cited in Carolyn DeMarco, "Endometriosis: Options for Treating a Puzzling Condition," *Sojourner: The Women's Forum* 17, no. 7 (March 1992): 19H.

9 The cartoon appears in Ballweg and the Endometriosis Association, *Overcoming Endometriosis*, 72.

10 See, for example, Craig A. Molgaard, Amanda L. Golbeck, and Louise Gresham, "Current Concepts in Endometriosis," *Western Journal of Medicine* 143 (July 1985): 42–46.

11 Joe Vincent Meigs, "Endometriosis: Its Significance," *Annals of Surgery* 114 (1940): 869.

12 On the discourses on menstruation, see Janice Delaney, Mary Jane Lupton, and Emily Toth, *The Curse: A Cultural History of Menstruation* (Urbana: University of Illinois Press, 1988).

13 Emily Martin, "The Egg and the Sperm: How Science has Constructed a Romance Based on Stereotypical Male–Female Roles," *Signs* 16, no. 3 (Spring 1991): 486; idem, *The Woman in the Body: A Cultural Analysis of Reproduction* (Boston: Beacon Press, 1987).

14 Dr. John Sampson's theory of retrograde menstruation, formulated in 1921, is the oldest and still most widely accepted explanation for endometriosis. Accord-

ing to Sampson, during menstruation a certain amount of menstrual fluid is forced backward from the uterus through the fallopian tubes and showered on the pelvic organs and pelvic lining. See Weinstein, *Living with Endometriosis*, 23–25.

15 Meigs, "Endometriosis: Its Significance," 868.

16 Edward Walker, Wayne Katon, Lindy Michael Jones, and Joan Russo, "Relationship between Endometriosis and Affective Disorder," *American Journal of Psychiatry* 146, no. 3 (March 1989): 380–81.

17 Molgaard et al., "Current Concepts in Endometriosis," 43.

18 Dorothy Otnow Lewis, Florence Comite, Catherine Mallouh, Laura Zadunaisky, Karen Hutchinson-Williams, Bruce D. Cherksey, and Catherine Yeager, "Bipolar Mood Disorder and Endometriosis: Preliminary Findings," *American Journal of Psychiatry* 144, no. 12 (December 1987): 1588.

19 For another argument along these lines, see Hillary Allen, "At the Mercy of Her Hormones: Premenstrual Tension and the Law," *m/f* 9 (1984): 21–43.

20 Meigs, "Endometriosis: Its Significance," 866, 869.

21 Ibid., 866.

22 Roger B. Scott and Richard W. Te Linde, "External Endometriosis: The Scourge of the Private Patient," *Annals of Surgery* 131 (May 1950): 701.

23 Ibid., 700.

24 Ibid.

25 A few of the exceptions I have come across are Diana E. Houston, "Evidence for the Risk of Pelvic Endometriosis by Age, Race and Socioeconomic Status," *Epidemiologic Reviews* 6 (1984): 167–91; and Donald L. Chatman, "Endometriosis in the Black Woman," *American Journal of Obstetrics and Gynecology* 125 (1976): 987–89.

26 Veasy C. Buttram, interview, *Houston Chronicle*, December 1980, as cited in Houston, "Evidence for the Risk of Pelvic Endometriosis," 182.

27 Meigs, "Endometriosis: Its Significance," 866.

28 Houston, "Evidence for the Risk of Pelvic Endometriosis," 178. Houston argues, on the basis of many case studies, that the rate at which endometriosis afflicts teenage women is unknown.

29 Veasy C. Buttram Jr., "An Expanded Classification of Endometriosis," *Fertility and Sterility* 30, no. 2 (August 1978): 241.

30 Idem, "An Expanded Classification of Endometriosis," 242.

31 Mary Lou Ballweg and Meri Lan, "Joe with Endo" in Ballweg and the Endometriosis Association, *Overcoming Endometriosis*, 181.

32 This information is based on visits to several fertility clinics in the New York area and Atlanta.

33 For a social and discursive analysis of the desperate infertile woman, see Sarah Franklin, "Deconstructing 'Desperateness': The Social Construction of Infertility in Popular Representations of New Reproductive Technologies," in *The New Reproductive Technologies*, ed. by Maureen McNeil, Ian Varcoe, and Steven Yearly (New York: St. Martin's Press, 1990), 200–29.

34 Similar analyses have pointed out the invisibility of women in the discourses around AIDS, abortion, and reproductive technologies. See Paula A. Treichler,

"Beyond Cosmo: AIDS, Identity, and Inscriptions of Gender," *Camera Obscura* 28 (January 1992): 21–75; Faye D. Ginsburg, *Contested Lives: The Abortion Debate in an American Community* (Berkeley: University of California Press, 1989), 1–315; Deborah Lynn Steinberg, "The Depersonalization of Women through the Administration of In Vitro Fertilization," in McNeil et al., *The New Reproductive Technologies*; and Valerie Hartouni, "Containing Women: Reproductive Discourse in the 1980s," in *Technoculture*, ed. by Constance Penley and Andrew Ross (Minneapolis: University of Minnesota Press, 1992).

35 Joe Vincent Meigs, "Endometriosis: Etiologic Role of Marriage Age and Parity; Conservative Treatment," *Obstetrics and Gynecology* 2, no. 1 (July 1953): 46–53.

36 F. P. Lloyd, "Endometriosis in the Negro Woman: A Five Year Study," *American Journal of Obstetrics and Gynecology* 89 (1964): 468–69.

37 For example, Stephen Corson writes that "incidence rates [of endometriosis] in England and Australia were less than those in the United States, and rates for Caucasians were higher than those for blacks": Stephen L. Corson, "Use of the Laparoscope in the Infertile Patient," *Fertility and Sterility* 32, no. 4 (October 1979): 364.

38 Houston, "Evidence for the Risk of Pelvic Endometriosis," 179.

39 Ibid.

40 Chatman, "Endometriosis in the Black Woman."

41 A recent study by Chatman challenges the view that endometriosis is uncommon in blacks after finding pelvic endometriosis in over 20 percent of his private black patients undergoing diagnostic laparoscopy. Diana Houston, meanwhile, calls for more specific studies with identified variables of race and class and a definition of the epidemiologic characteristics to understand the etiology of the disease.

42 Rayna Rapp, "Constructing Amniocentesis: Maternal and Medical Discourses," in *Uncertain Terms: Negotiating Gender in American Culture*, ed. by Faye D. Ginsburg and Anna Lowenhaupt Tsing (Boston: Beacon Press, 1990), 40.

43 Angela Gilliam, "Women's Equality and National Liberation," in *Third World Women and the Politics of Feminism*, ed. by Chandra Talpade Mohanty, Ann Russo, and Lourdes Torres (Bloomington: Indiana University Press, 1991), 224.

44 For more documentation, including archival footage, see Ana Maria Garcia, dir., *La Operación*, Pandora Films, 1982 (40 mins., color).

45 Maria Milagros Lopez, "Sterilization and Cesarean Operations in Puerto Rico: Women's Bodies and Strategies of Development," paper presented at "Cross Talk: A Multicultural Feminist Symposium," organized by Ella Shohat, The New Museum of Contemporary Art and The Drawing Center, New York City, June 1993.

46 Angela Davis, *Women, Race, and Class* (New York: Random House, 1981), 213–16.

47 Cheryl Johnson-Odim, "Race, Identity, and Feminist Struggles," in Mohanty et al., *Third World Women and the Politics of Feminism*, 323.

48 Robert L. Barbieri, "New Therapy for Endometriosis," *New England Journal of Medicine* 318, no. 8 (25 February 1988): 512.

49 It should be pointed out that most hormonal treatment, including birth-control pills, is not covered by health insurance. Drugs such as GnRH, meanwhile, are still considered experimental.

50 See the section "New Directions: Is Endometriosis What We Think It Is?" in Ballweg and the Endometriosis Association, *Overcoming Endometriosis*, 197–233.

51 Thomsen, "Lasers versus Female Complaints."

52 Camran Nezhat, "Laser Overview and the Carbon Dioxide Laser," in Ballweg and the Endometriosis Association, *Overcoming Endometriosis*, 63–68.

53 Ibid.

54 Ibid.

55 Matt Clark and Ginny Caroll, "Conquering Endometriosis: Lasers Battle the 'Career Women's Disease,'" *Newsweek*, 13 October 1986, 95.

56 Thomsen, "Lasers versus Female Complaints," 90–91.

57 Michelle Bekey, "Lasers for Ladies," *Health*, vol. 15, May 1983, 16; cartoon by Bob Hiemstra.

58 "Laser Laparoscopy Offers New Hope for Infertility," *American Family Physician*, vol. 27, April 1983, 267.

59 Lisa Cartwright, "'Experiments of Destruction': Cinematic Inscriptions of Physiology," *Representations* 40 (Fall 1992): 138.

60 Ibid.

61 Francis Bacon, *Advancement of Learning and Novom Organum* (New York: Colonial Press, 1899), 135.

62 Joseph Breuer and Sigmund Freud, *Studies on Hysteria*, trans. by James Strachey and Anna Freud (New York: Basic Books, 1957), 139.

63 For the relations between science, spectacle, and the discourses of discovery, particularly as manifested in metaphors such as the "virgin land" and the "dark continent," see Ella Shohat, "Imaging Terra Incognita: The Disciplinary Gaze of Empire," *Public Culture* 3 (Spring 1991): 41–70.

64 Thomsen, "Lasers versus Female Complaints," 91; "Laser Laparoscopy Offers New Hope for Infertility," 267–68.

65 "Laser Laparoscopy Offers New Hope for Infertility," 267–68.

66 Camran Nezhat, "Foreword," in Ballweg and the Endometriosis Association, *Overcoming Endometriosis*, xv.

67 One is reminded of the Spanish proverb, *"Abre tu cuerpo veras un puerco,"* which translates as "Open your body and you'll see a pig."

68 Although I did not conduct extensive research, I certainly found some clear tendencies in the reception of video laparoscopy.

69 I should emphasize that not all laser surgeons use video laparoscopy, and when they do, not all give these procedures to the patients. I spoke largely with self-help groups in the New York area and read letters written to the Fertility and Endocrinology Center in Atlanta. My research, in this sense, does not attempt to represent *all* patients or to cover a whole broad spectrum of patients' responses to their own images.

70 Ballweg, from a letter written to the Endometriosis Association, in *Overcoming Endometriosis*, 170.

71 Ballweg and the Endometriosis Association, *Overcoming Endometriosis*, 170.

72 I am using this phrase in its empowering sense as discussed in bell hooks, *Talking Back: Thinking Feminist, Thinking Black* (Boston: South End Press, 1989).

73 See for example, Alexandra Juhasz, "WAVE in the Media Environment: Camcorder Activism and the Making of HIV TV," *Camera Obscura* 28 (January 1992): 135–52; Juanita Mohammed, "WAVE in the Media Environment: Camcorder Activism in AIDS Education," *Camera Obscura* 28 (January 1992): 153–56.

DISORIENTING CLEOPATRA

A Modern Trope of Identity

The name "Cleopatra" provokes passions of all kinds. One of the not-so-minor passions concerns her looks and, by implication, the issue of her origins and identity. What did the ancient queen look like? Was she hauntingly beautiful? Was she white or black? Was she of Macedonian Greek or Egyptian ancestry? Emphatic and categorical answers to these questions would suggest a scientific hubris about the very possibility of possessing "Historical Truth" in general, and more specifically, about a complete cognitive mastery concerning Cleopatra and her world. No matter how science might strive for objectivity, history, as we have come to recognize, involves not only facts but also narratives, discourses, and worldviews. Unlike a certain postmodernism, however, this essay does not nihilistically profess the impossibility of access to any "fact" or "truth" (in non-capital letters). Throughout my work I have tried to inquire into how facts are established and how they are juxtaposed with other facts and narrated as a part of a larger narrative complex. Fragmentary and situated, scientific knowledge must rely partially on interpretation and on the "reading" of facts. Any look at the past within this conjuncture must be correlated with issues of worldview and the discourses shared by the "readers" of history.[1]

Here I will examine contemporary writings that attempt to dispel the mystery surrounding Cleopatra's looks and origins. Engaging with the subject of Cleopatra almost necessarily entails addressing the question of image making and visual representation. For millennia, her story of love and death, of power and sexuality, of domination and subordination, and of the imperial intercourse between Greek, Egyptian, and Roman civilizations has excited the popular imagination, triggering passionate opinions about her identity. The historical and the fantastical have mutually nourished each other. The uncertainty about her looks, meanwhile, has allowed each generation to shape her image in the form of its desire. Each age, one might say, has its own Cleopatra, to the point that one can study the thoughts and discourses of an epoch through its Cleopatra fantasies. The ancient queen therefore constitutes more than a historical figure who can be relegated to the domain of archaeology and Egyptology; rather, she allegorizes highly charged issues having to do with sexuality, gender, race, and nation, issues that reach far beyond the geocultural space of her times. Here I will largely focus on the representation of Cleopatra over the past century, as it became enmeshed in the heights of imperialism as well as in the subsequent emergence of postcolonial nations and their diasporas. Locating the battle over her looks and origins within colonial domination, anticolonial struggles, and postcolonial racial frictions, as I will try to show, adds yet another dimension for comprehending the investment in Cleopatra's identity.

To engage contemporary debates over Cleopatra in depth, however, one must take her representation in popular culture seriously. Written within a cultural studies framework, this essay insists on the importance of "reading" Cleopatra within modernity, and especially in the context of mass-media technologies. Since the late nineteenth century, Cleopatra has emerged as a mass-mediated figure. She has been visualized, evoked, or alluded to in numerous photographs, postcards, films, advertisements, commercials, television series, fashion magazines, and websites. Recently, for example, Cleopatra appeared in the futurist TV series 2525, in which an exotic dancer named Cleopatra, frozen in the year 2001, wakes up five centuries later and courageously battles to reclaim the surface of the earth for mankind from evil creatures known as Bailies. The advent of the various media technologies—film and television, video and digital—has in no way diminished the passion for the ancient queen. Cleopatra's image-making industry has achieved a remarkable global dissemination, to the point that her image has infiltrated households across the most diverse cultural geographies.

CLEOPATRA BETWEEN EUROCENTRISM AND AFROCENTRISM

> The grandmother of Cleopatra was a concubine; her mother is not known for certain. Given all the uncertainties of her ancestry, one scholar has estimated her blood has 32 parts Greek, 27 parts Macedonian and 5 parts Persian. It is a reasonable guess. If she was Black, no one mentioned it.[2]

Over the past decades, Cleopatra has been the subject of a vocal debate about blood, race, and origins. Although many texts acknowledge the impossibility of fully establishing her origins, most authors nevertheless proceed to offer their own firm assertions. Scientific and artistic investments in a particular visuality for Cleopatra suggest that her figure has transformed into a metaphorical site for contemporary racial battles, especially in the postcolonial "West." Within the imagined geography of modernity, the tired dichotomies of East versus West, Africa versus Europe, and Black versus White continue to inform the way ancient civilizations are diacritically constructed. Establishing her blackness, Africanness, and Egyptianness, on the one hand, or her whiteness, Macedonian Greekness, and Europeanness, on the other, is seen as scoring a point for either side in the "culture wars." Visible in the mass media, these charged debates have often been entangled with the clash over the emergence of Afrocentrism as a scholarly field. In 1991, *Newsweek*, for example, dedicated a few pages to the question of whether Cleopatra was black as part of its review of the Afrocentric highlighting of African civilizational achievements. The Afrocentric project has relocated ancient Egypt within the terrain of African civilization, arguing that Egypt was "stolen" from Africa and placed in the Near East by nineteenth-century scholars whose racism prevented them from crediting Africans with such monumental achievements as building the pyramids. *Newsweek*'s overall stance implied that such Afrocentric claims, and particularly those arguing that European civilization actually derived from Africa, were disregarded or denied by Western scholars. The magazine included a question-and-answer section asking whether Egyptians were black and answering that Egypt was home to blacks, Asians, and Semites, but that Cleopatra "was probably Greek."[3] While accepting the partial blackness of Egypt, the *Newsweek* article seems to Eurocentrically suggest that Greek civilization precludes blacks, or even that "Greek" automatically implies "whiteness."

The media debate over Cleopatra's complexion has everything to do with multicultural contestations over the curriculum, pedagogy, and historiography. What is at stake in the Cleopatra debate is whether the teaching of history can be interrogated and revised or only standardized in a "business-as-usual" manner. The black-versus-white Cleopatra dispute cannot therefore be examined simply within the realm of antiquity. It must be seen, as well, within the colonial context and its aftermath. The contemporary investment in Cleopatra's blackness, Egyptianness, and Africanness exists in dialectical relation to the prior insistence on her whiteness, Greekness, and Europeanness. Over the past few centuries, innumerable artworks, popular representations, and historiographical accounts have either assumed or even asserted her whiteness. Authors such as Jack Lindsay trace Cleopatra's ancestry to the Ptolemies of Egypt.[4] Cleopatra, for Lindsay, was mainly of "Macedonian blood," though he admits that some questions remain about her grandmother's ethnicity. At the same time, Lindsay deflects any argument suggesting that Cleopatra's grandmother could have been Egyptian when he writes that "she certainly had no Egyptian blood." His case rests on the assumption that only one Ptolemy had had an Egyptian mistress, and generally the mistresses of the Ptolemies were Greek. Lindsay adds, furthermore, that we are not certain about the identity of Cleopatra's mother while also quarreling with the assumption that Cleopatra was the daughter of "an unnamed mistress." Since Cleopatra was never "taunted" for being the daughter of a concubine even during "the furious propaganda-charges and insults of her later years," Lindsay concludes that her mother must have been "properly married" to her father, Ptolemy XII.

The author of another Cleopatra biography, Michael Grant, also believes that, although Cleopatra lived and ruled in Egypt, she did not possess "a drop of Egyptian blood in her veins."[5] As a Ptolemy, she was brought up as a Greek and was "to a very considerable extent of Greek race." Grant also brings up the issue of the identity of Cleopatra's mother, concluding that she must have been Cleopatra V Tryphaena—the first wife of Cleopatra's father. Grant rejects the possibility that a mistress could have been Cleopatra's mother on the same ground as Lindsay: It is unlikely Cleopatra was an illegitimate child because the negative Roman propaganda against her never mentioned it. Although Grant adamantly insists that Cleopatra had no "Egyptian blood," he does suggest that she was racially mixed and quite "dark," a fact he attributes to her Macedonian forebears who "were of very mixed blood." He concludes, significantly, that, although the "racial ingredients" of Cleopatra's Macedonian identity might have been mixed, culturally she was entirely Greek. In his book *From Alexander to Cleopatra*, however, Grant does give an account of customs that could be read to suggest that Greek men frequently took Egyptian women as mistresses. "When Greek men went overseas as colonists and settlers," he writes, "they frequently did not take their wives and families with them."[6] He points out, furthermore, that while extramarital relations were out of the question for women, the husbands were "allowed casual adultery, especially with slaves and prostitutes." Although Grant himself does not draw this conclusion, his account suggests the occurrence of "racial mixing" not only in Macedonia but also in Egypt, a fact that carries significant implications for the discourses about Cleopatra's ethnic and racial makeup.

A few texts, however, have pushed to the foreground the possibility of Cleopatra's mixed origins. Sarah B. Pomeroy, for example, describes Cleopatra as an anomaly among Romans because she could not fit neatly into any category.[7] Roman society made an important distinction between women of one's class, whom men might marry, and courtesans, but because Cleopatra was "coming like the courtesans from the Hellenized East" she was called, oxymoronically, "*regina meretrix* (courtesan queen)." The Ptolemies, furthermore, did take Egyptian women as mistresses, a point raised by Pomeroy but generally denied by writers such as Grant and Lindsay. Pomeroy describes a situation in which a Greek "coming to Egypt without friends or kin would naturally develop an attachment to his slave concubine and his children by her." Generally, Greek men in Egypt could not find Greek wives and thus "married native women or took foreign slaves as concubines." Greek–Egyptian miscegenation, in other words, must have occurred in Egypt, since slaveowners sometimes had children with their female Egyptian slaves. Alan Cameron, in the same vein, tells the story of a black concubine, Didyme, a royal mistress of Ethiopian origin whose beauty was praised in Asclepiades's poem.[8] Although intermarriage between Greeks and Egyptians was not socially accepted, as the case of Didyme shows, unions between "natives" and Greeks did occur, even in the highest social ranks. According to Cameron, it has generally gone unnoticed that one of the Ptolemaic kings (Ptolemy Philadelphus) had a "native"—that is, Egyptian—mistress. Despite a few such scholarly accounts of Egyptian society as permeated by racial and ethnic hybridity, the passion for a white Cleopatra persists. The recent documentary *Cleo-*

patra's World (History Channel, 2001), for example, interviewed Margaret George, author of *The Memoirs of Cleopatra*, who stated categorically that "Cleopatra had no Egyptian blood; therefore, she could not be Black."

The debate about Cleopatra's complexion has intersected, predictably enough, with the debate over Martin Bernal's *Black Athena* concerning the Enlightenment invention of classical Greece as purely "European." Although Bernal's work does not refer to Cleopatra, the media hype has called Cleopatra to the witness stand. In a 1992 *New Republic* article, Mary Lefkowitz attempted to discredit Bernal's argument by linking him to various Afrocentric claims, one of which assumed Cleopatra's blackness. To buttress her critique, Lefkowitz recounts the offense a student took at the screening of *Cleopatra* at the ancient history film series due to the casting of a white actress—Elizabeth Taylor—to play the role of Cleopatra, whom the student believed to have been black. In response to this, Lefkowitz writes, rather patronizingly,

> We did our best to persuade the student that, on the basis of Cleopatra's ancestry (and her name), Cleopatra was a member of the Macedonian Greek dynasty that had imposed itself on Egypt, and that despite her fluency in the Egyptian language, the style of her dress, and the luxury of her court, she was in origin a Greek.[9]

Lefkowitz here seems to categorically deny any possibility of even partial Egyptian or black ancestry for Cleopatra, possibly traced not only to Egypt but also to Greece/Macedonia. Her dismissal elides the literary and archaeological evidence of the interwovenness of central African blacks in various societies throughout the Greco-Roman world.[10] Even some of those who insist on the full Macedonian Greekness of Cleopatra also acknowledge a certain racial hybridity in Macedonia. Thus, even if one assumes that Cleopatra had "no drop of Egyptian blood," it would be difficult to categorically reject any trace of mixedness in her lineage and, by implication, a certain contribution of Afrocentric scholarship.

At the same time, what is striking about the debate—whether in the Eurocentric or Afrocentric discourse—is the way categories of race as a biological marker are often conflated with those of ethnicity and nationality as symptoms of geographical, cultural, and social affiliations. In many ways, then, both of these opposite claims—that Cleopatra was Egyptian and therefore black, and that she was Greek and therefore white—are equally problematic. Both simplistically equate Egyptianness with blackness and Greekness with whiteness, essentializing cultural geographies.

Assuming Cleopatra's whiteness entails a disregard for what even such authors as Grant, who insist on Cleopatra's Greekness, do recognize: the fact that Macedonians were racially quite mixed. Both claims, similarly, seem to neglect mixing on the other side—among the Egyptians. The Eurocentric investment in Cleopatra's pure whiteness and the Afrocentric insistence on her pure blackness strangely mirror each other. More recently, the question of hybridity also entered the renewed debate over Bernal's work. In the 2001 *Times Literary Supplement*, Bernal both aligns and distances himself from some of the Afrocentric claims. In his response to Lefkowitz, he writes:

> Lefkowitz places great emphasis on what she sees as my closeness to Afrocentrism. It is true that I respect the Afrocentrists' attachment for almost 200 years to their own version of the Ancient Model, holding that ancient Egyptians were black, in the face of disparagement not only from the white academic Establishment but also from blacks who have accommodated themselves to it. This does not mean that I accept some of the wilder views held by a number of them, for example that Cleopatra was black or that melanin is necessary for creativity.[11]

Referring to Cleopatra only once in this debate, Bernal goes on to suggest the hybridity of both Egypt and Greece. In some respects, he points out, Lefkowitz's arguments are closer to the Afrocentrists' than his. Lefkowitz shares with most Afrocentrists the view of the "Africanness of Egypt," since they both object to the notion of the mixing of culture from different continents. "What is anathema for Mary Lefkowitz is the claim made in *Black Athena* that the 'Glory that was Greece' was the result of intercontinental hybridity."

The debate over Cleopatra's identity, as we have seen, assumes whiteness and blackness as unmistakable polarities devoid of in-between shades, while also projecting Greece and Egypt as racially pure spaces. Thus, to Michael Foss's emphatic statement that, "If Cleopatra was Black, no one mentioned it," one might answer: If Cleopatra was white, no one mentioned that, either. The "proof" for Cleopatra's whiteness often marshals the lack of reference to her blackness in the negative Roman campaign against Cleopatra. Such argument assumes simplistically that the fact of blackness constituted negativity within Roman discourses. Yet as some authors have demonstrated, the Greco-Roman world was not plagued by the same color prejudice that infects the modem world.[12] Invoking Roman propaganda against Cleopatra as evidence of her pure whiteness rests on several other problematic suppositions: that the Romans knew everything that needs to be known about the sexual practices of all Macedonians prior to their arrival in Egypt and of every member of the Ptolemaic dynasty in Egypt during the three centuries separating Alexander's conquest of Egypt and Cleopatra's birth; that any such account, especially of "official history," can guarantee the knowledge of racial purity not merely of Cleopatra but of any individual; that the concepts of blackness and whiteness in Cleopatra's time carried negative and positive connotations akin to Europe's racialized discourses that have emerged in the wake of its colonization of the Americas, Africa, and Asia; that the definition of whiteness and blackness as identity markers in the ancient Mediterranean deeply impacted cultural belonging and social stature to the extent that it necessitated the identification of individuals as either black or white; that the content and meaning of blackness and whiteness in the ancient Mediterranean can be easily established within clear-cut racial dichotomies; that blackness and whiteness have possessed a fixed meaning over millennia; that the definition of Egyptian in Cleopatra's time necessarily meant being black; and that the definition of Greek necessarily meant being white.

The Eurocentric dismissal of Cleopatra's possible blackness raises questions similar in nature to those that can be posed to the Afrocentric insistence on Cleopatra's blackness: Which paradigms would define blackness and whiteness as racial-biological categories? Is it merely a matter of visuality—that is, skin tone, facial features, hair quality, and other physical characteristics? Or is it also a matter of blood quantum even in the absence of visible (white or black) traits detectable by the naked eye? Adopting such a discursive framework would require a number of scientific procedures: determining the amount of melanin to mark the racial borderline between blackness and whiteness; drawing a scientific representation of diverse features—nose, lips, hair—that would indicate blackness and whiteness; providing a systemic measurement of the amount of black and white "blood" and other, less visible organs (such as brains) in a person to determine his or her racial makeup in those instances where the "racial truth" might elude the gazing scientists; measuring and ranking of the living and the dead to produce a global map that would delineate the genealogical separateness of races. To put it bluntly, the attempt to cast a purely white or black Cleopatra would send us back not to antiquity but, rather, to nineteenth-century racialist discourses whose biological essentialism would then have to be extended retroactively into antiquity. In the nineteenth century, Eurocentric racism gained the aura associated with science as "objective" knowledge free from the taint of the subjective and contingent. The same epoch saw the birth of biological racism; ancient prejudices were given a scientific stamp. Biological determinism argued that socioeconomic differences among races, classes, and sexes were the product of inherited genetic traits; the social was an epiphenomenon of biology. Decadence was attributed to race mixture; the "mestizo" became the personification of the dialectics of empire and emancipation and was dreaded by racists as a monster and as an infertile hybrid. Blood and genetics overdetermined European culture in the nineteenth century, policing identity borders against the anarchic fluidity of racial-sexual exchange.

The contemporary dichotomous discussions of Cleopatra's identity, then, reproduce the scientific racism and legal codifications that formed one of the most repugnant features of colonial discourse. Classifying Cleopatra's racial heritage according to the amount of melanin visible to the naked eye would suggest that Cleopatra's identity would have to be graphed in terms of blood proportion: How much black blood would be sufficient to determine her blackness—one eighth or simply one drop? Can we now invoke such blood categories to determine the racial makeup of ancient populations in a Mediterranean space characterized by millennia of mixing of peoples and cultures from the continents of Africa, Asia, and Europe—that is, in a region where mixing took place before, during, and after Cleopatra's age? The categorical dismissal not only of any blackness in Cleopatra's complexion, but also of the possibility of any trace of blackness in her "blood"—whether from Macedonia, Egypt, or both—raises further questions having to do with the relationship between antiquity and modernity. Rather than a project of antiquity, determining Cleopatra's race in exclusivist terms constitutes, I would argue, a project of modernity.

REVISITING MEDITERRANEAN SYNCRETISM

Within colonialist discourse, metaphors, tropes, and allegorical motifs have played a constitutive role in "figuring" European superiority. They have also played a crucial if contradictory role in constructing Eurocentric hierarchies. Although tropes can be repressive, a defense mechanism against literal meaning, they also constitute an arena of contestation: Each is open to perpetuation, rejection, or subversion. The trope of lightness/darkness, for example, underlines the Enlightenment ideal of rational clarity. It envisions non-European worlds as less luminous—whence, the notion of Africa as the "dark continent" and of Asians as "twilight people."

Earlier religious Manicheisms of good and evil became transmuted into the philosophical binarism of rationality and light versus irrationality and darkness. Sight and vision are attributed to Europe, while those outside the Continent are otherized as living in "obscurity," blind to rational and moral knowledge. Color, complexion, and even climatic hierarchies emerge, privileging light and day over darkness and night, light skin over dark skin, as well as temperate over tropical climes.[13] The idea of race can be seen as less a reality than a trope—a trope of difference.[14] Apart from the association of "race" with metaphors of pedigree and horse breeding, "race" also "tropes" through schematic exaggeration. People are not literally black, red, white, or yellow but display a wide spectrum of nuanced tones. Hollywood, interestingly, literalized such tropes, painting actors and actresses with red, black, brown, or yellow makeup while not applying white color to white, thus leaving whiteness as an unmarked norm. The notion of colors as clearly distinct, furthermore, is itself a trope. In fact, some "black" people are lighter than some "white" people. A cognate trope, as we see in the discourses about Cleopatra, is the notion of racial "blood," which historically has served to signify class ("blue blood"), race ("black blood"), or religious affiliation ("Jewish blood"). Still, the troped nature of "blood" did not prevent the U.S. army, as late as World War Two, from literally segregating "black" blood plasma from "white" blood plasma. Anxieties about other kinds of mixing, about the exchange of other fluids and colors, were projected onto a blood that never ceased being red. Despite their quasi-fictive nature, racial tropes, then, exercise real influence in the world.

Representing Cleopatra's complexion and establishing her identity, as we have seen, involves a particular construction of race within her geocultural space. The dichotomous discourse about her racial identity depends on the ways Greece and Egypt are imagined. Cleopatra's identity is caught up in the battle over the "true origins" of "History" and of "Civilization," between Eurocentrism's claim for Greece as point of origin and Afrocentrism's claim for Egypt. Yet positing history as "beginning" in Greece or Egypt—that is, in one location—is itself problematic, since world history has no single point of origin.[15] Even during the Classical period, history was played out around the globe, in China, in the Indus Valley, in Mesopotamia, in Africa, in what we now call the Americas, and indeed wherever there were human beings. Rather than the "Age" of antiquity, we should speak of the "ages" of antiquity.[16] Positing an alternative Afrocentric version of history, in this sense, reproduces the logic of a centered history on one level, but on another level inverts it, and, given the negative legacy of anti-African prejudice, reaffirms a genealogically productive past. Less important than the "origins" of civilization here is the "beginning" of political consciousness, with debates about Greece and Egypt becoming proxy battles for cultural prestige. Issues of origin become entangled with the political genealogy of diasporic identity.

In historical and discursive terms, the advent of colonialism inspired a retroactive rewriting of African history and its relation to Classical Greek civilization. History was recast to conform to colonialist norms in the name of an eternal "West" unique since its moment of conception. Whole continents were turned into eternal "slave continents." Bernal describes the process in relation to Africa in *Black Athena*:

> If it had been scientifically "proved" that Blacks were biologically incapable of civilization, how could one explain Ancient Egypt—which was inconveniently placed on the African continent? There were two, or rather, three solutions. The first was to deny that the Ancient Egyptians were black; the second was to deny that the Ancient Egyptians had created a civilization; the third was to make doubly sure by denying both. The last has been preferred by most 19th and 20th century historians.[17]

Bernal distinguishes between the "ancient model," which simply assumed Classical Greek civilization's deep indebtedness to both African (Egyptian and Ethiopian) and Semitic (Hebraic and Phoenician) civilizations, and the "Aryan model" that developed in the wake of slavery and colonialism. The Aryan model had to perform ingenious acrobatics to "purify" Classical Greece of all African and Asian "contaminations." It had to explain away, for example, the innumerable Greek homages to Afro-Asiatic cultures, Homer's description of the "blameless Ethiopians," Moses's marriage to a daughter of Kush, and the frequent references to the "*kalos kagathos* (handsome and good)" Africans in Classical literature.[18]

The revulsion at the idea of Cleopatra's possible Africanness is embedded in a Eurocentric discourse that has systematically degraded Africa as deficient according to Europe's own arbitrary criteria (the presence of monumental architecture, literate culture) and hierarchies (melody over percussion, brick over thatch, clothing over body decoration). Yet even by these dubious standards, precolonial Africa was clearly a continent of rich and diverse culture—the scene of high material achievements (witness the ruins of Zimbabwe), widespread commercial exchange, complex religious beliefs and social systems, and diverse forms of writing (pictograms, ideograms, object scripts such as Alele and Ngombo). Scholars have also established the complexity of Dogon astronomical knowledge: The *sigui* ritual, introduced by the mythical ancestor of the Dogons, Dyongu Seru, has been found to analogize and reflect the orbiting cycle of the star Sirius B.[19] And the Moorish Spaniard Leo Africanus, writing in the early sixteenth century, described the "magnificent and well-furnished court" of the king of Timbuktu, and "the great store of doctors, judges, priests, and other learned men . . . bountifully maintained at the King's cost and charges."[20]

The idea that Europe is Europe, Africa is Africa, and never the twain shall meet, meanwhile, is a myth. There had been considerable contact between Africa and Europe over the centuries, and the relative state of development of the two continents, prior to 1492, was roughly equal. Africa had a varied and productive economy, with strong metallurgical and textile industries. Africans developed iron-working and blast-furnace technology even before 600 B.C., prefiguring techniques used in Europe only in the nineteenth century.[21] The textile exports of the eastern Congo, in the early seventeenth century, were as large as those of European textile-manufacturing centers such as Leiden. Indeed, in the early years of the Atlantic trade, Europe had little to sell Africa that Africa did not already produce.[22] The "inferiority" of Africa and the African was thus an ideological invention. It demanded, as Cedric Robinson suggests, the

> eradication within Western historical consciousness of the significance of Nubia for Egypt's formation, of Egypt in the development of Greek civilization, of Africa for imperial Rome, and more pointedly of Islam's influence on Europe's economic, political and intellectual history.[23]

The point here is not that Africa should be complimented for "satisfying" competitive Eurocentric criteria for "civilization." Rather, it is to call attention to the constructed nature of the supposedly unbridgeable gap between Europe and Africa.[24]

The denial of racial and ethnic mixing in antiquity, in other words, must be seen within the broader context of the rise of colonialism and the emergence of a new Eurocentric epistemology that denied cultural syncretism and insisted on the essentialist clash of civilizations. Although a Eurocentric narrative constructs an artificial wall of separation between European and non-European cultures, in fact Europe itself is a synthesis of many cultures, Western and non-Western. The notion of a "pure" Europe originating in Classical Greece is premised on crucial exclusions, from the African and Asiatic influences that shaped Classical Greece itself, to the osmotic Sephardic-Judaic-Islamic culture that played such a crucial role during the so-called Dark Ages (an ethnocentric label for a period of Oriental ascendancy), the Middle Ages, and the Renaissance. All of the celebrated "stations" of European progress—Greece, Rome, Christianity, Renaissance, Enlightenment—are moments of cultural syncretism. The "West," then, is itself a collective heritage, an omnivorous mélange of cultures. It did not simply absorb non-European influences; it was constituted by them.[25]

Yet within a Eurocentric perspective, Greece is constructed as purely European and therefore white, while within Afrocentrism, Egypt is African and therefore by definition black. Both of these segregationist logics, however, ignore the question of cultural syncretism, especially within the space of the Mediterranean. Even if we were willing to assert Cleopatra's pure whiteness or blackness, what would we say about her culture? Just as advancing the idea of "pure blood" anywhere is historically suspect, so is the idea of pure culture. Like most cultural worlds, Cleopatra's was complex: The porous cultural borders between the civilizations of Greece and Egypt allowed for clash, dialogue, borrowing, and, ultimately, mutual transformation. The assumption that three hundred years of Greek Macedonian existence in Egypt did not produce cultural mixing sufficient to render Cleopatra a syncretic figure is highly questionable. Some writers, meanwhile, have stated that although Cleopatra spoke Egyptian, she was Greek. Yet even if her origins were indeed "pure Macedonian Greek," such a discourse implies that cohabitation in one place for generations, as well as the mastery of its native language and culture, are all irrelevant to shaping one's identity, for identity is squarely defined by biological and geographical origins. As with Cleopatra's color debate, here, too, nineteenth-century anthropological discourses, attuned only to ethno-cultural genealogies and to the mapping of fixed and essentialist notions of identity, affect and petrify the configuring of Cleopatra's cultural belonging.

The debate over Cleopatra's identity would profoundly benefit from a more complex discourse on her multiple cultural affiliations. Like her city Alexandria, Cleopatra can be said to have belonged to at least two cultures, each a palimpsest of diverse cultures. Travel, commerce, learning, translation, and conquest, along with rape and marriage, all resulted in new unions and the amalgamation of populations and cultures. The East-versus-West dichotomy, furthermore, cannot be projected onto Cleopatra's world or onto a millennial history of cultural mélange. We must transcend the tendency to erect totalizing and essentialist narratives of culture to chart Cleopatra's identity. A more historicized view of Egypt and

Greece, such as that attempted here, locates Cleopatra within a dynamic, dialogical, and fluid conception of cultural identity.

ENLIGHTENMENT AESTHETICS AND VISUAL CULTURE

By denying the possibility of any African black ancestry for Cleopatra, contemporary debates, as we have seen, betray an investment in Cleopatra's whiteness. A certain unspoken syllogism seems to operate here: Cleopatra possessed attractive looks; attractive looks are white; therefore, Cleopatra must have been white. The debate over Cleopatra's race inevitably spills over, in this sense, into rival visions of beauty, each armed with its normative definition. The passion for a white Cleopatra, to my mind, can be historically located in Enlightenment aesthetics and nineteenth-century racialist scientific discourses.[26] A gendered racism left its mark on Enlightenment aesthetics replete with homages to the ideal of whiteness. The measurements and rankings characteristic of the new sciences were wedded to aesthetic value judgments derived from an Apollonian reading of a de-Dionysianized Greece. Aryanists like Carl Gustav Carus measured the divine in humanity through resemblance to Greek statues. The auratic religion of art, meanwhile, also worshiped at the shrine of whiteness, within a normative gaze that has systematically devalued non-European appearance and aesthetics.[27] For Comte Arthur de Gobineau, the "white race originally possessed the monopoly of beauty, intelligence and strength."[28] For Georges-Louis Leclerc de Buffon, "[Nature] in her most perfect exertions made men white."[29] Friedrich Bluembach called white Europeans "Caucasians" because he believed that the Caucasus Mountains were the original home of the most beautiful human species.[30] Where but among Caucasians, the British surgeon Charles White asked rhetorically, does one find "that nobly arched head, containing such a quantity of brain. . . . In what other quarter of the globe shall we find the blush that overspreads the soft features of the beautiful women of Europe?"[31] Although White's tumescent descriptions clearly hierarchize male brains over female beauty, they ultimately embrace white women for their genetic membership in the family of (white) Man.

As a result of the rise of biologistic evolutionary concepts of races, as well as of ranking and measurement science, Cleopatra's features were subjected to a dissecting scrutiny. The passionate debates over Cleopatra's nose, for example, coincided with the emergence of racialized configurations of beauty. "Everything that poetry can do," writes William Maginn, "is done, to make us forget the faults of Cleopatra, and to think that a world was lost for that *petit nez retroussé*."[32] Cleopatra's visual representation has sometimes involved a cleansing operation, ridding the ancient queen of so-called non-European features, such as the hooked nose, in a way that parallels the visual remodeling of an Aryan appearance for Christ, deemed more appropriate for a supreme being. Lord Berners's novel *The Romance of the Nose* offers a redemptive narrative for Cleopatra's nose.[33] He describes Cleopatra as the smartest and most beautiful woman in the world, "But alas, that nose!" To fix her monstrous nose, she has Apollodorus perform plastic surgery. He parades thirty slave girls before Cleopatra to help her select her future nose, but she chooses for her model a perfect artistic representation—a copy of a stone bust of a Syrian woman. On seeing her new nose, Cleopatra takes her clothes off and performs cartwheels. Other writers, seeing Cleopatra's large nose as a kind of disfigurement, attempted to redeem her unfortunate features with heightened descriptions of her greatness. Anatole France wrote that the medals featuring Cleopatra

all represent her with large, harsh features, and an exceedingly long nose. . . . [I]f we are to believe the medals, this nose was all out of proportion; but we will not believe them; no, not if people should put before us all the collections of medals in the Bibliothèque Nationale, the British Museum, and the Cabinet of Vienna. . . . The features which caused Caesar to forget the empire of the world were not spoilt by a ridiculous nose.[34]

Not all cultures have necessarily seen hooked noses as ugly. Different epochs and diverse geocultural spaces, as we know, have possessed variegated aesthetic norms inseparable from gendered ideologies of the body and sexuality. That relativity of beauty was already advanced in antiquity is implicit in Sextus Empiricus's suggestion that the Ethiopians preferred the blackest and the most flat-nosed, while the Persians preferred the whitest and the most hooked-nosed.[35] Contemporary writers, even when gesturing toward the difficulty of actually defining beauty, nevertheless express their strong convictions about Cleopatra's beauty or ugliness. The only really reliable representations of Cleopatra, according to Lucy Hughes-Hallett, are preserved on coins, including coins from Cleopatra's own mint. Although these coins intended to flatter her, they still showed her "with an enormous hooked nose, and a kind of witch-like chin that curves up to meet the nose, and really cannot be described as attractive by any standards."[36] Evoking the possibility of multiple aesthetic standards, Hughes-

Hallett acknowledges relativism but in the same breath endorses beauty norms informed by Greco-Roman-Aryanist tradition, specifically the idea of the straight or the turned-up nose as a model of beauty. Witches, lest one forget, were portrayed with the same "hideous" features—the hooked nose that meets the curved chin—as Jews within a mythological discourse inflected by both anti-Semitism and sexism. If Cleopatra in fact had a hooked nose, a curved-up chin, or dark skin, we would certainly not know it from the mass-mediated culture that has spread Eurocentric images of beauty globally, to the extent that even the acknowledgment of the relativity of beauty still affirms an implicitly hegemonic perspective. The question, then, is not simply whether Cleopatra was or was not considered beautiful in her time, but how such gendered and raced discussions of looks are emblematic of Eurocentric visual culture.

Since its very beginnings, cinema has been obsessed with ancient civilizations. Cinema, itself the product of Western scientific discoveries, made palpable to audiences the master narrative of the progress of Western civilization, often through biographical narratives about explorers, inventors, and scientists. As the self-articulated product of scientific ingenuity, cinema saw itself as the avatar of a new kind of interdisciplinary science that could make "other" worlds accessible. It could chart a map of the world like the cartographer; it could chronicle events like the historian; it could "dig" into the distant past like the archaeologist; and it could anatomize customs of "exotic" peoples like the anthropologist. In its role as pedagogue, dominant cinema promised to initiate the Western spectator into unknown cultures, visualized as lived (à la Hegel) "outside of history." Cinema thus became the epistemological mediator between the cultural space of the Western spectator and that of the cultures represented on the screen, linking separate spaces and figurally separate temporalities in a single moment of exposure.

In this sense, cinema performed the role of a celluloid archivist. Linking a new, apprentice art to ancient times and "distant" places, it resuscitated forgotten civilizations—both on screen and through the architectural design of pseudo-Egyptian movie palaces. Made in a period when colonized people were beginning to assert a counter-identity vis-à-vis their colonizers, these films suppress contemporary conflicts in favor of a romantic, nostalgic search for the lost Eastern origins of the West. This contextual feature may explain a structuring absence in Hollywood's representations of Egypt, Babylonia, and the (biblical) Holy Land: the absence on the screen of contemporary colonized Arab geography and its nationalist struggles.

The films define the Orient as ancient and mysterious, epitomized by an iconography of papyruses, sphinxes, and mummies, whose existence and revival depend on the revivifying "look" and "reading" of the Westerner. The putative rescue of the past, in other words, suppresses the present and thus legitimates by default the availability of Oriental space for Western geopolitical maneuvers. The filmic mummified zone of ancient civilizations, in sum, played an active role in generating an imperial gaze.

As a visual medium the cinema had no choice but to be concerned with Cleopatra's complexion and facial features. The visual adaptation of oral and written narratives, even of historical figures, forces the painter and the photographer to take a stance. The nature of cinema requires a selection of actors and a process of casting that inevitably locates face and body in concepts of race. In the tradition of Western popular culture, cinema continued the iconography of a white Cleopatra. Given the ideology of stardom, Hollywood's politics of casting could not entertain the possibility of a non-white Cleopatra. The grandeur of a larger-than-life historical figure had to be reflected allegorically in a larger-than-life glamorous star, a position that, until recently, excluded non-white women. Neither a revered queen nor an adored star could be imagined and visualized as non-white, which would make her, presumably, "smaller-than-life." The screen's segregated space also enforced a taboo on mixed romance. The Production Code of the Motion Picture Producers and Distributors of America, Inc., 1930–34, explicitly states: "Miscegenation (sex relations between the white and black races) is forbidden." The code reflected segregationist laws that assumed the fictitious categories of "white" and "black" bloods and that defined miscegenation as a "crime of blood." Erotic (hetero-)sexual interaction on the screen prior to the late 1960s was severely limited by apartheid-style racial codes. The delegitimizing of a romantic union between "whites" and other "races" was linked to a broader exclusionary social practice in which the biological definition of race was embedded in the political concept of race and the gendered hierarchy of civilizations.

Inherited from colonialist discourse, the hegemonic white-is-beautiful aesthetic has been displayed in countless colonial adventure novels and films. *Trader Horn* (1930) and *King Kong* (1933), for example, show "natives" in naked adoration of the fetish of white beauty. Hollywood's ideology of casting conformed to the Aryanist aesthetic ideal. If the historical Cleopatra did in fact have such "negative" features, Hollywood's beauty norms would not have permitted such a "denigrating" image of a queen/star. Hollywood's fairy-tale logic translates the hero's or heroine's moral goodness and triumphant spirit into a presumed visual superiority. In the context of imperial narratives, Cleopatra's physical traits inevitably provoke a debate on visual representation. Does the idea that Cleopatra was not black mean she looked like actresses such as Theda Bara, Claudette Colbert, Vivian Leigh, and Elizabeth Taylor, who have played her? Even if we accept her Greekness, and therefore her presumed whiteness, in which mode is her whiteness represented? Do these actresses incarnate antiquity's notions of Greek, Egyptian, or Roman beauty? Casting within the star system clearly involved aesthetic norms that lauded a specific vision of beauty. In the silent era, pale-skinned actresses such as Lillian Gish and Mary Pickford were iconic versions of the virginal white female, emerging in diacritical relation to the image of the repellent black savage. The idolized pale heroine also emerged in contradistinction to the darker vamp, associated with actresses such as Theda Bara (figure 33), Nita Naldi, and Alia Nazimova, and generally with darker "white ethnics." Characterized by heavy makeup, with eyes and lips made to appear dangerously seductive and virtually vampiric, this look established a touch of darkness within the realm of intra-white erotica.

Representation of blackness as desirable, however, remained a taboo—beyond the pale, so to speak, a "falling" outside of the exotic bounds. While absent from the spotlight, as "producers" of desire, women of color were present as consumers of desire. Since the late nineteenth century, the cosmetic industry had been targeting the African American community to maximize its markets.[37] Deploying specific advertising strategies to sell cosmetics to black women, images of refinement and social mobility were linked with whiteness.[38] Advertisements for skin lighteners, for example, nourished a fantasy of passing and of freedom from the shackles of black history and color. Advertisements targeted at middle-class white women, meanwhile, evoked the "exotic"—an imaginary space of otherness; of seductively mysterious geographies; of travel, adventure, and exploration. For women mostly confined to their domestic space, the exotic allure helped fashion an image of an aristocratic woman, her horizons broadening as she roamed freely in the expanding world of imperial powers.[39] Advertisements for cosmetics marketed certain exotic alterities—Oriental, Pacific Island—while retaining a core of white normativity. In the early 1930s, for example, Hollywood and Max Factor developed exotic makeup lines that resulted in their flaunting of dark-haired stars such as Hedy Lamarr, Dolores Del Rio, Dorothy Lamour, and Rita Hayworth instead of the monochromatic white looks of bleached platinum blondes.[40] The

33 Cleopatra as vamp:
Theda Bara (1917)

34 From screen to ad:
Homegrown Cleopatras

gesture toward other possible beauty norms commodified difference, but only to a point. Produced to appeal to women of diverse ethnicities, Cleopatra's image was only slightly darker than the average pale female complexion adorning numerous advertisements, yet it was never too dark, and it certainly never betrayed "non-white" features—for example, a hooked or wide nose (figure 34). Hollywood's ethnic simulacra fabricated a spectacle of difference while eliding numerous "others" in the narrative. As with the cosmetics industry's selection of models, Hollywood's politics of casting effectively submerged the multiculturalism at the center of American national formation, offering instead a visually coded racial hierarchy.

The debate over Cleopatra's looks, then, suggests the intense relations between race, gender, and sexuality. After all, discourses on ancient Rome have not tried in the same way to dissect images of Caesar's or Antony's bodily fragments. Nor does the concept of "fatal beauty" extend equally to masculinity. In recent years, feminist readings have emphasized Cleopatra's achievement as an intellectual and as a leader blessed with an impressive array of talents, including speaking many languages without having to rely on interpreters. Hughes-Hallett, for example, highlights Cleopatra's intellectual power, critiquing the misplaced emphasis on her looks. Feminist readings of Cleopatra stand out against the backdrop of the fetishistic millennial gaze focused mostly on Cleopatra's eroticizing beauty.[41] In numerous representations, Cleopatra's body has served as a metaphor for a feminized ancient Egypt. In Cecil B. DeMille's *Cleopatra* (1934), Caesar addresses Cleopatra as he orders her: "Egypt, sit down!" And toward the end of the film, as Antony falls on his sword, believing that Cleopatra has betrayed him, he gasps: "I am dying, Egypt, dying." The camera surveys her body voyeuristically, as her Roman men address her or as she prepares for her death. Dressed in black in a low-cut décolletage, she sits on her throne, removes from a basket a one-foot-long asp, and applies it to her breast. No matter what the historical facts about the reptile and the breast, imagining a phallic snake on Cleopatra's bosom reinforces a masculinist representation of history and of the triumph of the Roman Empire. In such representations, Cleopatra's power—and the power of Egypt—lies largely in her sexuality. With her death, an entire world vanishes.

In the nineteenth century, European representations of ancient civilizations, stimulated by archaeological discoveries, projected the imperial present onto past encounters between the West and East through gendered tropes. The nineteenth-century Romantic depiction of the ancient Orient of Babylonia and Egypt, reproduced in Griffith's *Intolerance* (1916) and

DeMille's *Cleopatra* (1934), displayed the "East" as feminine. In De Mille's *Cleopatra*, Caesar's countrymen tell him that "the woman is making an Egyptian out of you," and Brutus insists that "Rome cannot be turned into another Orient"—all within a framework that associates Rome with masculinity and Egypt with femininity (figure 35). The subjugation of Cleopatra and Egypt in the Cleopatra films has contemporary colonial overtones: The Roman court seems to consist of aristocratic Englishmen, who make sarcastic jibes at the idea that the presumably black Cleopatra could ever rule Rome. And this despite the fact that Hollywood aesthetic conventions, as we have already suggested, visualized Cleopatra as a European-looking white woman, in the same manner that Christ was gradually de-Semitized in western iconography.

Casting a powerful star to play Cleopatra produces tensions between gender and racial ideologies. Joseph L. Mankiewicz's *Cleopatra* seems to endow the ancient queen and the contemporary star with the power of the gaze. From behind a wall, Cleopatra (Elizabeth Taylor) spies on a conversation in which Caesar discusses the queen he has just met, making the spectator aware of what Caesar does not know. Within this cinematic structuring of a knowledge gap between the character and the spectator, the viewer is sutured into Cleopatra's point of view. Her eyes peer through two small holes in the wall, invisible, as it were, behind a mural of an Egyptian drawing of a larger-than-life female face. Made up to resemble ancient Egyptian paintings, Taylor's eyes look through the eye of the mural figure, giving "three-dimensionality" to the two-dimensional painting in a shot that matches Taylor's eyes and the mural figure's eye in shape and color, highlighting the star's famous violet-blue eyes (figure 36). As the spectator gazes at the spying "bluest eyes," merging a contemporary white star with an ancient Egyptian queen, Caesar's dialogue informs us that Cleopatra has Macedonian origins and that she has "not a drop of Egyptian blood." In this moment of a semi-Aryanist visualizing of Cleopatra, her character gains a provisional power of the gaze, of the kind usually associated with masculinity. More typically, however, Hollywood films authorize a male voyeuristic gaze into an inaccessible private space (for example, the panoptical harem in the 1955 film *Kismet*). Endowing Taylor/Cleopatra with the surveillance power deviates from the Hollywoodian harem fantasy of a hetero-masculinist utopia of sexual omnipotence. Yet Cleopatra's momentary gazing power is taken away once she is no longer the delegate of a supremacist whiteness, and then she is induced, as it were, to enact the traditional positioning of the female star—that is, the gazed upon. Through-

35 The iconography of a feminized Egypt: *Cleopatra* (1934)

36 The queen's/star's "bluest eyes" behind the Egyptian eye:
Cleopatra (1963)

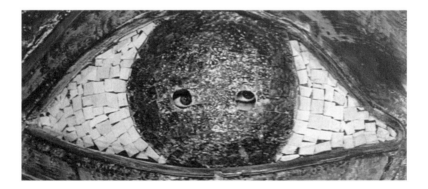

out the film *Cleopatra*, the queen/star's body is subjected to spectatorial scopophilia, as when Taylor/Cleopatra takes off her clothes and luxuriates in her bath, the blue water at a level slightly above her breasts. (Three decades later, this eroticized image of Taylor's Cleopatra in the bath was invoked in an advertisement for Taylor's own perfume Passion.) Taylor's body, like Cleopatra's, becomes an ambivalent site, at once empowered by the economics of her (white) sexuality and disempowered by the masculinist culture of objectifying surveillance.

It is only against the backdrop of this long history of glorification of whiteness and the devaluation of blackness that one can appreciate the emotional force of the counter-expression "Black Is Beautiful" and the provocative challenge of the very notion of a black Cleopatra. The norms of Eurocentric aesthetics exiled women of color from their own bodies. Until the late 1960s, the overwhelming majority of Anglo-American fashion journals, films, TV shows, and commercials promoted a canonical notion of beauty within which white women (and secondarily white men) constituted the only legitimate objects of desire. In so doing, the media extended a longstanding philosophical valorization of whiteness. In a century in which popular culture has reached a previously unknown degree of mass-mediation, Cleopatra's representation has to be discussed not only in terms of the historical efforts to reconstruct how she really did look, but also in terms of the very real power to produce and project her image onto the consuming world. Such representations, as I have tried to suggest, have real repercussions and reverberations in the world, and here, too, we must see Cleopatra not merely as a figure of antiquity but also as a trope of modernity.

ALLEGORIES OF NATION AND DIASPORA

Claiming a specific race and nation for Cleopatra is always a relational act, performed in contradistinction to alternative claims. The articulation of national identity has relied heavily on a symbolic language of origins and belonging, but its writing of the past has often clashed with other nationalist imaginaries. The very way the question about Cleopatra's identity is posed reveals the depth of a structural binarist thought: Was she black or white, African or European, Greek or Egyptian, Macedonian or Greek? The emotions expressed in favor of any one, unique identity for Cleopatra demarcate a particular territorial or cultural border. Contemporary Cleopatra representations, to my mind, are haunted by such dichotomies, which can be understood as both imposing and resisting exclusionary hegemonic practices. The Cleopatra quarrels can be read, in this sense, as allegories of reinventing national and diasporic identities and their place on the global map.

During the same years that the major Cleopatra films were produced, U.S. racial discourses could allow for blacks only in subordinate roles. In the same year that Claudette Colbert played Cleopatra, she also acted as the maternal queen of a household in *Imitation of Life*, served by a black, Aunt Jemima–like maid whose daughter Piola passes for white. In the 1960s film *Cleopatra*, meanwhile, blacks were more visible in the spectacular extravaganza sequences, performing exotic dance and laboring as slaves/servants—as if the ancient Mediterranean, too, were organized around the modern racial hierarchies typical of the colonial black Atlantic. Only in the 1970s, when popular culture both appropriated and gave voice to Black Power icons and Afrocentric symbols, did a kind of black Cleopatra make it to the screen. Her representation, however, was retrofitted to conform to the parodic tone of the blaxploitation genre, usually the domain of black (hetero-)masculinity, here hosting a contemporary dark queen.

In the film *Cleopatra Jones* and the sequel, *Cleopatra Jones and the Casino of Gold*, the supermodel Tamara Dobson stars as a CIA agent who fights drug traffickers and the underworld. While most blaxploitation films focused on the prowess of black men, here special agent Cleopatra Jones magically defeats evil empires with her kung fu, high kicking, and quick thinking. The films reverse Hollywood's moral codification of complexion, mocking the tendency to associate white characters with good and black characters with evil. White actresses are cast in the roles of the female antagonists who head criminal cartels, be it Shelley Winters as the black-leather-clad white lesbian in *Cleopatra Jones* or Stella Stevens as the blonde dragon lady nicknamed "Snow White" in *Cleopatra Jones and the Casino of Gold*. A few sequences in *Cleopatra Jones* playfully allude to the decade-earlier superproduction of Mankiewicz's *Cleopatra*, as when black Cleopatra, her hair wraps and eye makeup reminiscent of Elizabeth Taylor, winks at black children in the street, an allusion to the sequence of Cleopatra's introduction to Rome that ends with Cleopatra/Taylor winking at Caesar (and the spectator). *Cleopatra Jones and the Casino of Gold*, meanwhile, has the black heroine kill the blonde villain in her own luxurious turquoise bath/swimming pool, a reference to Taylor's famous shot in the

Mankiewicz film. While the bath sequence of the 1960s superproduction was designed as a monument to Taylor/Cleopatra's beauty and sensuality, the Cleopatra Jones's bath sequence stages the demise of white power and ultimately pokes fun at the spectator's libidinal investment in Eurocentric beauty norms (figure 37).

Afro-diasoporic popular culture offers a certain playful subversion of Hollywood's racialized dream factory, of its mythologizing whiteness, which operates through the glamorizing of white stars in general, and through the totemic whiteness of Cleopatra more specifically.[42] The African American heroine in the Cleopatra Jones films is visually associated with signs of the Black Power Movement—Afro hairstyle, clenched fist, and Dashiki clothing. Casting the tall and Afro-haired Tamara Dobson, whose visual presence evokes the famous images of the black revolutionary Angela Davis, contributes to this sense of parodic demystification of both the white queen and the white star (figure 38). Within the film's overarching U.S. nationalism, however, "Angela Davis," tamed and domesticated, is refashioned to correspond to the existing social order: Here she works for the CIA, incarnated by the ultimate white patriarch, her boss. It is he who enables the powerful and sexy Cleopatra Jones to rescue her own "Egypt"—the black community. Racial conflicts and black rebellion are appropriated as an American familial saga, just as the TV series *Roots* was framed as the saga of an American family. Black feminist texts, however, have embraced Cleopatra as a sister, signifying black subjectivity, whether through reclaiming desire as in Barbara Chase-Riboud's poems "Cleopatra" and "Anthony," or through empowerment, as in Shelley P. Haley's reading Cleopatra as a black feminist reacting to oppression and exploitation.[43]

Cleopatra has been claimed not only by black diasporic nationalists, but also by several other nationalist discourses.[44] Greece and Macedonia have made competing claims about Alexander the Great, whose ancient kingdom in the fourth century B.C. expanded beyond the Balkans into Africa and Asia and who symbolically embodies a glorious national past. The debate over a purely Macedonian or Greek Cleopatra—Alexander's descendent—is embedded in the present-day Balkans, a region torn by ethnonationalist conflicts. The Balkans' battle over ethno-national identity is enmeshed in diverse exclusionary logics. A certain East-versus-West dichotomy equates Christianity with Europe and the West, leaving Balkan Muslims as Easterners "outside" European identity. The foundation of a Macedonian nation-state is also premised on consolidating a separate iden-

37 Sabotaging white beauty: Elizabeth Taylor in *Cleopatra*, 1963 (left), and Stella Stevens in *Cleopatra Jones and the Casino of Gold*, 1975 (right)

38 Tamara Dobson and Black Power: *Cleopatra Jones* (1973)

tity vis-à-vis Greece. The figure of Alexander the Great constitutes a defining genealogy for the Macedonian nation, invested in invoking ancient civilizational origins prior to the Ottoman domination of the region. The unwanted traces of that history, within this perspective, still mark the Balkans, traces made "visible" in its "foreign" Muslim population. Finally, within this exclusionary perspective the triumphant achievements of Western culture originate from ancient Greece, in which Macedonia played a pivotal role. The Balkan desire for a "Western" identity is itself dependent on the Enlightenment reinvention of Greece as a pure European space, cleansed of African, Semitic, Phoenician, and other "Eastern" elements. Integration with western Europe enables the Balkan imaginary to de-Orientalize itself. The ancient Macedonian/Greek presence in Egypt, similarly, is read as a purely "European" history. Cleopatra's life in Egypt, therefore, is merely a footnote, for she is seen as a pure Macedonian or Greek—that is, European. The lineage of Alexander-Cleopatra in Egypt encodes an imaginary nationalist identity in which the Balkan region frees itself from the shackles of the "Oriental" past by Occidentalizing itself.[45] Thus, although a millennia separates the historical figures of Alexander and Cleopatra and the Muslim Ottoman rule of the Balkans, the reading of the complex Mediterranean cultural network—and, specifically, that of ancient Greece/Egypt—remains entangled in modern nationalist clashes.

Although the land of Egypt had other powerful queens, the special passion reserved for Cleopatra can be located partially in the intersection between what has come to be seen as East (Egypt) and West (Rome). Yet the cult-figure adoration that Cleopatra has received in Western popular culture has hardly been universal, even in Egypt, her birthplace. In 1933, the same year that Cecil B. DeMille gave expression to the Eurocentric representation of Cleopatra and to the clash between Egypt and Rome, the well-known Egyptian writer Taha Hussein articulated a more complex understanding of the meeting of civilizations:

> Three elements have formed the literary spirit of Egypt since it was Arabized. The first of them is the purely Egyptian element which we have inherited from the ancient Egyptian. . . . The second . . . is the Arab element, which came to us through its language and religion and civilization. . . . It is our language, and a thousand times closer to us than the language of the ancient Egyptians. . . . The third element . . . is the foreign element which has always influenced Egyptian life, and will always do so. It is what has come to Egypt from its contacts with the civilized peoples in the east and west . . . Greeks, and

Romans, Jews and Phoenicians in ancient times, Arabs, Turks and Crusaders in the Middle Ages, Europe and America in the modern age. . . . I would like Egyptian education to be firmly based on a certain harmony between these three elements.[46]

Such Egyptian intellectuals, associated with the rise of modernity and nationalism, have attempted to portray a relatively syncretic view of Egyptian identity. Although, in line with nationalist thought, they assumed an Egyptian "core" versus "foreign" elements, these writers did not posit a simplistic binarism of Egyptian versus Greek cultures, eschewing purist notions of civilization, culture, and history. Since the late nineteenth century, modern Arabic literature mixed old with new genres and forms within a cultural project of figuring modernity and nationalism. The emergence of new Arabic poetry and literature gave expression to a new consciousness of Arabness within the modern world. Intellectuals and writers such as Ahmad Shawqi and Taha Hussein were simultaneously engaged in resisting colonialism and in forming nationalism in a manner that drew partly on contemporaneous British and French discourses of modernity. Within this context, ancient Egypt corresponded to the Romanticism of nationalist discourses engaged in a teleological search for origins and genealogies. Also, as Albert Hourani suggests, since Arab nationalist movements revolted against the present as well as the immediate past, they were able to appeal to the memory of a more distant, pre-Islamic past.[47] Archaeological excavations, furthermore, brought visible evidence of the multiple layers of history that could now be claimed not only by European Egyptologists, but also by Egyptian intellectuals, whose nationalism, it should be added, was not divorced from the Enlightenment vision of progress.

In the era of colonialism and neocolonialism, Arab Egyptian intellectuals were embracing an ancient Egypt that Egyptologists had too often detached from contemporary Egypt, as if contemporary Egyptians only "happened" to live on top of a grand civilization. Archaeological rescue narratives of ancient Egypt had the collateral effect of celebrating the possession of a colonized space. The camera itself, meanwhile, played an important role in revealing to the world the unearthing of buried civilizations, imbuing every sight with the wide-eyed freshness of the new machine. Yet the pioneers of the new science and of the recorded image rarely questioned the constellation of power relations that allowed them to represent other lands and cultures. No one questioned whether and how Egyptian land, history, and culture should be represented, for example, or asked

39 "Westernmost Colossus of the Temple of Re, Abu Simbel, 1850": Photograph, Maxime Du Camp

what Egyptian people might have to say about the matter. Photographers such as George Bridges, Louis de Clercq, and Maxime Du Camp, and filmmakers such as Thomas Edison and the Lumière brothers, did not simply document other territories; they also documented the cultural baggage they carried with them. Their visual interpretations were deeply embedded in the discourses of their respective European empires. Travel photographers did not just chart territories for military and governmental purposes; their photos also registered the advances of scientific activities, especially archaeological excavations. Fascination with ancient monuments was mingled with admiration for the camera's capacity to provide a vivid sense of distant regions and remote times. A photo in Du Camp's album *Egypte, Nubie, Palestine et Syrie* (1852), "Westernmost Colossus of the Temple of Re, Abu Simbel, 1850" (figure 39), shows the photographer's assistant atop the crown of Ramses II, illustrating both relative scale and a moment of mastery and possession.

Egyptian nationalist pride mingled with an anticolonial feeling, meanwhile, surfaced with the literal unearthing of ancient Egypt. Central in articulating Egyptian nationalism, some Egyptian writers were inspired by the uncovering of ancient Egyptian worlds, such as the discovery of Tutankhamen's tomb in 1922. Ahmad Shawqi sought to highlight the continuity of Egyptian life from the pharaohs to the present. In one of his poems, written for the unveiling of a monument in a public garden in Cairo, Shawqi evokes the Sphinx's unchanged gaze at Egyptian history:

> Speak! And perhaps your speech will guide us. . . . Have you not seen Pharaoh in his might, claiming descent from the sun and the moon, giving shade to the civilization of our ancestors. . . . You have seen Caesar in his tyranny over us, making us slaves, his men driving us before them as one drives donkeys, and then defeated by a small band of noble conquerors.[48]

Although modern Arabic writers since the late nineteenth century were influenced by English and French Romantic poetry, their "reading" of ancient Egypt differed from that of European Romantics. If Percy Bysshe Shelley's poem "Ozymandias" speaks of a remnant of lost omnipotent grandeur as a metaphor for man's destiny and for the poet's genial sensibility, Egyptian writers unearthed the stones of ancient Egypt as living testimony to a contemporaneous rise of the Egyptian nation. Thus, even some of the twentieth-century romanticization of Cleopatra in Egyptian popular culture stems less from an isolated Egyptian history than from Egypt's relation to Europe—whether through dialogical borrowings or in dialectical opposition to French and British hegemony.

With the incursion of French and British imperialism into Egypt, Cleopatra became imbued with an even denser allegorical meaning. Cleopatra did not enter twentieth-century Egyptian popular culture merely as a past Egyptian queen; she also entered as an Egyptian symbolic figure for a latter-day anti-imperial struggle. In Ahmad Shawqi's play *Masra' Klyubatra* (The Killing of Cleopatra, 1929), the ancient queen is far from the silent-screen vamp incarnated a decade earlier by Theda Barra (1917). Instead, she is a national heroine defending her country against imperial European aggression. Rewriting Shakespeare's play, Shawqi makes his Cleopatra a military strategist whose flight from Actium is meant to lead the two Roman forces into a battle from which Egypt will emerge triumphant, with the Mediterranean Sea at its disposal. More recently, Wole Soyinka suggested that Shakespeare's play already demonstrated Egyptian patriotism and therefore did not require a critical rewriting.[49] Arabic literature has shown a special fascination with Shakespeare, evocatively speculating that Shakespeare might really have been an Arab, Shaykh al-Zubayr, given his vivid capturing of the tones, smells, tastes, and textures alien to wintry Europe, as well as his knowing invocation of the *Book of the Dead* in scenes portraying Cleopatra's reflection on death.[50] Written in an anticolonial context, Shawqi's play placed greater emphasis on resistance to Rome, allegorizing Egypt's struggle for national independence. At the same time, the theatrical play did not ignore the romance between Cleopatra (Munira Mahdia) and Antony, played by the young Muhamad Abdel Wahab, who became Egypt's leading singer, composer, and film star. Abdel Wahab as Antony sang his successful operetta *Ana Antunio* (I Am Antony),[51] with accompanying music that syncretized Arabic quarter-tones with Western instrumentation. While *The Killing of Cleopatra* highlighted a nationalist Egyptian spirit, the composition, in other words, revealed the popular fusion between Arabic and European musical traditions and was ultimately premised on a syncretic vision of Egyptian culture.

In conclusion, it seems that the historical Cleopatra not only dazed and disoriented her lovers, but that she has also dazed and disoriented archaeologists, Egyptologists, historians, artists, writers, and filmmakers. Each age and each culture seems to projects its own Cleopatra, visualizing her in a new way. Looking at the history of Cleopatra's representations, consequently, is richly informative about how her image has been "screened" through different grids and discourses. The fact that diverse movements have passionately claimed Cleopatra suggests not only the historical queen's incredible impact on history, but also the various ways in which history itself is refiltered and allegorized through the present concerns of its readers/writers. While it is important to search into the actual historical record concerning Cleopatra, it is also vital to trace the ways in which she and her world have been represented and configured over time. The desire to fix Cleopatra within one single complexion, or nation, or race—in a word, within one identity—proves to be futile, not simply in relation to the historical Cleopatra, but also in relation to the very project of imagining and accounting for the complex intercultural space with which she has been imbricated from the outset. The various interpretations of Cleopatra, as I have tried to show, reveal in an uncanny way the discursive grids that operate at given historical moments and in given geographical places. Each "take" on Cleopatra unmasks not only a facet of Cleopatra, but also a facet of the representer and, more important, reveals the nature of the prisms through which Cleopatra has been seen and imagined.

NOTES

This essay was completed with the help of a Senior Faculty Development Grant, Tisch School of the Arts, Office of the Dean, New York University, 2002–03.

1 See Ella Shohat and Robert Stam, *Unthinking Eurocentrism: Multiculturalism*

and the Media (London and New York: Routledge, 1994). This essay assumes the definition of the concept of *Eurocentrism* as delineated in that book.

2 Michael Foss, *The Search for Cleopatra* (New York: Arcade Publishing, 1997).

3 "Was Cleopatra Black?" *Newsweek*, 23 September 1991, esp. 42, 44.

4 Jack Lindsay, *Cleopatra* (London: Constable, 1971), 2–4.

5 Michael Grant, *Cleopatra: A Biography* (Sheffield: Phoenix Press, 2000), esp. xiii, 4, 5.

6 Michael Grant, *From Alexander to Cleopatra: The Hellenistic World* (New York: Scribner, 1982).

7 Sarah B. Pomeroy, *Women in Hellenistic Egypt: From Alexander to Cleopatra* (Detroit: Wayne State University Press, 1990), 27 (*regina meretrix*), 55 (Didyme), 132 (Greek attachment to concubines), 137 (intermarriage).

8 Alan Cameron, "Two Mistresses of Ptolemy Philadelphus," *Greek, Roman and Byzantine Studies* 31 (fall 1990), 288 (skin color), 289 (Didyme). Asclepiades wrote the following poem dedicated to Didyme: "If she is black, what of it? So are coals. But when we warm them, they gleam like budding roses."

9 Mary Lefkowitz, "Not out of Africa," *New Republic* 220 (1992), 30.

10 See Frank M. Snowden Jr., *Blacks in Antiquity: Ethiopians in the Greco-Roman Experience* (Cambridge, Mass.: Belknap Press of Harvard University Press, 1970), 2.

11 Martin Bernal, "Black Athena is the Ancient Model," *Times Literary Supplement*, May 11, 2001, 10.

12 According to Snowden (1970), 169, numerous classicists and anthropologists noted the absence of color prejudice in the Greco-Roman world. J. Bryce claimed that in the Roman Empire, we hear little, if any, repugnance toward the dark-skinned Africans. E. Baring argued that color antipathy formed no bar to social intercourse in antiquity. For E.E Sikes, the ancients were apparently quite free from the antipathy of color bar. A. Zimmem saw the Greeks as having no prejudice. W. L. Westermann observed that Greek society has no color line, while T. J. Haarhoff observed that there never has been any color prejudice in Italy. For Kluckholn, the Greeks did not fall into the error of biological racism, color was no stigma, and men were classified not as black or white but as free or servile. And H. C. Baldry suggested that the Greeks were spared the modern curse of color prejudice.

13 Somewhat contradictorily, it is not the clear-skied Mediterranean but the cold, cloudy North that forms the locus of rationality and morality, while the jungle and wilderness are projected as the tangled sites of violent impulse and anarchic lust. And all of these binarisms—reflecting the id versus the superego on the scale of civilizations—are mapped onto others: sane/insane, pure/impure, reasonable/hysterical, healthy/sick.

14 See also Henry Louis Gates Jr., *Figures in Black* (New York: Oxford University Press, 1988).

15 Some physical anthropologists, interestingly, speculate that the first human being was African and a woman. See Donald C. Johnson and Maitland A. Edey, *Lucy, the Beginnings of Humankind* (New York: Simon and Schuster, 1981). Ethiopian commentators from the region where "Lucy" was "discovered" criticized the choice of a European name (a choice triggered by the Beatles' song "Lucy in the Sky with Diamonds"). The African American filmmaker Alice Sharon Larkin points out that had she been making a documentary about "Lucy," she would have called her "what the Ethiopian children call her—Wonderful," and she would have had contemporary Ethiopian women talk about Lucy. See Larkin, "Black Women Filmmakers Defining Ourselves: Feminism in our own Voice," in Deidre Pribram, ed., *Female Spectators: Looking at Film and Television* (London: Verso, 1988), 16.

16 See Samir Amin, *Eurocentrism* (New York: Monthly Review Press, 1989). The Americas, furthermore, are dotted with antique ruins, with the pyramids and acropoles of Mesoamerica and "Turtle Island," but Eurocentric education rarely calls attention to them. Who tells us that Peruvian monumental architecture existed before Stonehenge? Or that when ancient Greece was falling under Roman hegemony, the Native American Adena culture had been flourishing for over 1,000 years? See David E. Stannard, *American Holocaust: Columbus and the Conquest of the New World* (New York: Oxord University Press, 1992), 41.

17 Martin Bernal, *Black Athena* (New Brunswick, N.J.: Rutgers University Press, 1987), 241.

18 Frank Snowden, *Before Color Prejudice: The Ancient View of Blacks* (Cambridge, Mass.: Harvard University Press, 1983) documents contacts between the Africans of Kush and the Egyptians, Syrians, Greeks, and Romans from the third millennium B.C. onward.

19 Jean Rouch filmed the ritual in 1967 in the *La caverne de Bongo* (1969). V. Y. Mudimbe sums up some of the debates about the Dogon in *The Invention of Africa: Gnosis, Philosophy, and the Order of Knowledge* (Bloomington: Indiana University Press, 1988).

20 Leo Africanus, *History and Description of Africa*, quoted in David Killingray, *A Plague of Europeans* (Middlesex, 1973), 12–13.

21 John Thornton, *Africa and Africans in the Making of the Atlantic World, 1400–1680* (Cambridge: Cambridge University Press, 1992), 46.

22 Ibid., 43–71.

23 Cedric J. Robinson, *Black Marxism: The Making of the Black Radical Tradition* (London: Zed Press, 1983, distributed in the United States by Biblio Distribution Center; Totowa, N.J.), 4.

24 Patrick Buchanan was assuming this gap when he made his notorious comment that "Zulu immigrants to Virginia would be harder to assimilate than Englishmen." In the *New York Times* (8 March 1992), Stephen L. Carter pointed out that many Zulus in multilingual South Africa speak better English than the Europeans of whom Buchanan is so enamored. In a subsequent letter to the editor (dated 9 March 1992), Lorna Hahn pointed out that there are descendants of Zulus in present-day Virginia who not only actively participate in public life but who "even became conservative Republicans." One must also interrogate the conservative fondness for invoking the Zulus for their rhetorical purposes, as in

Saul Bellow's equally notorious observation about the lack of a "Zulu Proust." Is the word "Zulu" preferred because it has comic resonances for the Eurocentric ear or because it phonetically includes "zoo"?

25 Western art, then, has always been indebted to and transformed by non-Western art. In the case of modernism especially, aesthetic ideas have moved (at least) in two directions—whence, the Moorish influence on the poetry of courtly love, the African influence on modernist painting, the impact of Asian forms (Kabuki, No drama, Balinese theater, ideographic writing) on European theater and film, and the influence of Africanized forms not only on the Hollywood musical but also on such choreographers as Martha Graham and George Balanchine. See also Pieterse Jan Nederveen, *Empire and Emancipation: Power and Liberation on a World Scale* (London: Pluto, 1989).

26 My discussion here of Enlightenment aesthetics is based on Shohat and Stam 1994.

27 See also Cornel West, *Prophesy Deliverance: An Afro-American Revolutionary Christianity* (Philadlephia: Westminster Press, 1982); Clyde Taylor, "Black Cinema in the Post-Aesthetic Era," in Jim Pines and Paul Willemen, eds., *Questions of Third Cinema* (London: BFI, 1989); Bell Hooks, *Black Looks: Race and Representation* (Boston: South End Press, 1992).

28 Quoted in Brian V. Street, *The Savage in Literature: Representations of "Primitive" Society in English Fiction, 1858–1920* (London and Boston: Routledge, 1975), 99.

29 George-Louis Leclerc de Buffon, *The History of Man and Quadrupeds*, trans. by William Smellie (London, 1812), 422.

30 George L. Mosse, *Toward the Final Solution: A History of European Racism* (New York: H. Fertig, 1978), 44.

31 Charles White, *Account of the Regular Gradation in Man*, quoted in Stephen Jay Gould, *The Mismeasure of Man* (New York: Norton, 1981), 42.

32 William Maginn and Shelton R. Mackenzie, "Lady Macbeth," from *The Shakespeare Papers of the Late William Maginn* (New York: Redfield, 1856), 184.

33 John Bourchier, Lord Berners, *The Romance of a Nose* (London, 1941).

34 Anatole France, from the preface to Theophile Gautier, *Cleopatra* (Paris, 1899).

35 Snowden 1970, 7, 178.

36 An interview with Hughes-Hallett 1990 for the documentary *Intimate Portrait—Cleopatra, Race and Beauty*, broadcast on Lifetime TV, 1997.

37 Kathy Lee Peiss, "Making Faces: The Cosmetics Industry and the Cultural Construction of Gender, 1890–1930," *Genders* 7 (1990), 143–69, 158–59.

38 The image of Cleopatra has been recycled by diverse advertisements and by now has entered cyberspace, as, for example, "The Story of Cleopatra's Secret," a site designed by an Egyptian woman to sell a hair-removal product (www.cleosecret.com).

39 Over the past decade, numerous books on the subject of female travelers have appeared. For extended discussion and a bibliography, see Shohat and Stam 1994; Caren Kaplan, *Questions of Travel: Postmodern Discourses of Displace-*

ment (Durham, N.C.: Duke University Press, 1996); Inderpal Grewal, *Home and Harem: Nation, Gender, Empire, and the Cultures of Travel* (Durham, N.C.: Duke University Press, 1996).

40 Sarah Berry, *Screen Style: Consumer Fashion and Feminity in 1930s Hollywood* (Minneapolis: University of Minnesota Press, 2000), 95.

41 See, for example, Mary Hamer, "Disowning Cleopatra," in Susan Walker and Sally-Ann Ashton, eds., *Cleopatra Reassessed.* The British Museum Occasional Papers #103 (London: British Museum, 2003).

42 Recently Jay Roach's parodic film *Austin Powers: Goldmember* (2002) pays homage to 1970s popular culture, including blaxpliotation films. The film's hero, Austin Powers (Mike Myers), is joined by the heroine Foxy Cleopatra (Beyoncé Knowles) fighting Dr. Evil and his clone.

43 Barbara Chase-Riboud's poems "Cleopatra" and "Anthony," in *Erotique Noire, Black Erotics*, edited by Miriam Decosta-Willis, Reginald Martin, and Rose-ann P. Bell (New York: Anchor Books, 1969). Shelley P. Haley, "Black Feminist Thought and Classics: Re-membering, Re-claiming, Re-empowering," in *Feminist Theory and the Classics*, edited by Nancy Sorkin Rabinowitz and Amy Richlin (New York: Routledge, 1993), 28–30.

44 In Israel, Roni Somech, an Iraqi-Israeli poet, also wrote a poem about Cleopatra. In collaboration with the composer and singer Yair Dalal, he gave expression to another diasporic existence in which Arab culture was denied to Arab Jews (also known as "Blacks") by Euro-Israel.

45 For a discussion of Balkan self-Occidentalizing, see Busan I. Bjelic, ed., Balkan as Metaphor: *Between Globalization and Fragmentation* (Cambridge, Mass.: MIT Press, 2002).

46 Albert Hourani, *A History of the Arab Peoples* (Cambridge, Mass.: Harvard University Press, 1991), 341–42.

47 Ibid., 342–43.

48 Ibid., 342.

49 Wole Soyinka, "Shakespeare and the Living Dramatist," in idem., *Art, Dialogue, and Outrage: Essays on Literature and Culture* (New York: Pantheon Books, 1993), 207–11.

50 Soyinka also looks at other theories to endow Shakespeare with Arab paternity, focusing on the content of the literature. "Only an Arab," it is claimed, "could have understood or depicted a Jew so 'convincingly'" as in the *The Merchant of Venice.* Similarly, the focus is sometimes placed on Othello: The Moor's dignity even in folly has been held up as convincing proof that no European could have fleshed out this specific psychology of a jealousy complicated by racial insecurity but a man from beneath the skin—an Arab at the very least. See Soyinka 1993, 151. Qaddafi, it should also be noted, has been a prominent advocate of the idea of Shakespeare the Arab.

51 Sa'eed Darwish, who died during work on the theatrical play, first composed the music. The young Abdel Wahab was asked to take over. In 1973, he wrote another song about Cleopatra.

TABOO MEMORIES,
DIASPORIC VISIONS

Columbus, Palestine, and Arab-Jews

Dr. Solomon Schechter [Cambridge expert in Rabbinical literature a century ago] agreed to look at them, but chiefly out of politeness, for he was still skeptical about the value of the "Egyptian fragments." But it so happened that he was taken completely by surprise. One of the documents immediately caught his interest, and next morning, after examining [it] . . . he realized that he had stumbled upon a sensational discovery. . . . The discovery has so excited Schechter that he had already begun thinking of travelling to Cairo to acquire whatever remained of the documents. . . . Schechter was fortunate that Cromer [the British administrator of Egypt] himself took interest in the success of his mission. The precise details of what transpired between Schechter and British officialdom and the leaders of the Cairo's Jewish community are hazy, but soon enough . . . they granted him permission to remove everything he wanted from the Geniza [a synagogue chamber where the community books, papers, and documents were kept for centuries], every last paper and parchment, without condition or payment. It has sometimes been suggested that Schechter succeeded so easily in his mission because the custodians of the Synagogue of Ben Ezra had no idea of the real value of the Geniza documents—a species of argument that was widely used in the nineteenth century to justify the acquisition of historical artifacts by colonial powers. . . . Considering that there had been an active and lucrative trade in Geniza documents . . . and impoverished as they were, it is hard to believe that they would willingly have parted with a treasure which was, after all, the last remaining asset left to them by their ancestors. In all likelihood the decision was taken for them by the leaders of their community, and they were left with no alternative but acquiescence. As for those leaders . . . like the elites of so many other groups in the colonized world, they evidently decided to seize the main chance at a time when the balance of power—the ships and the guns— lay overwhelmingly with England. . . . Schechter . . . filled out about thirty sacks and boxes with the materials and with the help of the British embassy in Cairo he shipped them off to Cambridge. A few months later he returned himself—laden . . . "with spoils of the Egyptians."[1]

I begin my essay with the account of the emptying out of the Jewish Egyptian Geniza "archive" as narrated in Amitav Ghosh's *In an Antique Land*. The genealogy of the word "Geniza" in Hebrew, it is speculated, is rooted in the Persian word *gange*, which refers to a storage place. Jews in the region commonly deposited unusable sacred manuscripts or even everyday documents, or fragments of them, in a specially designated room in the synagogue. Papers bearing the scriptural traces of God's name, no matter how decayed, could not be simply trashed. They had to be laid to rest, in a full burial ceremony. Storage was either a transitory place for documents or their permanent home. *In an Antique Land* calls attention to one such Judeo-Arabic document: the correspondence about family and trade affairs by a twelfth-century Jewish Tunisian merchant, Abraham Ben-Yiju, preserved in the Geniza of Ben Ezra synagogue in Cairo. Ghosh traces the letters in an effort to piece together moments from the life of Ben-Yiju across the regions of the Mediterranean and the Indian Ocean. Like their forebears, the leaders of the old Cairo (Fustat) synagogue treated the community texts with great respect, placing them in the Geniza room built in 1025. The room was not emptied of its contents during a period of eight hundred years; the last document was deposited around 1875. The thoroughly hybrid documents were largely inscribed in Arabic and Hebrew, with some documents featuring both languages, where it was not uncommon to find the Arabic registered in Hebrew script and vice versa. The surviving fragments formed part of Cairo's Jewish community life and history, a tissue of its threaded connections to all those other worlds with which it had interacted. The Geniza did not function as an archive in the common definition of the word, but the dense layers of documents accumulated over the centuries, layers upon layers and generations upon generations, converted it, post factum, into an archive. The Geniza, furthermore, became "minutes," as it were, of a cultural meeting, a stenographic record of the historical interactions of this Cairo community.

Colonialism did not pass over Egypt's Jewish community. Egypt's strategic location turned it into the object of interest for imperial powers, soon becoming a focus of attraction not only for Napoleon's battalions and their British competitors, but also for an army of researchers, artists, and diverse travelers afflicted with Egyptomania. Egypt's past—its spoils of mummies, sphinxes, and pyramids—was visited by "discoverers" who dug, uncovered, and studied Egypt within assumptions produced by the Enlightenment's conceptual apparatus. The field of Egyptology was premised on the rescue of ancient Egypt from oblivion, legitimating the initiation of a new act within the ongoing drama: the transfer of cultural artifacts, and "treasures," from their original location to the centers of the West for scholarship and commerce. It is within this cultural-colonial context that the "discovery" of the Geniza took place, in a period when the digging of the Suez Canal under imperial orchestration was at its height. The Judaica antiquity collector Jacob Saphir, whose travel to Egypt led to the ground-shaking discovery by Solomon Schechter of Cambridge University, had organized the first voyage that brought the Geniza treasure to the attention of scholars in the West, in 1864. It took thirty years for the implementation of the operation to transfer the Geniza's contents under Schechter, who received the British Crown signature from the administrator Evelyn Baring Cromer, the virtual ruler of Egypt. With the help of the British Embassy, the boxes were filled and sent to Cambridge and catalogued in the Taylor-Schechter collection. Other documents were taken from the Jewish burial ground in Egypt. By World War One, the Cairo Geniza was stripped of all of its documents, which were then distributed in Europe and America, with a large part of the documents going into private collections.

Within this Enlightenment project, under the banner of progress and science, there was not a shred of doubt about the legitimate right of archaeologists and antiquity traders to uproot papyruses, mummies, or tombstones. Within this ultimately Eurocentric framework, such acts were not conceived as theft or dispossession; on the contrary, they were perceived as applying the principles of universalism and humanism. The inhabitants, it was assumed, did not understand or appreciate the value of the treasures around them. Within this context, there was nothing unusual about such a colonial raid on the archive—in this case, a very literal archive, indeed. What is unusual, however, is how the two groups of co-religionists, the European Ashkenazi Jews (British in this case) and Sephardi Arab-Jews (Egyptians), fell out on opposite sides of the colonial divide. European Jews' closeness to Western powers permitted the dispossession of Arab-Jews even before the advent of Zionism as a Eurocentric national project, which later would presume to take under its aegis the Eastern Jews. For the Geniza scholars, the documents represented a world devoid of life. They were not seen as part of a societal tissue, an organ in a breathing, living, and creating community body. The documents were torn from their historical producers without this violation provoking any debate.

The Jewish studies experts who organized the dislocation of the Geniza to Cambridge from its region of belonging in Cairo inadvertently began a process of symbolic displacement of Jews of the East from their geocultural space. In this historical episode, the culture of the Egyptian Jewish community was partially "disappeared" through the confiscation of its documents. At the time the Geniza was removed, two years after its "discovery" in 1896, Egyptian Jews for millennia had already been an ingrained part of the geocultural landscape of the region. The British Jewish scholars, like their non-Jewish compatriots, cast an imperial gaze at the Egyptian Jews, the very people who had produced and sustained the Geniza for almost a thousand years, and whose documents the scholars were appropriating, but whom the scholars described as "aborigines" and "scoundrels" whose religious leaders had the "unpleasant" habit of kissing other men "on the mouth."[2] While the Geniza documents testify to the rootedness of the Jews in a vast region stretching from the Mediterranean to the Indian Ocean, the textual "witnesses" themselves ironically were uprooted and displaced. At times the actual pages from the same manuscript "wandered" to widely distant destinations: Cambridge, England, St. Petersburg, Russia, and Philadelphia, Pennsylvania. The document as a proof or a testimony vanished from the Jewish Egyptian geography that invented it. The palimpsestic "archive" that provides a record of so many lives and ideas, and that tells of so many worlds, has enabled the writing of the past of Eastern Jews who created it. Yet, paradoxically, the Geniza's dislocation from the geocultural space in which it was created also made possible the erasure of the very tangible evidence of the Jewish past from that same geocultural space.

The phrase "the Geniza's discovery (*gilui ha-gniza*)" permeates dominant Jewish historiography. Echoing the colonialist term "discovery" that assumes a European point of view, the term "discovery" obscures the fact that the Geniza was known to its producers. While the word "archive" tends to be associated with a conscious act of accumulating, classifying, and organizing documents, the Geniza was perceived as an unconscious act of accumulation, and thus as a kind of a detritus site. In the introduction to his monumental work *A Mediterranean Society*, S. D. Goitein, the foremost Geniza scholar, contrasts the concept of the archive with the Geniza.[3] Whereas the former houses documents soon after their writing, made accessible for study, the latter were deposited after their owners lost interest in them, and often long after their writing. It is precisely because the Geniza is not an organized archive that Goitein dubs it a "treasure." In his definition, two worlds—the modern and the pre-modern—collide around the signification of preservation. Yet, this kind of salvage project is marked by erasure and fragmentation. The Geniza's discovery and rescue can be seen from another perspective: as its exiling. Indeed, in historical terms, the "diasporization" of the Geniza anticipated by half a century the exiling of its owners. In a traumatic turn of events in the wake of the Israeli-Arab conflict, Arab-Jews had to abandon the regions in which they had lived for millennia. After the British withdrawal from Palestine, and the establishment of the State of Israel in 1948, Arabs and Jews were newly staged as enemy identities. If at the time of the "Geniza discovery" Egyptian Jews were still seen as part of the colonized Arab world, with the partition of Palestine, Arab-Jews, in a historical shift, suddenly became simply "Jews."

The historical episode of emptying out the Geniza suggests not only that alliances and opposition between communities evolve historically, but also their narrativizations differ when seen in the light of the present. And as certain strands within a cultural fabric become taboo, this narrativization involves destroying connections that once existed. The process of constructing a national historical memory also entails destroying a different, prior historical memory at whose expense the nationalist narrative articulates itself. Although a large proportion of the Geniza texts were written in Judeo-Arabic, the process of dispersing the community resulted in the paradoxical effect of "disappearing" a language that the generation of displaced from Arab countries are the last to speak. The rupture that affected Judeo-Arabic culture was not merely a result of the dispersal of its people from the Arab world. Within Zionist discourse, Judeo-Arab culture was disdained as a sign of "*galut* (diaspora)"—a negative term within Euro-

Israeli Zionist discourse. The reemergence of new political maps therefore also brought about the emergence of different geographies of identity and a new rewriting of the boundaries of belonging.

The European "discovery" and "rescue" of the Geniza from its Egyptian producers testifies to a dramatic turn in the relationship between Ashkenazi Jews and Levantine Jews in the modern era. Over the centuries, Ashkenazi Jewish religious scholars had corresponded and consulted with the Jewish religious centers of the Islamic world. But since the Enlightenment, with the partial secularization of European Jewry, Ashkenazi-Sephardi relations entered a new transcultural semantics. The traditional difference between these two cultural and liturgical worlds, even their mutual prejudices, had not been articulated before within a context of power relations under the auspices of colonialism and, later, Zionism, all part of the spreading Eurocentric vision of the world. In the post-Enlightenment era, the gradual integration of European Jews at the universities produced a new field of inquiry, Judaic studies, which was not simply secular but Eurocentric. Ashkenazi-Jewish scholars became central to the representation of Jewish history, including Arab-Jewish history. Eurocentric norms of scholarship established typically colonial relations that have taken a heavy toll on the representation of Arab-Jewish history and identity. In this essay, I will attempt to demonstrate some of the contradictions and antinomies produced for Arab-Jewish culture since the arrival of colonialism and nationalism. I hope to disentangle the complexities of Arab-Jewish identity by unsettling some of the borders erected by almost a century of Eurocentric Zionist historiography, with its fatal binarisms such as civilization versus savagery, modernity versus tradition, and West versus East.

TOWARD A RELATIONAL APPROACH TO IDENTITY

Recent postcolonial theory has at times shied away from grounding its writings in historical context and cultural specificity. While innumerable poststructuralist essays elaborate abstract versions of "difference" and "alterity," few offer a communally participatory and politicized knowledge of non-European cultures. At the same time, however, the professionalized study of compartmentalized historical periods and geographical regions (as in Middle East studies and Latin American studies) has often resulted in an overly specific focus that overlooks the interconnectedness of histories, geographies, and cultural identities. In *Unthinking Eurocentrism*,

Robert Stam and I argue for a relational approach to multicultural studies that does not segregate historical periods and geographical regions into neatly fenced-off areas of expertise, and that speaks of communities not in isolation but, rather, "in relation."[4] Rather than pit a rotating chain of resisting communities against a Western dominant (a strategy that privileges the "West," if only as constant antagonist), we argue for stressing the horizontal and vertical links that thread communities and histories together in a conflictual network. Analyzing the overlapping multiplicities of identities and affiliations that link diverse resistant discourses helps us transcend some of the politically debilitating effects of disciplinary and community boundaries.

The kind of connections we have in mind operates on a number of levels. First, it is important to make connections in temporal terms. While postcolonial studies privilege the imperial era of the nineteenth and twentieth centuries, one might argue for grounding the discussion in a longer history of multiply located colonialisms and resistances, tracing the issues at least as far back as 1492. We propose connections, second, in spatial and geographical terms, placing debates about identity and representation in a broader context that embraces the Americas, Asia, and Africa. We also argue for connections in disciplinary and conceptual terms, forging links between debates usually compartmentalized (at least in the United States): on the one hand, postcolonial theory associated with issues of colonial discourse, imperial imaginary, and national narrations, and on the other, the diverse "ethnic studies" that focus on issues of "minorities," race, and multiculturalism. The point is to place the often ghettoized discourses about geographies ("here" versus "there") and about time ("now" versus "then") in illuminating dialogue. A relational approach, one that operates at once within, between, and beyond the nation-state framework, calls attention to the conflictual, hybrid interplay of communities within and across borders.

My subtitle "Columbus, Palestine, and Arab-Jews" already juxtaposes disparate entities to underline the ways in which nation-states have imposed a coherent sense of national identity precisely because of their fragile sense of cultural, even geographical, belonging. The formation of the postcolonial nation-state, especially in the wake of colonial partitions, often involved a double process of joining diverse ethnicities and regions that had been separate under colonialism and, at the same time, partitioning regions in a way that forced regional redefinitions (Iraq/Kuwait) or a cross-shuffling of populations (Pakistan/India or Israel/Palestine in relation

40 *Green Card* (1992), artwork by Inigo Manglano-Ovalle, laminated c-print

to Palestinians and Arab-Jews). Given the "minority"/"majority" battles "from within" and the war waged by border crossers (refugees, exiles, immigrants) "from without," Eurocentric historiography has played a crucial role in handing out passports to its legitimate races, ethnicities, nations. In the words of the Palestinian Mahmoud Darwish's well-known poem, "Jawaz Safar (Passport)": "Stripped of my name, my identity? On a soil I nourished with my own hands?" The same colonial logic that dismantled Palestine had already dismantled the "Turtle Island" of the Americas. Thus, the first illegal alien, Columbus,[5] remains a celebrated discoverer, while indigenous Mexicans "infiltrate" a barbed border to a homeland that was once theirs and Native Americans are exiled in their own land (figure 40).

By way of demonstration of the "relational" method, I will focus on Sephardi Arab-Jewish (known in the Israeli context as Mizrahi) identity as it intersects with other communities and discourses in diverse contexts over time. I will take as a point of departure the 1992 quincentennial commemorations of the expulsion of Sephardi Jews from Spain to argue that any revisionist effort to articulate Arab-Jewish identity in a contemporary context that has posited Arab and Jew as antonyms can be disentangled only through a series of positionings vis-à-vis diverse communities and identities (Arab Muslim, Arab Christian, Palestinian, Euro-Israeli, Euro-American Jewish, indigenous American, African American, Chicano/a) that would challenge the devastating consequences that the Zionist-Orientalist binarism of East versus West, Arab versus Jew, has had for Arab-Jews (or Jewish Arabs). Linking, delinking, and relinking, at once spatially and temporally, thus becomes part of adversary scholarship working against taboo formulations, policed identities, and censored affiliations.

STAGING THE QUINCENTENARY

"Your Highnesses completed the war against the Moors," Columbus wrote in a letter addressed to the Spanish throne, "after having chased all the Jews . . . and sent me to the said regions of India in order to convert the people there to our Holy Faith."[6] In 1492, the defeat of the Muslims and the expulsion of Sephardi Jews from Spain converged with the conquest of what came to be called the New World. But while the celebrations of Columbus's voyages have provoked lively opposition (ranging from multicultural debates about the Eurocentric notion of "discovery" to satirical performances by Native Americans landing in Europe and claiming it as their discovered continent), the Eurocentric framing of the "other 1492" has not been questioned. Apart from some enthusiastic scholastic energy dedicated to the dubious pride in whether Columbus once and for all can be claimed as a (secret) Jew, expulsion events navigated within the calm seas of Old World paradigms. Furthermore, the two separate quincentenary commemorations, both of which took place in the Americas, Europe, and the Middle East, have seldom acknowledged the historical and discursive linkages between these two constellations of events. To examine the relationship between contemporary discourses about the two "1492s" might therefore illuminate the role that scholarly and popular narratives of history play in nation-building myths and geopolitical alliances.

The Spanish Christian war against Muslims and Jews was politically, economically, and ideologically linked to the caravels' arrival in Hispaniola. Triumphant over the Muslims, Spain invested in the project of Columbus, whose voyages were financed partly by wealth taken from the defeated Muslims and confiscated from Jews through the Inquisition.[7] The Reconquista's policies of settling Christians in the newly (re)conquered areas of Spain, as well as the gradual institutionalization of expulsion, conversion, and killing of Muslims and Jews in Christian territories, prepared the grounds for similar Conquista practices across the Atlantic. Under the marital-political union of Ferdinand (Aragon) and Isabella (Castille), victorious Christian Spain, soon to become an empire, strengthened its sense of nationhood, subjugating indigenous Americans and Africans. Discourses about Muslims and Jews during Spain's continental expansion crossed the Atlantic, arming the conquistadors with a ready-made "us versus them" ideology aimed at the regions of India, but in fact applied first toward the indigenous of the accidentally "discovered" continent. The colonial misrecognition inherent in the name "Indian" underlines the linked imaginaries of the East and West Indies. (Perhaps not coincidentally, in Ridley Scott's film *1492: The Conquest of Paradise* [1992], Orientalist, "Ali Baba"–style music accompanies the encounter with Caribbean "Indians.") India awaited its colonized turn with the arrival of Vasco de Gama (1498) and the Portuguese conquest of Goa (1510). If in the fifteenth century the only European hope for conquering the East—given the Muslim domination of the continental route—was via sailing to the West, the nineteenth-century consolidation of European imperialism in the East was facilitated by Europe's previous self-aggrandizing at the expense of the Americas and Africa. The colonization of the Americas and Africa made possible Europe's modernization, subsequently allowing the colonization of North Africa (the Maghreb) and the so-called Near East (Mashreq.) "The Indian Ocean trade, and the Culture that supported it," writes Amitav Ghosh, "had long since been destroyed by European navies. Transcontinental trade was no longer a shared enterprise; the merchant shipping of the high seas was now entirely controlled by the naval powers of Europe."[8]

Although Moorish Spain testifies to syncretic multiculturalism *avant la lettre*, the Reconquista ideology of "Limpieza de Sangre" (cleansing of the blood) as an early exercise in European "self-purification," sought to expel, or forcibly convert, Muslims and Jews. The Crusades, which inaugurated "Europe" by reconquering the Mediterranean area, catalyzed Europeans' awareness of their own geocultural identity and established the principle that wars conducted in the interests of the Holy Church were axiomatically just. The campaigns against Muslims and Jews as well as against other "agents of Satan," heretics and witches, made available a mammoth apparatus of racism and sexism for recycling in the "new" continents. Anti-Semitism and anti-infidelism provided a conceptual and disciplinary framework that, after being turned against Europe's immediate or internal others, was then projected outward against Europe's distant or external others.[9] Prince Henry ("the Navigator"), the pioneer of Portuguese exploration, had himself been a Crusader against the Moors at the battle of Ceuta. Amerigo Vespucci, writing about his voyages, similarly drew on the stock of Jewish and Muslim stereotypes to characterize the savage, the infidel, the indigenous man as a dangerous sexual omnivore and the indigenous woman as a luringly yielding nature.[10] In this sense, the metonymic links between Jews and Muslims—their literal neighboring and shared histories—are turned into metaphorical and analogical links in relation to the peoples of the Americas.[11] The point is not that there is a complete equivalence between Europe's oppressive relations toward Jews and Muslims and toward indigenous peoples. The point is that European Christian demonology prefigured colonialist racism. Indeed, we can even discern a partial congruency between the phantasmatic imagery projected onto the Jewish and Muslim "enemy" and onto the indigenous American and Black African "savage," all imaged to various degrees as "blood drinkers," "cannibals," "sorcerers," and "devils."[12]

One of the rare contemporary representations that expose ecclesiastic participation in genocidal measures, the Mexican film *El Santo Oficio* (The Holy Office, 1973), features the attempt by the Holy See to spread the Inquisition into the New World. Although the film focuses on the recently converted Sephardis, the Conversos, it also shows that they are persecuted alongside heretics, witches, and indigenous infidels. Consumed by enthusiastic spectators, their burning at the stake is performed as a public spectacle of discipline and punishment, just as lynching was consumed as a popular entertainment by some whites in the United States. Screened at a Los Angeles ceremonial opening for a conference dedicated to the quincentennial expulsion of Sephardi Jews (organized by the International Jewish Committee Sepharad '92), *El Santo Oficio* provoked strong emotions. Its documentation of Sephardi Jewish rituals practiced in secrecy, and its visual details of torture, rape, and massacre were not received, however, in the spirit of the linkages I have charted here. The audience, consisting largely of Euro-American, Jewish, and a substantially smaller number of Sephardi American educators, scholars, and community workers, was eager to consume the narrative evidence of the singular nature of the Jewish experience. To point out the links between the Inquisition and the genocide of the indigenous peoples of the Americas, and the devastation of African peoples, would have been tantamount to promiscuously intermingling the sacred with the profane. At the reception that followed the film, Chicano waiters plied the guests with food. The simplistic category of "them" (Spanish Christians), however, stood in remarkably ironic relation to the indigenous faces of the waiters; their presence suggesting that the charting of Sephardi Conversos' history must be negotiated in relation to that of other Conversos.

The importance of rupturing the boundaries of these histories becomes even clearer in the actual intersection of diverse histories of forced conversions in the Americas. For example, the case of Chicano and Mexican families of partly Sephardi Jewish origins suggests that at times the links are quite literal. Recent research by the Southwest Jewish Archives in the United States points out that Sephardi traditions remain alive in predominantly Roman Catholic Mexican American families, although the family members are not always conscious of the origins of the rituals. They are uncertain why, for example, their grandmothers make unleavened bread called *"pan semita,"* or Semite bread, and why their rural grandparents in New Mexico or Texas slaughter a lamb in the spring and smear its blood on the doorway. Revealing that some Chicanos and Mexicans are the descendants of secret Jews is a taboo that results in contemporary secrecy even among those who are aware of their ancestry.[13] The issue of forced conversions in the Americas and the consequent cultural syncretism implicates and challenges Jewish as well as Catholic Euro-indigenous institutions. The hybridity of Chicano and Mexican culture, however, does not necessarily facilitate the admission of another complex hybridity, one crossing Jewish-Catholic boundaries.

If the genocide of indigenous Americans and Africans is no more than a bit of historical marginalia, the linked persecutions in Iberia of Sephardi Jews and Muslims, of Conversos and Moriscos,[14] are also submerged. The quincentennial elision of the Arab Muslim part of the narrative was especially striking. During the centuries-long Reconquista, not all Muslims and Jews withdrew with the Arab forces. Those Muslims who remained after the change of rule were known as *mudejars*, deriving from the Arabic *mudajjin*, "permitted to remain," with a suggestion of "tamed," "domesticated." The Spanish Inquisition, institutionalized in 1478, did not pass over the Muslims. Apart from the 1492 expulsion of 3 million Muslims and 300,000 Sephardi Jews, in 1499 mass burning of Islamic books and forced conversions took place, and in 1502 the Muslims of Granada were given the choice of baptism or exile. In 1525–26, Muslims of other provinces were given the same choice. In 1566, there was a revival of anti-Muslim legislation, and between 1609 and 1614 came edicts of expulsions. In other words, the same inquisitional measures taken against the Jewish Conversos who were found to be practicing Judaism secretly were taken against the Moriscos found to be practicing Islam, measures that culminated in edicts of expulsion addressed specifically to Muslims. As a result, many fled to North Africa, where, like Sephardi Jews, they maintained certain aspects of their Hispanicized Arab culture.[15]

This well-documented history[16] found little echo in the events promoted by the International Jewish Committee Sepharad '92, whose major funds came from the United States, Spain, and Israel. Spain, which still has to come to terms with its present-day racist immigration policies toward— among others—Arab North Africans, embraced its "Golden Age" after centuries of denial, while reserving a mea culpa only for the official spokespeople of "the Jews." As for all other representatives, including conservative upper-middle-class Zionist Sephardim, the elision of comparative discussions of the Muslim and Jewish (Sephardi) situations in Christian Spain was largely rooted, I would argue, in present-day Middle Eastern politics. The 1992 commemorations entailed a serious contemporary battle over the representations of "Jewish identity" in terms of an East–West axis, a battle that dates back to the nineteenth-century beginnings of Zionist nationalism.

THE TRAUMA OF DISMEMBERMENT

When Zionist historiography does refer to Islamic–Jewish history, it consists of a morbidly selective "tracing the dots" from pogrom to pogrom. (The word "pogrom" itself derives from and reflects the Eastern European Jewish experience.)[17] Subordinated to a Eurocentric historiography, most quincentenary events lamented yet another tragic episode in a homogeneous, static history of relentless persecution. Not surprisingly, the screening of *El Santo Oficio* at the expulsion conference elicited such overheard remarks as: "You think it's different today?" and "That's also what the Nazis did to us. That's what the Arabs would do if they could." (This is a curious claim, since the Arab Muslims had a millennium-long opportunity to install an inquisition against Middle Eastern Jews—or against Christian minorities—but never did.) Such common remarks underline the commemoration's role as a stage for demonstrating (Euro-)Israeli nationalism as the only possible logical answer to horrific events in the history of Jews. The inquisition of Sephardi Jews is seen merely as a foreshadowing of the Jewish Holocaust. In this paradigm, the traumas left by Nazi genocidal practices are simplistically projected onto the experiences of Jews in Muslim countries and onto the Israeli–Palestinian conflict.[18]

My point here is not to idealize the situation of the Jews within Islam but, rather, to suggest that Zionist discourse has subsumed Islamic–Jewish history into a Christian–Jewish history while also undermining comparative studies of Middle Eastern Jews in the context of diverse religious and ethnic minorities in Muslim geographies. On the occasion of

the quincentenary, the Zionist perspective privileged Sephardi Jewish relations with European Christianity over those with Arab Islam, projecting
Eurocentric maps of Christians and Jews as West and Muslims as East and
ignoring the fact that, at the time of the expulsion, syncretic Jewish communities were flourishing within Muslim spaces. Quincentennial events
not only rendered the interrelations between Jewish Conversos and indigenous American Conversos invisible, but they also undermined the Sephardi Jewish and Muslim cultural syncreticism. The only Muslim country
that received quincentennial attention was Turkey, partly because Sultan
Beyazid II ordered his governors in 1492 to receive the expelled Jews
cordially. But no less important are Turkey's contemporary regional alliances, its fissured national identity between East and West. Unlike Arab
Muslim countries, where expelled Sephardim also settled (Morocco, Tunisia, Egypt), Turkey has not participated in the Israeli–Arab conflict or in
the non-allied embargo that for decades regionally isolated Israel until the
recent orchestration of Arab diplomatic recognition. Yet even in the case of
Turkey, the quincentennial's emphasis was less on Muslim-Jewish relations than on the voyages of refuge and, anachronistically, on the Turkish
(national) as opposed to Muslim (religious) shelter.

In this rewriting of history, present-day Muslim Arabs constitute merely
one more "non-Jewish" obstacle to the Jewish Israeli national trajectory.
The idea of the unique, common victimization of all Jews at all times provides a crucial underpinning of official Israeli discourse. The notion of
uniqueness precludes analogies and metonymies, thus producing a selective reading of "Jewish history"—one that hijacks Mashreqian and Maghrebian Jews from their Judeo-Islamic geography and subordinates that geography to that of the European Ashkenazi *shtetl*. This double process entails
the performance of commonalities among Jews in the public sphere so as
to suggest a homogeneous national past, while silencing any deviance into
a more globalized and historicized narrative that would see Jews not simply through their religious commonalities but also in relation to their contextual cultures, institutions, and practices. Given this approach, and given
the Israeli-Arab conflict, no wonder that the Jews of Islam—and, more
specifically, Arab-Jews—have posed a challenge to any simplistic definition
of Jewish and, particularly, of the emergent Jewish Euro-Israeli identity.

The selective readings of Middle Eastern history, in other words, make
two processes apparent: the rejection of an Arab and Muslim context for
Jewish institutions, identity, and history, and their unproblematized subordination into a "universal" Jewish experience. In the Zionist "proof" of a

41 Yemeni Jews arriving in the "Promised Land" (1949)

single Jewish experience, there are no parallels or overlappings with other religious and ethnic communities, whether in terms of a Jewish hyphenated and syncretic culture or in terms of linked analogous oppressions. All Jews are defined as closer to each other than to the cultures of which they have been a part. Thus, the religious Jewish aspect of diverse, intricate, and interwoven Jewish identities has been given primacy, a categorization tantamount to dismembering the identity of a community. And indeed, the Euro-Israeli separation of the "Jewish" part from the "Middle Eastern" part in the case of Middle Eastern Jews has resulted in practically dismantling the Jewish communities of the Muslim world, as well as in pressures exerted on Mizrahim (Orientals) to realign their Jewish identity according to Zionist Euro-Israeli paradigms (figure 41). Since the beginnings of European Zionism, the Jews of Islam have faced, for the first time in their history, the imposed dilemma of choosing between Jewishness and Arabness in a geopolitical context that has perpetuated the equation between Arabness and Middle Easternness and Islam, on the one hand, and between Jewishness and Europeanness and Westernness, on the other.[19]

The master narrative of universal Jewish victimization has been crucial for legitimizing an anomalous nationalist project of "ingathering of the Diaspora from the four corners of the globe," but it can also be defined as forcing displacements of peoples from such diverse geographies, languages, cultures, and histories—a project in which, in other words, a state created a nation. It has also been crucial for the claim that the "Jewish nation" faces a common "historical enemy"—the Muslim Arab—implying a double-edged amnesia with regard to both the Judeo-Islamic history and the colonial partition of Palestine. False analogies between the Arabs and Nazis—and, in 1992, Inquisitors—becomes not merely a staple of Zionist rhetoric, but also a symptom of a Jewish European nightmare projected onto the structurally distinct political dynamics of the Israeli–Palestinian conflict. In a historical context of Jews experiencing an utterly distinct history within the Muslim world from that which haunted the European memories of Jews, and in a context of the massacres and dispossession of Palestinian people, the conflation of the Muslim Arab with the archetypical (European) oppressors of Jew downplays the colonial-settler history of Euro-Israel itself.

The neat division of Israel as West and Palestine as East, I would argue, ignores some of the fundamental contradictions within Zionist discourse itself.[20] Central to Zionism is the notion of return to origins located in the Middle East.[21] Thus, Zionism often points to its linguistic return to Semitic Hebrew, and to its sustaining of a religious idiom intimately linked with the topography of the Middle East, as a "proof" of the Eastern origins of European Jews—a crucial aspect of the Zionist claim for the land. And although Jews have often been depicted in anti-Semitic discourse as an alien "Eastern" people within the West, the paradox of Israel is that it presumed to "end a diaspora" characterized by Jewish ritualistic nostalgia for the East, only to found a state whose ideological and geopolitical orientation has been almost exclusively Western. Theodor Herzl called for a Western-style capitalist-democratic miniature state, to be made possible by the grace of imperial patrons such as England or Germany, while David Ben-Gurion formulated his visionary utopia of Israel as that of a "Switzerland of the Middle East." Although European Jews have historically been the victims of anti-Semitic Orientalism, Israel as a state has become the perpetrator of Orientalist attitudes and actions whose consequences have been the dispossession of Palestinians. The ideological roots of Zionism can be traced to the conditions of nineteenth- and early-twentieth-century Europe, not only as a reaction against anti-Semitism, but also to the rapid expansion of capitalism and of European empire building. Israel, in this sense, has clearly been allied to First World imperialist interests, has deployed Eurocentric-inflected discourse, and has exercised colonialist policies toward Palestinian land and people.

The question is further complicated by the socialist pretensions—and, at times, socialist achievements—of Zionism. In nationalist Zionist discourse, the conflict between the socialist ideology of Zionism and the real praxis of Euro-Jewish colonization in Palestine was resolved through the reassuring thesis that the Arab masses, subjected to feudalism and exploited by their own countrymen, could only benefit from the emanation of Zionist praxis.[22] This presentation embodies the historically positive self-image of Israelis as involved in a non-colonial enterprise and therefore morally superior in their aspirations. Furthermore, the hegemonic socialist-humanist discourse has hidden the negative dialectics of wealth and poverty between First World and Third World Jews behind a mystifying facade of egalitarianism. The Zionist mission of ending the Jewish exile from the "Promised Land" was never the beneficent enterprise portrayed by official discourse, since from the first decade of the twentieth century Arab-Jews were perceived as a source of cheap labor that could replace the dispossessed Palestinian fellahin (figure 42).[23] The "Jews in the form of Arabs"[24] thus could prevent any Palestinian declaration that the land belongs to those who work it and contribute to the Jewish national demographic needs. The Eurocentric projection of Middle Eastern Jews as coming to the "land of milk and honey" from desolate backwaters, from societies lacking all contact with scientific-technological civilization, once again set up an Orientalist rescue trope. Zionist discourse has cultivated the impression that Arab-Jewish culture before Zionism was static and passive and, like the fallow land of Palestine, as suggested by Edward Said, lying in wait for the impregnating infusion of European dynamism.[25] While presenting Palestine as an empty land to be transformed by Jewish labor, the Zionist "Founding Fathers" presented Arab-Jews as passive vessels to be shaped by the revivifying spirit of Promethean Zionism.

The Euro-Zionist problematic relation to the question of East and West has generated a deployment of opposing paradigms that often results in hysterical responses to any questioning of its projected "Western identity." Zionism viewed Europe both as ideal ego and as the signifier of ghettoes, persecutions, and Holocaust. Within this perspective, the "Diaspora Jew" was an extraterritorial, rootless wanderer, someone living "outside of history." Posited in gendered language as the masculine redeemer of the passive Diaspora Jew, the mythologized sabra simultaneously signified the destruction of the diasporic Jewish entity. The prototypical newly emerging Jew in Palestine—physically strong with blond hair and blue eyes; healthy looking and cleansed of all "Jewish inferiority complexes"; and a cultivator of the land—was conceived as an antithesis to the virtually anti-Semitic Zionist image of the "Diaspora Jew." The sabra prototype (figure 43), partly influenced by the Romantic ideals of German *Jugendkultur*, generated a

42 The path to modernization: Yeminis on the way to the Joint Transitional Camp,
Aden, 1949 (top); Moroccans entering housing project in Mitzpe Ramon, Israel,
1964 (bottom)

43 The *sabra* embraces the land: *Oded the Wanderer* (1933)

culture in which any expression of weakness came to be disdained as *galuti*, or that which belongs to the Diaspora. Zionism, in other words, viewed itself as an embodiment of European nationalist ideals to be realized outside Europe, in the East, and in relation to the pariahs of Europe, the Jews. Thus, the sabra was celebrated as eternal youth devoid of parents, as though born from a spontaneous generation of nature, as, for example, in Moshe Shamir's key nationalist novel of the 1948 generation *Bemo Yadav* (In His Own Hands), which introduces the hero as follows: "Elik was born from the sea." In this paradoxical, idiosyncratic version of the Freudian *Familienroman*, Euro-Zionist parents raised their children to see themselves as historical foundlings worthy of more dignified, romantic, and powerful progenitors. Zionism posited itself as an extension of Europe in the Middle East, carrying its Enlightenment banner of the civilizing mission.

If the West has been viewed ambivalently as the place of oppression to be liberated from as well as a kind of an object of desire to form a "normal" part of it, the East has also signified a contemporary ambivalence. On the one hand, is it a place associated with "backwardness," "underdevelopment," a land swamped, in the words of 1950s propaganda films, with "mosquitoes, scorpions, and Arabs." On the other hand, the East has symbolized solace, the return to geographical origins, and reunification with biblical history. The obsessive negation of the "Diaspora," which began with the Haskalah (European Jewish Enlightenment) and the return to the homeland of Zion, led at times to the exotic affirmation of Arab "primitiveness" as a desirable image to be appropriated by the native-born sabra. The Arab was projected as the incarnation of the ancient, the pre-exiled Jews, the Semite not yet corrupted by wanderings in exile, and therefore, to a certain extent, as the authentic Jew.[26] The Arab as presumably preserving archaic ways and rootedness in the land of the Bible, in contrast with the landless ghetto Jew, provoked a qualified identification with the Arab as a desired object of imitation for Zionist youth in Palestine/Eretz Israel and as a reunification with the remnant of the free and proud ancient Hebrew.

This projection, however, coexisted with a simultaneous denial of Palestine. The role of archaeology in Israeli culture, it should be pointed out, has been crucial in disinterring remnants of the biblical past of Palestine, at times enlisted in the political effort to demonstrate a historical right to the "land of Israel." In dramatic contrast to Jewish archaeology of the text,[27] this idea of physical archaeology as demonstrating a geography of identity carries with it the obverse notion of the physical homeland as text to be allegorically read, within Zionist hermeneutics, as a "deed to the land." Corollary to this is the notion of historical "strata" within a political geology. The deep stratum, in the literal and figurative sense, is associated with the Israeli Jews, while the surface level is associated with the Arabs, as a recent "superficial" historical element without millennial "roots." Since the Arabs are seen as "guests" in the land, their presence must be downplayed, much as the surface of the land has at times been "remodeled" to hide or bury remnants of Arab life and Palestinian villages, in certain instances, have been replaced with Israeli ones or completely erased. The linguistic, lexical expression of this digging into the land is the toponymic archaeology of place names. Some Arabic names of villages, it was discovered, were close to or based on the biblical Hebrew names; in some cases, therefore, Arabic names were replaced with old-new Hebrew ones.

PARTING WORLDS, SUBVERSIVE RETURNS

Yet despite the importance of the idea of return, it is no less important to see Zionist representation of Palestine in relation to other settlers' narratives. Palestine is linked to the Americas in more ways than would at first appear. The Columbus masternarrative prepared the ground for an enthusiastic reception of Zionist discourse within Euro-America. The Israeli-Palestinian conflict as a whole touches, I would argue, on some sensitive historical nerves within "America" itself. As a product of schizophrenic masternarratives—colonial settler state on the one hand, and anticolonial republic on the other—"America" has been subliminally more attuned to the Zionist than to the Palestinian nationalist discourse. Zionist discourse contains a liberatory narrative vis-à-vis Europe that in many ways is pertinent to the Puritans. The New World of the Middle East, like the New World of America, was concerned with creating a New Man. The image of the sabra as a new (Jewish) man evokes the American Adam. The American hero was celebrated as prelapsarian Adam, as a New Man emancipated from history (i.e., European history) before whom all the world and time lay available, much as the sabra was conceived as the antithesis of the "Old World" European Jew. In this sense, one might suggest an analogy between the cultural discourse about the innocent national beginning of America and that of Israel. The American Adam and the sabra masculinist archetypes implied not only their status as creators, blessed with the divine prerogative of naming the elements of the scene about them, but also their fundamental innocence. The notions of an American Adam and an Israeli sabra elided a number of crucial facts—notably, that there were other civilizations in the Promised Land; that the settlers were not creating "being from nothingness"; and that the settlers, in both cases, had scarcely jettisoned all their Old World cultural baggage, their deeply ingrained Eurocentric attitudes and discourses. Here the gendered metaphor of the "virgin land," present both in Zionist and American pioneer discourses, suggests that the land is implicitly available for defloration and fecundation. Assumed to lack owners, the land therefore becomes the property of its "discoverer" and cultivators, who transform the wilderness into a garden, those who "make the desert bloom."

In the case of Zionist discourse, the concept of "return to the motherland," as I have pointed out, suggests a double relation to the land, having to do with an ambivalent relation to the "East" as the place of Judaic origins and as the locus for implementing the "West." The sabra embodied the humanitarian and liberationist project of Zionism, carrying the same banner of the "civilizing mission" that European powers proclaimed during their surge into "found lands." The classical images of sabra pioneers as settlers on the Middle Eastern frontiers, fighting Indian-like Arabs, along with the reverberations of the early American biblical discourse encapsulated in such notions as "Adam," "(New) Canaan," and "Promised Land," have all facilitated the feeling of Israel as an extension of "us"—the United States. Furthermore, both the United States and Israel fought against Brit-

44 Repression of a Black Panthers' demonstration, Jerusalem (1971):
Photograph by Shimshon Wigoder

ish colonialism while also practicing colonial policies toward the indigenous peoples. Finally, I would argue for a triangular structural analogy by
which the Palestinians represent the aboriginal "Indians" of Euro-Israeli
discourse, while the Sephardim or Mizrahim, as imported cheap labor,
constitute the "blacks" of Israel.[28] (Taking their name from the American
movement, the Israeli "Black Panthers," for example, sabotaged the myth
of the melting pot by showing that there was in Israel not one but two Jewish communities—one white, one black; figure 44.) The manifest Palestinian refusal to play the assigned role of the presumably doomed "Indians"
of the transplanted (far) Western narrative has testified to an alternative.
The story of the Jewish victims of Zionism also remains to be heard.[29]

   The same historical process that dispossessed Palestinians of their property, lands, and national-political rights was intimately linked to the process that affected the dispossession of Arab-Jews from their property,
lands, and rootedness in Arab countries, as well as their uprootedness
from that history and culture within Israel itself.[30] But while Palestinians
have fostered the collective militancy of nostalgia in exile (be it *fil dakhel*,
under Israeli occupation, or *fil kharij*, under Syrian, Egyptian, American
passports or on the basis of laissez-passer), Arab-Jews, trapped in a no-exit
situation, have been forbidden to nourish memories of at least partially
belonging to the peoples across the river Jordan, across the mountains of
Lebanon, and across the Sinai desert and Suez Canal. The pervasive notion
of "one people" reunited in their ancient homeland actively disauthorizes

any affectionate memory of life before the State of Israel. Quincentennial events luxuriated in the landscapes, sounds, and smells of the lost Andalusian home, but silence muffled an even longer historical imaginary in Cairo, Baghdad, and Damascus, and hid an even more recent loss. For centuries, both Muslim and Jewish poets eulogized Andalusia by referring to the keys they persisted carrying in exile. Yet in contemporary Palestinian poetry, Andalusia is far from being only a closed chapter of Arab grandeur, for it allegorizes Palestine. In the words of Mahmoud Darwish's poem "Al Kamanjat (The Violins)": "The violins weep with the gypsies heading for Andalusia / the violins weep for the Arabs departing Andalusia. / The violins weep for a lost epoch that will not return / the violins weep for a lost homeland that could be regained." But the parallelism between Andalusia and Palestine stops precisely at the point of reclaiming a Palestinian future, for Andalusia remains in the past.

The 1992 discussions of expulsion brought out the "wandering Jew" motif as perennially displaced people. But the Jews of the Middle East and North Africa for the most part had stable, "non-wandering" lives in the Islamic world. As splendidly captured in *In an Antique Land*, the Sephardim or the Jews-within-Islam who moved within the regions of Asia and Africa, from the Mediterranean to the Indian Ocean, did so more for commercial, religious, or scholarly purposes than for reasons of persecution. Ironically, the major traumatic displacement took place in recent years when Arab-Jews were uprooted, dispossessed, and dislodged due to the collaboration between Israel and some of the Arab governments under the orchestration of Western colonial powers who termed their solution to the "question of Palestine" a "population exchange" (figure 45).[31] That no one asked either the Palestinians or the Arab-Jews whether they wished to be exchanged is yet another typical narrative of Third World histories of partition. Sephardim/Mizrahim who have managed to leave Israel, often in (an indirect) response to institutionalized racism there, have dislocated themselves yet again, this time to the United States, Europe, and Latin America. In a sudden historical twist, today it is to the Muslim Arab countries of their origins to which most Middle Eastern Jews cannot travel, let alone fantasize a return—the ultimate taboo.[32]

The cultural commonalities between Middle Eastern Jews and Muslims are a thorny reminder of the Middle Eastern/North African character of the majority of Jews in Israel today. Not surprisingly, quincentenary events in Europe, the Middle East, and the Americas have centered on the Spanishness of Sephardi culture (largely on Ladino or Judeo-Español language,

45 Like Arab, like Jew: A Yemeni woman in an Israeli transit camp (1949)

cuisine, and music) while marginalizing the fact that Jews in Iberia formed part of a larger Judeo-Islamic civilizational space of North Africa and the European Balkan area of the Ottoman Empire. Major Sephardi texts in philosophy, linguistics, poetry, and medicine were written in Arabic. They reflect specific Muslim influences as well as a strong sense of Jewish Arab cultural identity, seen especially in the development of the Judeo-Arab script used in religious correspondence between Jewish scholars across the regions of Islam, as well as in the emergence of some specific local Jewish-Arabic dialects.[33] The Jews of Iberia had come from the East and South of the Mediterranean—some with the Romans; others largely with the Muslims—and returned there when they fled the Inquisition. Over 70 percent returned to the regions of the Ottoman Empire, while the rest went to western Europe and the Americas.[34] Thus, a historiography that speaks of a pan-Jewish culture is often the same historiography that speaks of "Arab versus Jew" without acknowledging Arab-Jewish existence.

The erasure of the Arab dimension of Sephardim-Mizrahim has been crucial to the Zionist perspective since the Middle Easternness of Jews questions the very definitions and boundaries of the Euro-Israeli national project. Euro-Israel has ended up in a paradoxical situation in which its "Orientals" have had closer cultural and historical links to the presumed enemy—the "Arab"—than to the Ashkenazi Jews with whom they were coaxed and coerced into nationhood. The taboo around the Arabness of Sephardi history and culture is clearly manifested in Israeli academic and media attacks on Sephardi/Mizrahi intellectuals who refuse to define themselves simply as Israelis and who dare to assert their Arabness in the public sphere.[35] The Ashkenazi-Israeli anxiety about Sephardi-Mizrahi identity (expressed by both right and left) underlines that Sephardi Jews have represented a problematic entity for Euro-Israeli hegemony. Although Zionism collapses the Sephardim/Mizrahim and the Ashkenazim into a single people, at the same time the Mizrahi difference has destabilized Zionist claims that it represents a single Jewish people, premised not only on a common religious background but also on common nationality. The strong cultural and historical links that Middle Eastern Jews have shared with the Arab Muslim world—stronger in many respects than those they shared with the European Jews—threatened the conception of a homogeneous nation akin to those on which European nationalist movements were based. As an integral part of the topography, language, culture, and history of the Middle East, Mizrahim have also threatened the Euro-Israeli self-image that sees itself as a prolongation of Europe "in" the Middle East, but not "of" it.

Fearing an encroachment from the East on the West, the Israeli establishment attempted to repress the Middle Easternness of Jews as part of an effort to Westernize the Israeli nation and to mark clear borders of identity between Jews as Westerners and Arabs as Easterners. Arabness and Orientalness have been consistently stigmatized as evils to be uprooted, creating a situation in which Arab-Jews were urged to see Judaism and Zionism as synonyms and Jewishness and Arabness as antonyms. Thus, Arab-Jews were prodded to choose between anti-Zionist Arabness and a pro-Zionist Jewishness for the first time in history. Distinguishing the "evil" East (the Muslim Arab) from the "good East" (the Jewish Arab), Israel has taken upon itself the "cleansing" of Arab-Jews of their Arabness and redeeming them from their "primal sin" of belonging to the Orient. This conceptualization of East and West has important implications in this age of the "peace process," since it avoids the inherent question of the majority of the population within Israel being from the Middle East—Palestinians citizens of Israel as well as Mizrahi-Sephardi Jews. For peace as it is defined now does not entail a true democracy in terms of adequate representation of these populations and in terms of changing the educational, cultural, and political orientation within the State of Israel.

The leitmotif of Zionist texts was the cry to be a "normal civilized nation," without the presumably myriad "distortions" and forms of pariahdom typical of the *gola* (Diaspora), of the state of being a non-nation-state.

The *Ostjuden*, perennially marginalized by Europe, realized their desire to become Europe, ironically, in the Middle East, this time on the back of their own *Ostjuden*, the Eastern Jews. The Israeli establishment therefore has made systematic efforts to suppress Sephardi-Mizrahi cultural identity. The Zionist establishment, since its early encounter with Palestinian (Sephardi) Jews, has systematically attempted to eradicate the Middle Easternness of those other Jews—for example, by marginalizing their histories in school curricula and by rendering Mizrahi cultural production and grassroots political activities invisible in the media. However, Mizrahi popular culture, despite its obvious shifts since the partition of Palestine, has clearly manifested its vibrant intertextual dialogue with Arab, Turkish, Iranian, and Indian popular cultures. Oriental Arabic music produced by Mizrahim—at times in collaboration with Israeli Palestinians—is consumed by Palestinians in Israel and across the borders in the Arab world, often without being labeled as originating in Israel. This creativity is partly nourished through an enthusiastic consumption of Jordanian, Lebanese, and Egyptian television programs, films, and Arabic video-music performances, which rupture the Euro-Israeli public sphere in a kind of subliminal transgression of a forbidden nostalgia. In fact, recent musical groups such as the Moroccan Israeli Sfatayim (Lips) traveled to Morocco to produce a music video sung in Moroccan Arabic against the scenery of the cities and villages that Moroccan Jews have left behind, just as Israeli-born Iraqi singers such as Ya'aqub Nishawi sing old and contemporary Iraqi music. This desire for "return of the Diaspora" ironically evokes an attitude that reverses the biblical expression of nostalgia for Zion. Now it becomes: "By the waters of Zion, where we sat down, and there we wept, when we remembered Babylon."[36]

Arab Muslim historiography, meanwhile, has ironically echoed the logic of Zionist paradigms, looking only superficially into the culture and identity of Arab-Jews both in the Arab world and, more recently, within Israel. Thus, Ghosh, the visiting Indian anthropologist, notices what is otherwise unnoticeable: that in the Geniza's home country, Egypt, "nobody took the slightest notice of its dispersal. In some profound sense, the Islamic high culture of Masr [Arabic for Egypt] has never really noticed, never found a place for the parallel history the Geniza represented, and its removal only confirmed a particular vision of the past. . . . Now it was Masr, which had sustained the Geniza for almost a millennium, that was left with no traces of its riches: not a single scrap or shred of paper to remind her of the aspect of her past. It was as though the borders that were to divide Palestine several decades later had already been drawn, through time rather than territory, to allocate a choice of Histories."[37] The amnesia of this recent history in most contemporary Arab culture has fed into an Israeli and Arab refusal of the hybrid, the in-between. Even Israeli Arab-Jews, such as the Iraqi Israeli writer Samir Naqash, who still writes his novels in Arabic, are "rejected" from membership in the Arab geocultural region seen simply as "Israeli." The "Jews of Islam" thus exist today as part of a historiography in which their relations to the Arab Islamic world exist only in the past tense. Colonial partitions and nationalist ideologies have left little room for the inconvenient "minority" of Arab-Jews. Even the Geniza itself, presumably rescued from obscurity and decay at the hands of its own producers, has been used to mobilize a nationalist narrative in which every text or fragmented document is to be deciphered for a Zionist transformation "*mi-gola le-geoola* (from Diaspora to redemption)."

The historiographical work of Euro-Jewish scholars such as S. D. Goitein and E. Strauss might have facilitated the entry of an Indian anthropologist such as Ghosh into the Indian Ocean world of the twelfth-century Tunisian Jewish trader Abraham Ben-Yiju, who, unlike Ghosh, traveled in an era when "Europe" did not dominate the channels of scholarly communication. But the Geniza scholarship was shaped and used within a context of Zionist Enlightenment readings of the otherized Jews of the Levant—the very same Jews whose cultural practices made possible the Geniza scholarship of Western academic institutions. Within these asymmetrical power relations, Euro-Jewish scholars infused the colonized history with national meaning and telos, while, ironically, Arab-Jews were simultaneously being displaced and, in Israel, subjected to a school system in which Jewish history textbooks featured barely a single chapter on their history (figure 46).

Today, Mizrahim inhabit the pages of Euro-Israeli sociological and anthropological accounts as maladjusted criminals and superstitious exotics, firmly detached from Arab history that looms only as deformed vestiges in the lives of Israelis of Asian and African origins. Sociology and anthropology detect such traces of underdevelopment, while national historiography tells the story of the past as a moral tale full of national purpose. Such scholarly bifurcation cannot possibly account for an Arab-Jewish identity that is at once past and present, here and there. Perhaps it is not a coincidence that the author of *In an Antique Land*, a hybrid of anthropology and history, ends up splitting the subjects of ethnography and historiography: the first focusing on present-day Egyptian Muslims, and the second on past Arab-Jews. At the end of his book, Ghosh somehow ends his narrative

46 Meir Gal, "Nine Out of Four Hundred" (1997): The title refers to the number of pages dedicated to Mizrahim in Jewish history textbooks in Israel

at the very point where the subject of his historiography could have turned into a subject of his ethnography. The anthropological accounts of Ghosh's visits to Egypt are paralleled by the historiographical chronicle of Ben-Yiju's travel within the Judeo-Islamic world. On his final trip to Egypt, Ghosh notices Arab-Jewish pilgrims from Israel coming to Egypt to visit the tomb of the cabbalist mystic Sidi Abu-Hasira, a site holy for both Muslims and Jews, with many similar festivities. Yet for one reason or another, he never meets them. Perhaps Ghosh's missed rendezvous, his packing up and leaving Egypt precisely as the Arab-Jews visit Abu-Haseira's holy site, is revelatory of the difficulties of representing a multi-diasporic identity, the dangers of border crossing in the war zone. Arab-Jews thus continue to "travel" in historical narratives, inextricable from a legendary Islamic civilization. As the postcolonial story unfolds, however, Arab-Jews suddenly cease to exist, as though they have reached their final destination—the State of Israel—and nothing more needs to be said.

In contrast to the negatively connoted term "Orientals" (in the United States), in Israel, "Orientals (Mizrahim)" signifies radical politics, evoking a common experience shared by all Asian and African Jews in Israel, despite their different origins. On the part of radical Sephardi movements, this new term also suggests a resistant discourse that calls for linkages to the East as opposed to the hegemonic discourse of "we of the West." The names of the 1980s movements East for Peace and the Oriental Front in Israel; Perspectives Judeo-Arabes in France; and World Organization of Jews from Islamic Countries in the United States point to the assertion of the past and a future interwovenness with the East. Mizrahim, along with Palestinians within Israel proper (Israeli Palestinians), compose the majority of the citizens of a state that has rigidly imposed an anti–Middle Eastern agenda. In a first-of-its-kind meeting with Palestinians held at the symbolic site of Toledo, Spain, in 1989, Sephardi/Arab-Jewish representatives insisted that a comprehensive peace would mean more than settling political borders: It would require the erasure of the East-West cultural borders between Israel and Palestine and the remapping of national and ethnic-racial identities against the deep scars of colonizing partitions. A critical examination of national histories may thus open a cultural space for working against taboo memories and fostering diasporic visions.

NOTES

Parts of this essay appeared in preliminary form in *Middle East Report*, no. 178 (September–October 1992), and *Third Text*, no. 21 (Winter 1992–93). An earlier version was included in Keith Ansell-Pearson, Benita Parry, and Judith Squires, eds., *Cultural Readings of Imperialism: Edward Said and the Gravity of History* (London: Lawrence and Wishart, 1997).

1 Amitav Ghosh, *In an Antique Land* (New York: Alfred A. Knopf, 1992), 89–94. Some of my comments here were made in a public conversation with Ghosh dedicated to his book. The conversation also included Tim Mitchell and was organized and moderated by Kamala Visweswaran and Parag Amladi, CUNY TV, March 1994.

2 Ghosh, *In an Antique Land*, 85, 93

3 See S. D. Goitein, *A Mediterranean Society*, revised and edited by Jacob Lassner (Berkeley: University of California Press, 1999).

4 I thank Robert Stam for allowing me to use some "shared territory" from our book *Unthinking Eurocentrism: Multiculturalism and the Media* (London: Routledge, 1994).

5 See, for example, "Green Card" artwork by Inigo Manglano-Ovalle.

6 As quoted in Jean Comby, "1492: Le Choc des Cultures et l'Evagelization du Monde," *Dossiers de1'episcopat Francais*, no. 14 (October 1990).

7 See Charles Duff, *The Truth about Columbus* (New York: Random House, 1936).

8 Ghosh, *In an Antique Land*, 81.

9 Jan Pieterse makes the more general point that many of the themes of European imperialism traced antecedents to the European and Mediterranean

sphere. Thus the theme of civilization against barbarism was a carry over from Greek and Roman antiquity; the theme of Christianity against pagans was the keynote of European expansion culminating in the Crusades; and the Christian theme of "mission" was fused with "civilization" in the *mission civilisatrice.* See Jan P. Nederveen Pieterse, *Empire and Emancipation* (London: Pluto, 1990), 240.

10 For details, see Jan Carew, *Fulcrums of Change: Origins of Racism in the Americas and Other Essays* (Trenton, N.J.: Africa World Press, 1988).

11 The indigenous peoples of the Americas similarly were officially protected from massacres by the throne only once they converted to Christianity.

12 The presumed "godlessness" of the indigenous people became a pretext for enslavement and dispossession. While Jews and Muslims were diabolized, the indigenous Americans were accused of devil worship. The brutalities practiced by official Christianity toward Jews and Muslims have to be seen therefore on the same continuum as the forced conversions of indigenous peoples of the Americas who, like the Jews and Muslims in Christian Spain, were obliged to feign allegiance to Catholicism.

13 Pat Kossan, "Jewish Roots of Hispanics-Delicate Topic," *Phoenix Gazette,* 14 April 1992, sec. C.

14 Moors who converted to Christianity.

15 Spanish Muslim culture in Christian Spain, like Sephardi Jewish culture, was expressed in Spanish, as well.

16 On that history, see, for example, W. Montgomery Watt and Pierre Cachia, *A History of Islamic Spain* (Edinburgh: Edinburgh University Press, 1977); James T. Monroe, *Hispano-Arabic Poetry* (Berkeley: University of California Press, 1974).

17 This picture of an ageless and relentless oppression and humiliation ignores the fact that, on the whole, Jews of Islam—a minority among several other religious and ethnic communities in the Middle East and North Africa—lived relatively comfortably within Arab Muslim society.

18 For a more complex analysis, see, for example, Ilan Halevi, *A History of the Jews: Ancient and Modern* (London: Zed Books, 1987); Maxime Rodinson, *Cult, Ghetto, and State: The Persistence of the Jewish Question* (London: Al Saqi Books, 1983); Ammiel Alacaly, *After Jews and Arabs: Remaking Levantine Culture* (Minneapolis: University of Minnesota Press, 1993).

19 See Ella Shohat, "Sephardim in Israel: Zionism from the Standpoint of its Jewish Victims" *Social Text* 19–20 (Fall 1988).

20 For more on the question of East and West in Zionist discourse, see Ella Shohat, *Israeli Cinema: East/West and the Politics of Representation* (Austin: University of Texas Press, 1989).

21 In the early days of Zionism, other "empty" territories were proposed for Jewish settlement; typically they were located in the colonized world. However, one of Herzl's famous proposals for settlement—Uganda—created a crisis for the Zionist Congress known as the Uganda crisis.

22 See Maxime Rodinson, *Israel: A Colonial-Settler State?* Translated by David Thorstad. (New York: Monad Press, 1973).

23 See Yoseff Meir, *Ha-Tnu'a ha-Tzionit ve-Yehudei Teman* (The Zionist Move-

ment and the Jews of Yemen) (Tel Aviv: Sifriat Afikim, 1982); G. N. Giladi, *Discord in Zion: Conflict between Ashkenazi and Sephardi Jews in Israel* (London: Scorpion Publishing, 1990).

24 The phrase was already in use in the first decade of this century by the early engineers (such as Shmuel Yaveneli) of "Aliya" of Jews from the regions of the Ottoman Empire. See Meir, *The Zionist Movement and the Jews of Yemen*.

25 See Edward Said, *The Question of Palestine* (New York: Times Books, 1979).

26 For a similar discourse addressed to bedouins, see Smadar Lavie, *The Poetics of Military Occupation: Mezina Allegories of Bedouin Identity under Israeli and Egyptian Rule* (Berkeley: University of California Press, 1990).

27 See, for example, Jacques Derrida, "Edmund Jabès and the Question of the Book," in *Writing and Difference*, trans. Alan Bass (Chicago: University of Chicago Press, 1978), 64–78; George Steiner, "Our Homeland, the Text," *Salmagundi* 66 (Winter–Spring 1985): 4–25.

28 In recent years, the term *shhorim* (blacks) has also applied to the Orthodox religious Ashkenazi codes of dressing. I should point out that the sartorial codes favoring dark colors of centuries-ago Poland were never part of Judeo Levantine culture. And over the past decade, since the massive arrival of Ethiopian Jews, the pejorative term "blacks," or *kushim*, has been used against Ethiopian Jews.

29 I specifically address the relationship between the Palestinian and the Sephardi-Mizrahi questions vis-à-vis Zionism in my essay on Sephardi identity in Israel, "Zionism from the Standpoint of Its Jewish Victims," *Social Text* 19–20 (Fall 1988). The title of that article refers to Edward Said's "Zionism from the Standpoint of Its Victims," *Social Text* 1 (1979), which also appeared as a chapter in his book *The Question of Palestine* (New York: Vintage Books, 1992). Both essays have been republished in Anne McClintock, Aamir Mufti, and Ella Shohat, eds., *Dangerous Liaisons: Gender, Nation and Postcolonial Perspectives* (Minneapolis: University of Minnesota Press, 1997).

30 Neither Palestinians nor Arab-Jews have been compensated for their lost property.

31 See, for example, Abbas Shiblak, *The Lure of Zion: The Case of the Iraqi Jews* (London: Al Saqi Books, 1986); Giladi, *Discord in Zion*.

32 Thus, for example, when Shimon Ballas wrote the novel *Vehu Aher* (And He Is an Other) (Tel Aviv: Zmora Bitan, 1991), which partially concerned an Iraqi Jew who remained in Iraq after the dislodging of his community and converted to Islam, he was vehemently attacked in a rush to censor the imaginary.

33 Jewish Arabic language was written in Hebrew script, but the script differs from the contemporary Hebrew script that became a lingua franca after the revival of modern Hebrew and its spread through Zionist institutions. Young Sephardim have largely lost familiarity with this script. Today, Sephardi prayer texts are printed in the common (Ashkenazi) script, even when the text is in Judeo-Arabic.

34 Most cultural expression in the Arab world, needless to say, was not in Ladino/Español. In fact, it makes one wonder whether this widespread misrepresentation of Arab-Jewish history led Bharati Mukerjee, author of *The Middleman and Other Stories*, to have her Iraqi Jewish protagonist Alfie Judah say that "[speaking] a form of Spanish" in "old Baghdad" was good preparation for the Southwest."

35 For example, attacks on Ballas after the publication of *And He Is an Other* and on myself after the publication of my book *Israeli Cinema: East/West and the Politics of Representation* in Hebrew (*Ha-Kolno'a ha-Israeli: Historia ve-Idiologia* [Israeli Cinema: History and Ideology] [Tel Aviv: Breirot, 1991]).

36 See Ella Shohat, "Dislocated Identities: Reflections of an Arab-Jew," published in *Movement Research: Performance Journal* 5 (fall–winter 1992).

37 Ghosh, *In an Antique Land*, 95.

NOTES ON THE "POST-COLONIAL"

The academic opposition to the Gulf War mobilized a number of familiar terms—"imperialism," "neocolonialism," "neo-imperialism"—in a verbal counterstrike against the New World Order. But conspicuously absent from the discussion was the term "postcolonial," even from speeches made by its otherwise prominent advocates. Given the extraordinary circulation of the term at recent academic conferences and in publications and curricular reformulations, this sudden invisibility was somewhat puzzling. Was this absence sheer coincidence? Or is there something about the term "postcolonial" that does not lend itself to a geopolitical critique, or to a critique of the dominant media's Gulf War macro-narratives? When lines drawn in the sand still haunt Third World geographies, it is urgent to ask how we can chart the meaning of the "postcolonial." It is from my particular position as an academic Arab-Jew whose cultural topographies are (dis)located in Iraq, Israel/Palestine, and the United States that I would like to explore some of the theoretical and political ambiguities of the "postcolonial."

Despite its dizzying multiplicity of positionalities, postcolonial theory curiously has not addressed the politics of location of the very term "post-colonial." In what follows, I propose to begin an interrogation of the term "postcolonial," raising questions about its ahistorical and universalizing deployments and its potentially depoliticizing implications. The rising institutional endorsement of the term "postcolonial" and of postcolonial studies as an emergent discipline (evident in Modern Language Association job announcements calling for specialization in "postcolonial literature") is fraught with ambiguities. My recent experience as a member of the multicultural international studies committee at one of the branches of the City University of New York illustrates some of these ambiguities. In response to our proposal, the generally conservative members of the college curriculum committee strongly resisted any language that invoked issues such as "imperialism and Third Worldist critique," "neocolonialism and resisting cultural practices," and "the geopolitics of cultural exchange." They were visibly relieved, however, at the sight of the word "postcolonial." Only the diplomatic gesture of relinquishing the terrorizing terms "imperialism" and "neocolonialism" in favor of the pastoral "postcolonial" guaranteed approval.

My intention is not merely to anatomize the term "postcolonial" semantically, but also to situate it geographically, historically, and institutionally while raising doubts about its political agency. The question at stake is this: Which perspectives are being advanced in the "postcolonial?" For what purposes? And with what slippages? In this brief discussion, my point is neither to examine the variety of provocative writings produced under the rubric postcolonial theory, nor simply to essentialize the term "postcolonial." Rather, it is to unfold the term's slippery political significations, which occasionally escape the clearly oppositional intentions of its theoretical practitioners. I will argue for a more limited, historically and theoretically specific usage of the term "postcolonial," one that situates it in a relational context vis-à-vis other (equally problematic) categories.

The "postcolonial" did not emerge to fill an empty space in the language of political-cultural analysis. On the contrary, its wide adoption during the late 1980s coincided with and dependend on the eclipse of an older paradigm—that of the "Third World." The terminological shift indicates the professional prestige and theoretical aura the issues have acquired, in contrast to the more activist aura once enjoyed by "Third World" within progressive academic circles. Coined in the '50s in France by analogy to the Third Estate (the commoners, all those who were neither the nobility nor the clergy), the term "Third World" gained international currency in both academic and political contexts, particularly in reference to anticolonial nationalist movements of the '50s through the '70s, as well as to the political-economic analysis of dependency theory and world system theory (André Gunder Frank, Immanuel Wallerstein, Samir Amin).

The past decade has witnessed a terminological crisis around the concept of the Third World. The three-worlds theory is indeed, as many critics have suggested, highly problematic.[1] For one thing, the historical processes of the past three decades offered a number of very complex and politically ambiguous developments. The period of so-called Third World euphoria—a brief moment in which it seemed that First World leftists and Third World guerrillas would walk arm in arm toward global revolution— has given way to the collapse of the Soviet communist model, the crisis of existing socialisms, the frustration of the hoped-for tricontinental revolution (with Ho Chi Minh, Frantz Fanon, and Che Guevara as talismanic figures), the realization that the wretched of the earth are not unanimously revolutionary (or necessarily allies to one another), and the recognition that international geopolitics and the global economic system have obliged even socialist regimes to make some kind of peace with transnational capitalism. And despite the broad patterns of geopolitical hegemony, power relations in the Third World are also dispersed and contradictory. The First World–Third World struggle, furthermore, takes place not only between nations (India-Pakistan, Iraq-Kuwait), but also within nations, with the constantly changing relations between dominant and subaltern groups, settler and indigenous populations. It also takes place in a situation marked by waves of post-independence immigrations to First World countries (Britain, France, Germany, and the United States) and to more prosperous Third World countries (the Gulf states.) The notion of the three worlds, in short, flattens heterogeneities, masks contradictions, and elides differences.

This crisis in "Third World" thinking helps explain the current enthusiasm for the term "postcolonial," a new designation for critical discourses that thematize issues emerging from colonial relations and their aftermath and covering a long historical span (including the present.) Dropping the suffix "-ism" from "postcolonialism," the adjective "postcolonial" is frequently attached to the nouns "theory," "space," "condition," and "intellectual," often substituting for the adjective "Third World" in relation to the noun "intellectual." The qualifier "Third World," by contrast, more frequently accompanies the nouns "nations," "countries," and "peoples."

More recently, "the postcolonial" has been transformed into a noun, used both in the singular and the plural ("postcolonials"), designating the subjects of the "postcolonial condition."[2] The final consecration of the term came with the erasure of the hyphen. Often buttressed by the theoretically connoted substantive "postcoloniality," the "postcolonial" is largely visible in Anglo-American academic (cultural) studies in publications of discursive-cultural analyses inflected by poststructuralism.[3]

Echoing "postmodernity," "postcoloniality" marks a contemporary state, situation, condition, or epoch.[4] The prefix "post-," then, aligns "postcolonialism" with a series of other "posts"—"poststructuralism," "postmodernism," "post-Marxism," "post-feminism," "post-deconstructionism"— all of which share the notion of a movement beyond. Yet while these "posts" refer largely to the supercession of outmoded philosophical, aesthetic, and political theories, the "postcolonial" implies both going beyond anticolonial nationalist theory and a movement beyond a specific point in history: that of colonialism and Third World nationalist struggles. In that sense, the prefix "post-" aligns the "postcolonial" with another genre of "posts": "postwar," "post–Cold War," "post-independence," "postrevolution," all of which underline a passage into a new period and a closure of a certain historical event or age, officially stamped with dates. Although periodizations and the relationship between theories of an era and the practices that constitute that era always form contested terrains, it seems to me that the two genres of the "post" are nonetheless distinct in their referential emphasis, the former on disciplinary advances characteristic of intellectual history, and the second on the strict chronologies of history *tout court*. This unarticulated tension between the philosophical and the historical teleologies in the "postcolonial," I would argue, partially underlies some of the conceptual ambiguities of the term.

Since the "post" in "postcolonial" suggests "after" the demise of colonialism, it is imbued, quite apart from its users' intentions, with an ambiguous spatio-temporality. Spreading from India into Anglo-American academic contexts, the "postcolonial" tends to be associated with Third World countries that gained independence after World War Two. However, it also refers to the Third World diasporic circumstances of the past four decades —from forced exile to "voluntary" immigration—within First World metropolises. In some postcolonial texts, such as *The Empire Writes Back: Theory and Practice in Post-Colonial Literatures*, the authors expand the term "postcolonial" to include all English literary productions by societies affected by colonialism:

The literatures of African countries, Australia, Bangladesh, Canada, Caribbean countries, India, Malasia, Malta, New Zealand, Pakistan, Singapore, South Pacific Island countries, and Sri Lanka are all post-colonial literatures. The literature of the USA should also be placed in this category. Perhaps because of its current position of power, and the neo-colonizing role it has played, its postcolonial nature has not been generally recognized. But its relationship with the metropolitan centre as it evolved over the last two centuries has been paradigmatic for post-colonial literature everywhere. What each of these literatures has in common beyond their special and distinctive regional characteristics is that they emerged in their present form out of the experience of colonization and asserted themselves by foregrounding the tension with the imperial power, and by emphasizing their differences from the assumptions of the imperial centre. It is this which makes them distinctively post-colonial.[5]

This problematic formulation collapses very different national-racial formations—the United States, Australia, and Canada, on the one hand, and Nigeria, Jamaica, and India, on the other—as equally "postcolonial." Positioning Australia and India in relation to an imperial center simply because both were colonies, for example, equates the relations of the colonized white settlers to the Europeans at the "center" with that of the colonized indigenous populations to the Europeans. It also assumes that white settler states and emerging Third World nations broke away from the "center" in the same way. Similarly, white Australians and aboriginal Australians are placed in the same "periphery," as though they were co-habitatants vis-à-vis the "center." The critical differences between Europe's genocidal oppression of Aborigines in Australia, indigenous peoples of the Americas, and Afro-diasporic communities, *and* Europe's domination of European elites in the colonies are leveled with an easy stroke of the "post." The term "postcolonial" in this sense masks the white settlers' colonialist-racist policies toward indigenous peoples not only before independence but also after the official break from the imperial center, while also de-emphasizing neocolonial global positionings of First World settler states.

I am not suggesting that this expanded use of the "postcolonial" is typical or paradigmatic.[6] The phrase "post-colonial society" might equally evoke Third World nation-states after independence. However, the disorienting space of the "postcolonial" generates odd couplings of the "post" and particular geographies, blurring the assignment of perspectives. Does the "post" indicate the perspective and location of the ex-colonized (Algerian), the ex-colonizer (French), the ex-colonial settler (*Pied Noir*), or the displaced hybrid in First World metropolitans (Algerian in France)? Since the experience of colonialism and imperialism is shared, albeit asymmetrically, by (ex-)colonizer and (ex-)colonized, it becomes an easy move to apply the "post" also to First World European countries. Since most of the world is now living after the period of colonialism, the "postcolonial" can easily become a universalizing category that neutralizes significant geopolitical differences between France and Algeria, Britain and Iraq, or the United States and Brazil, since they are all living in a "postcolonial epoch." This inadvertent effacement of perspectives, I should add, results in a curious ambiguity in scholarly work. While colonial discourse refers to the discourse produced by colonizers in both the colony and the motherland and, at times, to its contemporary discursive manifestations in literature and mass-mediated culture, "postcolonial discourse" does not refer to colonialist discourse after the end of colonialism. Rather, it evokes the contemporary theoretical writings, placed in both the First World and the Third World generally on the left and that attempt to transcend the (presumed) binarisms of Third Worldist militancy.

Apart from its dubious spatiality, the "postcolonial" renders a problematic temporality. First, the lack of historical specificity in the "post" leads to a collapsing of diverse chronologies. Colonial settler states such as those found in the Americas, Australia, New Zealand, and South Africa gained their independence, for the most part, in the eighteenth century and nineteenth century. Most countries in Africa and Asia, in contrast, gained independence in the twentieth century, some in the 1930s (Iraq), others in the 1940s (India, Lebanon), and still others in the 1960s (Algeria, Senegal) and 1970s (Angola, Mozambique), while others have yet to achieve it. When exactly, then, does the "postcolonial" begin? Which region is privileged in such a beginning? What are the relationships between these diverse beginnings? The vague starting point of the "postcolonial" makes certain differentiations difficult. It equates early independence won by settler colonial states, in which Europeans formed their new nation-states in non-European territories at the expense of indigenous populations, with that of nation-states whose indigenous populations struggled for independence against Europe but won it, for the most part, with the twentieth century collapse of European empires.

If one formulates the "post" in the "postcolonial" in relation to Third Worldist nationalist struggles of the 1950s and 1960s, then, what time frame would apply to contemporary anticolonial and antiracist struggles carried out under the banner of national and racial oppression—for example, for Palestinian writers such as Sahar Khalifeh and Mahmoud Darwish, who write contemporaneously with "postcolonial" writers? Should one suggest that they are pre-"postcolonial"? The unified temporality of "post-coloniality" risks reproducing the colonial discourse of an allochronic other, living in another time, still lagging behind us—the genuine postcolonials. The globalizing gesture of the "postcolonial condition," or "postcoloniality," downplays multiplicities of location and temporality, as well as the possible discursive and political linkages betweeen "postcolonial" theories and contemporary anticolonial or anti-neocolonial struggles and discourses. In other words, contemporary anticolonial and anti-neocolonial resistant discourses from Central America and the Middle East to Southern Africa and the Philippines cannot be theoretically dismissed as epigons, as a mere repetition of the all too familiar discourses of the '50s and '60s. Despite their partly shared discourses with Third World nationalism, these contemporary struggles also must be historicized, analyzed in a present-day context, when the "nonaligned" discourse of revolutions is no longer in the air. Such an approach would transcend the implicit suggestion of a temporal "gap" between "postcolonial" and the pre-"postcolonial" discourses, as exemplified in the mélange of resistant discourses and struggles in the Intifada.[7] What has to be negotiated, then, is the relationship of difference and sameness, rupture and continuity.

Since on one level the "post" signifies "after," it potentially inhibits forceful articulations of what one might call "neo-coloniality." Formal independence for colonized countries has rarely meant the end of First World hegemony. Egypt's formal independence in 1923 did not prevent the European, especially British, domination that provoked the 1952 revolution. Anwar Sadat's opening to the Americans and the Camp David Accords in the 1970s were perceived by Arab intellectuals as a reversion to pre-Nasser imperialism, as was Egyptian collaboration with the United States during the Gulf War.[8] The purpose of the Carter Doctrine was to partially protect perennial U.S. oil interests (*our* oil) in the Gulf, which, with the help of petro-Islamicist regimes, have sought to control any force that might pose a threat.[9] In Latin America, similarly, formal "creole" independence did not prevent Monroe Doctrine–style military interventions or Anglo-American free-trade hegemony. This process sets the history of Central America and South America and the Caribbean apart from the rest of the colonial settler states, for despite shared historical origins with North America, including the genocide of the indigenous population, the enslavement of Africans, and a multiracial and multiethnic composition, these regions have been subjected to political and economic structural domination, on some levels more severe, paradoxically, than that of recently independent Third World countries such as Libya and even India. Not accidentally, Mexican intellectuals and independent labor unions have excoriated the Gringostroika of the recent Trade Liberalization Treaty.[10] Formal independence did not obviate the need for Cuban-style or Nicaraguan-style revolutions, or for the Independista movement in Puerto Rico. The term "revolution," once popular in the Third World context, specifically assumed a post-colonial moment initiated by official independence, but whose content had been a suffocating neocolonial hegemony.

The term "postcolonial" carries with it the implication that colonialism is now a matter of the past, undermining colonialism's economic, political, and cultural deformative traces in the present. The "postcolonial" inadvertently glosses over the fact that global hegemony, even in the post–cold war era, persists in forms other than overt colonial rule. As a signifier of a new historical epoch, the term "postcolonial," when compared with neocolonialism, comes equipped with little evocation of contemporary power relations. It lacks a political content that can account for 1980s- and 1990s-style U.S. militaristic involvements in Granada, Panama, and Kuwait-Iraq, and for the symbiotic links between U.S. political and economic interests and those of local elites. In certain contexts, furthermore, racial and national oppressions reflect clear colonial patterns—for example, the oppression of blacks by Anglo-Dutch Europeans in South Africa and in the Americas and the oppression of Palestinians and Middle Eastern Jews by Euro-Israel. The "postcolonial" leaves no space, finally, for the struggles of Aborigines in Australia and indigenous peoples throughout the Americas —in other words, of Fourth World peoples dominated by both First World multinational corporations and by Third World nation-states.

The hegemonic structures and conceptual frameworks generated over the past five hundred years cannot be vanquished by waving the magic wand of the "postcolonial." The 1992 unification of Europe, for example, strengthens cooperation among ex-colonizing countries such as Britain, France, Germany, and Italy against illegal immigration, practicing stricter border patrol against infiltration by diverse Third World peoples: Algerians, Tunisians, Egyptians, Pakistanis, Sri Lankans, Indians, Turks, Senegalese, Malians, and Nigerians. The colonial masternarrative, meanwhile, is being triumphantly restaged. Millions of dollars are poured into international events planned for the quincentenary of Columbus's so-called voyages of discovery, climaxing in the Grand Regatta, a fleet of tall ships from forty countries leaving from Spain and arriving in New York Harbor for U.S. Independence Day, the Fourth of July. At the same time, an anticolonial narrative is being performed via view-from-the-shore projects, the Native American commemorations of annihilated communities throughout the United States and the American continent, and plans for setting up blockades at the arrival of the replicas of Columbus's caravels as they sail into U.S. ports. What, then, is the meaning of "postcoloniality" when certain structural conflicts persist? Despite different historical contexts, the conflict between the Native American claim to the land as a sacred and communal trust and the Euro-American view of land as alienable property remains structurally the same. How, then, does one negotiate sameness and difference within the framework of a "postcolonial" whose "post" emphasizes rupture and deemphasizes sameness?

Contemporary cultures are marked by the tension between the official end of direct colonial rule and its presence and regeneration through hegemonizing neocolonialism within the First World and toward the Third World, often channeled through the nationalist patriarchal elites. The "colonial" in the "postcolonial" tends to be relegated to the past and marked with a closure—an implied temporal border that undermines a potential oppositional thrust. For whatever the philosophical connotations of the "post" as an ambiguous locus of continuities and discontinuities,[11] its denotation of "after"—the teleological lure of the "post"—evokes a celebratory clearing of a conceptual space that on one level conflicts with the notion of "neo."

The "neocolonial," like the "postcolonial," also suggests continuities and discontinuities, but its emphasis is on the new modes and forms of the old colonialist practices, not on a "beyond." Although one can easily imagine the "postcolonial" traveling into Third World countries (more likely via the Anglo-American academy than via India), the "postcolonial" has little currency in African, Middle Eastern, and Latin American intellectual circles, except occasionally in the restricted historical sense of the period immediately following the end of colonial rule. Perhaps it is the less intense experience of neocolonialism, accompanied by the strong sense of relatively unthreatened multitudes of cultures, languages, and ethnicities in India, that allowed for the recurrent usage of the prefix "post-" over that of the "neo-." Now that debt-ridden India, where "postcolonial discourse" has flourished, has had to place itself under the tutelage of the International Monetary Fund, and now that its nonaligned foreign policy is giving way to political and economic cooperation with the United States, one wonders whether the term "neocolonial" will become more pervasive than "postcolonial."[12]

The "postcolonial" also forms a critical locus for moving beyond anticolonial nationalist modernizing narratives that inscribe Europe as an object of critique toward a discursive analysis and historiography that addresses decentered multiplicities of power relations (for example, between colonized women and men, or between colonized peasantry and the bourgeoisie). The significance of such intellectual projects stands in ironic contrast to the term "postcolonial" itself, which linguistically reproduces, once again, the centrality of the colonial narrative. The "postcolonial" implies a narrative of progression in which colonialism remains the central point of reference in a march of time that is arranged neatly from the "pre" to the "post" but that leaves ambiguous its relation to new forms of colonialism—that is, neocolonialism.

Considering the term "postcolonial" in relation to other terms, such as "neocolonial" and "post-independence," allows for mutual illumination of the concepts. Although "neocolonial," like "postcolonial," implies a passage, it has the advantage of emphasizing a repetition with difference, a regeneration of colonialism through other means. The term "neocolonialism" usefully designates broad relations of geo-economic hegemony. When examined in relation to "neocolonialism," the term "postcolonial" undermines a critique of contemporary colonialist structures of domination more available through the repetition and revival of the "neo." The term "post-independence," meanwhile, invokes an achieved history of resistance, shifting the analytical focus to the emergent nation-state. In this sense, the term "post-independence," precisely because it implies a nation-state telos, provides expanded analytical space for confronting such explosive issues as religion, ethnicity, patriarchy, gender, and sexual orientation, none of which can be reduced to epiphenomena of colonialism and neocolonialism. Whereas "postcolonial" suggests a distance from colonialism, "post-independence" celebrates the nation-state, but by attributing power to the nation-state, it also makes Third World regimes accountable.

The operation of simultaneously privileging and distancing the colonial narrative, moving beyond it, structures the "in-between" framework of the "postcolonial." This in-betweenness becomes evident through a kind of commutation test. While one can posit the duality between colonizer and colonized and even neocolonizer and neocolonized, it does not make much sense to speak of postcolonizers and postcolonized. "Colonialism" and "neocolonialism" imply both oppression and the possibility of resistance. Transcending such dichotomies, the term "postcolonial" posits no clear domination and calls for no clear opposition. It is this structured ambivalence of the "postcolonial," of positing a simultaneously close and distant temporal relation to the "colonial," that is appealing in a post-structuralist academic context. It is also this fleeting quality, however, that makes the "postcolonial" an uneasy term for a geopolitical critique of the centralized distribution of power in the world.

Postcolonial theory has dealt most significantly with cultural contradictions, ambiguities, and ambivalences.[13] Through a major shift in emphasis, it accounts for the experiences of displacement of Third World peoples in the metropolitan centers and the cultural syncretisms generated by the First World/Third World intersections, issues less adequately addressed by Third World nationalist and world systems discourses, which are more rooted in the categories of political economy. The "beyond" of postcolonial theory, in this sense, seems most meaningful when placed in relation to Third World nationalist discourse. The term "postcolonial" would be more precise, therefore, if articulated as "post–First World/Third World theory," or "post-anticolonial critique," as a movement beyond a relatively binaristic, fixed, and stable mapping of power relations between "colonizer and colonized" and "center and periphery." Such rearticulations suggest a more nuanced discourse, which allows for movement, mobility, and fluidity. Here, the prefix "post-" would make sense less as "after" than as following, going beyond and commenting on a certain intellectual movement (Third Worldist anticolonial critique) rather than beyond a certain point in history (colonialism). For here, "neocolonialism" would be a less passive form of addressing the situation of neocolonized countries and a politically more active mode of engagement.

Postcolonial theory has formed not only a vibrant space for critical, even resistant, scholarship, but also a contested space, particularly since some practitioners of various ethnic studies feel somewhat displaced by the rise of postcolonial studies in North American English departments. If the rising institutional endorsement of the term "postcolonial" is, on the one hand, a success story for the PCS (politically correct), is it not also a partial containment of the POCS (people of color)? Before "poco" (postcolonialism) becomes the new academic buzzword, it is urgent to address such schisms, specifically in the North American context,[14] where one has the impression that the "postcolonial" is privileged precisely because it seems safely distant from "the belly of the beast," the United States. The recognition of these cracks and fissures is crucial if ethnic studies and postcolonial studies scholars are to forge more effective institutional alliances.

Having raised these questions about the term "postcolonial," it remains to address some related concepts and to explore their spatio-temporal implications. The foregrounding of "hybridity" and "syncretism" in postcolonial studies calls attention to the mutual imbrication of "central" and "peripheral" cultures. "Hybridity" and "syncretism" allow negotiation of the multiplicity of identities and subject positionings that result from displacement, immigration, and exile, without policing the borders of identity along essentialist and originary lines. It is largely diasporic Third World intellectuals in the First World—hybrids themselves, not coincidentally—who elaborate a framework that situates the Third World intellectual within a multiplicity of cultural positionalities and perspectives. Nor is it a coincidence, by the same token, that in Latin America "syncretism" and "hybridity" had already been invoked decades ago by diverse Latin American modernisms, which spoke of neologistic culture, of *créolité*, of *mestizaje*, and of anthropophagy.[15] The culturally syncretic protagonists of the Brazilian modernists of the 1920s, the "heroes without character" coined by Mario de Andrade, might be seen as "postcolonial hybrids" *avant la lettre*. The cannibalist theories of the Brazilian modernists, and their elaborations in the tropicalist movement of the late 1960s and early 1970s, simply assumed that New Worlders were culturally mixed, a contentious amalgam of indigenous, African, European, Asian, and Arab identities.

At the same time, the problematic spatio-temporality implicit in the term "postcolonial" has repercussions for the conceptualization of the past in post(anti)colonial theory. The rupture implicit in the "post" has been reflected in the relationship between past and present in postcolonial discourse, with particular reference to notions of hybridity. At times, the antiessentialist emphasis on hybrid identities comes dangerously close to dismissing all searches for communitarian origins as an archaeological excavation of an idealized, irretrievable past. Yet on another level, while avoiding any nostalgia for a prelapsarian community or for any unitary and transparent identity predating the fall, we must also ask whether it is possible to forge a collective resistance without inscribing a communal past. Rap-music narratives and video representations that construct resistant invocations of Africa and slavery are a case in point. For communities that have undergone brutal ruptures and are now in the process of forging a collective identity, no matter how hybrid that identity has been before,

during, and after colonialism, the retrieval and reinscription of a fragmented past becomes a crucial contemporary site for forging a resistant
collective identity. A notion of the past might thus be negotiated differently—not as a static fetishized phase to be literally reproduced, but as
fragmented sets of narrated memories and experiences on the basis of
which to mobilize contemporary communities. A celebration of syncretism and hybridity per se, if not articulated in conjunction with questions
of hegemony and neocolonial power relations, runs the risk of appearing
to sanctify the fait accompli of colonial violence.

The current metropolitan discursive privileging of palimpsestic syncretisms must also be negotiated in relation to Fourth World peoples. It must
account, for example, for the paradoxical situation of the indigenous Ka-
yapo in the Amazon forest who, on the one hand, use video cameras and
thus demonstrate their cultural hybridity and their capacity for mimicry,
but who, on the other, use mimicry precisely in order to stage the urgency
of *preserving* the essential practices and contours of their culture, including
their relation to the rain forest and the communal possession of land. The
de facto acceptance of hybridity as a product of colonial conquest and post-
independence dislocations, as well as the recognition of the impossibility
of return to an authentic past, do not mean that the politico-cultural movements of various racial-ethnic communities should stop researching and
recycling their precolonial languages and cultures.[16] Postcolonial theory's celebration of hybridity risks an antiessentialist condescension toward those communities obliged by circumstances to assert, for their very
survival, a lost and even irretrievable past. In such cases, the assertion of
culture prior to conquest forms part of the fight against continuing forms
of annihilation. If the logic of the poststructuralist/postcolonial argument
were taken literally, then the Zuni in Mexico and the United States would
be censured for their search for the traces of an original culture, and the
Maori in New Zealand would be criticized for their turn to Aboriginal
language and culture as part of their own regeneration. The question, in
other words, is not whether there is such a thing as an originary homogeneous past, and whether it would be possible to return to it, or even
whether the past is unjustifiably idealized. Rather, the question is: Who is
mobilizing what in the articulation of the past, deploying what identities,
identifications, and representations, and in the name of what political
vision and goals?

Negotiating locations, identities, and positionalities in relation to the violence of neocolonialism is crucial if hybridity is not to become a figure for

the consecration of hegemony. As a descriptive catch-all term, "hybridity" per se fails to discriminate between the diverse modalities of hybridity—for example, forced assimilation, internalized self-rejection, political coopta- tion, social conformism, cultural mimicry, and creative transcendence. The reversal of biologically and religiously racist tropes—the hybrid, the syncretic—on the one hand, and the reversal of anticolonialist purist no- tions of identity, on the other, should not obscure the problematic agency of "postcolonial hybridity." In contexts such as Latin America, nationhood was officially articulated in hybrid terms, through an integrationist ide- ology that glossed over institutional and discursive racism. At the same time, hybridity has also been used as part of resistant critique; for example, by the modernist and tropicalist movements in Latin America. As in the term "postcolonial," the question of location and perspective has to be addressed—that is, the differences between hybridities or, more specifi- cally, hybridities of Europeans and their offshoots around the world and that of (ex-)colonized peoples. Furthermore, the differences among and between Third World diasporas must be addressed—for example, between African American hybrids who speak English in the First World and those of Afro-Cubans and Afro-Brazilians who speak Spanish and Portuguese in the Third World.

"Hybridity," like the "postcolonial," is susceptible to a blurring of per- spectives. "Hybridity" must be examined in a non-universalizing, differen- tial manner, contextualized within present neocolonial hegemonies. The cultural inquiry generated by the hybridity–syncretism discourse needs to be relinked to macro-level geopolitical analysis. It requires articulation with the ubiquity of Anglo-American informational media (Cable News Network, British Broadcasting Corporation, Associated Press), as well as with events of the magnitude of the Gulf War, with its massive and trau- matic transfers of populations. The collapse of Second World socialism, it should be pointed out, has not altered neocolonial policies, and on some levels it has generated increased anxiety among such Third World commu- nities as the Palestinians and South African blacks concerning their strug- gle for independence without a Second World counterbalance.

The circulation of "postcolonial" as a theoretical frame tends to suggest a supercession of neocolonialism and the Third World and Fourth World as unfashionable, even irrelevant, categories. Yet with all its problems, the term "Third World" does still retain heuristic value as a convenient label for the imperialized formations, including those within the First World.

The term "Third World" is most meaningful in broad political-economic terms and becomes blurred when one addresses the differently modulated politics in the realm of culture, the overlapping contradictory spaces of intermingling identities. The concept of "Third World" is schematically productive if it is placed under erasure, as it were, seen as provisional and ultimately inadequate.

At this point in time, replacing the term "Third World" with the "postcolonial" is a liability. Despite differences and contradictions among and within Third World countries, the term "Third World" contains a common project of (linked) resistances to (neo)colonialisms. Within the North American context, more specifically, it has become a term of empowerment for intercommunal coalitions of various peoples of color.[17] Perhaps it is this sense of a common project around which to mobilize that is missing from post(anti)colonial discussions. If the terms "postcolonial" and "post-independence" stress, in different ways, a rupture in relation to colonialism, and "neocolonial" emphasizes continuities, "Third World" usefully evokes structural commonalities of struggles. The invocation of the "Third World" implies a belief that the shared history of (neo)colonialism and internal racism forms sufficient common ground for alliances among such diverse peoples. If one does not believe or envision such commonalities, then the term "Third World" should indeed be discarded. It is this difference of alliance and mobilization between the concepts "Third World" and "postcolonial" that suggests a relational usage of the terms. My assertion of the political relevance of such categories as "neocolonialism," and even that of the more problematic Third World and Fourth World peoples, is meant not to suggest a submission to intellectual inertia, but to point to a need to deploy all of the concepts in differential and contingent manners.

In sum, the concept of the "postcolonial" must be interrogated and contextualized historically, geopolitically, and culturally. My argument is not necessarily that one conceptual frame is "wrong" and the other is "right," but that each frame illuminates only partial aspects of systemic modes of domination, of overlapping collective identities, and of contemporary global relations. Each addresses specific and even contradictory dynamics between and within different world zones. There is a need for more flexible relations among the various conceptual frameworks—a mobile set of grids, a diverse set of disciplinary as well as cultural-geopolitical lenses—adequate to these complexities. Flexible yet critical usage that can address the politics of location is important not only for pointing out historical and geographical contradictions and differences, but also for reaffirming historical and geographical links, structural analogies, and openings for agency and resistance.

NOTES

1 See, for example, Aijaz Ahmad, "Jameson's Rhetoric of Otherness and the 'National Allegory,'" *Social Text* 17 (Fall 1987); Arjun Appadurai, "Disjuncture and Difference in the Global Cultural Economy," *Public Culture* 2, no. 2 (1990); Robert Stam, "Eurocentrism, Afrocentrism, Polycentrism: Theories of Third Cinema," *Quarterly Review of Film and Video* 13, nos. 1–3 (Spring 1991); Chandra Talpade Mohanty, "Cartographies of Struggle: Third World Women and the Politics of Feminism," in *Third World Women and the Politics of Feminism*, ed. by Chandra Talpade Mohanty, Ann Russo, and Lourdes Torres (Bloomington: Indiana University Press, 1991).

2 Does that condition echo the language of existentialism, or is it the echo of postmodemism?

3 The relationships between "postcolonial," "postcoloniality," and "postcolonialism" have yet to be addressed rigorously.

4 For a reading of the relationships between postmodernism and postcolonialism, see Kwame Anthony Appiah, "Is the Post- in Postmodernism the Post- in Postcolonial?" *Critical Inquiry* 17 (Winter 1991).

5 Bill Ashcroft, Gareth Griffiths, and Helen Tiffin, *The Empire Writes Back: Theory and Practice in Post-Colonial Literatures* (London: Routledge, 1989), 2.

6 For a radical formulation of resistant postcolonial, see Gayatri Chakravorty Spivak, "Poststructuralism, Marginality, Postcoloniality and Value," in *Literary Theory Today*, ed. by Peter Collier and Helga Geyer-Ryan (London: Polity Press, 1990).

7 Read, for example, Zachary Lockman and Joel Benin, eds., *Intifada: The Palestinian Uprising against Israeli Occupation* (Boston: South End Press, 1989), esp. Edward W. Said, "Intifada and Independence," 5–22; Said, *After the Last Sky* (Boston: Pantheon Books, 1985).

8 This perspective explains the harsh repression of movements in opposition to the U.S.-Egypt alliance during the war. In fact, the Camp David Treaty is intimately linked to the open-door economic policy, with its dismantling of the Egyptian public sector. Referred to as the shadow government of Egypt, the U.S. Agency for International Development is partly responsible for the positions that Egyptian and most Arab governments took during the Gulf War.

9 The rigid imposition of Islamic law in Saudi Arabia is linked to efforts to mask the regime's anti-regional collaboration with imperial interests.

10 The term "Gringostroika" was coined by the Mexican multimedia artist Guillermo Gómez-Peña.

11 For discussions of the "post," see, for example, Robert Young, "Poststructuralism: The End of Theory," *Oxford Literary Review* 5, nos. 1–2 (1982); R. Radha-

krishnan, "The Postmodern Event and the End of Logocentrism," *boundary 2* 12, no. 1 (Fall 1983); Geoffrey Bennington, "Postal Politics and the Institution of the Nation," in *Nation and Narration*, ed. by Homi K. Bhabha (London: Routledge, 1990).

12 As these notes on the "postcolonial" originally went to print, a relevant article appeared in *The Nation*. See Praful Bidwai, "India's Passage to Washington," *The Nation*, 20 January 1992.

13 See, for example. Homi K. Bhabha, "The Commitment to Theory," in *Questions of Third Cinema*, ed. by Jim Pines and Paul Willemen (London: British Film Institute, 1989); Trinh T. Minh-ha, *Woman, Native, Other* (Bloomington: Indiana University Press, 1989).

14 The "postcolonial" replacement of the "Third World" is ambiguous, especially when poststructuralist and postcolonial theories are confidently deployed with little understanding of the historical and material legacy of colonialism, neocolonialism, racism, and anticolonial resistance. These slippages have contributed to facile dismissals of Frantz Fanon's formulations as vulgar.

15 On the Brazilian modernists and the concept of anthropophagy, see Robert Stam, *Subversive Pleasures: Bakhtin, Cultural Criticism and Film* (Baltimore: Johns Hopkins University Press, 1989).

16 For another critical consideration of hybridity and memory, see also Manthia Diawara, "The Nature of Mother in Dreaming Rivers," *Third Text* 13 (Winter 1990–91).

17 In his " 'Third World Literature' and the Nationalist Ideology" (*Journal of Arts and Ideas* 17–18 [June 1989]), Aijaz Ahmad offers an important critique of the usages of "Third World" in the U.S. academy. Unfortunately, he ignores the crucial issue of empowerment taking place under the rubric "Third World" among diverse peoples of color in North American intellectual and academic communities.

POST-FANON AND THE COLONIAL

A Situational Diagnosis

> One must make a "situational diagnosis."
> —Frantz Fanon, *Toward the African Revolution*

In this essay, I would like to engage Frantz Fanon's work, both critically and passionately, at a specific historical moment: at a time when the metanarratives of anticolonial revolution have long since been eclipsed and reconfigured, yet when issues of colonialism, racism, and neo-imperialism still persist. Eschewing the tiresome dichotomy between a Third World Marxist salute to *The Wretched of the Earth* and a modish psychoanalytical embrace of *Black Skin, White Masks*, this essay proposes a multilevel reflection on Fanon's writing. Fanon's books must be viewed not dichotomously but, rather, in relation to one another. The theoretical grids deployed in the two books highlight different dimensions of an intricate colonial situation. Given the various historical and discursive shifts since Fanon's time, how can one assume the fundamental validity of the antiracist and anticolonialist Third Worldist movement embodied by Fanon? And how can one also probe the various fissures having to do with gender, religion, class, ethnicity, and sexuality, rending the formerly colonized world? In what ways can one develop a more historicized, culturally specific, and contingent approach to the variegated yet interrelated texts and geographies featured in Fanon's work?

Rather than adopt a stagist approach that suggests that we necessarily know better than Fanon, or take a presentist approach that turns him into a contemporary postmodernist postcolonial, I will look at his work from multiple perspectives and registers in terms of various forms of relationality—between texts, between discourses, between disciplines, between histories, between geographies, and between communities. What Fanon called "situational diagnosis," and what I call "relationality," leads, I believe, to productive questions about Fanon's choices of where, when, and in relation to what and whom he opens up or closes down his analogies and comparisons. "Relationality" here has a double reference: to relationality within Fanon's work itself and to relationality as a method of reading Fanon, one that can amplify and extrapolate that work in new directions and, at times, even against the grain of Fanon's own text. This approach will hopefully help avoid a number of pitfalls and simplifications of reducing Fanon to the various caricatural figures sometimes encountered in the literature: (1) the pyromaniac advocate of senseless violence; (2) the crypto-totalitarian prophet of the "Third World gulag"; (3) the Manichean partisan of simplistic dichotomies; and (4) the trendy advocate of the sinuous hybridities of the "posts." Fanon's critique of the binarist character of racism and of the colonial situation—for example, of an Algeria ripped in two—has too often been used to charge Fanon himself with simplistic binarism. I hope, meanwhile, to demonstrate Fanon's complex account of colonialism, the multifaceted web of identifications, ambivalences, and negotiations in both his theory and his practice.

BETWEEN DISCOURSES

All of Fanon's arguments have to be situated historically within multiple discursive contexts, in relation to various reigning theories and intellectual currents. Even Fanon's word "situational" is itself situated, for example, in that it echoes Jean-Paul Sartre's idea of "situated freedom" and the title of his famous collection *Situations*. At the same time, we are reminded of some of the linguistic notions of Mikhail Bakhtin and Valentin Voloshinov. In *Marxism and the Philosophy of Language*, the two Russian theorists rejected the Saussurean idea of the "sign," seen as overly static and binarist, in favor of a more dynamic "situated utterance." The phrase synthesizes a phenomenological sensitivity to human "situatedness"—the idea that we all, individually and collectively, occupy specific points in time and space—with the discursive turn of semiotics, this time not of the sign but, instead, of the historically situated and socially inflected "utterance" that exists in relation to a speaker and an addressee, both immersed in history, located in a specific place and period.

To understand Fanon's text, one has to engage diverse philosophical traditions and note both the ways in which he disrupts those narratives and remains enmeshed within them. Thus, Fanon, in the fragmentary way allowed him by his short span of life, both absorbed and surpassed a series of intellectual currents. Fanon embraced psychoanalysis but pointed to the ethnocentrism of its Oedipalism. He absorbed Marxism but pointed to the Eurocentric limits of its class analysis. He incorporated existentialism but pointed to the social aporia engendered by a subjectivist voluntarism, seen as irrelevant for colonized people. If Fanon's word "situational" calls up Sartre, it also calls up Fanon's own critique of Sartre and phenomenology as *insufficiently* situated, as failing to acknowledge the specific nature of the constraints on human freedom typical of the colonized world. And finally, Fanon applauded certain features of Negritude while denouncing its originary, nostalgic, and binarist penchant for pitting African emotion against European reason. What we see over and over is that Fanon takes a preexisting discourse and interrogates it, often transforming its terms by bringing race and colonialism on board.

Participating in diverse intellectual dialogues and streams of thought, including aspects of Hegelianism, Marxism, psychoanalysis, Negritude, socialism, pan-Africanism, existentialism, and phenomenology, Fanon performed the precocious deconstruction of what would later be called "masternarratives." In this sense, Fanon can be seen as preparing the way for a certain poststructuralism, including the work of the Algerian Jew Jacques Derrida, whose deconstruction is usually traced back exclusively to Heidegger. Profoundly interdisciplinary, Fanon's work drew on psychiatry, philosophy, sociology, ethnography, history, literature, and film, anticipating in a sense the whole field of cultural studies.[1] In some ways, not unlike Roland Barthes's semiological readings in *Mythologies*, Fanon offers a reading of colonialist mythologies, its grammar and rhetoric, as in the case of the "myth of the Negro." Fanon's text conducts an explicit conversation with diverse intellectuals: with Sartre on existentialism and phenomenology; with Sigmund Freud and Jacques Lacan on psychoanalysis; with Marx on historical materialism. Undoubtedly, phenomenology and existentialism were one of Fanon's most crucial intertexts. He politicized and "Third Worldized" phenomenology, turning it into a viable prism through which to look at the lived existence of the black man, and to an extent of the black woman, within white society, or of the Arab man, and to an extent, the Arab woman, within French colonialism.

Fanon's critique of Sartre emerged against the backdrop of African national independence movements. While critiquing Negritude as a purely reactive phenomenon, Fanon also rejected Sartre's white patronage of the Negritude Movement. In "Orphée Noir" (Black Orpheus), his influential preface to Léopold Senghor's 1948 anthology of Negritude poetry, Sartre used pronouns, or "shifters" in linguistics, in a shifting way, moving back and forth between "our" and "your" when addressing the (white) reader.[2] At the same time, Sartre deployed a static universalizing discourse when speaking about Negritude to blacks, implying that "all of us" are marching together toward the telos of emancipation. Just as Sartre's *Anti-Semite and Jew* suggested that anti-Semitism would come to an end with the dawn of socialism, his "Black Orpheus" also predicted the end of racism with the demise of colonialism and the advent of a true universalism. Within Sartre's Hegelian millenarian view, Blackness and Jewishness both functioned as the antithesis in the master–slave dialectical process. Sartre thus called for the transcendence of all particularist identities in the name of universal socialist revolution.

The Sartrean model of "anti-Semite and Jew" forms a taken-for-granted matrix of analysis lurking in the background of *Black Skin, White Masks*. Fanon cites Sartre on the designated space for blacks in the dialectical imagination:

> In fact, Negritude appears as the minor term of a dialectical progression. The theoretical and practical assertion of the supremacy of the white man is its thesis; the position of negritude as an antithetical value is the moment of negativity. But this negative moment is insufficient by itself, and the Negroes who employ it know this very well; they know it is intended to prepare the synthesis or realization of the human in a society without races. Thus negritude is the root of its own destruction, it is a transition and not a conclusion, a means and not an ultimate end.[3]

Echoing Sartre's claims that "the Jew is one whom other men consider a Jew" and that "it is not the Jewish character that provokes anti-Semitism, on the contrary, it is the Anti-Semite who creates the Jew," Fanon, too, writes that "it is the racist who creates his inferior" and "the black soul is a white man's artifact."[4] Although *Anti-Semite and Jew* affected Fanon's parallel anatomy of the generative processes of identity, for Fanon understanding the "black" required understanding the specificities of white racism toward blacks. Thus, Fanon both repeats and transcends Sartre's idea of the negative dialectic between Jew and anti-Semite. In this sense, Fanon echoes Albert Memmi's objections to Sartre's claim that the anti-Semite invents the Jew. For Memmi, a Tunisian Jew, Sartre's Jew has no history or culture apart from that produced by the hostile otherizing of the anti-Semite.[5] The Jew in Sartrean discourse becomes virtually an ahistorical entity, devoid of cultural specificity and existing only in function of the anti-Semite.

Fanon similarly deconstructs Sartre's view that the "black" might constitute only a transitional stage in the inexorable march toward the universal: "I am not a potentiality of something, I am wholly what I am. I do not have to look for the universal. No probability has any place inside me. My Negro consciousness does not hold itself out as a lack. It is its own follower."[6] Predicated on the denial of the Black experience, this falsely universalizing discourse for Fanon constituted a symptom of intellectual subordination to imperial reason. A colorless universalism, de facto, meant whiteness. This kind of universalism placed the (white) intellectual in a position of superiority, as the spokesperson for the Universal, as the omnipotent agent advancing the dialectics of History. Corporeal visibility and the history of displacement, however, produced the particularities of being black in the world. By situating black neurosis within a larger race drama between whites and blacks, for example, Fanon could address the pathologies of colonialism itself. In this way, the phenomenon of race could be approached at once psychoanalytically and historically without constituting merely a negation or lacuna in a universalizing synthesis.[7] Fanon, in other words, accepts Sartre's reversing and dismantling of the *Cogito ergo sum*, i.e., the "I think, therefore I am" thesis, but he also begins to "race," as it were, the meaning of the "I exist."

Throughout his work, Fanon articulates the complex entrappings of the colonizer/colonized dialectics, negotiating the colonized identity both within and beyond Sartre's thought. Fanon does view the oppressed partly as a function of "*le regard*," of projected hatreds, while also avoiding any essentialist definition of identity for the black, Jew, or Arab. Yet for Fanon, the act of struggling for liberation transforms the colonized, now no longer confined to the space created, constructed, and imagined by the colonizer. The emergence of anticolonial movements composed a new "grammar" in which blacks spoke as subjects, substituting the paradigmatic object in the white syntax. Blackness thus could no longer be defined simply as the product of racism, and the revolutionary black or Arab could no longer simply be an exemplum of "being for others." On one level, then, Fanon's discourse can be seen as a historicized variant of Sartre's; it aspires to break away from the negative space allotted by racism and anti-Semitism. On another level, however, Fanon conceives of black existence in a way that transgresses Sartre's Universal in that Fanon refuses to abandon the particular. Racial or ethnic specificity in Fanon's work is not eliminated but, rather, transfigured. By the time of *The Wretched of the Earth*, Fanon's categories of blackness vis-à-vis whiteness give way to a language of national affiliations: Angolans, Algerians, Senegalese. The colonized's subjectivity is gained and performed through the disruption of the colonial order. Thus, in *Toward the African Revolution*, Fanon writes, "It is the white man who creates the Negro. But it is the Negro who creates 'Negritude.' "[8]

Black Skin, White Masks reveals Fanon's penchant for a "situational diagnosis," especially in his rendering of the Antillean's multiple positionalities vis-à-vis Africa and Europe. Fanon's departure from Martinique in 1943 to fight alongside the Allies arguably catalyzed his insight into the conjunctural, relational nature of identity, specifically within the colonial system. Unlike certain exponents of Negritude (e.g., Senghor), Fanon found the discourse of transcendent harmony unconvincing. In contrast to the investment in an African essence, Fanon highlights a shifting black existence. In France, he writes, "I subjected myself to an objective examination, I discovered my blackness, my ethnic characteristics; and I was battered down by tom toms, cannibalism, intellectual deficiency, fetishism, racial defects, slave ships, and above all else, above all *Y'a bon Banania*."[9] Similarly, Fanon dissects the instability of identification as a geographically contingent phenomenon: "Attend showings of a Tarzan film in the Antilles and in Europe. In the Antilles, the young Negro identifies himself de facto with Tarzan against the Negroes. This is much more difficult for him in a European theatre, for the rest of the audience, which is white, automatically identifies him with the savages on the screen."[10] While psychoanalytical feminist film theory spoke of the "to-be-looked-at-ness" (Laura Mulvey) of women's screen performance, Fanon had called attention to the "to-be-looked-at-ness" of spectators themselves. His example suggests that diasporic blacks are shackled by their complexion, denuded by a white gaze ("Look, a Negro! . . . I am being dissected under white eyes, the only real eyes. I am *fixed* . . . I am laid bare.") But returning the gaze, Fanon also speaks of diasporic experience in its variegated particularities.[11]

Fanon's physical movement between the Caribbean and France, and subsequently between France and North Africa, entails a theoretical methodological shift. Although he never completely abandoned the hybrid psychoanalytical–phenomenological method, Fanon's later work is also inflected by a Marxizing phenomenological paradigm. Here one becomes aware, again, of the relationality of theoretical and disciplinary grids, each with its blindnesses and insights. When reflecting through a psychoanalytical frame, for example, Fanon grants agency to the white man, arguing that the white creates the black man. But when he writes within a materialist, economic frame, Fanon grants agency to the black man, arguing in effect that the black creates the white man: "Europe is literally the creation of the Third World."[12] With both frames, however, Fanon disturbs the sheltered narcissism of Eurocentric thinking.

Fanon must also be read against the backdrop of his discipline and his profession. In Fanon's time, the dominant models of psychoanalysis were premised on a universalist construction of the psyche, eliding various social permutations. Normative psychoanalysis extrapolated to the world at large, to put it somewhat crudely, the neuroses of the Viennese bourgeoisie. Fanon's writing on psychiatry, as well as his therapeutic practice, gradually began to engage with the cultural specificity of his patients. Freud's Eurocentric analysis of the unconscious (e.g., in *Totem and Taboo*) aligned it with primitivism, invoking analogies between the individual id and uncivilized tribes. Fanon's approach, in contrast, was uninterested in a "universal" Oedipus complex. Both Fanon's answer to Octave Mannoni and Fanon's project as a whole can be viewed as an exercise in refuting Prospero's representation of Caliban. Fanon's provocative yet in some ways misguided claim that the Oedipus complex is irrelevant to Martinique perhaps should be taken not literally but, instead, as a warning of the pitfalls of any psychoanalytic theory oblivious to sociopolitical context.

Fanon's psychoanalytical writing and psychiatric practices ground the Freudian drama in culture and history. In *Black Skins, White Masks*, Fanon coined the term "situational neurosis" to unmask, as it were, the social alienation triggered by the white mask worn on a black face.[13] In response he proposed his situational analysis, a strategy further developed and theorized in North Africa. In collaboration with his Algerian Jewish colleague

Jacques Azoulay, Fanon attempted to "diagnose" the false universalism of standard French psychiatric methods. For the two authors, institutional therapy formed part of a colonial assimilationist policy. Conscious of the importance of linguistic and cultural difference within this process, Fanon was invested in the real and symbolic context of mental illness in ways that anticipate the later work of the "anti-psychiatry" movement embodied by such figures as R. D. Laing, David Cooper, and Felix Guattari. Fanon was acutely aware of the limitations of his own practice in the psychiatric ward in Algiers, especially of his lack of command of Berber or Arabic. (Fanon began studying Arabic but never achieved fluency and therefore had to rely on interpreters.) Within the French ward system, as with the colonial system as a whole, questions of language and power had devastating repercussions for the psyche, although they were hardly deemed relevant to the therapeutic process.

As with a Freudian-Lacanian discourse, language would seem always to stand in the realm of the symbolic and thus presumably could not be touched by the gravity of history. Yet the very presence of an interpreter, for example, carried a specific weight for Algerians, for whom the French language embodied French power, obliging the colonized, whether in the courthouse, in prison, in school, or in the mental institution, to meet the colonizer on the latter's linguistic turf. Although the Frenchified Algerian elite could join the colonizer in a linguistic rendezvous, the encounter was trapped in an absurd theater of polite mimicry performed against the din of machine guns. Healing traumatized and tortured Algerians was necessarily inscribed on the act of translation in a situation where the doctors' native tongue tended to be French and the patients', Arabic—all in a situation, ironically, in which the French language was itself a factor in the colonial production of pathologies.

In a 1954 article entitled "Social Ward," Fanon and his collaborator, Azoulay, situated their own method, critiquing their former psychiatric practice of administering French therapies to Algerian patients. Largely developed for French women, who constituted the majority of patients in French wards and hospitals, such therapies, Fanon and Azoulay argued, were simply inappropriate for Algerian patients. Occupational therapy based on music or games had been modeled on French cultural norms, leading Fanon to bring local Arab musicians into the ward. To endow psychoanalysis with cultural content, furthermore, Fanon studied Arab/ African approaches to insanity—in which the insane were viewed as possessed by *jinns* (from which derives the English word "genie")—as well as the healing role played by the *taleb* or the *marabout*. Adopting a dialectical approach, Fanon and Azoulay tried to synthesize local practices with European psychiatric treatment, thus anticipating what would later be called integrative medicine. Although Fanon was not fluent in the Arabic language or deeply conversant in Algerian cultural codes, in other words, he was searching for a therapeutic practice attuned to cultural difference.[14] Fanon and Azoulay came to realize that they had been the unconscious "carriers" of the French assimilationist model within the mental institution itself. But within this asymmetrical situation, Fanon at least tried to unravel the fictitious universalism of psychoanalysis and psychiatry by placing theory and practice in dialogue.[15]

BETWEEN COMMUNITIES

Fanon's textual and disciplinary dialogism must be situated biographically, as his voyage across continents informs his intellectual trajectory. To draw out a non-Eurocentric relationality is to take Fanon's own logic even further by placing it in relation to the Caribbean and North Africa without having always to make stopovers, as it were, in Paris. What happens when diverse racialized communities are positioned in mutual relation without passing through the white "center"? Rather than discern only a single axis at a time, as though each existed autonomously (Fanon of Martinique–France, on the one hand, and Fanon of Algeria–France, on the other), we could look for a multidirectional, multichronotopic set of axes. Communities in Fanon's text, I argue, do not constitute essentialist entities. Rather, they exist situationally, in shifting relations expressed through metaphors, metonymies, allegories, disjunctions, comparisons, analogies, and disanalogies.

Black Skin, White Masks reveals a strong feature of Fanon's work: his penchant for placing diverse ethnicities and communities in comparative relation to one another. "The Negro is comparison," writes Fanon, suggesting that, "not only must the black man be black, he must be black *in relation* to the white man."[16] Even Fanon's *Black Skin, White Masks* does not concern only black existence. His text is thick with tales of parallel subjugations and the advocacy of brotherly solidarity within humanistic norms. (We will return to the gendered dimensions of Fanon in a moment.) Written in the context of postwar Martinique and France, the "Fact of Blackness"[17] and "The Negro and Psychotherapy" chapters in *Black Skin, White Masks* stress the relation between blackness and white racism, on the one hand, and between Jewishness and anti-Semitism, on the other. Within a contemporary context in which Jews and blacks are often discussed as if they have always been antonyms, it is valuable to read Fanon at a different historical conjuncture: one that allowed—indeed, almost necessitated—his linking of their shared oppression by European racism. Citing his philosophy professor, a native of the Antilles, Fanon writes: "Whenever you hear anyone abuse the Jews, pay attention, because he is talking about you. . . . An anti-Semite is inevitably anti-Negro."[18] Fanon's recollection, addressed also to an implied black reader, resonates against the backdrop of the genocide of Jews only a decade earlier, during a war that also placed Senegalese, Tunisian, Ghanaian, and Indian soldiers together on the front line, defending the very same civilization that had dispossessed and even massacred them.

Fanon's analogy can also be seen in a broader context, as part of a larger black diasporic pattern of cross-cultural identifications found, for example, in the black allegorization of Jewish biblical stories of slavery, exodus, and the Promised Land, or in Rastafarian evocations of Jewish narratives of captivity, diaspora, and longing to return, as in the theme "by the waters of Babylon." But only a sense of a longer historical durée can give us a full sense of the meaning of the following Fanon statement: "Since I was not satisfied to be racialized, by a lucky turn of fate I was humanized. I joined the Jew, my brother in misery."[19] Fanon's comparative framework opens up a rich field of ethnic relational studies. The imagery of black corporeality, for example, reflects the embodied history of enslavement, while the imagery of Jewish intellectualism reflects a more conceptual theological inquisition. European anti-Semitism, it can be argued, provided the model and matrix for anti-black racism in the Black Atlantic.[20] Anti-Semitism, including its anti-Arab variant, provided a conceptual and disciplinary apparatus, which, after being aimed at Europe's internal "others" (the Jews and Muslims) was then displaced outward against Europe's external others (the indigenous peoples of Africa and the Americas). Preexisting patterns of ethnic, religious, and gender otherizing—for example, of women, witches, heretics, and infidels—were transferred from Europe to its colonies. Indeed, one can discern a partial congruence between the phantasmatic imagery projected onto both the Jews and Muslims, on the one hand, and onto the red and black savages, on the other: blood drinkers, cannibals, sorcerers, devils.

Although Fanon's text does not offer precisely this reading of history, it is significant that his effort to explore the cognate problem of black identity is articulated in relation to other "others." Fanon draws parallels between the anti-Semite and the racist, invoking, with regard to the black, Sartre's argument that the Jew is a Jew because of the other's fixating gaze. As a result, "the Jew," according to Sartre, "has a personality like the rest of us, and on top of that he is Jewish. It amounts to a doubling of the fundamental relationship with the other. The Jew is over-determined."[21] In this vein, Fanon discusses the inauthenticity and alienation of the black, who like the Jew possesses an emotional life split in two, in search of "a dream of universal brotherhood in a world that rejects him." The attempts by the Jew, for Sartre, or by the black, for Fanon, to assimilate into an anti-Semitic or racist society lead only to the pathologies of self-hatred and inferiority complexes. For Sartre, "It is the anti-Semite who makes the Jew," just as for Fanon it is, to an extent, the white who makes the black. On this level, as we saw earlier, Fanon extends Sartre's dialectics of identity. But Fanon also goes beyond the black–Jewish analogy, attempting to sketch the specificities of anti-black racism in contradistinction to the Jewish experience of anti-Semitism.

Fanon further existentializes Sartre's analytical model in *Anti-Semite and Jew*. In contrast to that of the assimilated (European) Jew, the situation of the black, no matter how assimilated within white society, was visibly overdetermined. Of primordial importance for Fanon within this logic, then, is the *visibility* of the black body. Fanon, as we saw, partly adheres to Sartre's nonessentialist idea that the Jew—and by extension, the black—is the product of *"le regard d'autrui"* (the look of the others). But while he accepts Sartre's insight into the construction of subjectivity in function of the "other," Fanon adds a new wrinkle. The Jew, he reminds Sartre, is also "a white man, apart from a few debatable features, he can sometimes pass unnoticed. . . . I am not the slave of the idea others have of me, but of my appearance."[22] Significant distinctions separate anti-Semitic and anti-black imageries precisely in terms of corporeality. Fanon writes that "whoever says rape says Negro,"[23] in contrast to the imaginary of both the white body and the not-quite-white body of the (European) Jew: "An erection on Rodin's Thinker is a shocking thought. One cannot decently 'have a hard on' everywhere. The Negro symbolizes the biological danger; the Jew, the intellectual danger."[24] According to Fanon, Jews are feared for their presumed "control over everything," while blacks are feared for their presumed "tremendous sexual powers."[25] The Jew in this sense comes to function as superego, seen as possessing self-control and the potency to control others even in an invisible fashion, while the black is projected as id, lacking in self-control and therefore carrying the visible danger of havoc and chaos. Comparing the violence toward Jews and blacks, Fanon thus writes:

> No anti-Semite would conceive of . . . castrating the Jew. He is killed or sterilized. . . . The Jew is attacked in his religious identity, in his history, in his race, in his relations with his ancestors and with his posterity; when one sterilizes a Jew, one cuts off the source; every time that a Jew is persecuted, it is the whole race that is persecuted in his person. But it is in his corporeality that the Negro is attacked. It is as a concrete personality that he is lynched. It is as an actual being that he is a threat. The Jewish menace is replaced by the fear of the sexual potency of the Negro.[26]

Apart from the fact that Fanon "centers" on the male anatomy as his normative frame for comparative study, leaving the vagina a textual lacuna, some of his comparisons require rearticulation in light of recent scholarship concerning the history of racial discourses. Nineteenth-century biologistic sciences, for example, placed corporeality at the core, not just as part of anti-black racism but also of widely varied forms of racism. Racist science "proved" inferiority using data on brain size, height, head shape, buttocks, genitalia, and so forth. Corporeal offenses such as rape, moreover, permeated colonial discourse directed against a wide array of peoples. (In *Toward an African Revolution*, not coincidentally, Fanon does extend his earlier discussion of the racist imagery of blacks to that of the Arab man as rapist and the Arab woman as prostitute.) Stigmatized corporeal practices, especially sexual and culinary practices, were attributed to diverse non-European others, whether to the indigenous peoples of the Americas and Africa (cannibalism) or to the Jews, figured as blood-sucking capitalists or Christian-blood drinkers (e.g., "The Blood Libel"). Even the exaggeratedly outsized phallic nose of the anti-Semitic stereotype, given the formulaic proportionality between nose and penis, evokes a sexual sleaziness that warns against sexual crossings between Jews and Aryans.[27]

In his phenomenological effort to demarcate the experience of (European) Jews and blacks in a racist society (including its anti-Semitic variant), Fanon underestimates the extent to which European Jews too have been marked biologically, including sexually. Apart from the fact that not all European Jews can pass for European Christians, even on the level of appearance, the question of biology was never simple. Anti-Semitic discourse constructed the Jew as a biological aberration, as deformed, grotesque, and abnormal, culminating in the Nazi obsession for detecting and quantifying "Jewish blood." As in racist discourses about Muslim Arab men, the circumcised penis hidden beneath clothing provoked manifest anxiety; the racist could not easily rely on the naked eye to detect the passing Jew. In a demonstration against Leon Blum, the French Jewish prime minister who came to power in 1936, the Pied Noir cried: "Down with Leon Blum and all the circumcised."[28] In Vichy France, assimilated Jews were sometimes forced to strip and expose their penile Jewishness, the only visible mark of difference. The notion of innate Jewish greed, meanwhile, was also linked to deviant genitalia. The European Jewish body, long associated in anti-Semitic discourse with aberrant, abnormal genitalia, was seen as diseased, mutilated, and often linked, like that of the prostitute, with specific forms of sexual pollution such as syphilis.

The imageries of Jews and blacks, furthermore, contaminate each other in that Jews were often perceived as black in anti-Semitic discourse. The medieval Catholic imaginary, which contrasted the "black" synagogue with the white church, transmuted itself in the nineteenth century into the image of the "Black Jew," common in racist tracts. Hermann Wegener called Jews "White Negroes," and Julius Streicher, one of the most notorious anti-Semites of the Weimar Republic and the Third Reich, argued in 1928 for the identity of language and facial features between Jews and blacks: "The swollen lips remind us again of the close relationship between Jews and Blacks. Speech takes place with a racially determined intonation."[29] My point is that, along with the deep discursive links between anti-Semitism and anti-black racism, Jews were also attacked in their corporality. And acknowledging this issue should not completely upset the marked difference between the (white) Jew and the black as drawn by Fanon, in terms of the everyday experience of the epidermis. Jewishness and blackness, in sum, are both attacked in their biology, only differently.

For Fanon, analogies of oppression between Jews and blacks also come with dis-analogies. Affinities in victimization, furthermore, do not guarantee solidarity or identification and may even result in a rolling series of hateful transferences among the diverse oppressed themselves. Fanon begins to touch on the question of the black in the eyes of the Jew. In speaking of Michel Salomon, Fanon writes that "he is a Jew, he has a 'millennial experience of anti-Semitism,' and yet he is racist."[30] Fanon's attention to a "racist Jew" in a period following the Jewish Holocaust may seem oxymoronic. But it also anticipates the later fissures in the alliances among the oppressed and offers a discursive foreshadowing of the latter-day tensions between blacks and Jews. (Recent history, unfortunately, has given us myriad examples of both Jewish forms of racism and of black modes of anti-Jewishness.) Yet Fanon's very mention of a racist Jew stresses the vitality of locating racism's specificities, including among the oppressed, asking us to reflect on the parallel and distinct forms of racism among minorities compared with that of "normal" white Christian racism. Fanon's text anticipates the gradual entry of the Jew—however tenuous and contradictory—into the terrain of whiteness or Europeanness in the post–World War Two era, simultaneously with Israel joining the Western imaginary. Here one may find in Fanon's text the germ of still another contemporary field—whiteness studies—and more specifically the study of the gradual whitening of the Jew.

Rather like the chains of negative desire in a Corneille play—A loves B who loves C who loves D who loves A—Fanon occasionally suggests a negative chain of community relationalities: "The Frenchman does not like the Jew who does not like the Arab, who does not like the Negro."[31] But he locates this chain in the French divide and conquer strategy. "The Jew," Fanon writes, "is told: 'You are not the same class as the Arab because you are really white and because you have Einstein and Bergson.'"[32] Fanon insightfully locates the whitening of the Jew within a negative dialectic vis-à-vis the colonized Arab, just as Arab anti-Jewishness is reinforced when the "Arab is told: 'If you are poor, it is because the Jew has bled you and taken everything from you.'" Meanwhile, "the Negro," Fanon writes, "is told: 'You are the best soldiers in the French Empire; the Arabs think that they are better than you, but they are wrong.'"[33] Reflecting in *Black Skin, White Masks* on his experience in North Africa during World War Two, Fanon also noted Arab racism—a place, one might note, where blacks were commonly referred to as *al-'abeed* (literally, slaves), but also a place where communities were largely identified in terms of religious and ethnic affiliations rather than in terms of race. Fanon recognized the complexity of the hierarchies that ultimately placed the French on top, followed by assimilated Jews, then by assimilated Muslims, and unassimilated Jews, and then Muslims at the bottom.

At the same time, in *Black Skin, White Masks* Fanon notices another hierarchy having to do less with epidermis than with the cultural hierarchies that favor the Martinican over the Arab: "Many times I have been stopped in broad daylight by policemen who mistook me for an Arab; when they discovered my origins, they were obsequious in their apologies; 'Of course, we know that a Martinician is quite different from an Arab.' I always protested violently, but I was always told, 'You don't know them.'"[34] Fanon's categorization sometimes blurs the distinction between the racial, the national, and the religious, thus implying a structuring absence of possible cross figures between blackness, Jewishness, and Arabness. Fanon, for example, often contrasts Arabness with Jewishness, and blackness with Jewishness, as if these categories were mutually exclusive and in excess of each other. Throughout *Black Skin, White Masks*, Fanon tends to speak of "Jews" as part of a European Christian cultural geography, even as he addresses French colonialism, thus overlooking diverse Jewish geographies, cultures, and appearances—specifically, that of Asian or African Jews, black Jews, or Arab-Jews, many of whom were living in North Africa in Fanon's own time, and some of whom would have, in other contexts, been perceived as black.[35] Extremely diverse notions of Jewish, black, or Arab histories and identities, furthermore, cannot be reduced to responses to anti-Semitism or racism. Rather, they have to be articulated in relation to particular locations within specific historical contexts. Charting the operations of racism toward diverse communities, while also reproducing the dominant categories used to define these communities, inadvertently grants the racist agency in defining the very categories of belonging, hindering the study of the intricate nature of these categories, or of the porous borders between them. My point is that Fanon's critique of Sartre's ungrounded particularities may also be addressed to the insufficient or intermittent situatedness of identities in Fanon's own text, especially in his early work.

Fanon's discourse of community identity, meanwhile, shifts, demonstrating features of a "situational diagnosis." Indeed, in *Black Skin, White Masks* Fanon distinguishes between experiencing the black body in the Caribbean or Africa, where blacks form the majority, and experiencing it in France, as a minority. In Fanon's insights into the varied racialized experiences of diasporic life we may trace antecedents of diasporic comparative studies. Fanon offers a path for "reading" communities as a conjunctural shaping of comparisons. As Fanon moves into the revolutionary context of North Africa his writings begin to move beyond the black-white dichotomy, and beyond the Martinican-French axis, to address more historically specific notions of communities. By the time of *The Wretched of the Earth*, Fanon supplements the black-Jewish axis of *Black Skin, White Masks* with the Arab-black axis. In *A Dying Colonialism*, Fanon also speaks of specific Jews in a specific context—"Algeria's Jews"[36]—and touches on a more mobile notion of ethnic, racial, national, and religious identity. He even briefly refers to the unsettling situation of minorities caught in the gears of colonialism's dualistic machines. The colonial effort to opportunistically contrast the "bad Arab" with the "good Kabyl" paralleled the construction of "bad Muslim" and "good Jew" in Algeria. Thus, citing Constantine Jews, Fanon writes:

> One of the most pernicious maneuvers of colonialism in Algeria was and remains the division between Jews and Moslems. . . . Jews have been in Algeria for more than two thousand years; they are thus an integral part of the Algerian people. . . . Moslems and Jews, children of the same earth, must not fall into the trap of provocation. Rather, they must make a common front against it, not letting themselves be duped by those who, not long ago, were offhandedly contemplating the total extermination.[37]

When Fanon writes within the Martinique-France axis, in other words, he formulates Jewishness in a rather ahistorical and Eurocentric fashion. But within the Algerian context, he seems to differentiate between the one-fifth of Jews who are French and four-fifths of Algerian Arab-Jews who are Arab Algerians. Fanon was writing, we must recall, in a context where colonial Algerian society comprised a clear-cut class, racial, and ethnic hierarchy, headed by the native French; followed by the naturalized French; then by the Italian, Spanish, Maltese, and other Europeans; and only then by indigenous Algerian Jews; with Muslims (whether Arabs or Berbers) at the social bottom.[38] Both anti-Jewishness and anti-Arabness formed an integral part of French colonial discourse. Apart from the electoral anxiety of the Pied Noir in fin-de-siècle Algeria (given the décret Crémieux, granting Algerian Jews voting rights), anti-Jewishness displaced and allegorized fears of the Algerian Muslims' demand for political representation onto Jews, foreshadowing the horrifying prospect of Muslims, like Jews, acquiring voting power.[39]

Despite Fanon's awareness of the insecure space occupied by indigenous minorities within national culture, his revolutionary paradigm rendered difficult a relational discussion of the place assigned to religion and ethnicity within the imagined nation-state. The pitfalls of this kind of revolutionary paradigm become obvious when we think about the post-independence role of Islamicism, or the fragile positioning of such communities as Berbers and Jews in Algeria or that of Kurds, Assyrians, Chaldeans, Turkmens, and Jews in Iraq. From a perspective that assumes a wide spectrum of complex power relations among, between, and within communities, Third World nationalism has had complex implications for minorities, especially where colonial partitions were involved.[40] While Fanon rightly denounced the fixing gaze of colonialist racism, anticolonialist nationalism also imposed fixing homogenous definitions on the nation, with disastrous consequences for ethnic, national, religious, racial, gender, and sexual minorities.

National culture in Fanon's text is rendered, curiously, almost in the same biologistic discourse that Fanon criticizes elsewhere: "A non-existent culture can hardly have any bearing on reality, or to influence reality. The first necessity is the re-establishment of the nation in order to give life to national culture in the strictly biological sense of the phrase."[41] But the biological trope of the organically unitary nation is impregnated with ruptures and splits within the imagined corpus. The opportunistic postponements and wait-your-turn exclusions of nationalism—first the nation, then class or ethnicity or gender—have come to haunt Third World liberation struggles through the return of what had been repressed during the foundational period of the nation-state. Thus, we find the ongoing conflict between, for example, Berbers and Arab Algerians, or the disillusionment of Algerian women, who believed that their participation in the anticolonial struggle would guarantee their empowerment once independence was won. Undoubtedly, the idea of a homogeneous nation was crucial for legitimizing realpolitik demands within a colonial context premised on the ideology of (French or British) nationalist coherency, which could be confronted only by mirroring counterclaims. Yet in the process, various minorities were rendered invisible and subordinate. Fanon's chapter on the "pitfalls of the national bourgeoisie," by the same token, bears the traces of a Marxism that downplays the historical relevance of such categories as ethnicity or gender.

BETWEEN GEOGRAPHIES

A relational approach to Fanon's thinking also has implications for the intersection of gender and geography, especially along the Martinique–France–Algeria axis. In the early text, the Martinican woman serves as a key antagonist within Fanon's narrative, while in the later text, the Algerian woman performs as the protagonist. Written at a time when marriage between a *Béké* and a black in Martinique was virtually unthinkable, *Black Skin, White Masks* examines the desire of the black woman for the white man, and the desire of the black man for the white woman. Revealing selective empathy, Fanon unmasks the negrophobic environment that drives the black man into the arms of the white woman, but he extends no such understanding for the black woman driven into the arms of the white man. Fanon's censuring of Abdoulaye Sadji's Nini and Mayotte Capécia's desire for the white man as a pathological form of social mobility is more passionately proffered than any criticism of the black man's desire to marry a light-skinned woman. It would seem that Fanon (dis)places the lactification neurosis and the burden of miscegenation-as-betrayal on the black/mulatta woman alone. Several recent writings have critiqued this gendered limitation of Fanon's analysis of Capécia's semifictional, auto-biographical *Je suis martiniquaise*, while others have performed a gendered analysis of Fanon's writings on Algerian women and the veil. But rather than discuss each female figure in isolation, I want to facilitate a dialogue— a threshold encounter, as it were—between Fanon's diasporic Martinican and the Arab Algerian female figures, an encounter that never takes place explicitly in Fanon's text. My goal is not simply to point to Fanon's misogy-nist blind spots or to suggest his theoretical lacuna, but, rather, to explore the intersection of gender and nation, of sexuality and geography, within the larger discursive frame of revolutionary discourses. Rather than see *Black Skin, White Masks* and the later texts about Algeria as discontinuous, I want to read them in relation, in terms of their gendered allegorizations.

Fanon's devaluation of Capécia and his valorization of the Algerian woman do not explicitly revolve around Arab versus Caribbean racial iden-tity. The two women, after all, might even look alike. (Some Caribbean women of mixed race and North African women have features and color in common.) Fanon's disdain for Capécia as a traitor to the race, on the one hand, and his enthusiastic embrace of the faithful Algerian revolutionary woman, on the other, is in some ways symptomatic of revolutionary mas-culinist discourse. While the Algerian woman's deployment of her body as a weapon against Europe arouses his passionate ode to a metaphorically feminized land (exemplified in the notion of "Algeria unveiled"), which fuses the female body with the national geography, the Martinican woman provokes his anxiety concerning the transgression of racial and sexual borders. He salutes the revolutionary Algerian woman for responding to colonial violence, for passing through political borders, for fashioning her own body as a border, and ultimately for refusing to facilitate a fluid con-tact between colonizer and colonized—precisely the taboo violated by Ca-pécia's exchange of bodily fluids with the Frenchman. Fanon's revolution-ary female figure is viewed as a vehicle for freedom, while the Martinican woman becomes an obstacle to the liberation of the black man. Capécia's figure is looked on as a morbid body neurotically immersed in narcissism and infantilism and associated with amputation, mutilation, and castration.[42] Capécia's erotic preference for the white man, in this sense, is safely de-eroticized, revealing worries about the unmanning, as it were, of the black man.[43]

Fanon's discussion of cross-racial desire is haunted by metaphors of sterility and aridity. His language virtually resonates with the colonial trope of the mulatto/mulatta as sterile, but later salvaged as a moment or an opening to restructure social life.[44] Fanon's text at times bears the traces of a Romantic eros/tanatos characteristic of a certain revolutionary imaginary,[45] promising a revolutionary redemption through a virile anticolonialist action. Interestingly, however, it is largely narrated through a cross-gender identification with the female figure, as Fanon's prose vividly captures the nuances of inhabiting the body of veiled or unveiled woman. Fanon also describes the Algerian woman's corporeal conflicts—her estrangement from her unveiled body—as she sacrifices herself for the nation. For Fanon, the Algerian woman who "walks stark naked" into the European city "relearns her body," reestablishing it in totally revolutionary fashion. Fanon paints a desired form of womanhood, the shape-shifting Algerian woman overflowing with eroticized life force as she carries out her deadly mission. Through his identification with the Algerian woman, Fanon configures a revolutionary subjectivity that is cross-national, cross-racial, and even at times cross-gendered.

Anticolonialist intellectuals, while not usually preoccupied with revolutionizing gender and sexual hierarchies, did nonetheless deploy a discourse rich in gender and sexual tropes. Revolutionary discourse often spoke of the revolution in analogies drawn from the realm of heterosexual relationship, as when Gamal Abdel Nasser, in a conversation with Che Guevara, said that "mobilizing the masses came in the romance stage of revolution. The day of the revolution was the consummation of the romance—the wedding night. But after that you had to make the marriage succeed. You had to earn money, build a house, and produce children."[46] Both Fanon and Aimé Césaire, meanwhile, referred to the rape and ravage brought on by colonialism. Césaire excoriated "that collection of adventurers who slashed and violated and spat on Africa to make the stripping of her easier."[47] While addressing the dispossession of colonial land and people, Fanon condenses the horrors of colonialism through a portrayal of the colonizer's brutality toward colonized women: "The Algerian woman is at the heart of the combat. Arrested, tortured, raped, shot down, she testifies to the violence of the occupier and to his inhumanity."[48] Third Worldist intellectuals answered the colonial narratives of the rape and rescue of white women, and at times of dark women, from violent dark men and cultures. They countered such narratives by recalling the actual history of the sexual violence and dispossession performed against colonized women. The revolutionary man subverted the gendered rhetoric that had often justified colonialism's "mission of progress," yet his rhetoric, too, relied on similar narratives and tropes, but only in an inverted fashion. Third Worldist revolutionary discourse mounted its own (hetero)masculinist discourses of rape and rescue to articulate and legitimize the revolution. More than a metonymy, rape here was metaphor.[49]

Fanon marshals the metaphor of "Algeria unveiled" in a chapter devoted to the Algerian woman's revolutionary defiance, analyzing the shifting significations of the veil in the anticolonial war. "Unveiling," both as a metaphor and metonymy, refers to the militant Algerian women masquerading as Europeans to fight against Europe, camouflaging the true purpose of their unveiling. The dialectics of veiling and unveiling transmutes into the metaphorical locus of domination and resistance. Forming part of a divide-and-conquer modernizing strategy, France's obsessive desire to literally unveil Algerian women is decoded as an attempt to denude Algeria and, in Fanon's words, to "penetrate the native society."[50] Fanon describes the battle over the veil in sexualized language:

> Every rejected veil disclosed to the eyes of the colonialists horizons until then forbidden, and revealed to them, piece by piece, the flesh of Algeria laid bare. . . . Every veil that fell, every body that became liberated from the traditional embrace of the *haik*, every face that offered itself to the bold and impatient glance of the occupier, was a negative expression of the fact that Algeria was beginning to deny herself and was accepting the rape of the colonizer.[51]

France's historical unveiling of Algerian women, in other words, is read as a symbolic unveiling of the nation, but it leaves "veiled" the question of woman's entangled agency within a patriarchal revolution and language.

The rhetoric of the veil, meanwhile, carries sexual and epistemological connotations. It implies that only Algerians truly "know" their women, who therefore must be reclaimed from the colonizer—a discourse that allows colonized men to assert their symbolic possession over the nation. The account of the anticolonial struggle, in other words, remains inscribed on the body of the woman, made to bear the symbolic burden of represent-

ing the suffering corpus of the nation. To battle the literal and metaphorical rape performed by the colonizer, Fanon enlists an eroticized image of
the revolutionary woman: "The shoulders of the unveiled Algerian woman
are thrust back with easy freedom. She walks with a graceful, measured
stride, neither too fast nor too slow. Her legs are bare, not confined by the
veil, given back to themselves, and her lips are free."[52] Unlike the trea-
sonous figure of Capécia, the revolutionary Algerian woman sacrifices for
the nation, respecting the taboo on cross-racial desire erected by both
colonialists and nationalists. Although sexualized by the French, she deploys that sexualization against the colonial power, preserving herself for
the revolution and for the revolutionary man. The female body in such
instances is largely figured as an object of competing virilities, between the
potent Frenchman and the emasculated colonized man fighting to regain
potency. Fanon embraces the bodily versatility of Algerian women: their
chameleonic readiness to veil and unveil themselves and to disguise themselves as European to carry and plant bombs at will. This revolutionary
"passing" must be seen in contradistinction to Capécia's conformist passing in which the sexual embrace of a white man equals social intercourse
with the system he represents. In Fanon's text, Capécia emerges as a parallel figure to the racist Jew who turns his back on the oppressed. In this
sense, it matters less whether Capécia was in fact an alienated mixed-blood
woman, or whether Michel Salomon was racist; what matters more is
Fanon's notion of "passing" as a political rather than a biological category.

The exoticization of the mulatta within dominant French culture was intertwined with the erasure or castration of the mulatto/black man. Fanon's
text fires back: "I marry white culture, white beauty, white whiteness. When
my restless hands caress those white breasts, they grasp white civilization
and dignity and make them mine."[53] In this homosocial dual, women—
including and, here, especially the silenced white woman—are vanquished
possessions in a fantasized triumph over the white man. Fanon the man
forcefully recounts a heterosexual fantasy, but Fanon the analyst only
places the black man's wounded ego on the couch to garner a therapeutic
massage. Yet Fanon's analysis of the black man's desire for the white
woman as a trophy of white culture passes over its corollary: the black
man's rejection of the black woman. In his writing, Fanon does not subject
his own marriage to a French white woman to the same scrutiny brought to
bear on Capécia. Rather, he explains his marriage in terms of affinities and
the magical accidents of love. If Simone de Beauvoir in the *Second Sex*
deploys blackness as a metaphor for women's enslavement, Fanon's fe-

male figure allegorizes the state of blacks in the colonized world. In between these two rhetorical modes, the voice of the black woman, or the Third World woman, however, remains a blank space—or, to recall the African American women's dictum, "And some of us are brave."

Despite his concern with the literal rape of the colonized woman, and the figurative rape of African land, Fanon on the whole is more invested in contesting the white projection of the black man as rapist than in contesting the projections that make the black woman or the colonized woman "rapable." Fanon's critique of Mannoni's "Prospero Complex," in anticipation of Césaire's revisionist version of Shakespeare's *The Tempest*, disputes Prospero's assumption that Caliban is just waiting for the chance to molest Miranda. (Interestingly, the figure of Caliban, in Shakespeare, like Fanon's text, mixed references to the Caribbean and to Algiers). Like Shakespeare and like Mannoni, Césaire and Fanon in their critical rewriting or reading of *The Tempest* fail to imagine a sister for Caliban, a possible Calibana, or even an Ariela. When Fanon speaks of his Algerian Calibana it is mainly as the trigger for Prospero's lust and scorn, and for Caliban's virility and impotence.

When Fanon writes about rape both as a metaphor for the colonized nation and as an index of the colonizer's actual violence, his text produces striking silences. In one of the case studies of the mental disorders wrought by colonialism, Fanon addresses a specific rape incident, focusing on the "impotence in an Algerian following the rape of his wife."[54] Fanon dedicates narrative space to the impotency of the FLN man whose wife was raped by the French police as part of interrogating her about her husband. Her story unfolds through his. If Freud invokes rape only within the realm of female fantasy, Fanon's raped Algerian woman receives no narrative space of her own. Fanon also does not analyze the mental and biological disorders engendered by colonialism in relation to female sexuality. In "The Colonial War and Mental Disorders," Fanon briefly speaks of "Menstruation Trouble in Women," suggesting that "this pathology is very well known, and we shall not spend much time on it. Either the women affected remain three or four months without menstruation, or else considerable pain accompanies it, which has repercussions on character and conduct."[55] Fanon does acknowledge the repercussions of colonial war for women's mental disorders but simultaneously does not see it as fit for serious scientific investigation. At the same time, in a context where "revolution" carries the latent potential of attaining heterosexual virility, it is also not a surprising coincidence that stories of sexual violence committed against colonized women are privileged over those of violence toward colonized men. The same sexual blinders that lead Fanon to claim that "there is no homosexuality in Martinique" lead him, and the cohort of other revolutionaries, to leave out of bounds any discussion of sexual violence performed against imprisoned colonized men by the colonizers, not to mention among the colonized themselves.[56] And if colonial discourse attributed rape to the black man, or to the colonized man, Fanonian anticolonial discourse acknowledges only one kind of rape—heterosexual rape by Frenchmen of the Algerian women—repressing other modes of speaking of rape.

Texts by Third World women have focused precisely on some of the issues elided in Fanon's anticolonial text. Although the practice of rape was shaped and intensified by the colonialist class and gender hierarchy, its agents were also colonized men themselves. Rather than have the woman carry the allegory of the birth of the nation, women's narratives have focused on concrete birth and maternity, entangled in sexual and class taboos and obstacles, often shaping open-ended narratives, far from the euphoric telos of the nationalist narrative. Although the revolutionary woman for Fanon constitutes a historic rupture with traditional Algerian gender codes, his narrative relies on a unified identity of the Algerian woman, ignoring differences based on class, region, and ethnicity. Colonialism, as many Arab feminists have pointed out, affected these diverse women in different ways. In rural Berber-speaking regions of Algeria, women usually conducted their lives without recourse to the veil. The colonialist discourse and modernization policies of unveiling consequently had far more impact in the urban centers. Fanon's analysis of the veil as a signifying object does redeem it from a Eurocentric imaginary that would simply project Arab women as passive and in need of rescue. Yet the same Fanon who privileges the peasantry (in contrast to the Marxist emphasis on the proletariat) overlooks not merely the issue of power relations between men and women, but also those affecting women of variegated regions and classes in Algeria.

Fanon enshrines the Algerian woman in terms parallel to the FLN discourse that glorified women for their contribution to the revolution but violated their rights with the nascent nation-state. Women were praised for doing what women had traditionally done: sacrificing themselves. At the same time, in spite of invoking a familiar paradigm, the very act of participating in the revolution for many Third World women did strengthen their sense of empowerment. No longer were they simply fighting for independence; they were also battling for a social revolution. Although the revolutionary project was hopeful for the women working within anticolonial movements, the project was also locally and globally intertwined with multiple oppressions and resistances. When Third World women mounted gender critiques, their male compatriots generally accused them of becoming "Westernized." Therefore, while still resisting the colonized situation of their "nation," revolutionary women opened a way to crack the narrative of the "nation" or of "race" as a unified entity. The demise of Third Worldist euphoria, including its liberationist promise for women, has encouraged a public "outing" of what was previously whispered, revealing that decolonization has not led to liberation on gender and sexual grounds. Reading the Algerian woman of Fanon's text against the backdrop of the history of Algerian women speaks volumes concerning the muffling of women's voices, the failure to appreciate their multi-fronted struggle.

At the same time, juxtaposing Fanon's Algerian woman in relation to Capécia requires additional historical contextualization. Fanon was writing about the pathologies of race and sexuality after having served as a soldier for Free France, in a war in which he was wounded and during which he came to perceive the illusory nature of the ideals of *La Republique.* Not unlike the experience of African Americans who spilled blood in the name of freedom during World War Two, only to find their own blood literally segregated from "white blood" in the army blood supply, Fanon discovered that he had fought a war for a free France that was about as racist as Vichy France. The participation of diverse colonized soldiers fighting on behalf of the colonialist allies indirectly energized postwar movements, leading to a demand for an end to colonialism and racism, whether practiced by France, Britain, or the United States. In *Je suis martiniquaise,* Capécia's heroine shares her white lover's right-wing political sympathies. She looks down at the blacks who fought against the Vichy regime in Martinique, describing the black population as becoming arrogant after the war. Capécia's text replicates the views of the *Békés,* whose enthusiastic support for Vichy was stirred by their hope of reducing the political power of the black mulatto middle class. (This paralleled the situation in Algeria, where the Pied Noirs succeeded in revoking the seventy-year-long décret Crémieux, stripping Algerian Jews of their citizenship during Vichy, led by Marshall Petain.) Fanon's rejection of Capécia must therefore be read as a response not only to her symbolic rejection of the black man and of her worshipful mimicry of the French bourgeoisie, but also to her embrace of the Vichy regime.[57] Fanon's criticism of Capécia-style assimilation resonates with his own "disobedience" to the Francophile assimilationism of the colored bourgeoisie in Martinique, a criticism extrapolated into another geographical context, and on another register, in Fanon's scrutiny of the "Pitfalls of Bourgeois Nationalism" in *The Wretched of the Earth*. Fanon's rebuff of Capécia, who denies not only her race but also her country, reflects his general antagonism toward collaborationist Martinicans who backed Vichy France. In criticizing Fanon's gender politics, we need not idealize Capécia, whose support for a fascist regime seems to color Fanon's take on her racial alienation and social arrivisme.

Can Fanon's rejection of Capécia be divorced from his ambivalent relation to a native land seen as yielding itself to the French? Fanon is less concerned with the ambiguities of Capécia's racial identity than with her "bad faith" and "inauthenticity," to use Sartrean language, or in Marxist terms, her "false consciousness." In a sense, Capécia forms a shadow alter ego for Fanon. She embodies the same diasporic relationality exemplified by Fanon; both are hybrid products of the mestizo syncretism of the Americas, and both address the issue of cross-racial desire. Both attempt to chart a way out, but end up on opposite ideological sides. Fanon's virtually dualistic account of the two female figures, at two distinct points of his work, testifies, in a displaced fashion, to his rebellion against an acquiescent diasporic existence. In Algeria, Fanon found a revolutionary politics worthy of his revolutionary enthusiasm. Fanon's Algerian woman, who emerges from the Medina, commonly referred to as "nigger town," and crosses barbed-wire borders only to expel the French comes to answer, as it were, to Fanon's earlier anxiety concerning Capécia's crossing of racial borders in a more hybrid and assimilationist "New World" context. There are, however, some fundamental differences between Fanon's Capécia and the Algerian woman as metaphors for the Caribbean and Africa, respectively. In contrast to the diasporic blacks of the Americas, born of the violent transport of enslaved people across the ocean and uprooted from their land, their community, language, and religion, the majority of colonized people in Asia and Africa, in Fanon's time, were usually resisting while still rooted in their land. Even if partly exiled on their land, even if partly dispossessed from their culture, their existence manifested a clearer evidence of historical continuity.

Could it be that Fanon had trouble coming to terms with his own diasporic background? Could it be that Africa signified a symbolic homecoming for a Caribbean intellectual? Edouard Glissant speaks of the way Caribbean writers are constantly making "detours," constantly exiting from their Caribbean beginnings, constantly moving elsewhere—to France, to the United States, and in Fanon's case, to Algeria. Fanon's embrace of the sacrificing Algerian woman restages, on one level, a desire for a sacrificial mother Africa who avenges and rescues the returning son of enslavement. But by placing her nursing figure on the pedestal, Fanon paradoxically expresses another ambivalence—this time toward the abandoning continent, Africa. In a kind of a compensatory recuperation, the valorized Algerian woman of Fanon's text enacts the historically dense contradictions of the transatlantic passage. The problem with Fanon's discourse here, arguably, lies less in the dualistic discourse about the two female figures than in how each figure is entangled in a larger geographical allegory.

BETWEEN TEMPORALITIES

The figures of black, Arab and Jew, the Algerian woman, and even Capécia must be seen as metonymic and metaphoric for Fanon's larger project of humanizing the enslaved,[58] the oppressed, the colonized, and even, perhaps, the colonizer. Fanon's revolutionary work of "restructuring the world"[59] is intertwined with an epistemological project of creating, in his words, a "new humanism."[60] The universalism of the old humanism, like the scientific objectivity of Western rationalism, according to Fanon, is directed against the colonized.[61] He calls for the colonized to "leave this Europe, where they are never done talking of Man, yet murder men everywhere they find them, at the corner of every one of their streets, in all the corners of the globe."[62] His powerful statement slices open the paradoxes inherent in Europe's humanist discourse and its narrative of progress. The universalism of the new humanism, in contrast, promises to redeem the colonized and thus, in Fanon's words, allow them to "rise above this absurd drama that others have staged around me . . . to reach out to the universal."[63] Thus, for Fanon, "The Negro is aiming for the Universal. . . . The Negro is universalizing himself."[64] Fanon articulates liberation not merely within the material realm of political struggle but also within an epistemological project that envisions a refurbished and truly universal humanism. And that underlying utopian project imbues Fanon's writing with a transformative, even cathartic, power. In this new universalism lies both the passionate force of Fanon's writings and, to an extent, its dissonances and aporias.

Suggesting the incongruity between Europe's Enlightenment ideal of humanism and its real-life dehumanizing of colonized people, Fanon's text formed an advance foray into what was to become the postmodernist critique of "universalism." It also performed the groundwork for dependency theory in such works as Walter Rodney's *How Europe Underdeveloped Africa*, Manning Marable's *How Capitalism Underdeveloped Black America*, and Eduardo Galeano's *The Open Veins of Latin America*. Deploying the method of materialist dialectics, Fanon eloquently reveals the underside of progress:

> The European opulence is literally scandalous, for it has been founded on slavery, it has been nourished with the blood of slaves and it comes directly from the soil and from the subsoil of that underdeveloped world. The well-being and the progress of Europe have been built up with the sweat and the dead bodies of negroes, Arabs, Indians, and the yellow races.[65]

Fanon subverts Europe's rescue fantasies "on behalf" of its colonized, seeing the West itself as depending on the non-West to generate its modernity. For Fanon, progress was a document of civilization, in Walter Benjamin's powerful aphorism, that hides a document of barbarism. The "victims of progress" thesis of Fanon's text inevitably raises the question of temporality. Does Fanon propose his New Humanism in relation to a precolonial past before European contamination or in relation to a future utopia to begin at degree zero? What are the implications of Fanon's demystifying Europe's false universalizations for the very idea of universalism? In what sense does the analysis of the negativities of Europe's progress impact on the linear narrative of progress? Does Fanon only dissect, or completely reject, or perhaps rethink, Europe's humanism? And how does he narrativize the Enlightenment?

Fanon's negotiation of the question of temporality often makes him sound more like Marx than Senghor. Indeed, the final chapter of *Black Skin, White Masks* opens with an epigraph from Marx's *The Eighteenth Brumaire of Louis Napoleon*, written as a response to Bonaparte's 1851 coup and as a summary of the French 1848 Revolution: "The social revolution . . . cannot draw its poetry from the past, but only from the future. It cannot begin with itself before it has stripped itself of all its superstitions concerning the past. . . . The revolutions of the nineteenth century have to let the dead bury the dead." Fanon conceptualizes the relations between past and future in a similar fashion: "The discovery of the existence of a Negro civilization in the fifteen century confers no patent of humanity on me. Like it or not, the past can in no way guide me in the present moment."[66] Subsequently, in *The Wretched of the Earth*, Fanon further developed his critique of the intellectual "slaves of the past": "I admit that all the proofs of a wonderful Songhai civilization will not change the fact that today the Songhais are underfed and illiterate, thrown between sky and water with empty heads and empty eyes."[67] Fanon's anticolonial poetics betray little nostalgia for an Edenic precolonial past. In his remarks on "national culture," Fanon offers an insight into the passionate investment with which native intellectuals defend an idealized version of the precolonial past. The colonized psyche, unlike that of the European intellectual, "is not conveniently sheltered behind a French or a German culture which has given full proof of its existence and which is uncontested."[68] Fanon, in other words, empathizes with the colonized intellectual's desire to rehabilitate an unjustly unrecognized past, but he refuses an intellectual project of archaeological recuperation.

Fanon was not a partisan of Negritude; nor can he be seen as anticipating an Afrocentric search for an originary past:[69]

> In no way should I dedicate myself to the revival of an unjustly unrecognized Negro civilization. I will not make myself the man of any past. I do not want to exalt the past at the expense of my present and of my future. It is not because the Indo-Chinese has discovered a culture of his own that he is in revolt. It is because "quite simply" it was, in more than one way, becoming impossible for him to breathe.[70]

In fact, Negritude can be seen as a positive inversion of philosophical postulations such as Hegel's that Africa did not participate in historical movement and progression and that its "Spirit" was "still involved in the conditions of mere nature."[71] Fanon's critique of what might be called the *hermeneutics of the ancient* can be similarly addressed to diverse contemporaneous racialized intellectuals—for example, Jewish thinkers in France such as Edmond Fleg, Emmanuel Levinas, and Eliane Amado Lévy-Valensi, who while critiquing the modern Christian West in its own language were also trying to redeem the place of Jews in the West by demonstrating the contribution of Judaism to universal culture.[72] Fanon's revolutionary project, meanwhile, sought a new third stage, a synthetic space that was neither derivative nor reactive. Just as Fanon critiques those who "throw [themselves] greedily upon Western culture,"[73] he also critiques those who fixate on the past: "The colonized man who writes for his people ought to use the past with the intention of opening the future, an invitation to action and a basis for hope."[74]

Fanon's revolutionary hope is predicated on the eclipse of Europe as the unique site of freedom and liberty:

Come, then, comrades, the European game has finally ended; we must find something different. We today can do everything, so long as we do not imitate Europe, so long as we are not obsessed by the desire to catch up with Europe. . . . Humanity is waiting for something from us other than such an imitation. . . . For Europe, for ourselves, and for humanity, comrades, we must turn over a new leaf, we must work out new concepts, and try to set afoot a new man.[75]

Despite this desire for new concepts, Fanon's "new humanism" ultimately faces the dilemma of whether to "mend or end" the Enlightenment's humanist project. To what extent, then, is his project revolutionary or merely reformative? Fanon invokes "humanism" as a rhetorical boomerang against Europe's writing the colonized out of humanity. His text resonates ambiguously toward the Enlightenment, however, and cannot be seen as ultimately rejecting it. Fanon even used the term "enlightenment" in *Wretched of the Earth*—in the more vernacular sense of bringing the light of education—in a context where to speak of black enlightenment was paradoxically subversive while also scorning a certain black enlightenment that internalized white prejudices about black bodies. Fanon's goal of turning a new historical page is itself diacritically embedded in Enlightenment thought in that he seems more concerned with false universalism than with universalism per se. Fanon thus speaks within the metanarrative of universalism not to negate it altogether but, rather, to negate its exclusivism.

Fanon's critique had precursors around the time of the French Revolution, when the Caribbean Islands became the scene of black critiques of the Enlightenment. The "Black Jacobins" in Haiti incorporated Enlightenment revolutionary discourse but insisted that it apply equally to all, regardless of race. Toussaint L'Ouverture proclaimed liberty and equality for the slaves in Haiti, insisting on their right to be part of republican modernity. C. L. R. James said of the "Black Jacobins" of Haiti that they "had caught the spirit of the thing: Liberty, Equality, Fraternity."[76] Fanon, like his teacher Aimé Césaire, carries on that critique from another location and angle. Here I will only briefly try to relationalize the discussion in temporal terms, sending Fanon's text back to the Caribbean and placing it within longstanding debates about race and revolution, even though Fanon himself does not explicitly engage those debates.

The Enlightenment and its offspring, the revolution, are highly contradictory; both combine compassionate sentiments and horrifying complicities with colonialism and enslavement. The gaps, fissures, and hypocrisies highlighted by L'Ouverture earlier and by Césaire and Fanon later cannot be viewed as mere oversights on the part of Enlightenment thought. They must instead be seen as constitutive of its Eurocentrism. The concept "all men are created equal" was foundational for legalizing both equality for some and inequality for the excluded, colonized, enslaved, and dispossessed. Some more consistent Enlightenment philosophers such as Michel de Montaigne and Denis Diderot inverted the trope of barbarism, considering the colonizers the real barbarians. Diderot even defended the right of the oppressed to revolt, thus anticipating later radical renegades such as Sartre and de Beauvoir.[77] More commonly, however, Enlightenment philosophers ignored the "progressive" subjugation of those who stood in reason's way, failing to address the dark underside of the Enlightenment. Contemporaneous with Europe's rise to world power, the Enlightenment, as Robert Stam and I suggest in *Unthinking Eurocentrism*, perpetuated, along with its progressive and liberatory "overside," an imperialist, diffusionist, hierarchical underside. The "social contract" delineated by such philosophers as Locke, Rousseau, and Mill was doubled by what Y. N. Kly calls the "antisocial contract" in which the idea of "equality among equals" came to entail an equal opportunity to disappropriate and dispossess. The Enlightenment, as Charles W. Mills suggests, put forward a "racial contract," found in the work of Locke as well as in Rousseau's *Discourse on Inequality* (1755), that naturalizes inequality.[78]

Although race is sublimated, it is also not an afterthought or aberration from ostensibly raceless Enlightenment ideals. Rather, it is a central shaping constituent of those ideals. Conventional disciplinary divisions, furthermore, "delink" the philosophy of Enlightenment thinkers from their anthropology when, in fact, the anthropology of such thinkers forms an essential feature of their work.[79] Their philosophical treatises must be read alongside these other texts, where they explicitly developed negative views about blacks and advanced colonialist ideas about the world.[80] Widely regarded as the most important moral and aesthetic theorist of the modern period, Immanuel Kant, for example, actually devoted most of his career not to philosophy but to anthropology and physical geography. He was central to the shaping of the modern concept of race, assuming the immutability of race. Hegel's master–slave dialectic, meanwhile, was written with oblivion to its contemporaneous Europe's imperial mastery and enslavement of Africans in the era of the definitive black revolt in Haiti. Enlightenment thinkers, whether explicitly or implicitly, tended to encode the dominant Eurocentric values.[81] Guaranteeing the political economy of the West, the exploitation of colonized slave laborers was accepted as a given by the very thinkers who proclaimed freedom to be a natural human state and an inalienable right. Both the French Revolution and the American Revolution, as political expressions of the Enlightenment, defined a falsely universalist set of values while posing as defending the "rights of man." Although the French model does not recognize "race" as a valid conceptual or institutional category, the Republic of "Liberté, Egalité, Fraternité" did install and encode a gendered ethnic and racial order. However, such ideals, as Fanon's writing suggests, were undercut by an originary discourse of the "*Nos ancêtres les Gaulois*" of the colonial history books that taught the Martinicans, the Senegalese, and the Vietnamese that "our ancestors, the Gauls, had blue eyes and blond hair." Colonialism, then, aided the global "travel" of the Enlightenment, whose ideals would seem to contradict colonialism's raison d'être. Yet, paradoxically, colonialist discourse itself was premised on Enlightenment categories such as "*la mission civilisatrice.*"

Against this intellectual backdrop, and given Fanon's French education, it would be difficult to imagine a Fanonian project unmarked by Enlightenment discourse. In some respects, a certain Enlightenment was profoundly liberating for a certain strata within Europe and even outside it. Over the past three centuries, those victimized by colonizing and patriarchal claims possessed a conceptual vehicle for pointing out the failed universality of the regimes that excluded them while returning to those same universal Enlightenment principles to press their own emancipatory claims. What sense, then, can we make out of a Fanonian revolutionary discourse that opens up fissures in Europe's universalist humanism yet is itself born of the totalizing narratives embedded in Enlightenment discourse? Fanon's critique of false universalization is hardly preoccupied with critiquing the deep generative matrix that resulted in what might be called the bad intellectual habit of false universalization. It can even be argued that his enlisting of Enlightenment premises boomerangs against aspects of his own, new humanistic project, which stands on the same grounds it sets out to critique. As Fanon seeks to liberate the black man, in a kind of gendered trickle-down liberation, he does so within the terms of a new humanist objectivity and melioristic teleology. Fanon's retrofitted universalism thus raises legitimate questions about its own exclusions—for example, its eliding or masking of questions of gender and sexuality. Moreover, the ultimate question of who, how, and what determines and regulates the "universal" remains obscure, forming a kind of a buried epistemology in Fanon's text. Fanon's anticolonial text, then, is caught in a negative dialectic vis-à-vis colonial discourse, which, after all, articulates the project of the anticolonial liberation movement, but still within the discursive apparatus of Enlightenment universalism, the very same framework that informs the colonialist narrative.

Fanon's desire to abandon "Europe," then, is itself diacritically shaped by his dialogue with the Enlightenment narrative of "West" and "the rest." Fanon's refutation of "Europe" still takes on board some Eurocentric assumptions. Writing in the heat of a combat, in a politically driven situation, Fanon posits "Europe" and its "others" as two axiomatically contradictory cultural geographies. Such a reading on Fanon's part results not simply from colonialism's bifurcated reality, but also from the assimilation of Enlightenment dichotomies that delink various geographies and histories. Fanon's call to leave "Europe," then, does not translate into interrogating the Enlightenment narrative concerning "Europe" as culturally self-generated. Yet, in fact, the "West" has always been thoroughly imbricated and even shaped by its dialogue with African and Asian, as well as with the indigenous American, traditions. (Even Enlightenment philosophy was at least partly shaped by the encounter with various indigenous American worldviews.)[82] The notion of a "pure" Europe originating in Classical Greece is itself premised on crucial exclusions, from the African and Semitic influences that shaped Classical Greece itself to the osmotic Sephardic-Judeo-Islamic culture that played such a crucial role in the Europe of the so-called Dark Ages (a Eurocentric designation for a period of Oriental ascendancy), and even in the Middle Ages and the Renaissance. Because of this cultural amalgamation, the "West" is itself a site of an omnivorous mélange of cultures.[83] More than simply absorbing non-European influences, the "West" was constituted by various non-European cultures.[84] Fanon's text, in other words, reproduces a rather Eurocentric narrative about Enlightenment discourse that elides the historical mixing that made Africa, Asia, and, later, indigenous America constitutively present within the formation of the West. Fanon deconstructs "Europe" on numerous grounds, but in some respects he remains locked within that narrative even when he is opposing it.

Given the historical circumstances within which Fanon was writing, his work does not advocate alternative narratives. Although at times Fanon cites specific traditions that might contribute to the revolution—for example, "the *Djammas*" (Arabic for community) as a model of political participation—he generally regards traditional culture as peripheral. As a modernization discourse, Marxizing Third Worldism was impatient with "tradition," seen as synonymous with underdevelopment and the retrograde. Bearing some traces of this discourse, Fanon's text invested little rhetorical energy in imagining a future that would draw on diverse Arab, Kabyle, African cultural resources.[85] Although in his institutional practice, as we saw earlier, Fanon gradually became aware of the vital role cultural specificity could play in the treatment of scarred psyches, his writing hardly engaged in a deep study of Algeria's palimpsestic Berber-Arab-Ottoman-Muslim heritage and its repercussions for modes of resistance or for their potential role within the proposed new humanism.[86] Fanon's "Algeria," not unlike "the Algerian woman," consequently winds up acquiring a relatively abstract character. The nation, and the woman, in this sense appear to reproduce some of Sartre's postulations concerning the "Jew" or the "black" as mere sequences within the historical dialectics—the very same discourse Fanon rejected earlier. Such an approach allows Fanon, like Sartre, to de-essentialize "national culture," seeing it contingently, as bound to disappear with the eviction of colonialism. But this approach also thwarts a more complex analysis of the dynamic role North African cultural and historical particularities played in molding both progressive and regressive outcomes. Fanon's increasing appeal to the universal, like that of Sartre, echoes the French Republican ideal of universality that recognizes only the abstract French subject. (Any regional, ethnic, or religious particularities were perceived as a threat to the Republic's cohesiveness; hence, the unease about "the particular," seen even now in the current debate over wearing the veil in public schools.) Fanon's anxiety about the role of the "past" within the revolutionary project, meanwhile, can be traced to the Marxist linear model of meliorism that increasingly informs his writing in Algeria and Tunisia.

The traumatic rupture brought on by colonialism would come to haunt the revolutionary project, revealing the difficulty of detaching the "future" from the "past" and the "universal" from the "particular." Fanon's melioristic teleology leads him to underestimate the ongoing force of the precolonial social paradigms, a force that would be marshaled in moments of crisis, often in response, precisely, to the breakdown of the modernizing revolution. (In fact, colonialist discourse found its somewhat unlikely heir in post-independence Third Worldist modernization discourse and development policies.) Fanon unpacks Europe's narrative of rescue and progress but in other ways refurbishes its concepts of redemptive moderniza-tion. On one level, Fanon anticipates the postmodernist skepticism about the Enlightenment master narrative and its pretense of speaking on behalf of the universal. Yet unlike the postmodernists, Fanon nourishes a utopian thought of a "total revolution" but also, interestingly, one devoid of a ready-made blueprint.[87]

Rather than "cleanse" Fanon's text of Enlightenment traces, it would be more productive, I have tried to suggest, to read Fanon in relation to these contradictions. More important, it would be productive to read the Enlight-enment itself in a non-Eurocentric fashion, as emerging partially from a historical encounter with diverse indigenous American social organi-zations. The ambiguity in Fanon concerning the Enlightenment can be traced to the key issue of whether the Enlightenment signifies a rupture, or an extension of Europe's colonialist relation to its "others." Fanon's text betrays two contradictory impulses toward the Enlightenment, precisely because the Enlightenment itself was inherently contradictory. Positive values, such as representative government, freedom, and equality before the law, could not be reconciled with negative practices of colonialism, genocide, slavery, and imperialism, clearly the very antithesis of such val-ues. The contradictions central to the Enlightenment as simultaneously the source of racism and totalitarianism, and its alternatives, thus shape Fanon's discursive oscillation. Fanon partially reproduces an Enlighten-ment discourse that assumes Europe as a diffusionist source of reason, science, freedom, and progress while also seeing the Enlightenment as nothing more than the barbarity of instrumental reason, which annihilates local difference in the name of the universal. This tension is perhaps inevitable in a revolutionary project that seeks an anticolonial humanist meliorism while also dissecting colonialist humanist meliorism. Can we imagine a Fanonian project of liberation that completely rewrites the En-lightenment narrative? It remains for us to shape the contemporary ver-sions of Fanon's vision. In any case, we still must engage Fanon to go beyond Fanon.

NOTES

Frantz Fanon refers to "situational diagnosis" when he cites Dr. E. Stern. He calls Dr. Stern's medical advice "a magnificent plan" and tries to apply it to the social-colonial realm. See Frantz Fanon, *Toward the African Revolution: Political Essays,* trans. by Haakon Chevalier (New York: Grove Press, 1964), 10. Fanon also speaks of "situational neurosis," writing that "the Negro's behavior makes him akin to an obsessive neurotic type, or, if one prefers, he puts himself into a complete situational neurosis" (*Black Skin, White Masks* [New York: Grove Press, 1967]), 60.

Different parts of this essay have been presented as lectures since the 1980s in numerous venues. I especially thank the Center for Modern and Contemporary Studies, University of California, Los Angeles; the MacArthur Interdisciplinary Program on Peace and International Cooperation, Institute of International Relations, University of Minnesota, Minneapolis; the Center for Cultural Studies, University of California, Santa Cruz; the University of Leicester, United Kingdom; the Regents Lecture Series and Seminars, University of California, Davis; and the Conference in Honor of Angela Davis, School of Justice Studies, Arizona State University, Tempe. The final version of this essay was presented at the conference "Finding Fanon: Critical Genealogies," organized by Isaac Julien and Mark Nash, New York University, New York, September 1996. I am grateful to Moncef Cheikh-Rouhou for his generous hospitality during my research in Tunisia, where I was also revising this essay. I am especially appreciative of his sharing with me his insights and memories of Fanon during his exile from Algeria, especially of Fanon's attendance at the Open Table Monday meetings organized by Moncef's father Habib Cheikh-Rouhou, founder and editor of *Assabah* paper.

1 For a similar point, see Robert Stam, "Fanon, Algeria, and the Cinema: The Politics of Identification," in *Multiculturalism, Postcolonialism, and Transnational Media*, ed, by Ella Shohat and Robert Stam (New Brunswick, N.J.: Rutgers University Press, 2003).

2 Leopold S. Senghor, ed., *Anthologie de la nouvelle poésie nègre et malgache de langue française* (Paris: Presses Universitaires de France, 1948).

3 Fanon, *Black Skin, White Masks*, 133.

4 Jean-Paul Sartre, *Anti-Semite and Jew*, trans. by George J. Becker (New York: Shocken Books, 1976), 143; Fanon, *Black Skin, White Masks*, 14, 93.

5 Edward Said lists Albert Memmi as an example of Westerners who have demonstrated sympathy or comprehension of foreign cultures, as one of those intellectuals who crossed to the other side, when in fact Memmi is a Tunisian Jew, in contrast to Ashkenazi French Jews who came with the French colonization to Algeria (*Culture and Imperialism* [New York: Alfred A. Knopf, 1993], xx).

6 Fanon, *Black Skin, White Masks*, 135.

7 See ibid., 160–65.

8 Fanon, *Toward the African Revolution*, 29.

9 Fanon, *Black Skin, White Masks*, 112. It should be noted that I kept the French original "*Y'a bon Banania*," which Fanon's English translator rendered "Sho' good eatin'."

10 Ibid., 152–53, n. 15.

11 Ibid., 116.

12 Fanon, *The Wretched of the Earth*, trans. by Constance Farrington (New York: Grove Press, 1972), 102.

13 Fanon, *Black Skins, White Masks*, 60.

14 See Hammadou Ghania, "Fanon-Blida, Blida-Fanon," *Revolution Africaine*, 11 December 1987, 14.

15 Frantz Fanon and Jacques Azoulay, "La sociotherapie dans un service d'hommes musulmans," *L'Information Psychiatrique* 30 (1954): 349–61. The article was reprinted in *L'Information Psychiatrique* 51 (December 1975).

16 Fanon, *Black Skin, White Masks*, 110, 211; emphasis added.

17 Translated by Charles Lamm Markmann as "The Fact of Blackness," the original French title of the fifth chapter of *Peau noir, masques blancs* was "L'experience vecue du Noir," which can be translated as "The Lived Experience of the Black." The French title clearly indicates Fanon's intertext of phenomenology, with traces of Merleau-Ponty.

18 Fanon, *Black Skin, White Masks*, 122.

19 Ibid.

20 After praising the Inquisition against the Jews and the expulsion of the Muslims, Columbus reached the "New World" already bent on enslaving and converting those he would meet in "the land of the great Khan."

21 Sartre, *Anti-Semite and Jew*, 108.

22 Fanon, *Black Skin, White Masks*, 93.

23 Ibid., 166.

24 Ibid., 165.

25 Ibid., 157.

26 Ibid., 162–63.

27 In the nineteenth century, one finds the feminized, menstruating Jewish male, on the one hand, and the hypersexualized phallic black man, on the other. Jewish and black female bodies are cast out of this imagery.

28 On anti-Semitism in colonial Algeria from 1870 to 1940, see Michel Abitbol, *From Cremieux to Petain* (Jerusalem: Zalman Shazar Center, 1993), in Hebrew.

29 Sander Gilman, "Black Bodies, White Bodies: Toward an Iconography of Female Sexuality in Late Nineteenth Century Art, Medicine and Literature," in Henry Louis Gates Jr., *"Race," Writing, and Difference* (Chicago: University of Chicago Press, 1986).

30 Fanon, *Black Skin, White Masks*, 201.

31 Ibid., 103. While stationed in North Africa with the Free France forces during World War Two, Fanon observed that being a "Negro" made it "quite impossible to make contact with the natives."

32 Ibid., 103.

33 Ibid.

34 Ibid., 91.

35 The same kind of racist French sociological discourses about North Africans cited by Fanon in *Toward the African Revolution* during the upheavals of the 1950s and 1960s were also cited, this time positively, by Euro-Israeli writers and intellectuals with regard to North African Jews displaced to Israel around that time. Euro-Israeli academics evoked the work of their French colleagues, even their warnings that Israel was making the same "fatal mistake" of the French by opening the "gates too wide to Africans," perceived as "a certain kind of human material" that would "debase" Israel, sealing its fate as "a Levantine state." See Ella Shohat, "Sephardim in Israel: Zionism from the Standpoint of Its Jewish Victims," *Social Text* 19–20 (fall 1988).

Set in the south of Israel, Menahem Golan's film *Fortuna* (1964) projected the French-Algerian schism on the local scene, related through a tragic love story between a French man and an Algerian woman, allegorizing the Israeli version of deterministic climate theories and the clashing geographies of North versus South. See Ella Shohat, *Israeli Cinema: East/West and the Politics of Representation* (Austin: University of Texas Press, 1989).

36 Frantz Fanon, *A Dying Colonialism*, trans. by Haakon Chevalier (New York: Grove Press, 1965), 155.

37 Ibid., 157.

38 See Abitbol, *From Cremieux to Petain*.

39 Algerian Jews, even before the arrival of Zionism and the establishment of the State of Israel, had already entered an ambivalent status. Due to the granting of French citizenship, some ended up identifying with the French, while others took up arms with the nationalist movement.

40 Interestingly, despite Fanon's carving out spaces of black identity through and in relation to Jewishness and Arabness, the question of Israel/Palestine remains absent in his text. While he was working at a hospital in Tunisia, rival colleagues and his director, Ben Soltan, tried to have Fanon fired by accusing him of being a Zionist undercover agent maltreating Arab patients on orders from Israel. However, these accusations were dismissed outright by the minister of health, Ben Salah. See Peter Geismar, *Fanon* (New York: New Dial Press, 1971), 139–40.

41 Fanon, *The Wretched of the Earth*, p. 245.

42 Fanon, *Black Skin, White Masks*, 10, 44, 56, 59.

43 Recently, Françoise Vergès addressed the question of virility and disavowal in Fanon in "Creole Skin, Black Masks: Fanon and Disavowal," *Critical Inquiry* 23 (Spring 1997). See also Maryse Condé, "Order, Disorder, Freedom and the West Indian Writer," *Yale French Studies* 2, no. 83 (1993).

44 Fanon, *Black Skin, White Masks*, 48. Fanon also writes, "There is a zone of non-being, an extraordinarily sterile and arid region, an utterly naked declivity where an authentic upheaval can be born" (ibid., 8).

45 Fanon, who received *shahid* (Arabic for "martyr") recognition from the Algerians, died prematurely of leukemia. But it is the treacherous death of another revolutionary icon, Che Guevara, that better evokes a virtually crucified martyrdom. Nasser, who apparently warned Che that Bolivia was not ripe for revolution, also asked him, "Why do you always talk about death? You are a young man. If necessary we should die for the revolution, but it would be much better if we could live for the revolution." See Mohamed Hassanein Haikal, *The Cairo Documents: The Inside Story of Nasser and His Relationship with World Leaders, Rebels, and Statesmen* (Garden City, N.Y.: Doubleday, 1973), 356. In the same conversation, Nasser, the pan-Arabist, expressed other pragmatic concerns, challenging Che's romanticism. He cautioned Guevara, who wanted to join the fight in the

Congo, that "it won't succeed. You will be easily detected, being a white man, and if we get other white men to go with you, you will be giving the imperialists the chance to say that there is no difference between you and most mercenaries" (ibid., 352).

46 Guevara reportedly responded with a grin, saying, "I've already broken two marriages": ibid., 353.

47 Aimé Césaire, "Introduction," in Victor Schoeler, *Esclavage et colonisation* (Paris: Presses Universitaires de France, 1948).

48 Fanon, *A Dying Colonialism*, 66.

49 I am reminded of Malcolm X's rejection of the red shades of his hair, signifiers of the literal and symbolic rape of the black mother.

50 Fanon, "Algeria Unveiled," in *A Dying Colonialism*, 42.

51 Ibid.

52 Fanon, *A Dying Colonialism*, 58. Fanon also suggests that the Algerian woman will return to the veil later to solve the practical problem of hiding a bomb, for the safety of anonymity, and to make the declaration that Algeria is not French. For the discussion of the usages of the veil, see Barbara Harlow, "Introduction," in Malek Alloula, *The Colonial Harem*, trans. by Myrna Godzich and Wlad Godzich (Minneapolis: University of Minnesota Press, 1986); Marnia Lazreg, "Feminism and Difference: The Perils of Writing as a Woman on Women of Algeria," *Feminist Studies* 14 (1988).

53 Fanon, *Black Skin, White Masks*, 63.

54 Fanon, *The Wretched of the Earth*, 254.

55 Ibid., 291–92.

56 See also Ella Shohat, "Imaging Terra Incognita: The Disciplinary Gaze of Empire," *Public Culture* 3 (Spring 1991): 41–70. Despite rumors concerning the subject, the common silence confirms the sensitive nature of male on male rape.

57 In *Black Skin, White Masks*, 52, Fanon suggests this link when he cites Capécia's text with irony: "A fine specimen of his kind; he talked about the family, work, the nation, our good Petain and our good God, all of which allowed him to make her pregnant according to form. God has made use of us, said the handsome swine, the handsome white man, the handsome officer. After which, under the name of God-Fearing Petanist proprieties, I shove her over to the next man." In a footnote, Fanon continues: "It is legitimate to say that Mayotte Capécia has definitely turned her back on her country" (ibid., 53n).

58 "Two centuries ago, I was lost to humanity I was a slave forever" (ibid., 120).

59 Ibid., 82.

60 Ibid., 7.

61 Fanon, *The Wretched of the Earth*, 77.

62 Ibid., 311.

63 Fanon, *Black Skin, White Masks*, 197.

64 Ibid., 186.

65 Fanon, *The Wretched of the Earth*, 96.

66 Fanon, *Black Skin, White Masks*, 223, 225.

67 Fanon, *The Wretched of the Earth*, 209.

68 Ibid.

69 Fanon was not a black nationalist, although he was often understood as one by figures such as Stokely Carmichael and Eldridge Cleaver of the Black Power Movement in the United States.

70 Fanon, *Black Skin, White Masks*, 226.

71 Hegel wrote that "Africa . . . has no movement or development to exhibit. . . . Africa, is the Unhistorical, Undeveloped, Spirit still involved in the conditions of mere nature" (Georg W. Friedrich Hegel, *The Philosophy of History*, trans. by John Sibree [New York: Dover, 1956], 99).

72 Their intellectual activities were often linked to Jewish revival via Zionism, seen especially in the Colloques d'Intellectuels Juifs de Langue Française.

73 Fanon, *The Wretched of the Earth*, 218.

74 Ibid., 232.

75 Ibid., 312, 315–16.

76 C. L. R James, *The Black Jacobins: Toussaint L'Ouverture and the San Domingo Revolution* (New York: Vintage Books, 1989), 81.

77 Two key works that unearth Diderot's often hidden contributions to these debates are Yves Bénot, *Diderot: De l'athéisme à l'anti-colonialisme* (Paris: La Découverte, 1970), and M. Duchet, *Diderot et l'Histore des Deux Indes ou l' écriture fragmentaire* (Paris: Éditions A-G. Nizet, 1978).

78 Charles W. Mills, *The Racial Contract* (Ithaca, N.Y.: Cornell University Press, 1997).

79 See Kant's 1775 essay "The Different Races of Mankind" (Von den Verschiedenen Rassen des Menschen). Kant even gives some useful advice on how to beat Negroes efficiently. And although he rarely traveled out of his native Königsberg, Kant could confidently speak of the "passivity" (*Gelassenheit*) of the Hindus and the "idleness" of the Africans.

80 See also Mills, *The Racial Contract*, and Emmanuel Chukwudi Eze, *Race and the Enlightenment* (Cambridge, Mass.: Blackwell, 1997).

81 While denouncing slavery in theory, some Enlightenment philosophers were complicit with it in practice.

82 For more on the contradiction of the Enlightenment, see Ella Shohat and Robert Stam, "Renegade Voices" and "Antinomies of Enlightenment and Progress," in idem, *Unthinking Eurocentrism* (New York: Routledge, 1994).

83 Since at least the early twentieth century, the debt European culture owes to non-Western civilizations has provided intellectual fodder for various commentators. For example, during the Harlem Renaissance, Alain Locke remarked upon the debt of Cubist painters such as Picasso and Braque to African painting and sculpture and also suggested that their appropriation of African tradition had in turn inspired African American artists to examine African sculpture (see Leonard Harris ed., *Philosophy of Alain Locke: Harlem Renaissance and Beyond* [Philadelphia: Temple University Press, 1991]). In a similar vein, one might also consider the influence of African music on Igor Stravinsky's symphonic music and the presence of jazz in George Gershwin's work.

84 Jan Pieterse makes a similar argument in "Unpacking the West: How European is Europe?" in *Racism, Modernity and Identity: On the Western Front*, ed. by Ali Rattansi and Sallie Westwood (Cambridge: Polity, 1994), 129–49.

85 Nor does he see the complexity of the modernizing secular project in places where religion, class, ethnicity, gender, and sexuality can easily come to a clash with such projects. The future that Fanon imagines is very much limited by his French cultural model of the overall framework of modernization and progress.

86 Although Fanon critiqued psychoanalysis (the family) and existentialism (the look and objectification) from the standpoint of race and colonialism, he devoted *The Wretched of the Earth* largely to linking the psychoanalytical with the historical.

87 On "total revolution," see Fanon, *Toward the African Revolution*, 43.

POST–THIRD WORLDIST CULTURE

Gender, Nation, and the Cinema

At a time when the *grands récits* of the West have been told and retold ad infinitum, when a certain postmodernism (Jean-François Lyotard) speaks of an "end" to metanarratives, and when Francis Fukuyama speaks of an "end of history," we must ask: Precisely whose narrative and whose history is being declared at an "end"?[1] Hegemonic Europe (*sensu latu*) clearly may have begun to deplete its strategic repertoire of stories, but "Third World" peoples, "First World" minoritarian communities, women, and gays and lesbians have only begun to tell, and deconstruct, theirs. For the so-called Third World, this cinematic counter-telling basically began with the postwar collapse of the European empires and the emergence of independent nation-states. In the face of Eurocentric historicizing, the Third World and its diasporas in the First World have rewritten their own histories, taken control over their own images, and spoken in their own voices, reclaiming and reaccentuating colonialism and its ramifications in the present in a vast project of remapping and renaming. Third World feminists, for their part, have participated in these counternarratives while insisting that colonialism and national resistance have impinged differently on men and women and that remapping and renaming is not without its fissures and contradictions.

Although relatively small in number, female directors and producers in the Third World already played a role in film production in the first half of this century: Aziza Amir (figure 47), Assia Daghir, and Fatima Rushdi in Egypt; Carmen Santos and Gilda de Abreu in Brazil; Emilia Saleny in Argentina; and Adela Sequeyro, Matilda Landeta, Candida Beltran Rondon, and Eva Liminano in Mexico. However, their films, even when they focused on female protagonists, were not explicitly feminist in the sense of a declared political project to empower women in the context of both patriarchy and (neo)colonialism. In the post-independence or postrevolutionary era, women, despite their growing contribution to the diverse aspects of film production, remained less visible than men in the role of film direction. Furthermore, Third Worldist revolutionary cinemas in places such as China, Cuba, Senegal, and Algeria were not generally shaped by an anticolonial feminist imaginary. As is the case with First World cinema, women's participation within Third World cinema has hardly been central, although their growing production since the 1980s corresponds to a worldwide burgeoning movement of independent work by women, made possible by the new, low-cost technology of video communication. But quite apart from this relative democratization through technology, postindependence history, with the gradual eclipse of Third Worldist nationalism and the growth of women's grassroots local organizing, also helps us to understand the emergence of what I call "post–Third Worldist" feminist film and video.[2]

I am interested in examining recent feminist film and video work within the context of post–Third Worldist film culture as a simultaneous critique both of Third Worldist anticolonial nationalism and of First World Eurocentric feminism. Challenging white feminist film theory and practice that emerged in a major way in the 1970s in First World metropolises, post–Third Worldist feminist works have refused a Eurocentric universalizing of "womanhood," and even of "feminism." Eschewing a discourse of universality, such feminisms claim a "location," arguing for specific forms of resistance in relation to diverse forms of oppression.[3] Aware of white women's advantageous positioning within (neo)colonialist and racist systems, feminist struggles in the Third World (including that in the First World) have not been premised on a facile discourse of global sisterhood and often have been made within the context of anticolonial and antiracist

47 Egyptian film producer Aziza Amir

struggles. But the growing feminist critique of Third World nationalisms translates those many disappointed hopes for women's empowerment invested in a Third Worldist national transformation. Navigating between the excommunication as "traitors to the nation" and "betraying the race" by patriarchal nationalism, and the imperial rescue fantasies of clitoridectomized and veiled women proffered by Eurocentric feminism, post–Third Worldist feminists have not suddenly metamorphosized into "Western" feminists. Feminists of color have, from the outset, been engaged in analysis and activism around the intersection of nation, race, and gender. Therefore, while still resisting the ongoing (neo)colonized situation of their "nation" or "race," post–Third Worldist feminist cultural practices also break away from the narrative of the "nation" as a unified entity to articulate a contextualized history for women in specific geographies of identity. Such feminist projects, in other words, are often posited in relation to ethnic, racial, regional, and national locations.

Feminist critique within national movements and ethnic communities has not formed part of the generally monocultural agenda of Euro-"feminism." In cinema studies, for example, what has been called "feminist film theory" since the 1970s has often suppressed the historical, economic, and cultural contradictions among women. Prestigious feminist film journals have too often ignored the scholarly and cultural feminist work performed in particular Third Worldist national and racial media contexts. Feminist work to empower women within the boundaries of their Third World communities was dismissed as merely nationalist, not "quite yet" feminist. Universalizing the parameters for feminism and using ahistorical psychoanalytical categories such as "desire," "fetishism," and "castration" led to a discussion of "the female body" and "the female spectator" detached from the conflictual diversity of women's experiences, agendas, and political visions. Any dialogue with feminist scholars or film-makers who insisted on working from and within particular locations was thus inhibited. Is it a coincidence that throughout the 1970s and most of the 1980s, it was Third World cinema conferences and film programs that first gave prominence to Third Worldist women filmmakers (for example, the Guadeloupian Sarah Maldoror, the Colombian Marta Rodriguez, the Lebanese Heiny Srour, the Cuban Sara Gomez, the Senegalese Safi Faye, the Indian Prema Karanth, the Sri Lankan Sumitra Peries, the Brazilian Helena Solberg-Ladd, the Egyptian Atteyat El-Abnoudi, the Tunisian Selma Baccar, the Puerto Rican Ana Maria Garcia) rather than feminist film programs and conferences? A discussion of Ana Maria Garcia's documen-tary *La Operación*, a film that focuses on U.S.-imposed sterilization policies in Puerto Rico, for example, reveals the historical and theoretical aporias of such concepts as "the female body" when not addressed in terms of race, class, and (neo)colonialism. Whereas a white "female body" might un-dergo surveillance by the reproductive machine, the dark "female body" is subjected to a *dis-reproductive* apparatus within a hidden, racially coded demographic agenda.

In fact, in the 1970s and most of the 1980s, prestigious feminist film journals paid little attention to the intersection of heterosexism with rac-ism and imperialism. That task was performed by some "Third World cinema" academics who published in those leftist film and cultural jour-nals that allotted space to Third World alternative cinema (for example, *Jump Cut, Cineaste,* the *Independent, Framework,* and *Critical Arts*). Coming in the wake of visible public debates about race and multiculturalism, the task force on "race" (established in 1988) at the Society for Cinema Stud-ies, along with the increasingly substantial representation of the work of women of color in Women Make Movies, a major New York–based dis-tribution outlet for independent work by women film and videomakers, began to have an impact on white feminist film scholars, some of whom gradually came to acknowledge and even address issues of gender in the context of race. Discourses about gender and race still tend *not* to be understood within an anticolonial history, however, while the diverse, re-cent post–Third Worldist feminist film and video practices tend to be comfortably subsumed as a mere "extension" of a "universal" feminist theory and practice. Applying old paradigms to new (dark) objects implies,

to some extent, "business as usual." Post–Third Worldist feminist practices are often absorbed into the preoccupations of Eurocentric feminist
theories within the homogenizing framework of the shared critique of
patriarchal discourse. Examining recent Third World feminist cultural
practices only in relation to writings under the rubric of "feminist theory"
reproduces a Eurocentric narrative for feminism whose beginnings inevitably always reside in the "West." Feminism is imagined as a coherent
single-axis issue, disseminated into the Third World. Burdened as it were
by national or ethnic hyphenated identities feminist work on racism and
colonialism is viewed as not really feminist at its core. It is dismissed as too
"specific" to qualify for the universal realm of "feminist theory" and as too
"inclusive" to qualify for the single-axis analytical frame. Feminists privileging the intersection of gender and sexualtiy with race, class, and nation
are regarded as "losing sight" of feminism.

Rather than merely "extending" a preexisting First World feminism, as a
certain Euro-"diffusionism" would have it,[4] post–Third Worldist cultural
theories and practices create a more complex space for feminisms, open to
the specificity of community culture and history. To counter some of the
patronizing attitudes toward (post–)Third World feminist filmmakers—
the dark women who now also do the "feminist thing"—it is necessary
to contextualize feminist work in national and racial discourses, locally
and globally inscribed within multiple oppressions and resistances. Third
World feminist histories can be understood as feminist if seen in conjunction with the resistance work these women have performed within
their communities and nations. Any serious discussion of feminist cinema must therefore engage the complex question of the "national." Third
Worldist films are often produced within the legal codes of the nation-
state, often in (hegemonic) national languages, recycling national intertexts (literatures, oral narratives, music), projecting national imaginaries.
But if First World filmmakers have seemed to float "above" petty nationalist concerns, it is because they take for granted the projection of a national
power that facilitates the making and the dissemination of their films. The
geopolitical positioning of Third World nation-states continues to imply
that their filmmakers cannot assume a substratum of national power.

Here, I am interested in examining the contemporary work of post–
Third Worldist feminist filmmakers and video makers in light of the ongoing critique of the racialized inequality of the geopolitical distribution of
resources and power. I am especially concerned with looking into the
dynamics of rupture and continuity with regard to the antecedent Third

Worldist film culture. These texts, I argue, challenge the masculinist contours of the "nation" in order to perform a feminist decolonization of Third Worldist historiography as much as they prolong a multicultural decolonization of feminist historiography. My attempt to forge a "beginning" of a post–Third Worldist narrative for recent film and video work by diverse Third World, multicultural, diasporic feminists is not intended as an exhaustive survey of the spectrum of generic practices. Rather, by highlighting works embedded in the intersection between gender and sexuality and nation and race, this essay attempts to situate such cultural practices. It looks at a moment of historical rupture and continuity, when the macronarrative of women's liberation has long since subsided, yet sexism and heterosexism prevail, and in an age when the metanarratives of anticolonial revolution have long since been eclipsed, yet (neo)colonialism and racism persist. What, then, are some of the new modes of a multicultural feminist aesthetics of resistance? And in what ways do they simultaneously continue and rupture previous Third Worldist film culture?

THE ECLIPSE OF THE REVOLUTIONARY PARADIGM

Third Worldist films by women assumed that revolution was crucial for the empowering of women, that the revolution was integral to feminist aspirations. Sarah Maldoror's short film *Monangambe* (Angola, 1970) narrates the visit of an Angolan woman to see her husband who has been imprisoned by the Portuguese, while her feature film *Sambizanga* (Angola, 1972), based on the struggle of the Popular Movement for the Liberation of Angola (MPLA) in Angola, depicts a woman coming to revolutionary consciousness. Heiny Srour's documentary *Sa'at al-Tahrir* (The Hour of Liberation, Oman, 1973) privileges the role of female fighters as it looks at the revolutionary struggle in Oman, and her *Leila wal- dhiab* (Leila and the Wolves, Lebanon, 1984) focuses on the role of women in the Palestine Liberation Movement. Helena Solberg-Ladd's *Nicaragua up from the Ashes* (United States, 1982) foregrounds the role of women in the Sandanista revolution. Often cited as part of the late 1970s and early 1980s Third Worldist debates about women's position in revolutionary movements, Sara Gomez's well-known film *De cierta manera* (One Way or Another, Cuba, 1975) interweaves documentary and fiction to forge a feminist critique of the Cuban revolution. Decidedly pro-revolutionary, the film's images of building and construction metaphorize the quest for further structural changes. Macho culture is dissected and analyzed within overlaid cultural histories (African, European, and Cuban) in an effort to revolutionize gender relations in the postrevolutionary era.

By the late 1960s and early 1970s, in the wake of the Vietnamese victory over the French, the Cuban revolution, and Algerian independence, Third Worldist film ideology was crystallized in a wave of militant manifestos—Glauber Rocha's "Aesthetic of Hunger" (1965), Fernando Solanas's and Octavio Getino's "Towards a Third Cinema" (1969), and Julio Garcia Espinosa's "For an Imperfect Cinema" (1969)—and in declarations from Third World film festivals calling for a tricontinental revolution in politics and an aesthetic and narrative revolution in film form (figure 48).[5] Within the spirit of a politicized auteurism, Rocha demanded a "hungry" cinema of "sad, ugly films"; Solanas and Getino urged militant guerrilla documentaries; and Espinosa advocated an "imperfect" cinema energized by the "low" forms of popular culture. But the resistant practices of such films are neither homogeneous nor static; they vary over time, from region to region, and in genre, from epic costume drama to personal, small-budget documentary. Their aesthetic strategies range from "progressive realist" to Brechtian deconstructivist to avant-gardist, tropicalist, and resistant postmodern.[6] In their search for an alternative to the dominating style of Hollywood, such films shared a certain preoccupation with First World feminist independent films that sought alternative images of women. The project of digging into "herstories" involved a search for new cinematic and narrative forms that challenged both the canonical documentaries and mainstream fiction films, subverting the notion of "narrative pleasure" based on the "male gaze." As with Third Worldist cinema and with First World independent production, post–Third Worldist feminist films and videos conduct a struggle on two fronts, at once aesthetic and political, synthesizing revisionist historiography with formal innovation.

The early period of Third Worldist euphoria has given way to the collapse of communism, the indefinite postponement of the devoutly wished "tricontinental revolution," the realization that the "wretched of the earth" are not unanimously revolutionary (or necessarily allies to one another), the appearance of an array of Third World despots, and the recognition that international geopolitics and the global economic system have forced even the "Second World" to be incorporated into transnational capitalism. Recent years have even witnessed a crisis around the term "Third World" itself: It is now seen as an inconvenient relic of a more militant period. Some have argued that Third World theory is an open-ended ideological interpellation that papers over class oppression in all three worlds while

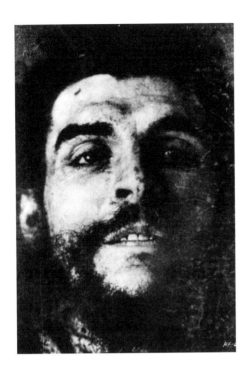

48 Revolutionary icon: Che Guevara in death (*The Hour of the Furnaces*, 1968)

limiting socialism to the now nonexistent Second World.[7] Three-worlds theory not only flattens heterogeneities, masks contradictions, and elides differences, but also obscures similarities (for example, the common presence of the Fourth World, or indigenous peoples, in both Third World and First World countries). Third World feminist critics such as Nawal El-Saadawi (Egypt), Vina Mazumdar (India), Kumari Jayawardena (Sri Lanka), Fatima Mernissi (Morocco), and Lelia Gonzales (Brazil) have explored these differences and similarities in a feminist light, pointing to the gendered limitations of Third World nationalism.

But even within the current situation of "dispersed hegemonies" (Arjun Appadurai) or "scattered hegemonies" (Inderpal Grewal and Caren Kaplan),[8] the historical thread or inertia of First World domination remains a powerful presence. Despite the imbrication of "First" and "Third" worlds, the global distribution of power still tends to make the First World countries cultural "transmitters" and the Third World countries "receivers." (One byproduct of this situation is that First World "minorities" have the power to project their cultural productions around the globe.) While the Third World is inundated with North American films, TV series, popular music, and news programs, the First World receives precious little of the vast cultural production of the Third World, and what it does receive is usually mediated by multinational corporations.[9] These processes are not entirely negative, of course. The same multinational corporations that disseminate inane blockbusters and canned sitcoms also spread Afro-diasporic music, such as reggae and rap, around the globe. The problem lies less in the exchange and more in the unequal terms on which the exchange take place.[10]

At the same time, the media-imperialism thesis, which was dominant in the 1970s, needs drastic retooling. First, it is simplistic to imagine an active First World forcing its products on a passive Third World. Second, global mass culture does not so much replace local culture as coexist with it, providing a cultural lingua franca re-marked by a "local" accent.[11] Third, there are powerful reverse currents as a number of Third World countries (Mexico, Brazil, India, Egypt) dominate their own markets and even become cultural exporters.[12] One must distinguish, furthermore, between the ownership and control of the media—an issue of political economy— and the specifically cultural issue of the implications of this domination for the people on the receiving end. The "hypodermic needle" theory is as inadequate for the Third World as it is for the First World. Everywhere, spectators actively engage with texts, and specific communities both incorporate and transform foreign influences.[13] In a world of transnational communications, the central problem becomes one of tension between cultural homogenization and cultural heterogenization, in which hegemonic tendencies, well documented by Marxist analysts like Armand Mattelart and Herbert Schiller, are simultaneously "indigenized" within a complex, disjunctive global cultural economy. At the same time, discernible patterns of domination channel the "fluidities" even of a "multipolar" world; the same hegemony that unifies the world through global networks of circulating goods and information also distributes them according to hierarchical structures of power, even if those hegemonies are now more subtle and dispersed.

Although all cultural practices are on one level products of specific national contexts, Third World filmmakers (men and women) have been forced to engage in the question of the national precisely because they lack the taken-for-granted power available to First World nation-states. At the same time, the topos of a unitary nation often camouflages the possible contradictions among different sectors of Third World society. The nation-states of the Americas, of Africa, and of Asia often "cover" the existence not only of women, but also of indigenous nations (Fourth World) within them. Moreover, the exaltation of "the national" provides no criteria for distinguishing exactly what is worth retaining in the "national tradition." A sentimental defense of patriarchal social institutions simply because they are "ours" can hardly be seen as emancipatory. Indeed, some Third World films criticize exactly such institutions: *Xala* (1990) criticizes polygamy; *Finzan* (1989) and *Fire Eyes* (1993) critique female genital mutilation; films like *Allah Tantou* (1992) focus on the political repression exercised even by a pan-Africanist hero like Sekou Toure; and Ousmane Sembene's *Guelwaar* (1992) satirizes religious divisions within the Third World nation. Third, all countries, including Third World countries, are heterogeneous, at once urban and rural, male and female, religious and secular, native and immigrant. The view of the nation as unitary muffles the "polyphony" of social and ethnic voices within heteroglot cultures. Third World feminists especially have highlighted the ways in which the subject of the Third World nationalist revolution has been covertly posited as masculine and heterosexual. Fourth, the precise nature of the national "essence" to be recuperated is elusive and chimerical. Some locate it in the precolonial past or in the country's rural interior (e.g., the African village), or in a prior stage of development (the preindustrial), or in a non-European ethnicity (e.g., the indigenous or African strata in the nation-states of the Americas); and each narrative of origins has had its gender implications. Recent debates have emphasized the ways in which national identity is mediated, textualized, constructed, and "imagined," just as the traditions valorized by nationalism are "invented."[14] Any definition of nationality, then, must see it as partly discursive in nature; must take class, gender, and sexuality into account; must allow for racial difference and cultural heterogeneity; and must be dynamic, seeing "the nation" as an evolving, imaginary construct rather than an originary essence.

The decline of the Third Worldist euphoria, which marked feminist films like *One Way or Another*, *The Hour of Liberation*, and *Nicaragua up from the Ashes*, brought with it a rethinking of political, cultural, and aesthetic possibilities, as the rhetoric of revolution began to be greeted with a certain skepticism. Meanwhile, the socialist-inflected national liberation struggles of the the 1960s and 1970s were harassed economically and militarily, violently discouraged from becoming revolutionary models for post-independence societies. A combination of pressure from the International Monetary Fund, cooptation, and "low-intensity warfare" obliged even socialist regimes to make a sort of peace with transnational capitalism. Some regimes repressed those who wanted to go beyond a purely nationalist bourgeois revolution to restructure class, gender, religion, and ethnic relations. As a result of external pressures and internal self-questioning, the cinema also gave expression to these mutations, with the anticolonial thrust of earlier films gradually giving way to more diversified themes and perspectives. This is not to say that artists and intellectuals became less politicized; instead, cultural and political critique took new and different forms. Contemporary cultural practices of post–Third World and multicultural feminists intervene at a precise juncture in the history of the Third World.

THIRD WORLDISM UNDER FEMINIST EYES

Largely produced by men, Third Worldist films were not generally concerned with a feminist critique of nationalist discourse. It would be a mistake to idealize the sexual politics of anticolonialist films like *Jamila* (1956; figure 49) and the classic *The Battle of Algiers*, for example. On one level, it is true that Algerian women are granted revolutionary agency. In one sequence, three Algerian women fighters are able to pass for French women and consequently slip through the French checkpoints with bombs in their baskets. The French soldiers treat the Algerians with disciminatory scorn and suspicion but greet the Europeans with amiable "*bonjours.*" The soldiers' sexism leads them to misperceive the three women as French and flirtatious when, in fact, they are Algerian and revolutionary. *The Battle of Algiers* thus underlines the racial and sexual taboos of desire within colonial segregation. As Algerians, the women are the objects of the military as well as the sexual gaze; they are publicly desirable for the soldiers, however, only when they masquerade as French. They use their knowledge of European codes to trick the Europeans, putting their own "looks" and the soldiers' "looking" (and failure to see) to revolutionary purpose. (Masquerade also serves the Algerian male fighters, who veil themselves as Algerian women to better hide their weapons.) Within the psychodynamics of oppression, the colonized knows the mind of the oppressor, while the converse tends not to be the case. In *The Battle of Algiers*, the women deploy this cognitive asymmetry to their own advantage, consciously manipulating ethnic, national, and gender stereotypes in the service of their struggle.

On another level, however, the women in the film largely carry out the orders of the male revolutionaries. They certainly appear heroic but only insofar as they perform their sacrificial service for the "nation." The film does not ultimately address the two-fronted nature of their struggle within a nationalist but still patriarchal revolution.[15] In privileging the nation-alist struggle, *The Battle of Algiers* elides the gender, class, and religious tensions that fissured the revolutionary process, failing to realize that, as Anne McClintock puts it, "nationalisms are from the outset constituted in gender power," and "women who are not empowered to organize dur-ing the struggle will not be empowered to organize after the struggle."[16] The final shots of a dancing Algerian woman waving the Algerian flag and taunting the French troops, accompanied by a voiceover announcing, "July 2, 1962: Independence. The Algerian Nation is born," has the woman "carry" the allegory of the "birth" of the Algerian nation. But the film does not raise the contradictions that plagued the revolution both before and after victory. The nationalist representation of courage and unity relies on the image of the revolutionary woman precisely because her figure might otherwise evoke a weak link, the fact of a fissured revolu-tion in which unity vis-à-vis the colonizer does not preclude contradictions among the colonized (figure 50).

Third Worldist films often favored the generic and gendered space of heroic confrontations, whether set in the streets, the casbah, the moun-tains, or the jungle. The minimal presence of women corresponded to the place assigned to women both in the anticolonialist revolutions and within Third Worldist discourse, leaving women's homebound struggles unac-knowledged. Women occasionally carried the bombs, as in *The Battle of Algiers*, but only in the name of a "Nation." More often, women were made to carry the "burden" of national allegory (the woman dancing with the flag in *The Battle of Algiers*; the Argentine prostitute whose image is under-scored by the national anthem in *Hour of the Furnaces*; the mestiza journal-ist in *Cubagua* as embodiment of the Venezuelan nation) or scapegoated as personifications of imperialism (the allegorical "whore of Babylon" figure in Rocha's films). Gender contradictions have been subordinated to anti-colonial struggle. Women were expected to "wait their turn."

A recent Tunisian film, *Samt al-Qusur* (The Silences of the Palace, 1994), by Moufida Tlatli, exemplifies some of the feminist critiques of the repre-sentation of the "nation" in anticolonial revolutionary films. (It is the first film that Tlatli, a film editor who worked on major Tunisian films of the post-independence Cinema Jedid [New Cinema] generation, has directed.) Rather than privileging explicit, violent encounters with the French, which would necessarily have to be set in male-dominated spaces of battle, the film presents 1950s Tunisian women at the height of the national struggle as restricted to the domestic sphere. Yet it also challenges middle-class

49 In the name of the nation: *Jamila, the Algerian* (Egypt, 1956)

50 Woman as national allegory: *The Battle of Algiers* (1966)

assumptions about the domestic sphere as belonging to the isolated wife–mother of a (heterosexual) couple. *The Silences of the Palace* focuses on working-class women, the servants of the rich, French-oriented Bey elite, subjugated to hopeless servitude, including at times sexual servitude, but for whom life outside the palace, without the guarantee of shelter and food, would mean the even worse misery of, for example, prostitution (figure 51). Although they are bound to silence about what they see and know within the palace, the film highlights their survival as a community. As an alternative family, their emotional closeness in crisis and happiness and their supportive involvement in decision making show their ways of coping with a no-exit situation. They become a non-patriarchal family within a patriarchal context. Whether through singing as they cook for an exhibitionist banquet, through praying as one of them heals a child who has fallen sick, or through dancing and eating in a joyous moment, the film represents women who did not plant bombs but whose social positioning turns into a critique of failed revolutionary hopes as seen in the post-colonial era. The information about the battles against the besieging French are mediated through the radio and by vendors, who report to the always "besieged" women on what might lead to an all-encompassing national transformation.

Yet this period of anticolonial struggle is framed as a recollection narrative of a woman singer, a daughter of one of the female servants, illuminating the continuous pressures exerted on women of her class. (With some exceptions, female singers and dancers are still regarded in the Middle East as just a little above prostitutes.) The gendered and classed oppression that she had witnessed as an adolescent in colonized Tunisia led her to hope that things would be different in an independent Tunisia. Such hopes were encouraged by the promises made by the middle-class male intellectual, a tutor for the Bey's family, who suggested that in the new Tunisia, not knowing her father's name would not be a barrier to establishing a new life. Their passionate relationship in the heat of revolution, where the "new" is on the verge of being born, is undercut by the framing narrative. Her history as a fatherless servant and her low status as a singer haunt her life in the post-independence era; the tutor lives with her but does not marry her, although he gives her the protection she needs as a woman in the public domain—a singer. The film opens on her sad, melancholy face singing a famous Umm Kulthum song from the 1960s, "Amal Hayati (The Hope of My Life)." Umm Kulthum, an Egyptian, was the leading Arab singer of the twentieth century (figure 52). Through her unusual musical talents—

51 Domestic space and national revolution: Moufida Tlatli's *The Silences of the Palace* (1994)

52 The Egyptian singer Umm Kulthum

أم كلثوم رائدة الفيلم
الغنائي .

including her deep knowledge of "*fusha* (literary)" Arabic—she rose from her small village to become "*kawkab al-sharq* (the star of the East)." Her singing accompanied the Arab world in all its national aspirations and catalyzed a sense of Arab unity that managed to transcend—at least, on the cultural level—social tensions and political conflicts. She was closely associated with the charismatic leadership of Gamal Abdel Nasser and his anti-imperial pan-Arab agenda, but the admiration, respect, and love she elicited has continued well after her death in 1975. Umm Kulthum's transcendental position, however, has not been shared by many female singers or stars in the Arab world.

The protagonist of *The Silences of the Palace* begins her public performance at the invitation of the masters of the palace. This invitation comes partly because of her singing talent but no less because of the sexual advances she begins to experience as soon as one of the masters notices that the child has turned into a young woman. The mother who manages to protect her daughter from sexual harassment is herself raped by one of the masters. On the day of the daughter's first major performance at the palace party, the mother dies of excessive bleeding from medical complications caused by aborting the product of the rape. In parallel scenes, the mother shouts from her excruciating pain, and the daughter courageously cries out a forbidden Tunisian nationalist song. The sequence ends with the mother's death and with her daughter leaving the palace for the promising outside world of young Tunisia. In post-independence Tunisia, the film implies, the daughter's situation has somewhat improved. She is no longer a servant but a singer who earns her living yet requires her boyfriend's protection against gender-based humiliation. Next to her mother's grave, the daughter articulates, in a voiceover, her awareness of some improvements in the conditions of her life compared with that of her mother. The daughter has gone through many abortions, despite her wish to become a mother, to keep her relationship with her boyfriend—the revolutionary man who does not transcend class for purposes of marriage. At the end of the film, she confesses at her mother's grave that this time she cannot let this piece of herself go. If, in the opening, the words of Umm Kulthum's song relay a desire for the dream not to end—"Leave me by your side / in your heart / and let me dream / wish time will not wake me up"—the film ends with an awakening to hopes unfulfilled with the birth of the nation. Birth is no longer allegorical, as in *The Battle of Algiers*, but concrete, entangled in taboos and obstacles, leaving an open-ended narrative far from the euphoric closure of the Nation.

Third World nationalist discourse has often assumed an unquestioned national identity, but most contemporary nation-states are "mixed" formations. A country like Brazil, arguably Third World in both racial (a *mestizo* majority) and economic terms (given its economically dependent status), is still dominated by a Europeanized elite. The United States, a First World country, which always had its Native American and African American minorities, is now becoming even more Third Worldized by waves of post-independence migrations. Contemporary U.S. life intertwines First World and Third World destinies. The song "Are My Hands Clean," by Sweet Honey in the Rock, traces the origins of a blouse on sale at Sears to cotton in El Salvador, oil in Venezuela, refineries in Trinidad, and factories in Haiti and South Carolina. Thus, there is no Third World, in Trinh T. Minh-ha's pithy formulation, without its First World, and no First World without its Third World. The First World–Third World struggle takes place not only *between* nations but also *within* them.

A number of recent diasporic film and video works link issues of post-colonial identity to issues of post–Third Worldist aesthetics and ideology. The Sankofa production *The Passion of Remembrance* (1986), by Maureen Blackwood and Isaac Julien, thematizes post–Third Worldist discourses and fractured diasporic identity—in this case, black British identity—by staging a "polylogue" between the 1960s black radical as the (somewhat puritanical) voice of nationalist militancy and the "new," more playful voices of gays and lesbians, all within a de-realized reflexive aesthetic. Film and video works such as Assia Djebar's *Nouba Nisa al Djebel Chenoua* (The Nouba of the Women of Mount Chenoua, 1977), Lourdes Portillo's *After the Earthquake* (1979), Lucía Salinas's *Canto u la vida* (Song to Life, 1990), Mona Hatoum's *Measures of Distance* (1988), Pratibha Parmar's *Khush* (1991; figure 53), Trinh T. Minh-ha's *Surname Viet Given Name Nam* (1989) and *Shoot for the Contents* (1991), Prajna Paramita Parasher's and Den Ellis's *Unbidden Voices* (1989), Lucinda Broadbent's *Sex and the Sandinistas* (1991), Mona Smith's *Honored by the Moon* (1990), Indu Krishnan's *Knowing Her Place* (1990), Christine Chang's *Be Good My Children* (1992), Teresa Osa's and Hidalgo de la Rivera's *Mujeria* (1992), and Marta N. Bautis's *Home Is the Struggle* (1991) break away from earlier macronarratives of national liberation, reenvisioning the nation as a heteroglossic multiplicity of trajectories. While remaining anticolonialist, these experimental films call attention to the diversity of experiences within and across

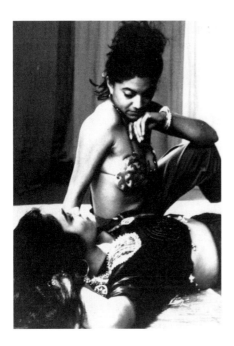

53 Double displacement: Pratibha Parmar's *Khush* (1991)

nations. Since colonialism had simultaneously aggregated communities fissured by glaring cultural differences and separated communities marked by equally glaring commonalities, these films suggest, many Third World nation-states were highly artificial and contradictory entities. The films produced in the First World, in particular, raise questions about dislocated identities in a world increasingly marked by the mobility of goods, ideas, and peoples attendant with the "multinationalization" of the global economy.

Third Worldists often fashioned their idea of the nation-state according to the European model, in this sense remaining complicit with a Eurocentric Enlightenment narrative. And the nation-states they built often failed to deliver on their promises. In terms of race, class, gender, and sexuality, in particular, many of them remained, on the whole, ethnocentric, patriarchal, bourgeois, and homophobic. At the same time, a view of Third World nationalism as the mere echo of European nationalism ignores the international realpolitik that made the end of colonialism coincide with the beginning of the nation-state. The formation of Third World nation-states often involved joining diverse ethnicities and regions previously separated under colonialism as well as partitioning regions, forcing regional redefinition and a cross-shuffling of populations. Furthermore, political geographies and state borders do not always coincide with what Edward Said calls "imaginary geographies"—whence, the existence of internal emigres, nostalgics, rebels (i.e., groups of people who share the same passport but whose relations to the nation-state are conflicted and ambivalent). In the postcolonial context of a constant flux of peoples, affiliation with the nation-state becomes highly partial and contingent.

While most Third Worldist films assumed the fundamental coherence of national identity, with the expulsion of the colonial intruder fully completing the process of national becoming, the postnationalist films call attention to the fault lines of gender, class, ethnicity, region, partition, migration, and exile. Many of the films explore the complex identities generated by exile—from one's own geography, from one's own history, from one's own body—within innovative narrative strategies. Fragmented cinematic forms homologize cultural disembodiment. Caren Kaplan's observations about a reconceived "minor" literature as deromanticizing solitude and rewriting "the connections between different parts of the self in order to make a world of possibilities out of the experience of displacement"[17] are exquisitely appropriate to two autobiographical films by Palestinians in exile: Elia Suleiman's *Homage by Assassination* (1992) and Mona Hatoum's *Measures of Distance* (1988). *Homage by Assassination* chronicles Suleiman's life in New York during the Persian Gulf War, foregrounding multiple failures of communication: a radio announcer's aborted efforts to reach the filmmaker by phone; the filmmaker's failed attempts to talk to his family in Nazareth (Israel/Palestine); his impotent look at old family photographs and despairing answering-machine jokes about the Palestinian situation. The glorious dream of nationhood and return is here reframed as a Palestinian flag on a TV monitor, the land as a map on a wall, and the return (*'awda*) as the "return" key on the computer keyboard. At one point, the filmmaker receives a fax from a friend, who narrates her family history as an ArabJew, her feelings during the bombing of Iraq and Scud attacks on Israel, and the story of her displacements from Iraq through Israel/Palestine, and then on to the United States.[18] Communications media become the imperfect means by which dislocated people struggle to retain their national imaginary while also fighting for a place in a new national context (the United States, Britain), in countries whose foreign policies have had concrete effects on their lives. *Homage by*

Assassination invokes the diverse spatialities and temporalities that mark the exile experience. A shot of two clocks, in New York and in Nazareth, points to the double time frame lived by the diasporic subject, a temporal doubleness underlined by an intertitle saying that, due to the Scud attacks, the filmmaker's mother is adjusting her gas mask at that very moment. The friend's letter similarly stresses the fractured spatio-temporality of being in the United States while identifying with relatives in both Iraq and Israel.

In *Measures of Distance*, the Palestinian video and performance artist Mona Hatoum explores the renewal of friendship between her mother and herself during a brief family reunion in Lebanon in the early 1980s. The film relates the fragmented memories of diverse generations: the mother's tales of the "used-to-be" Palestine, Hatoum's own childhood in Lebanon, the civil war in Lebanon, and the current dispersal of the daughters in the West. (She thus veers off from the conventions of the Orientalist films— from *The Sheik* through *The King and I* to *Out of Africa*—which privilege the itineraries of Western women travelers in the East rather than Eastern women in the West.) As images of the mother's handwritten Arabic letters to the daughter are superimposed on dissolves of the daughter's color slides of her mother in the shower, we hear an audiotape of their conversations in Arabic, along with excerpts of their letters as translated and read by the filmmaker in English.

The voiceover and script of *Measures of Distance* narrate a paradoxical state of geographical distance and emotional closeness. The textual, visual, and linguistic play between Arabic and English underlines the family's serial dislocations, from Palestine to Lebanon to Britain, where Mona Hatoum has been living since 1975, gradually unfolding the dispersion of Palestinians over very diverse geographies. The foregrounded letters, photographs, and audiotapes call attention to the means by which people in exile negotiate cultural identity. In the mother's voiceover, the repeated phrase "My dear Mona" evokes the diverse "measures of distance" implicit in the film's title. Meanwhile, background dialogue in Arabic— recalling their conversations about sexuality and Palestine during their Beirut reunion—recorded in the past but played in the present, parallels shower photos of the mother, also taken in the past but looked at in the present. The multiplication of temporalities continues in Hatoum's reading of a letter in English: To the moments of the letter's sending and its arrival is added the moment of Hatoum's voiceover translation of it for the

English-speaking viewer. Each layer of time evokes a distance at once temporal and spatial, historical and geographical; each dialogue is situated, produced, and received in precise historical circumstances.

The linguistic play also marks the distance between mother and daughter, while their separation instantiates the fragmented existence of a nation. When relentless bombing prevents the mother from mailing her letter, the screen fades to black, suggesting an abrupt end to communication. Yet the letter eventually arrives via messenger, while the voiceover narrates the exile's difficulties in maintaining contact with one's culture(s). The negotiation of time and place is here absolutely crucial. The video maker's voiceover reading her mother's letters in the present interferes with the dialogue recorded in the past in Lebanon. The background conversations in Arabic give a sense of present-tense immediacy, while the more predominant English voiceover speaks of the same conversation in the past tense. The Arabic speaker labors to focus on the Arabic conversation and read the Arabic scripts while also listening to the English. If the non-Arabic-speaking spectator misses some of the film's textual registers, the Arabic-speaking spectator is overwhelmed by competing images and sounds. This strategic refusal to translate Arabic is echoed in Suleiman's *Homage by Assassination*, where the director (in person) types out Arab proverbs on a computer screen, without providing any translation (figure 54). These exiled filmmakers thus cunningly provoke in the spectator the same alienation experienced by a displaced person, reminding us, through inversion, of the asymmetry in social power between exiles and their "host communities." At the same time, they catalyze a sense of community for the minoritarian speech community, a strategy especially suggestive in the case of diasporic filmmakers, who often wind up in the First World precisely because colonial or imperial power has turned them into displaced persons.

Measures of Distance also probes issues of sexuality and the female body in a kind of self-ethnography, its nostalgic rhetoric concerned less with the "public sphere" of national struggle than with the "private sphere" of sexuality, pregnancy, and children. The women's conversations about sexuality leave the father feeling displaced by what he dismisses as "women's nonsense." The daughter's photographs of her nude mother make him profoundly uncomfortable, as if the daughter, as the mother writes, "had trespassed on his possession." Videotaping such intimate conversations is not a common practice in Middle Eastern cinema—or, for that matter, in any cinema. (Western audiences often ask how Hatoum won her mother's

54 The scripted body of exile: Mona Hatoum's *Measures of Distance*, 1988 (top), and Elia Suleiman's *Homage by Assassination*, 1992 (bottom)

consent to use the nude photographs and how she broached the subject of sexuality.) Paradoxically, the exilic distance from the Middle East authorizes the exposure of intimacy. Displacement and separation make possible a transformative return to the inner sanctum of the home; mother and daughter are together again in the space of the text.

In Western popular culture, the Arab female body, whether in the form of the veiled, bare-breasted women who posed for French colonial photographers or the Orientalist harems and belly dancers of Hollywood film, has functioned as a sign of the exotic. But rather than adopt a patriarchal strategy of simply censuring female nudity, Hatoum deploys the diffusely sensuous, almost pointillist images of her mother's nakedness to tell a more complex story with nationalist overtones. She uses diverse strategies to veil the images from voyeuristic scrutiny: Already hazy images are concealed by text (fragments of the mother's correspondence, in Arabic script) and are difficult to decipher. The superimposed words in Arabic script serve to "envelop" her nudity. "Barring" the body, the script metaphorizes her inaccessibility, visually undercutting the intimacy that is verbally expressed in other registers. The fragmented nature of existence in exile is thus underlined by superimposed fragmentations: fragments of letters, dialogue, and the mother's *corps morcellé* (rendered as hands, breasts, and belly). The blurred and fragmented images evoke the dispersed collectivity of the national family itself.[19] Rather than evoke the longing for an ancestral home, *Measures of Distance*, like *Homage by Assassination*, affirms the process of re-creating identity in the liminal zone of exile.[20] Video layering makes it possible for Mona Hatoum to capture the fluid, multiple identities of the diasporic subject.

INTERROGATING THE AESTHETIC REGIME

Exile can also take the form of exile from one's own body. Dominant media have long disseminated the hegemonic white-is-beautiful aesthetic inherited from colonialist discourse, an aesthetic that exiled women of color from their own bodies. This normative gaze has systematically devalorized non-European appearance and aesthetics.[21] Popular sideshows and fairs were the heirs of a tradition of exhibitions of "real" human objects, a tradition that goes back to Columbus's importation of "New World" natives to Europe for scientific study and courtly entertainment. Exhibitions organized the world as a spectacle within an obsessively mimetic aesthetic.[22] Africans and Asians were exhibited as human figures bearing kinship to specific animal species, thus literalizing the colonialist zeugma that yoked "native" and "animal," the very fact of exhibition in cages implying that the cages' occupants were less than human. Lapps, Nubians, and Ethiopians were shown in Germany in anthropological-zoological exhibits.[23] The conjunction of "Darwinism, Barnumism, [and] pure and simple racism" resulted in the exhibition of Ota Benga, a Pygmy from the Kasai region, alongside the animals in the Bronx Zoo.[24] The 1894 Antwerp World's Fair featured a reconstructed Congolese village with sixteen "authentic" villagers. In many cases, the people exhibited died or fell seriously ill. "Freak shows," too, paraded before the bemused eyes of the West a variety of "exotic" pathologies.

A recent video, *The Couple in the Cage: A Gautinaui Odyssey* (1993), by Coco Fusco and Paula Heredia, "writes back" by readdressing the notion of pathology to its scientist "senders." The video is based on a satirical performance by Guillermo Gómez-Peña and Coco Fusco in which they place themselves in a cage in public squares and museums and perform as two newly discovered Gautinaui from an island in the Gulf of Mexico (figure 55). The video juxtaposes responses of spectators, many of whom take the caged humans to be "real," with archival footage from ethnographic films in a kind of a media jujitsu that returns the colonial gaze.

One of the best-known cases of the exhibition of an African woman is that of Saartjie Baartman, the "Hottentot Venus," who was exhibited on the entertainment circuit in England and France.[25] Although her protrusive buttocks constituted the main attraction, the rumored peculiarities of her genitalia also drew crowds, with her racial/sexual "anomaly" constantly being associated with animality.[26] The zoologist and anatomist George Cuvier studied her intimately and presumably dispassionately, and compared her buttocks to those of "female mandrills, baboons . . . which assume at certain epochs of their life a truly monstrous development."[27] After Baartman's death at twenty-five, Cuvier received official permission for an even closer look at her private parts and dissected her to produce a detailed description of her body, inside out.[28] Her genitalia still rest on a shelf in the Musée de l'Homme in Paris alongside the genitalia of *"une negresse"* and *"une peruvienne,"*[29] monuments to a kind of imperial necrophilia. The final placement of the female parts in the patriarchally designated "Museum of Man" provides a crowning irony.

A collage series by the artist Renee Green on the subject of the "Hottentot Venus" looks ironically at this specific form of colonizing the black female body. The supposedly oxymoronic naming of the "Hottentot Venus" was aggressive and Eurocentric. One of the collages turns this same "oxymoron" against its originators. The piece juxtaposes a photograph of a white man looking through a camera; a fragment of a nineteenth-century drawing of the torso of a white woman in a hoop skirt; a fragment of another torso, this time of the nude Hottentot; and finally, an image of the Grand Tetons (the Big Breasts). A text accompanying the collage calls attention to the undercurrents of desire within the scientific enterprise:

> The subinterpreter was married to a charming person, not only a Hottentot in figure, but in that respect a Venus among Hottentots. I was perfectly aghast at her development. I profess to be a scientific man, and was exceeding anxious to obtain accurate measurements of her shape.

The collage evokes a hierarchy of power. The man looking evokes Cuvier, the scientist who measured the historical Hottentot Venus. By fragment-

55 Returning the colonial gaze: Coco Fusco's and Guillermo Gómez-Peña's performance, *Two Undiscovered Amerindians* (1992)

56 Renee Green, *The Hottentot Venus* (1990–91): Mixed-media installation

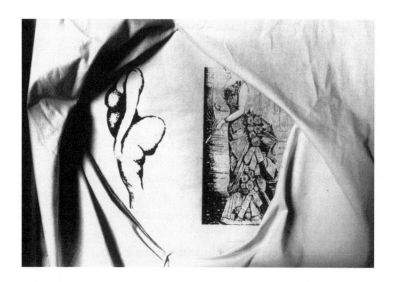

ing the African woman's buttocks, Green exaggerates what for the white scientists was already exaggerated. Juxtaposing this image with a fragmented depiction of a white woman whose fashionably hooped skirt also shapes artificially outsized buttocks (figure 56), she implies that both the African and the European woman have been constructed for masculinist pleasures: one as the acme of coy virginal beauty, adorned with flowers and a delicately held fan; the other, naked, imagined as an exemplum of gross corporeality supposedly to be looked at without pleasure, only for the sake of the austere discipline of science. Both drawings easily slide into the image of Nature, the Grand Tetons. The letter "A" appears next to the white woman, "B" next to the black, and "AB" next to the Grand Tetons, and a punning "C" ("see") next to the white man with camera. The strategic use of European representations of an African woman to underline social ironies about sexuality, gender, and race exploits a boomerang technique: A descendant of Africans literally reframes the prejudicial images of an earlier African woman as a kind of posthumous accusation.

The hegemony of the Eurocentric gaze, spread not only by First World media but even at times by Third World media, explains why *morena* women in Puerto Rico, like Arab-Jewish (Sephardi) women in Israel, paint their hair blond, and why Brazilian TV commercials are more suggestive of Scandinavia than of a black-majority country, and why "Miss Universe" contests can elect blond "queens" even in North African countries, and why Asian women perform cosmetic eye surgery to appear more white (the subject of Pam Tom's *Two Lies* (1989; figure 57). Multicultural feminists have criticized the internalized exile of Euro-"wannabees," who transform themselves through cosmetic surgery or by dyeing their hair. At the same time, however, there has also been a search for an open, nonessentialist approach to personal aesthetics (hence the debate over the partial "agency" involved in such transformations but highlighting the patterns that inform the agency exercised). The mythical norms of Eurocentric aesthetics come to inhabit the intimacy of self-consciousness, leaving severe psychic wounds. A patriarchal system contrived to generate neurotic self-dissatisfaction in *all* women (whence, anorexia, bulimia, and other pathologies of appearance) becomes especially oppressive for women of color by excluding them from the realms of legitimate images of desire.

Set in a Hollywood studio in the 1940s, Julie Dash's *Illusions* underscores these exclusionary practices by foregrounding a black singer who lends her singing voice to a white Hollywood star (figure 58). Like Hollywood's classic *Singin' in the Rain*, *Illusions* reflexively focuses on the cine-

57 The cosmetics of racism: Pam Tom's *Two Lies* (1989)

58 The racial dialectics of presence/absence: Julie Dash's *Illusions* (1983)

matic technique of post-synchronization, or dubbing. But while the former film exposes the intraethnic appropriation whereby the silent-movie queen Lina Lamont (Jean Hagen) appropriates the silky dubbed voice of Kathy Selden (Debbie Reynolds), *Illusions* reveals the racial dimension of constructing eroticized images of female stars. The film features two "submerged" black women: Mingon Dupree (Lonette McKee), invisible as an African American studio executive "passing for white," and Esther Jeeter (Rosanne Katon), the invisible singer hired to dub the singing parts for white film star (Lila Grant). Jeeter performs the vocals for a screen role denied her by Hollywood's institutional racism. Black talent and energy are sublimated into a haloed white image. But by reconnecting the black voice with the black image, the film makes the black presence "visible" and therefore "audible," while depicting the operation of the erasure and revealing the film's indebtedness to black performance. But if Gene Kelly can expose the injustice and bring harmony in the world of *Singin' in the Rain*, Lonette McKee—who is far from a "tragic mulatta" and is portrayed as a woman with agency, struggling to rewrite her community's history—has no such power in *Illusions* in a studio significantly named the "national studio." *Illusions* references the historical fading in of the African American image into Euro-American entertainment, suggesting that while black sounds were often welcome (for example, on the radio), black images remained taboo, as if their iconic presence would be incendiary after such a long disappearing act.

The existential life of the racialized body has been harsh, subject not only to the indignities of the auction block, to rape, branding, lynching, whipping, stun gunning, and other kinds of physical abuse, but also to the kind of cultural erasure enailed in aesthetic stigmatization. Many Third World and minoritarian feminist film and video projects offer strategies for coping with the psychic violence inflicted by Eurocentric aesthetics, calling attention to the sexualized and racialized body as the site of both brutal oppression and creative resistance. Black creativity turned the body, as a singular form of "cultural capital," into what Stuart Hall calls a "canvas of representation."[30] A number of recent independent films and videos—notably Ayoka Chenzira's *Hairpiece: A Film for Nappy-Headed People* (1985), Ngozi A. Onwurah's *Coffee Coloured Children* (1988), Deborah Gee's *Slaying the Dragon* (1988; figure 59), Shu Lea Cheang's *Color Schemes* (1989), Pam Tom's *Two Lies* (1989), Maureen Blackwood's *Perfect Image?* (1990), Helen Lee's *Sally's Beauty Spot* (1990), Camille Billop's *Older Women and Love* (1987), and Kathe Sandler's *A Question of Color* (1993)—meditate on

59 Media jujitsu: Deborah Gee's *Slaying the Dragon* (1988)

the racialized and sexualized body to narrate issues of identity. These semi-autobiographical texts link fragmented diasporic identities to larger issues of representation, recovering complex experiences in the face of the hostile condescension of Eurocentric mass culture. *Perfect Image*, for example, satirizes the mass-mediated ideal of a "perfect image" by focusing on the representation and self-representation of two black British women, one light-skinned and the other dark, lampooning the system that generates self-dissatisfaction in very diverse women, all of whom see themselves as "too" something—too dark, too light, too fat, too tall. Their constant shifting of personae evokes a diversity of women and thus prevents any essentialist stereotyping along color lines in the Afro-diasporic community.

Pathological syndromes of self-rejection—black skins/white masks—form the psychic fallout of racial hegemony. Given the construction of dark bodies as ugly and bestial, resistance takes the form of affirming black beauty. The Black Power Movement of the 1960s, for example, transformed kinky hair into proud Afro hair. Sandler's *A Question of Color* traces tensions around color-consciousness and internalized racism in the African American community, a process summed up in the popular dictum: "If you're white, you're all right / If you're yellow, you're mellow / If you're brown, stick around / But if you're black, stay back." (Such tensions formed the subject of Duke Ellington's musical composition "Black, Brown and Beige.") Hegemonic norms of skin color, hair texture, and facial features are expressed even within the community through such euphemisms as "good hair" (i.e., straight hair) and "nice features" (i.e., European-style features), and in inferentially prejudicial locutions like "dark *but* beautiful," or in admonitions not to "look like a Ubangi." The film registers the impact of the "Black Is Beautiful" movement while regarding the present moment as the contradictory site both of the resurgent Afrocentrism of some rap music along with lingering traces of old norms. One interview features a Nigerian cosmetic surgeon who de-Africanizes the appearance of black women while the film reflects on the valorization of light-skinned black women in rap video and MTV. Sandler also probes intimate relations to expose the social pathologies rooted in color hierarchies: the darker-skinned feel devalorized and desexualized; the lighter-skinned—to the extent that their own community assumes they feel superior to it—are obliged to "prove" their blackness. Filtering down from positions of dominance, chromatic hierarchies sow tensions among siblings and friends, all caught by Sandler's exceptionally sensitive direction.

In all of these films, internalized models of white beauty become the object of a corrosive critique. Not coincidentally, many of the films pay extraordinary attention to hair as the scene both of humiliation ("bad hair") and of creative self-fashioning, a "popular art form" articulating "aesthetic solutions," in Kobena Mercer's words, to the "problems created by ideologies of race and racism."[31] Since the advent of the Afro hairstyle of the late 1960s and 1970s, but especially recently, there have been reverse currents linked to the central role of African Americans in mass-mediated culture: whites who thicken their lips and sport dreadlocks, fades, or cornrows. From a multicultural feminist perspective, these cross-cultural transformations (cosmetic surgery, dyeing the hair) on one level are exempla of "internal exile" or "appropriation." But on another level, they evoke the possibility of an open, nonessentialist approach to looks and identity. Ayoka Chenzira's ten-minute animated short *Hairpiece: A Film for Nappy-Headed People* addresses hair and its vicissitudes to narrate African Americans' history of exile from the body as well as the utopia of empowerment through Afro-consciousness. In a dominant society where beautiful hair is that which "blows in the wind," *Hairpiece* suggests an isomorphism between vital, rebellious hair that refuses to conform to Eurocentric norms and the vital, rebellious people who "wear" the hair. Music by Aretha

Franklin, James Brown, and Michael Jackson accompanies a collage of black faces (from Sammy Davis to Angela Davis). Motown tunes underscore a quick-paced visual inventory of relaxers, gels, and curlers, devices painfully familiar to black people, and particularly to black women. The film's voiceover and "happy ending" might seem to imply an essentialist affirmation of "natural African beauty," but as Mercer points out in another context, "natural hair" is not itself African; it is a syncretic construct.[32] Afro-diasporic hairstyles, from the Afro to dreadlocks, are not emulations of "real" African styles but, rather, neologistic projections of diasporic identity. The styles displayed at the film's finale, far from being examples of "politically correct" hair, assert a cornucopia of diasporic looks, an empowering expression of a variegated collective body. Satirizing the black internalization of white aesthetic models, the film provokes a comic catharsis for spectators who have experienced the terror and pity of self-colonization.[33]

Ngozi A. Onwurah's lyrical semiautobiographical film *Coffee Coloured Children*, meanwhile, speaks of the black body as hemmed in by racism. The daughter of a white mother and an absent Nigerian father, the film's narrator recalls the pain of growing up in an all-white English neighborhood. The opening sequence immediately demonstrates the kind of racist harassment the family suffered: a Neo-Nazi youth defiles their front door with excrement while the mother, in voiceover, worries about protecting her children from feeling somehow responsible for the violence directed at them. The narrative conveys the traumatic self-hatred provoked by imposed paradigms. In one scene, the daughter doffs a blonde wig and white makeup in front of a mirror, trying to emulate a desired whiteness. If *The Battle of Algiers* made the mirror a revolutionary tool, here it becomes the speculum for a traumatized identity, literally that of a black skin masked with whiteness. The simple act of looking in a mirror is revealed to be multiply specular as one looks even at oneself through the eyes of many others—one's family, one's peers, one's racial others, as well as the panoptic eyes of the mass media and consumerist culture. The scars inflicted on the victims of this aesthetic hegemony are poignantly suggested in a bath sequence in which the children, using cleaning solutions, frantically try to scrub off a blackness lived as dirt.[34] The narrator's voiceover relating the cleansing ritual is superimposed on a close shot of rapid scrubbing, blurred to suggest bleeding, an apt image for colonialism's legacy inscribed on the body of children, a testament to the internalized stigmata of a devastating aesthetic regime.

While Third World and First World minoritarian women have experienced diverse histories and sexual regimes, they have also shared a common status as exotics in the colonial imaginary. They have been portrayed as wiggling bodies graced with Tutti-Frutti hats, as lascivious dark eyes peering from behind veils, as feathered dark bodies slipping into trances to accelerating rhythms. And while African women, disdained for their nudity, were in need of covering, Arab women, disdained for their covering, irnoically, were in need of denuding. In contrast to the Orientalist harem fantasy, all-female spaces have been represented very differently in feminist independent cinema, largely directed by Arab women. Documentaries such as Attiat El-Abnoudi's *Ahlam Mumkina* (Permissible Dreams, Egypt, 1989) and Claire Hunt's and Kim Longinotto's *Hidden Faces* (Britain, 1990) examine female agency within a patriarchal context. Both films feature sequences in which Egyptian women speaking together about their lives in the village recount in ironic terms their dreams and struggles with patriarchy. Through its critical look at the Egyptian feminist Nawal El Saadawi, *Hidden Faces* explores the problems of women working together to create alternative institutions. Elizabeth Fernea's *The Veiled Revolution* (1982) shows Egyptian women redefining not only the meaning of the veil but also the nature of their own sexuality. And the Moroccan filmmaker Farida Ben Lyazid's feature film *Bab Ila Sma Maftouh* (A Door to the Sky, 1988) offers a positive gloss on the notion of an all-female space, counterposing Islamic feminism to Orientalist fantasies (figure 60).

A Door to the Sky tells the story of a Moroccan woman, Nadia, who returns from Paris to her family home in Fez. That she arrives in Morocco dressed in punk clothing and hairstyle makes us expect an ironic tale about a Westernized Arab feeling out of place in her homeland. But instead, Nadia rediscovers Morocco and Islam and comes to appreciate the communitarian world of her female relatives, as well as her closeness with her father. She is instructed in the faith by an older woman, Kirana, who takes a flexible approach to Islam: "Everyone understands through his own mind and his own era." As Nadia awakens spiritually, she comes to see the oppressive aspects of Western society. At the same time, she sees Arab/ Muslim society as a possible space for fulfillment. Within the Islamic tradition of women using their wealth for social charity, she turns part of the family home into a shelter for battered women. The film is not uncritical of the patriarchal abuses of Islam—for example, the laws that count

60 Islamic feminism: Farida Benlyazid's *A Door to the Sky* (1988)

women as "half-persons" and that systematically favor the male in terms of marriage and divorce. The film's aesthetic, however, favors the rhythms of contemplation and spirituality, in slow camera movements that caress the contoured Arabic architecture of courtyards and fountains and soothing inner spaces. Dedicated to a historical Muslim woman, Fatima al-Fihra, the ninth-century founder of one of the world's oldest universities, in Fez, *A Door to the Sky* envisions an aesthetic that affirms Islamic culture while inscribing it with a feminist consciousness, offering an alternative both to the Western imaginary and to an Islamic fundamentalist representation of Muslim women. Whereas contemporary documentaries show all-female gatherings as a resistant site to patriarchy and fundamentalism, *A Door to the Sky* mobilizes all-female spaces to illuminate a liberatory project based on unearthing women's history within Islam, a history that includes female spirituality, prophecy, poetry, and intellectual creativity, as well as revolt, material power, and social and political leadership.[35]

A similar negotiation between past and present takes place in Tracey Moffat's *Nice Coloured Girls*, which interweaves tales about contemporary urban Australian Aborigine women and their "captains" (sugar daddies) with tales of aboriginal women and white men more than two hundred years before. Moffat interrogates the hackneyed conventions of the "Aborigine Film," proposing instead the formal experimentalism of *Nice Coloured Girls* itself.[36] And in sharp contrast to the colonial construction of the aboriginal "female body" seen as a metaphorical extension of an exoticized land, *Nice Coloured Girls* places dynamic, irreverent, resourceful Aborigine women at the center of the narrative, offering a multitemporal perspective on their "nasty" actions—mild forms of prostitution and conning white Australian men into spending money. By shuttling between present-day Australia and past texts, voices, and images, the film contextualizes their behavior in relation to the asymmetrical exchanges typical of colonial encounters. Two temporally and spatially distinct but conceptually interconnected frames—one associated with images of the sea (or its painterly representation) and set in the past, the other set in a pub in contemporary Australia—contextualize the encounter. In one early pub sequence, an Aborigine man and woman step behind a frosted glass door to smoke a joint. As their film-noirish silhouettes undulate to the diegetic pub music, a British-accented male voiceover reads excerpts from a historical journal describing an Aborigine woman's breasts, teeth, and face. The evocation of an earlier historical meeting conditions the viewer's comprehension of latter-day encounters.

Rather than search for an "authentic" Aborigine culture, *Nice Coloured Girls* constructs a "genealogy" of criminality. While from the vantage point of Eurocentric decorum the Aborigine women are amoral schemers, the historical context of settler colonialism and its sexualized relations to both land and women switches the ethical and emotional valence. In the pub, the women demonstrate their resilient capacity to survive and to outwit marginalization. Whereas images of the past are set inside a ship or in daylight on shore, images from the present are set in the nighttime city, pointing to the historical "neonization," as it were, of Aborigine space. The film can thus be seen as a "revenge" narrative in which Aborigine women trick Euro-Australian men into fantasizing a "fair" exchange of sex and goods, then take their money and run.

Racial and sexual relations from past (the initial encounter between Europeans and Aborigines, in 1788) and present (1987) are interwoven through overlapping images, music, texts, and voiceover. The opening sequence superimposes a text by an early English "explorer" over a dark urban skyscraper, accompanied by the sounds of rowing and of labored rhythmic breathing. While the male voiceover narrates excerpts from journals of the "discovery" of Australia in 1788, subtitles convey the thoughts of present-day Aborigine women. While the voiceover is in the first person, the subtitles relay a collective voice. The images reinforce the subtitled version, offering the women's perspective on their trapped "captains," deconstructing the journals not by correcting the historical record but rather through a discursive critique of their racist and masculinist thrust.

The title of *Nice Coloured Girls* is itself ironic, foreshadowing the film's subversion of the "positive" image of "nice" colored girls as the objects of colonial exoticization and the valorization of the "negative" image of "nastiness." The historical encounters are reconstructed in a minimalist, antirealist style, a symbolic evocation rather than a "realistic" depiction. By reflexively foregrounding the artifice of its production through stylized sets, excessive performance style, and ironic subtitles, the film undermines any expectation of sociologically "authentic" or ethnically "positive" representations. Image, sound, and text amplify and contextualize one another, militating against any authoritative history. The constant changes of discursive register—vérité-style hand-held camera, voiceover ethnographic texts, subtitled oral narratives, American soul music of obscure diegetic status—undermine any univocal mode of historical narration. *Nice Coloured Girls* challenges a whole series of discursive, generic, and disciplinary traditions. Looking at official Anglo-Australian discourse through the deconstructive eyes of the Aborigine women, this densely layered text mocks the prurient "ethnographic" fascination with aboriginal sexuality. Rather than reverse the dichotomy of sexualized Third World women and virginal European women by proposing an equally virginal image of Aborigine women, the film rejects the binaristic mode altogether. Finding the kernel of contemporary power relations in the colonial past, *Nice Coloured Girls* shows "nastiness" as a creative response to a specific economic and historical conjuncture.

A discourse that is "purely" feminist or "purely" nationalist, I have tried to argue, cannot apprehend the layered, dissonant identities of diasporic or post-independent feminist subjects. The diasporic and post–Third Worldist films of the 1980s and 1990s in this sense do not so much reject the "nation" as interrogate its repressions and limits, passing nationalist discourse through the grids of class, gender, sexuality, and diasporic identities. While often embedded in the autobiographical, they are not always narrated in the first person, nor are they "merely" personal. Rather, the boundaries between the personal and communal, like the generic boundaries between documentary and fiction, the biographic and the ethnographic, are constantly blurred. The diary form, the voiceover, the personal written text now bear witness to a collective memory of colonial violence and postcolonial displacement. While early Third Worldist films documented alternative histories through archival footage, interviews, testimonials, and historical reconstructions, generally limiting their attention to the public sphere, the films of the 1980s and 1990s use the camera less as a revolutionary weapon than as a monitor of the gendered and sexualized realms of the personal and the domestic, seen as integral but repressed aspects of national history. They display a certain skepticism toward metanarratives of liberation but do not necessarily abandon the notion that emancipation is worth fighting for. Rather than fleeing from contradiction, they install doubt and crisis at their very core. Rather than a grand anticolonial metanarrative, they favor heteroglossic proliferations of difference within polygeneric narratives, seen not as embodiments of a single truth but, rather, as energizing political and aesthetic forms of communitarian self-construction.

Since all political struggle in the postmodern era necessarily passes through the simulacral realm of mass culture, the media are absolutely central to any discussion of post–Third Worldist multicultural and transnational feminist practices. I have tried to link the often ghettoized debates concerning race and identity politics, on the one hand, and nationalism and postcolonial discourse, on the other, as part of an attempt to put in dialogue, as it were, diverse post–Third Worldist feminist critiques. The global nature of the colonizing process and the global reach of the contemporary media virtually oblige the cultural critic to move beyond the restrictive analytical framework of the nation-state. Within postmodern culture, the media not only set agendas and frame debates but also inflect desire, memory, and fantasy. The contemporary media shape identity; indeed, many argue that they now exist close to the very core of identity production. In a transnational world typified by the global circulation of images and sounds, goods, and peoples, media spectatorship has a complex impact on national identity, communal belonging, and political affiliations. By facilitating a mediated engagement with "distant" peoples, the media "deterritorialize" the process of imagining communities. And while the media can destroy community and fashion solitude by turning spectators into atomized consumers or self-entertaining monads, they can also fashion community and alternative affiliations. Just as the media can exoticize and disfigure cultures, they have the potential power not only to offer countervailing representations but also to open up parallel spaces for antiracist feminist transformation. In this historical moment of intense globalization and immense fragmentation, the alternative spectatorship established by the kind of film and video works I have discussed can mobilize desire, memory, and fantasy where identities are not only the given of where one comes from but also the political identification with where one is trying to go.

I thank Robert Stam for allowing me to use shared material from our coauthored book *Unthinking Eurocentrism* (New York: Routledge, 1994). I am also grateful to Chandra Talpade Mohanty and M. Jacqui Alexander, editors of *Feminist Genealogies, Colonial Legacies, Democratic Futures* in which this essay originally appeared, for their useful suggestions and insightful comments and for their truly dialogical spirit.

1 Despite his skepticism about "metanarratives," Lyotard supported the Persian Gulf War in a collective manifesto published in *Libération*, thus endorsing George H. W. Bush's metanarrative of a "New World Order."

2 I am proposing the term "post–Third Worldist" to point to a move beyond the ideology of Third Worldism. Whereas the term "postcolonial" implies a movement beyond anticolonial nationalist ideology and a movement beyond a specific point of colonial history, post–Third Worldism conveys a movement "beyond" a specific ideology: Third Worldist nationalism. A post–Third Worldist perspective assumes the fundamental validity of the anticolonial movement but also interrogates the fissures that rend the Third World nation. See "Notes on the Post-Colonial" in this volume.

3 For more on the concept of "location," see, for example, Chandra Talpade Mohanty, "Feminist Encounters: Locating the Politics of Experience," *Copyright* 1 (fall 1987); Michele Wallace, "The Politics of Location: Cinema/Theory/Literature/Ethnicity/Sexuality/Me," *Framework*, no. 36 (1989); Lata Mani, "Multiple Mediations: Feminist Scholarship in the Age of Multinational Reception," *Inscriptions* 5 (1989); and Inderpal Grewal, "Autobiographic Subjects and Diasporic Locations: *Meatless Days* and *Borderlands*," and Caren Kaplan, "The Politics of Location as Transnational Feminist Practice," both in Inderpal Grewal and Caren Kaplan, *Scattered Hegemonies: Postmodernity and Transnational Feminist Practice* (Minneapolis: University of Minnesota Press, 1994).

4 On "diffusionism," see J. M. Blaut, *The Colonizer's Model of the World: Geographical Diffusionism and Eurocentric History* (New York: Guilford Press, 1993).

5 The various film festivals—in Havana (dedicated to New Latin American cinema), in Carthage (for Arab and African cinemas), in Ougadogou (for African and Afro-diasporic cinemas)—gave further expression to these movements.

6 In relation to cinema, the term "Third World" has been empowering in that it calls attention to the collectively vast cinematic productions of Asia, Africa, and Latin America, as well as to the minoritarian cinema in the First World. While some, such as Roy Armes in *Third World Filmmaking and the West* (Berkeley: University of California Press, 1987), 407 n. 6, define "Third World cinema" broadly as the ensemble of films produced by Third World countries (including films produced before the very idea of the "Third World" was current), others, such as Paul Willemen, prefer to speak of "Third cinema" as an ideological project, that is, as a body of films adhering to a certain political and aesthetic program, whether or not they are produced by Third World peoples themselves (Jim Pines

and Paul Willemen, eds., *Questions of Third Cinema* [London: British Film Institute, 1989]). As long as they are not taken as "essential" entities but as collective projects to be forged, both "Third World cinema" and "Third cinema" retain important tactical and polemical uses for a politically inflected cultural practice. In purely classificatory terms, we might envision overlapping circles of denotation: (1) a core circle of "Third Worldist" films produced by and for Third World people (no matter where those people happen to be) and adhering to the principles of "Third cinema"; (2) a wider circle of the cinematic productions of Third World peoples (retroactively defined as such), whether or not the films adhere to the principles of Third cinema and irrespective of the period of their making; (3) another circle consisting of films made by First World or Second World people in support of Third World peoples and adhering to the principles of Third cinema; and (4) a final circle, somewhat anomalous in status, at once "inside" and "outside," comprising recent diasporic hybrid films (e.g., those of Mona Hatoum or Hanif Kureishi), which both build on and interrogate the conventions of "Third cinema." See Shohat and Stam, *Unthinking Eurocentrism*.

7 See Aijaz Ahmad, "Jameson's Rhetoric of Otherness and the National Allegory," *Social Text*, no. 17 (Fall 1987): 3–25; Julianne Burton, "Marginal Cinemas," *Screen* 26, nos. 3–4 (May–August 1985).

8 See Arjun Appadurai, "Disjuncture and Difference in the Global Cultural Economy," *Public Culture* 2, no. 2 (1990); Inderpal Grewal and Caren Kaplan, *Scattered Hegemonies*, which offers a feminist critique of global-local relations.

9 In the cinema, this hegemonizing process intensified shortly after World War One, when U.S. film-distribution companies (and, secondarily, European companies) began to dominate Third World markets, and was further accelerated after World War Two with the growth of transnational media corporations. The continuing economic dependence of Third World cinemas makes them vulnerable to neocolonial pressures. When dependent countries try to strengthen their own film industries by setting up trade barriers to foreign films, for example, First World countries can threaten retaliation in another economic area, such as the pricing or purchase of raw materials. Hollywood films, furthermore, often cover their costs in the domestic market and can therefore be profitably "dumped" on Third World markets at very low prices.

10 Although direct colonial rule has largely come to an end, much of the world remains entangled in neocolonial globalization. Partially as a result of colonialism, the contemporary global scene is now dominated by a coterie of powerful nation-states, consisting basically of western Europe, the United States, and Japan. This domination is economic (the "Group of Seven," the International Monetary Fund, the World Bank, the General Agreement on Tariffs and Trade), political (the five veto-holding members of the United Nations Security Council), military (the new "unipolar" North American Treaty Organization), and techno-informational-cultural (Hollywood, United Press International, Reuters, Agence-France Presse, Cable News Network). Neocolonial domination is enforced through deteriorating terms of trade and the "austerity programs" by which the

World Bank and the International Monetary Fund, often with the self-serving complicity of Third World elites, impose rules that First World countries themselves would never tolerate.

11 For a similar argument, see Grewal and Kaplan's introduction to *Scattered Hegemonies.*

12 The Indian TV version of the *Mahabharata* won a 90 percent domestic viewer share during a three-year run, and Brazil's Rede Globo now exports its *telenovelas* to more than eighty countries around the world.

13 For Appadurai, the global cultural situation is now more interactive. The United States is no longer the puppeteer of a world system of images but only one mode of a complex transnational construction of "imaginary landscapes." In this new conjuncture, he argues, the invention of tradition, ethnicity, and other identity markers becomes "slippery, as the search for certainties is regularly frustrated by the fluidities of transnational communication." See Appadurai, "Disjuncture and Difference in the Global Cultural Economy."

14 See Benedict Anderson, *Imagined Communities: Reflections on the Origin and Spread of Nationalism* (London: Verso, 1983); and E. J. Hobsbawm and Terence Ranger, eds., *The Invention of Tradition* (Cambridge: Cambridge University Press, 1983).

15 Pontecorvo returned to Algiers in 1991 to make *Gillo Pontecorvo Returns to Algiers*, a film about the evolution of Algeria during the twenty-five years that have elapsed since *Battle of Algiers* was filmed. It focuses on such topics as Islamic fundamentalism, the subordinate status of women, the veil, and so forth.

16 Anne McClintock, "No Longer in a Future Heaven: Women and Nationalism in South Africa," *Transition*, no. 51 (1991): 120.

17 Caren Kaplan, "Deterritorializations: The Rewriting of Home and Exile in Western Feminist Discourse," *Cultural Critique*, no. 6 (spring 1987): 198.

18 The friend in question is Ella Habiba Shohat.

19 Or as the letters put it: "This bloody war takes my daughters to the four comers of the world." This reference to the dispersion of the family, as metonym and metaphor for the displacement of a people, is particularly ironic given that Zionist disourse itself has often imaged its own national character through the notion of "the ingathering of exiles from the four comers of the globe."

20 In this sense, *Measures of Distance* goes against the tendency criticized by Hamid Naficy that turns nostalgia into a ritualized denial of history. See Hamid Naficy, "The Poetics and Practice of Iranian Nostalgia in Exile," *Diaspora*, no. 3 (1992).

21 See Cornel West, *Prophesy Deliverance: An Afro-American Revolutionary Christianity* (Philadelphia: Westminster, 1982); Clyde Taylor, "Black Cinema in the Post-Aesthetic Era," in Pines and Willemen, eds., *Questions of Third Cinema*; and bell hooks, *Black Looks: Race and Representation* (Boston: South End Press, 1992).

22 Egyptians at an Orientalist exposition were amazed to discover that the Egyptian pastries on sale were authentic. See Tim Mitchell, *Colonizing Egypt* (Berkeley: University of California Press, 1991), 10.

23 See Jan Nederveen Pieterse, *White on Black: Images of Africa and Blacks in*

Western Popular Culture (New Haven, Conn.: Yale University Press, 1992). On the colonial safari as a kind of traveling minisociety, see Donna Haraway, "Teddy Bear Patriarchy: Taxidermy in the Garden of Eden, New York City, 1908–1936," *Social Text*, no. 11 (winter 1984–85).

24 See Phillips Vemer Bradford and Harvey Blume, *Ota Benga: The Pygmy in the Zoo* (New York: St. Martin's Press, 1992).

25 The real name of the "Hottentot Venus" remains unknown, since it was never referred to by those who "studied" her.

26 For further discussion on science and the racial/sexual body, see Sander Gilman, "Black Bodies, White Bodies: Toward an Iconography of Female Sexuality in Late Nineteenth-Century Art, Medicine, and Literature," *Critical Inquiry* 12, no. 1 (Fall 1985); and in conjuction with early cinema, see Fatimah Tobing Rony, "Those Who Squat and Those Who Sit: The Iconography of Race in the 1895 Films of Felix-Louis Regnault," *Camera Obscura*, no. 28 (1992), special issue on "Imaging Technologies, Inscribing Science," ed. by Paula A. Treichler and Lisa Cartwright.

27 George Cuvier, "Flower and Murie on the Dissection of a Bushwoman," *Anthropological Review* 5 (July 1867): 268.

28 Richard Altick, *The Shows of London* (Cambridge, Mass.: Harvard University Press, 1978), 272.

29 Stephen Jay Gould, *The Flamingo's Smile* (New York: W. W. Norton, 1985), 292. On a recent visit to the Musée de l'Homme, I found no traces of the Hottentot Venus. Neither the official catalogue nor officials themselves acknowledged her existence.

30 Stuart Hall, "What Is This 'Black' in Black Popular Culture?" in *Black Popular Culture*, ed. by Gina Dent (Seattle: Bay Press, 1992), 27.

31 Kobena Mercer, "Black Hair/Style Politics," *New Formations*, no. 3 (winter 1987).

32 Ibid.

33 Not surprisingly, the film has been screened in museums and churches, and even for social workers and hair stylists, as a provocative contemplation of the intersection of fashion, politics, and identity.

34 This association is especially ironic given the colonial legacy of slavery and servitude in which black men (janitors) and women (maids) were obliged to clean up the "mess" created by white Europeans.

35 See Fatima Memissi, *The Forgotten Queens of Islam*, trans. by Mary Jo Lakeland (Minneapolis: University of Minnesota Press, 1993).

36 The juxtaposition of ethnographic diaries and writings and aboriginal images in *Nice Coloured Girls* is hardly coincidental, since the first photographic and cinematographic representations of Aborigines reflected the culture-bound ethnography of white settlers. (Walter Baldwin Spencer's 1901 footage of the Arrente tribe performing a kangaroo dance and rain ceremony marks the historical beginning of ethnographic filmmaking about the Aborigines.) See Karl C. Heider, *Ethnographic Film* (Austin: University of Texas Press, 1976), 19.

RUPTURE AND RETURN

Zionist Discourse and the Study of Arab-Jews

Eurocentric and Zionist norms of scholarship have had dire consequences for the representation of the history and identity of Arab-Jews/Mizrahim (i.e., Jews from Arab Muslim regions) vis-à-vis the question of Palestine. In previous publications I suggested some of the historical, political, economic, and discursive links between the question of Palestine and Arab-Jews and argued for a scholarship that investigates the erasure of such links. Here I will visit some moments in the hegemonic isolationist approach to the study of "Jewish History" as crucial to a quite anomalous project in which the state created the nation—not simply in the metaphorical sense of fabrication, but also in the literal sense of engineering the transplant of populations from all over the world. New modes of knowledge about Jews were essential in this enterprise, which placed Palestinians and European Zionist Jews at opposite poles of the civilizational clash. Yet Arab-Jews presented some challenges for Zionist scholarship, precisely because their presence "messed up" the Enlightenment paradigm that had already figured the modern Jew as cleansed from his or her *shtetl* past. In Palestine, freed of its progenitor, the Eastern European Jew (the *Ostjuden*), the New Jew paradoxically could live in the "East" without being of it.

Central to Zionist thinking was the concept of *Kibbutz Galuiot*—the "ingathering of the exiles." Following two millennia of homelessness and living presumably "outside of history," Jews could once again "enter history" as subjects, as "normal" actors on the world stage by returning to their ancient birth place, Eretz Israel. In this fashion, Jews could be healed from the deformative rupture produced by exilic existence. This transformation of *Mi-gola le-geoola*—from Diaspora to redemption—offered a teleological reading of Jewish history in which Zionism formed a redemptive vehicle for the renewal of Jewish life on a demarcated terrain, no longer simply spiritual and textual but, instead, national and political. The idea of Jewish return (which after the establishment of Israel was translated into legal language handing every Jew immediate access to citizenship) had been intertwined with the imaging of the empty land of Palestine. Its indigenous inhabitants could be bracketed or, alternatively, portrayed as intruders deemed to "return" to their Arab land of origins (a discourse that was encoded in the various transfer plans).

A corollary of the notion of Jewish return and continuity in Eretz Israel was the idea of rupture and discontinuity with diasporic existence. In order to be transformed into New Jews (later, Israelis), the "Diasporic Jews" had to abandon their diasporic culture, which, in the case of Arab-Jews, meant abandoning Arabness and acquiescing in assimilationist modernization for "their own good." Within this Promethean rescue narrative, concepts of "ingathering" and "modernization" naturalized and glossed over the historical, psychic, and epistemological violence generated by the Zionist vision of the New Jew.[1] This rescue narrative also elided Zionism's own role in provoking ruptures, dislocations, and fragmentation for Palestinian lives and—in a different way—for Middle Eastern and North African Jews. These ruptures were not only physical (the movement across borders) but also cultural (a rift in relation to previous cultural affiliations) as well as conceptual (in the very ways time and space, history, and geography were conceived).

In this essay I will examine some of the foundational premises and substratal axioms of Zionist discourse concerning Arab-Jews, arguing that writing a critical historiography in the wake of nationalism—both Arab and Jewish—requires the dismantling of a number of masternarratives. I will attempt to disentangle the complexities of the Mizrahi question by unsettling the conceptual borders erected by more than a century of Zionist discourse, with its lethal binarisms of savagery versus civilization, tradition versus modernity, East versus West, and Arab versus Jew. While one might examine the position of Mizrahim within the restrictive parameters of what Zionist scholarship constructed as "Jewish History," I have long argued against creating such a segregated discursive space for history, identity, and culture. Even if Mizrahi identity was "invented" within the process of the Zionist invention of the "Jewish nation," it is important to unsettle the ghettoized nationalist analytical framework.[2] A diasporized analysis would situate Arab-Jewish history, since the advent of Zionism and the partition of Palestine, within a constellation of multidirectional and palimpsestic cross-border movements. Although I do not focus here on contemporary intersections between Mizrahim and Palestinians, I am trying to offer a partial genealogy for today's ambivalent Mizrahi positioning as occupying the actantial slot of both dominated and dominators, simultaneously disempowered as "Orientals" or "blacks" vis-à-vis "white" Euro-Israelis and empowered as Jews in a Jewish state vis-à-vis Palestinians. In a sense, Mizrahim are both embedded in and in excess of Zionist history.

This essay offers another dimension to the critique of the denial of Palestinian right of return. It examines the Zionist foundational principle of the Jewish right of return in light of the contradictions that have emerged in the wake of the partition of Palestine for the Jewish minority in Arab Muslim states. Post-Zionist revisionist history has Eurocentrically ignored this question and in this sense has retained the contours of a Zionist narrative in which Arab-Jews are projected as if always already forming part of the Jewish nation. The critical project proposed here suggests that Mizrahim have been at least partly invented within Zionism, but it simultaneously refuses to accept the hegemonic Zionist and post-Zionist naturalizing of the place of Arab-Jews within Jewish nationalism. Furthermore, as Mizrahim are also actively reinventing their identity, a critical Mizrahi scholarship must invent a new understanding of the continuities and discontinuities entailed by the movement across national borders into Israel. The high-velocity history of the past century requires the rethinking of identity designations, intellectual grids, and disciplinary boundaries. Critical scholars especially need to dismantle the zoning of knowledge and rearticulate the relationships between the diverse interdisciplinary practices constituting multicultural Mizrahi inquiry.

My purpose has been to rearticulate a different conceptual framework, one formulated within a *multichronotopic* notion of time and space, high-lighting a dynamic palimpsest of identity formations. In this essay, I hope to suggest the contours of an intellectual and institutional space for critical analysis, called here "Mizrahi studies," whose *relational* approach would highlight a nonfinalized and conjunctural definition of identity as a poly-semic site of contradictory positionalities. In what follows, I will critically explore the dialectics of continuity and discontinuity, of rupture and re-turn, as central to Zionist discourse, especially concerning Jews from West Asia and North Africa. I will examine these dialectics through the follow-ing grids: (1) *dislocation*: spatiality and the question of naming; (2) *dis-placement*: the narrative of cross-border movement; (3) *dismemberment*: the erasure of the hyphen; (4) *dischronicity*: temporality and the paradoxes of modernization; (5) *dissonance*: methodology as discursive rupture; and (6) *disciplining*: the move toward Mizrahi studies as a relational inquiry.

DISLOCATION: SPATIALITY AND THE QUESTION OF NAMING

In the paradigmatically Zionist film *Sallah Shabbati* (Israel, 1964), the spectator is first introduced to the Oriental Jew when Sallah lands with his family in Israel. He comes from the Levant, but within the film's Euro-centric imaginary mapping, he comes from nowhere: first in the literal sense, since his place of origin remains unknown; and second, in the metaphorical sense, since Asian and African geographies are suggested to amount to nothing of substance. While the protagonist's Levantine es-sence forms the dynamic center of the narrative, his Levantine geography is crucially invisible. Sallah's physical presence in Israel only embodies that geography's absence, and highlights the process of erasure. Within the Zionist view, Jews from West Asia and North Africa arrive from obscure corners of the globe to Israel, the Promised Land, to which they have always already been destined. In this way, Mizrahim could be claimed as part of a continuous Jewish history and geography whose alpha and omega is in the Land of Israel, a land that the Zionist movement purported to represent. While superimposing a nationalist discourse on the spiritual messianic idea of Jewish renewal, Zionist ideologues sought not only the physical transfer of Palestinians to Arab countries, but also the transfer of Jews from Arab Muslim countries to Palestine. However, for the latter, physical dislocation was not adequate, since the displaced Jews had to undergo a metamorphosis. The establishment, in a contemporary retell-ing of the biblical Exodus from Egypt, called for "the death of the desert generation" in order to facilitate their birth as the New Jews/Israelis, as embodied by the sabra generation.

The question of continuity and discontinuity is central, therefore, to the Zionist vision of the nation-state. Yet one could argue that by provoking the geographical dispersal of Arab-Jews, by placing them in a new situation "on the ground," by attempting to reshape their identity as simply "Israeli," by disdaining and trying to uproot their Arabness, and by racializing them and discriminating against them as a group, the ingathering-of-exiles project itself provoked a dislocation that resulted in a series of traumatic ruptures and exilic identity formations. The Israeli establishment obliged Arab-Jews to redefine themselves in relation to new ideological paradigms and polarities, thus provoking the aporias of an identity constituted out of its own ruins. The Jews within Islam thought of themselves as Jews, but that Jewishness formed part of a larger Judeo-Islamic cultural fabric. Under pressure from Zionism, on the one hand, and Arab nationalism, on the other, that set of affiliations gradually changed, resulting in a transformed cultural semantics.

The identity crisis provoked by this physical, political, and cultural rupture is reflected in a terminological crisis in which no single term seems to fully represent a coherent entity. The very proliferation of terms suggests the difficulties of grappling with the complexities of this identity: non-Ashkenazi Jews; Sephardim; Jews of Islam; Arab-Jews; Middle Eastern, West Asian, or North African Jews; Asian and African Jews; non-European Jews; Third World Jews; Levantine Jews; Jews of the Mediterranean; Maghrebian and Mashreqian Jews (from the western and eastern parts of the Arab world); *Bnei Edot ha-Mizrah* (descendants of the Eastern communities); *yotzei artzot 'arav ve-ha-Islam* (those who left Arab and Muslim countries); blacks; *Israel ha-Shniya* (Second Israel); Mizrahiyim or Mizrahim; Iraqi Jews, Iranian Jews, Kurdish Jews, Palestinian Jews, Moroccan Jews, and so forth. Each term raises questions about the implicit history, politics, and discourses that generated the terms and that made them catchwords at specific conjunctures. Each term encodes a historical, geographical, and political point of view.

Prior to their arrival in Israel, Jews in Iraq, for example, had a different self-designation. They had thought of themselves as Jews, but that Jewish identity was diacritical: It played off and depended on a relation to other communities. Hyphens, even if silent, articulated a complexly embedded identity in relation to other communities: Baghdadi Jews (in contrast to Jews of other cities), Babylonian Jews (to mark historical roots in the region), Iraqi Jews (to mark national affiliation), or Arab-Jews (in contradistinction to Muslim and Christian Arabs, but also marking affiliation with the greater Arab civilization). The concept of Sephardiness was not part of the self-definition. That term referred strictly to the Jews of Spain who retained their Spanishness even outside Iberia—for example, in Turkey, Bulgaria, Egypt, Palestine, and Morocco. Yet a kind of transregional geocultural Jewish space, from the Mediterranean to the Indian Ocean, was shaped within which Jews, under the aegis of the larger Islamic world, traveled and exchanged goods and ideas. Culturally and politically interwoven into that world, their Jewishness was retained within that space. They were shaped by Arab Muslim culture, while also helping shape that culture in a dialogical process that generated their specific Judeo-Arab identity.

The rise of Zionism and Arab nationalism, along with the implementation of partitions as a colonial solution for regional conflicts, affected the identity designations of Jews in the Arab Muslim world. Arabness came to signify a national identity, requiring a realignment of Ottoman definitions. Their religion (Judaism) was rapidly turning into a national marker in the international arena, which gradually conflicted with their affiliation with the emerging Arab nation-state. With the rise of Arab nationalism, on the one hand, and Zionism, on the other, they have come to occupy an ambivalent positioning vis-à-vis both movements. The explosive politics after the partition of Palestine and the establishment of the State of Israel rendered their existence virtually impossible within a context of Arab nationalism. On arrival in Israel, shorn of any alternative passport, Arab-Jews entered a new linguistic and discursive environment, at once geopolitical (the Israel–Arab conflict), legal (Israeli citizenship), and cultural (East versus West). The normative term became "Israeli," not merely an indicator of a new passport, but also a signifier of a new cultural and ideological paradigm. Whereas Jewishness in Iraq, for example, formed part of a constellation of coexisting and complexly stratified ethnicities and religions, Jewishness in Israel was now the assumed cultural and political "dominant." Arabness became the marginalized category, and the religion of Arab-Jews, for the first time in their history, was now affiliated with the dominant power, equated with the very basis of national belonging. Their culture (their Arabness), meanwhile, became a marker of ethnic, even racial, otherness, a kind of embarrassing excess. If in the Arab world, prior to their "Exodus," their Jewishness (associated now with Zionism) was subjected to surveillance, in Israel their affiliation with an Arab cultural geography was similarly disciplined and punished.

The processes of spatial rupture and cultural displacement have affected and shifted identity designations.[3] Each term implies a different historical moment, geographical space, and ideological perspective. Throughout this essay, I will move back and forth between different namings, precisely because I am interested in situating identities rather than proposing an essential core identity. Since I am arguing for a conjunctural, historically situated definition of identity, I also want to highlight the processes and discourses that enabled such identity transformation. Although I have often used the term "Arab-Jews," it was not intended to suggest a reductive and essential Jewish or Arab identity. The aim in hyphenating Arab-Jewish identity is to call into question the Eurocentric nationalist paradigm that erased the hyphen and made it taboo. The term "Arab-Jew" obviously assumes an Arab cultural geography and therefore is not meant to cover, in a global sweep, the histories of *all* Jews. In fact, I have used the term in diacritical opposition to the term "Jewish History," arguing for Jewish histo*ries*. The term "Mizrahi history," meanwhile, implies a recent history, one produced within the ideological space of Israel and Zionism. And while one might rightly argue that there is no single Mizrahi history, the term highlights the dislocation and the shaping of a new hybrid identity, neither simply "Arab" nor simply "Jewish."

Each designation calls attention to a different dimension of a complex history and spatial trajectory, and each term foregrounds specific aspects of communal affiliation. Each frame illuminates only partial aspects of over-lapping collective identities shaped within the movement across borders. Each designation addresses specific and even contradictory dynamics between and within different world zones. Critical Mizrahi studies requires more flexible relations among the various conceptual frameworks—a mobile set of grids, a diverse set of disciplinary as well as cultural-geopolitical lenses—adequate to these complexities. Flexible, yet critical, usage of the terms that can address their politics of location is important not only for pointing out historical and geographical contradictions and differences, but also for reaffirming historical and geographical links and structural analogies.

DISPLACEMENT: NARRATIVES OF CROSS-BORDER MOVEMENT

The question of naming is also problematic in relation to the unprecedented movement across borders of West Asian and North African Jews from the late 1940s to the 1960s. Nationalist paradigms cannot capture the complexity of this historical moment, particularly for Arab-Jews. Perhaps due to the idiosyncrasies of the situation, for a community trapped between two nationalisms—Arab and Jewish—each term used to designate the displacement seems problematic. None of the terms—"*aliyah*" (ascendancy), "*yetzia*" (exit), "exodus," "expulsion," "immigration," "emigration," "exile," "refugees," "expatriates," and "population exchange"— seems adequate. In the case of the Palestinians, the forced mass exodus easily fits the term "refugee," since they never wanted to leave Palestine and have maintained the desire to return. In the case of Arab-Jews, the question of will, desire, and agency remains highly ambivalent and ambiguous. The very proliferation of terms suggests that it is not only a matter of legal definition of citizenship that is at stake, but also the issue of mental maps of belonging within the context of rival nationalisms. Did Arab-Jews want to stay? Did they want to leave? Did they exercise free will? Did they actually make a decision? Once in Israel, did they want to go back? Were they able to do so? And did they regret the impossibility of returning? Different answers to these questions imply distinct assumptions about questions of agency, memory, and space.

The displacement of Iraqi Jews, for example, was not simply the result of a decision made solely by Arab-Jews themselves.[4] Even if some Arab-Jews expressed a desire to go to Israel, the question is why, suddenly, after millennia of not doing so, would they leave overnight? The displacement for most Arab-Jews was the product of complex circumstances in which panic and disorientation, rather than desire for *aliyah* in the nationalist sense of the word, was the key factor. The "ingathering" seems less natural when one takes into account the circumstances that forced their departure: the efforts of the Zionist underground in Iraq to undermine the authority of community leaders such as hakham Sasson Khdhuri;[5] the Zionist policy of placing a "wedge" between the Jewish and Muslim communities, generating anti-Arab panic on the part of Jews;[6] the anti-Jewish propaganda, especially as channeled through the Istiklal, or Independence Party; the failure of most Arab intellectuals and leaders to clarify and act on the distinction between Jews and Zionists; their failure to actively secure the place of Jews in the Arab world; the persecution of communists, among them Jews who opposed Zionism; the secretive agreements between some Arab leaders and Israeli leaders concerning the idea of "population exchange"; and the misconceptions, on the part of many Arab-Jews, about the differences between their own religious identity, affiliation, or sentiments and the secular nation-state project of Zionism, a movement that had virtually nothing to do with those sentiments, even if it capitalized on a quasi-religious rhetoric.

The official term *"aliyah,"* therefore, is multiply misleading. It suggests a commitment to Zionism, when in fact the majority of Jews—and certainly Jews within the Levant—were decidedly not Zionists. Zionist discourse normalized the telos of a Jewish nation-state; the move toward its borders was represented as the ultimate Jewish act. When the actual departure of Arab-Jews is represented—as in the 1998 documentary series *Tekuma*, produced by the state TV channel in conjunction with the fiftieth anniversary of Israel—it is narrated as merely an act of devotion. Images of Yemeni Jews arriving at the camps set up by the Jewish Agency are juxtaposed with a voiceover that reductively speaks of messianic will and persecution. The Yemeni Jews are represented as *willing* to cross the desert and sacrifice their lives in order to get to the Promised Land, the State of Israel. Most Zionist writings highlight a kind of natural inevitability while erasing diverse Zionist tactics to actively dislodge these communities.

Even in much of Mizrahi literature and film, the historical complexity of the moment of dislocation, as well as its concomitant emotional, disorienting trauma, operates as a structuring absence. Such texts tend to delineate Jewish life in Israel and in the Arab world as separated existences taking place within disconnected cultural geographies. The production of split spaces that inform most narratives still manifests symptoms of a cultural schizophrenia—the difficulty with articulating the actual moment of departure—that crucial moment whereby overnight one's identity marker as an Iraqi or Yemeni ends and that of an Israeli suddenly begins. This difficulty of accommodating the two spaces within the same narrative is present even in texts that do refer to the move. Sammy Michael's Hebrew novel *Victoria* (1993), for example, describes the young heroine's life in Iraq from the turn of the century until the 1950s, after which she reenters the narrative as an elderly woman in present-day Israel. The event surrounding her dislocation, as well as the novelistic description of her move from Iraq to Israel, forms a textual silence in which the move to Israel is a taken-for-granted, obvious, and transparent act in the heroine's life. Yet the writer more clearly articulates the haunting memory of dislocation in interviews.[7] Michael speaks of a recurrent nightmare in which he is sitting in his favorite Baghdadi café—along the Tigris—a trigger for nostalgic longing. But when he comes to pay, he digs into his pocket and finds only Israeli coins, a telltale sign of his enemy Zionist affiliations. The discursive lacuna concerning the dislocation, however, characterizes most representations that assume the inevitable telos of *aliya* to the Jewish homeland without interrogating its semantics within a specifically Arab-Jewish history.

The term *"aliyah"* naturalizes both a negative and a positive pole: the will to escape persecution and the desire to go to the Jewish homeland. Yet this masternarrative excludes narratives that relay moments of refusal, questioning, or ambivalence toward the immanent dislocations. *"Aliya"* (literally, ascendancy) is borrowed from the realm of religion (*'aliyah la-regel*), which originally referred to the pilgrimage to the Temple and later to the holy sites of the land of Zion. Yet within Zionist discourse, *"aliyah"* has been transferred to the realm of citizenship and national identity. In this discursive conflation, the *'olim*, according to official ideology, benefited from spiritual and even material ascendancy, a view that contrasts sharply with the multifaceted devastation, the social descent (*yerida*) experienced by most Jews from Muslim countries. Zionist discourse about the transition of Arab-Jews to Israel deploys conceptual paradigms in which religious ideas such as redemption, ascent, and the ingathering are grafted onto nationalist paradigms. In this sense, even when scholars acknowledge that *aliyah* was not simply voluntary, they often deploy a term that subliminally encodes this Zionist vision.

At the same time, the dominant Arab nationalist discourse represented the mass exodus as an index of the Jewish betrayal of the Arab nation. Ironically, the Zionist view that Arabness and Jewishness were mutually exclusive gradually came to be shared by Arab nationalist discourse, placing Arab-Jews on the horns of a terrible dilemma. The rigidity of both paradigms has produced the particular Arab-Jewish tragedy, since neither paradigm can easily contain crossed or multiple identities and infinities.[8] The displacement of Arab-Jews from the Arab world took place, for the most part, without a fully conscious or comprehensive understanding on their part of what was at stake and what was yet to come. Arab-Jews often left their countries of origin with mingled excitement and terror but, most important, buffeted by manipulated confusion, misunderstandings, and projections provoked by a Zionism that blended messianic religiosity with secular nationalist purposes. Even Arab-Jewish Zionists at times failed to grasp this distinction and certainly never imagined the systematic racism that they were about to encounter in the "Jewish state." Therefore, some Arab-Jewish Zionist activists came to lament the day that they set foot in Israel.[9] The incorporation of the non-Ashkenazim into a new culture was far more ambiguous than any simple narrative of immigration and assimilation can convey. Although *aliyah* to Israel is celebrated by official ideology and sometimes seen by Sephardim/Mizrahim themselves as a return "home," in fact this return, within a longer historical perspective, can also be seen as a new mode of exile.

Arab-Jews, in my view, could never fully foresee what the impossibility of return to their countries of origin would mean.[10] The permission to leave—as in the case of Iraqi Jews—did not allow for a possible return either of individuals or of the community. Therefore, even the term "immigration" does not account for that massive crossing of borders. Iraqi Jews, for example, had to give up their citizenship (al-tasqit), losing their right to return. Within Israel, for at least four decades, performing even a symbolic return within the public sphere—the expression of nostalgia for an Arab past—became taboo. Meanwhile, the propagandistic description of the dislocation of Arab-Jews as a "population exchange," which supposedly justifies the creation of Palestinian refugees, is also fundamentally problematic. It elides the simple fact that neither Arab-Jews nor Palestinians were ever consulted about whether they wanted to be exchanged. Although following the partition of Palestine both movements across borders in opposite directions may be described as traumatic, the forced departure of Arab-Jews does not exactly parallel the circumstances of the Palestinian no-choice exodus during al-Nakbah (the catastrophe). Furthermore, the right of return for Palestinians has remained a central political issue, even an identity-shaping factor, while for Arab-Jews the idea of return became a murky issue even when limited to the discursive and cultural sphere. Yet despite these significant differences, the discursive naturalization of such terms as "aliyah" or "immigration" has to be reevaluated, since the questions of will, desire, and agency remain extremely complex, contingent, and ambivalent.

In sum, at the very core of the invention of Mizrahi identity, within the conceptual space of Zionism and within the physical space of Israel, lies an ambiguous relation to movement across the border. While for the Jews from the Muslim world the Land of Israel/Palestine was continuous with their cultural geography, the Eurocentric construct of the State of Israel on that land required discontinuity. The passage into the political space of Israel initiated Jews from Arab and Muslim lands into a new process within which they were transformed, almost overnight, into a new racialized ethnic identity. Therefore, a critical scholarship cannot afford to assume the Zionist masternarrative of choice and desire. Rather, it needs to look into the deep, anxious ambivalences generated by partition and the scars it left on the psyche of the displaced. Such scholarship probes the dialectics of continuity and discontinuity with regard to the Arab Muslim world as a palpitatingly vital issue that informs the transformation of Arab-Jews into Mizrahim, as they have ended up even if after the fact, in a largely colonial-settler enterprise.

DISMEMBERMENT: THE ERASURE OF THE HYPHEN

The masternarrative of unique Jewish victimization has been crucial for legitimizing an *anomalous* nationalist project of "ingathering of the exiles from the four corners of the globe." Yet this narrative has also legitimized the engendering of displacements of peoples from such diverse geographies, languages, cultures, and histories—a project in which in many ways a state created a nation. It has been argued that *all* nations are invented, yet I would suggest that *some* nations, such as Jewish Israel, are more invented than others. Zionist writings made great efforts to normalize not simply "the Jew" but also the very discourses that redefined the multitude of Jewish communities as the "Jewish nation." The metanarrative of the nation constructed one official past while simultaneously destroying other perspectives on that narrative. Non-canonical memories have been suppressed while previous affiliations have been severed. In the new conceptual vacuum, the hyphen, which made possible such terms as "Judeo-Muslim" and "Arab-Jew," was dropped while legitimating others— specifically, "Judeo-Christian," now a marker of a Western geopolitical culture.

Memories of a common past (biblical times), common language (Hebrew), and common land (Eretz Israel) were enlisted to serve a myth-making machine. The nation's memory was marshaled into suppressing any other possible memories from diverse pasts, languages, and lands. A state of perennial adrenal anxiety has marked the Zionist masternarrative. Foregrounding an exceptionalist victimization discourse, this narrative manufactured the Muslim Arab as a common perennial "historical enemy" facing the "Jewish nation." Zionist discourse has represented Palestinians, Arabs, or Muslims as merely one more "non-Jewish" obstacle to the Jewish Israeli national trajectory. Its historiography concerning Jews within Islam consists of a morbidly selective "tracing the dots" from pogrom to pogrom. The word "pogrom" itself, it must be noted, derives from and is reflective of the Eastern European Jewish experience. I do not mean to idealize the position of Jews within Islam. Rather, I argue that Zionist discourse in a sense has hijacked Jews from their Judeo-Islamic political geography and subordinated them into the European Jewish chronicle of *shtetl* and pogrom. This picture of an ageless, relentless oppression and humiliation, however, has produced a double-edged amnesia: one with regard to the Zionist settlement of Palestine, which for the most part disregarded the perspective and concerns of the inhabitants of Palestine, culminating in their dispossession and yielding almost a century of Palestinian antagonism to Zionism and Israel, now equated with Jews and Judaism; the second with regard to the Judeo-Islamic history, which deserves to be represented more complexly within a more *multiperspectival* approach.[11]

The Zionist conception of "Jewish History" presumes a unitary and universal notion of history, rather than a multiplicity of experiences differing from period to period and from context to context. Positing the vision of Jewish nationalism on a demarcated territory as a "natural evolution" is in itself a problematic claim, but positing this vision as a panacea for *all* Jews is especially bewildering. In the same period that the idea of Zionism was being formulated within a Christian European context, Jews in the Muslim world occupied a different position, one that did not necessarily require a nationalist articulation of their identity. (In this sense, one might argue that the concept of Jewish nationalism was politically irrelevant to their existence as Jews within the Islamic world.) The Zionist "proof" of a single Jewish experience, therefore, allows little space for comparative studies of Jews in relation to diverse religious and ethnic minorities, especially within Muslim spaces. The Zionist vision of a single Jewish experience leads to a historiographical narrative that excludes parallels and overlappings with non-Jewish religious and ethnic communities. Thus, this narrative ejects the idea of hyphenated and syncretic Jewish cultures, as well as the notion of linked and analogous oppressions between Jews and various communities. The selective reading of Judeo-Muslim history, in other words, makes two processes apparent: the unproblematized subordination of Jews within Islam to a "universal" Jewish experience and the rejection of an Arab and Muslim context for Jewish institutions, identities, and histories.

Contemporary cultural practices illustrate this process of dismemberment—that is, the attempt to represent the Jews within Islam detached from Muslim Arab culture, philosophy, and institutions. The exhibition of Turkish Jewish costumes at the Jewish Museum in New York (1989) provides such an example. The exhibition offered its viewers a vehicle for imaginary travel into distant geography and history via the colorful costume of the "other" Jews. Displaced from one geography to another, the museological project removed the costumes from their social habitus, displaying them as exotic objects, fetishistically isolated from the Muslim Ottoman context. This isolationist concept elides the embeddedness of Jewish life in the dominant Muslim culture. Jewish dress codes were shared with the ambient Muslim world—albeit at times with some differences, depending on the specific period. As cultural imperialism was marching into the Muslim world, there was still nothing obvious or natural about a discursive act of "separating" Jews from the Muslim world and unifying them with the culture of Ashkenazi Jews.

In fact, in the late nineteenth century, cultural dissonance seems to have been most afflicting the relationships among the coreligionists (Ashkenazi and Sephardi Jews) than among the co-regionists (Arab Muslims and Jews). Nowhere is it clearer than when the Alliance Israelite Universelle (AIU) was attempting to install what was regarded as an alien culture in the "Levant."[12] The AIU—the schooling system founded in Paris in 1860 by Westernized Ashkenazi Jews—was meant to provide a French curriculum for the Jews of the Levant and to carry the banner of enlightenment and the civilizing mission into the "desolated" regions of the world. The AIU began its programs by requiring its students to change their "outmoded" dress code and hairstyle, perceived as signs of backwardness. The Baghdadi Jewish establishment partially collaborated with the AIU mission to provide education for Baghdadi children, since this type of education was seen as useful within a world of rising Western powers. However, the establishment did not understand the learning of French culture and history to mean the abandonment of Judeo-Arab culture.[13] Consequently, it opposed the cultural power exercised by the AIU toward the students.

The negative reaction among Baghdadi Jews to the practices of the AIU was also shared by Arab Muslims. One of the articles in the Judeo-Arabic newspaper *Perah*, published in India, reports on the Muslims' response to the changes they began to perceive among upper-middle-class Jews: "From one day to the next the phenomenon [of shaving] is spreading so that the one who shaves his beard cannot be distinguished from the gentiles [Christians]. It has also become the occasion of ridicule by the Muslims in the marketplace who say: 'Wonder of wonders, the Jews have forsaken their religion. . . . See how the Jews have abandoned their religion (heaven forbid)—before, not one of them would touch his beard and earlocks, and now they cut them and throw them into the dustbin.' "[14] In contrast to contemporary representations of an inherent Muslim anti-

Semitism, one detects in this example a Muslim investment in maintaining Jewish identity as it had been known within the Muslim world. Both Muslims and Jews perceived Jewish identity as embedded within a larger Judeo-Islamic civilizational complex, while assimilation into Western style is seen as a betrayal of traditions at once culturally shared and religiously differentiated. In this respect, the Jewish French assimilationist practice is regarded as a violation of these norms. The Judeo-Arabic newspaper of the late nineteenth century cites the Muslim response as invoking the same code that the Jewish Baghdadi leaders also believed in. The anxiety that Arab-Jews manifest here, ironically, concerns their image in the eyes not of French Jews but of their Muslim neighbors, who were not seeking the assimilation of Arab-Jews.

Zionist historiography advanced the idea of a homogeneous national past and precluded any "deviance" into a more historicized and relational narrative that would see Jews not simply through their religious commonalties but also *in relation* to their non-Jewish contextual cultures, institutions, and practices. Thus, a historiography that assumes a pan-Jewish culture is often the same historiography that assumes the bifurcated discourse of "Arab versus Jew" without acknowledging a hyphenated Arab-Jewish existence. In this sense, the erasure of the hyphen was crucial to Zionist writings. The Arabness and the Orientalness of Jews posed a challenge to any simplistic definition of Jewish national identity, questioning the very axioms and boundaries of the Euro-Israeli national project. The cultural affinity that Arab-Jews shared with Arab Muslims—in many respects, stronger than that which they shared with European Jews—threatened the Zionist conception of a homogeneous nation modeled on the European nationalist definition of the nation-state. As an integral part of the topography, language, culture, and history of the "East," Eastern Jews have also threatened the Euro-Israeli self-image that has envisioned itself as a prolongation of "Europe," *in* the "East" but not *of* it. Arab-Jews, for the first time in their history, faced the imposed dilemma of choosing between Jewishness and Arabness in a geopolitical context that perpetuated the equation between Arabness, Middle Easterners, and Islam, on the one hand, and Jewishness, Europeaness, and Westernness, on the other. Thus, the religious Jewish aspect of what has been a culturally diverse Jewish identity has been given primacy, a reductive categorization tantamount to dismembering the identity of a community. The continuity of Jewish life meant the ceasing of Arab life for Arab-Jews in Israel—at least, in the public sphere. What was called by officialdom an "ingathering," then, was also a cultural dismembering, both within and between communities. But the Zionist reading of that dismemberment, both before and after the actual rupture, rendered it a healing and a return.

The past is subjected to contestation within diverse institutional force fields. Its narrators argue for a privileged ownership of the historical pain, collective memory, and the copyrights on their deployment. Memories that endanger the hegemonic discourse are forbidden, become taboo, and disappear from the public arena. These taboos are often internalized even by the scarred bodies that might potentially articulate history from a different angle and within a different frame. Zionist discourse, which argued for the "right for normalcy," narrated the historical past and envisioned a utopian future as a homogeneous, unified model. However, this regulation of "normalcy" created in its wake myriad forms of social "abnormalcy," the syndromes of which have included the silencing and kidnapping of the language of critical thinking. Rearticulating the terminology, concepts, and methods is crucial for producing transnational knowledge that undoes the Zionist normative apparatus.

DISCHRONICITY: TEMPORALITY AND THE PARADOXES OF MODERNIZATION

Discursively multifaceted, the ruptures provoked by Zionism were conceived at once geographically—dislodging the communities and transferring their bodies into a newly imagined political space of the *alt-neu-land* of Israel[15]—and historiographically, separating Jews from their culturally ossified habitus and integrating them into the dynamism of universal culture. The Zionist return to the old biblical land, in other words, was never premised on a simple return to the ways of biblical times, even when it was imbued with nostalgia for the ancient. Both bedouins and Yemeni Jews were romanticized within an exoticized temporality. As with all civilizing missions, the "inevitable" march of progress simultaneously produced in its wake the devastation of "primitive" worlds and the mourning for their disappearance. Undergirding these paradoxical conceptualizations was a modernizing assumption of what can be called "dischronicity," or the rupture of time, as though communities live in split time zones, some advanced and some lagging behind. The ideology of modernization thrives on a binarist demarcation of opposed concepts: modernity–tradition, underdevelopment–development, science–superstition, and technology–backwardness. In this sense, modernization functions as a bridge between two opposite temporal poles within a stagist narrative that paradoxically assumes the essential "developedness" of one community over another, while also generating programs to transform the "underdeveloped" into modernity.

In Israel, the ideology of modernization shaped both policy and identity within the formation of the nation-state. The modernization narrative has projected a Western national identity for a state geographically located in the Middle East and populated by Eastern European Jews as well as by a Middle Eastern majority—both Palestinians and non-Ashkenazi Jews. The dominant discourse of Euro-Israeli policy makers and scholars has suggested that Asian and African Jews—not unlike the Palestinian population —originate from "primitive," "backward," "underdeveloped," "premodern" societies and therefore, unlike Ashkenazim, require modernization.[16] But here modernization can also be seen as a euphemism, at best, for breaking away from Arab Levantine culture. Over the years, Euro-Israeli political leaders, writers, and scholars have frequently advanced the historiographically suspect idea that "Jews of the Orient," prior to their "ingathering" into Israel, were somehow "outside of" history. This discourse ironically echoes nineteenth-century assessments, such as those of Hegel, that Jews, like blacks, lived outside of the progressively unfolding spirit of Western civilization.

In the early 1950s, some of Israel's most celebrated intellectuals from Hebrew University in Jerusalem wrote essays addressing the "ethnic problem" and in the process recycled a number of the tropes typically projected onto colonized and non-European people. For Karl Frankenstein, for example, "The primitive mentality of many of the immigrants from backward countries" might be profitably compared to "the primitive expression of children, the retarded, or the mentally disturbed."[17] And in 1964, Kalman Katznelson published his openly racist book *The Ashkenazi Revolution*, in which he argued for the essential, irreversible genetic inferiority of the Sephardim, warning against mixed marriage as tainting the Ashkenazi race and calling for the Ashkenazim to protect their interests against a burgeoning Sephardi majority.[18]

In sociological and anthropological studies, the dispossession of Middle Eastern Jews of their culture has been justified by the concept of "the inevitable march of Western progress"—that is, those who have been living in a historically condemned temporality would inevitably disappear before the productive advances of modernity. Within traditional anthropology, one detects a desire to project the Mizrahim as living "allochronically" (Johannes Fabian)[19] in another time, often associated with earlier periods of individual life (childhood) or of human history (primitivism). From the perspective of official Zionism, the *aliyah* to Israel signifies leaving behind premodernity. Jews from Arab and Muslim countries enter modernity only when they appear on the map of the Hebrew state, just as the modern history of Palestine is seen as beginning with the Zionist renewal of the biblical mandate. In Israeli history textbooks, Middle Eastern Jewish history has been presumed to begin with the arrival of Jews to Israel.

Contemporary museological projects reproduce this teleological vision of history. The Babylon Jewish Museum in Or Yehuda, Israel, despite its name, is largely dedicated to the triumph of Zionism in Iraq.[20] The exhibition creates a disproportionate spatial gap between life in Babylon/Iraq before and after the arrival of Zionism. The walls dramatically expand on the few decades of Zionist activism in Iraq but minimally condense the millennia of Jewish history lived between the Dijla and Furat rivers. This linear narrative naturalizes the transition into the modern nation. The converging discourses of enlightenment, progress, and modernization are central to the Zionist masternarrative. A series of mutually reinforcing equations between modernity, science, technology, and the West has legitimized Zionism as an extension of the civilizing mission applied first to Palestine and then to Arab-Jews.

Discourses of progress were crucial to the colonization of Palestine and later played a central role in incorporating Arab-Jews into the Jewish nation. Rescue tropes such as "making the desert bloom" grounded the claim to Palestine in an argument that was both biblical and scientific, buttressed by archaeological evidence. Similarly, the "ingathering" project entailed not only a biblical messianic vision but also the idea of modernizing the "Land of the Fathers" and the "traditional Jews."[21] Zionist discourse portrayed Levantine Jewish culture as dormant and barren and, like the virgin land of Palestine, waiting langorously to receive the seed of European vitality. While presenting Palestine as an empty arid land to be transformed by Jewish toil, the Zionist "Founding Fathers" presented Arab-Jews as passive vessels to be shaped by the revivifying spirit of Zionism.

DISSONANCE: METHODOLOGY AS DISCURSIVE RUPTURE

The rupture shaping the lives of Arab-Jews, particularly since the partition of Palestine, has generated a scholarship that delineates their lives "before and after their arrival" to Israel. While one might debate the validity of the facts described in sociological, anthropological, or historical accounts, I

want to point to a discursive oscillation, a conceptual or even methodological schizophrenia that permeates such scholarship. Rather than a mere
coincidence, this disjuncture of paradigms is virtually necessitated by the
subliminal privileging of a Zionist vantage point.

Studies of the Jews of Yemen, for example, tend to highlight their
"clear separation" from Muslims, their "remoteness" and "isolation"
"amidst Arab tribesman" but cut off from other Jewish communities and
from the forces of modernity. In the foundational scholarship of. S. D.
Goiten, the Yemenite Jews were seen as preserving rabbinical Judaism of
the post-Biblical era.[22] A static, unchanging picture of an authentic Judaism emerged—a picture that has nourished much of the romanticization
of the Yemeni Jew as a figure of primitive origins. Studies of the Jews of
Yemen, for example, detail their oppression at Muslim hands, relating the
kidnapping of young Jewish women, their forced conversion to Islam, and
their imposed marriage to Muslim men. When these same Yemeni Jews
are studied within the Israeli framework, however, the writers abandon the
historical account of discrimination and shift into an anthropological account of folklore and tradition (the *mori*, henna, *gat* chewing).

A mixture of history and anthropology, Herbert S. Lewis's *After the Eagles
Landed: The Yemenites of Israel* celebrates the successful Yemeni adaptation
to Israeli society.[23] The terms "hybridity" and "syncretism," forgotten in
the millennial context of Yemeni Jewish-Muslim space, are invoked to seal
the recent marriage of Ashkenazi and Yemeni cultures in Israel—terms
that reencode assimilationist policy as happy mutual fusion. "I do not recall
ever hearing an older Yemenite complain about the work he or others had
to do in road building or forestation during the early years" (150). The
Yemenite positive qualities, in contrast to the Moroccans' resentful bit-
terness, propels his conclusion that "there is no sense in which these
Yemenites are a problem population. . . . They have successfully adapted to
the new world they came to in the 1950s, without retreat or breakdown."[24]
The book begins by addressing institutionalized discrimination in Yemen,
leaving out any parallel discussion of institutional discrimination in Israel.
Referring to the seventeenth-century Decree of Orphans, which took fatherless Jewish children in Yemen away from their families and communities and converted them to Islam, the author notes the resulting "great
hardship and fear . . . remembered vividly and with great pain today."[25] Yet
the text's tale of kidnapping and pain is highly selective. Although *After the
Eagles Landed* was written in 1989 and reissued in 1994, it fails to mention
one of the most traumatic kidnappings to afflict the Yemeni Jewish com-

munity between the late 1940s and the 1960s, which took place *not* in a Muslim country, but in the Jewish state. It is ironic in this sense that the author, who is so concerned about the memory of a tragedy in Yemen, is so silent about a more recent tragedy in Israel.

Disoriented by the new reality in Israel, Yemenis, as well as other Jews from Arab and Muslim countries, fell prey to doctors, nurses, and social workers, most of them on the state payroll. These representatives of the state's welfare institutions were involved in providing babies for adoption by Ashkenazi parents largely in Israel and the United States while telling the biological parents that the babies had died. The conspiracy was extensive enough to include the systematic issuance of fraudulent death certificates for the adopted babies and at times even fake burial sites for the babies who presumably had died, although the parents were never presented with the proof—the body. In this way, the government attempted to ensure that over several decades Mizrahi demands for investigation were silenced while information was hidden and manipulated by government bureaus. The act of kidnapping was not simply a result of financial interests to increase the state's revenues; it was also a result of a deeply ingrained belief in the inferiority of Jews from Arab and Muslim countries, seen as careless breeders with little sense of responsibility toward their own children. Doctors, nurses, and social workers in this sense saw themselves as missionaries of Western science and progress, faithful to their duty of carrying out the vision of modernity.[26] Transferring babies from the space of premodernity to that of modernity, where they would be raised according to nuclear-family values and Western behavioral norms, was perceived to be logical, rational, and scientific. Within this discursive framework, literally tearing babies away from the arms of their mothers seemed only natural, even redemptive. The act of kidnapping babies therefore operated on a continuum with the reigning academic discourses of the time. In this intersection of race, gender, and class, the displaced Jews from Muslim countries became victims of the logic of progress, bearing the marks of its pathologies on their bodies.

A severe human-rights violation—kidnapping—was subjected to systematic silencing and censorship.[27] The scholarly elision of this central experience is complicitous with the institutional silencing. Instead, anthropological texts tend typically to be organized around such concepts as kinship, marriage, rituals, religious values, and social attitudes. While not always embedded in the sociology of modernization, these texts tend to participate in a romanticizing anthropology invested in the exotic authenticity, and even the colorful simplicity, of its subjects. In this sense, the warm tone and rich texture of Orientalist ethnography contrasts with the metallic machinations of the sociology of modernization. Yet, both the romanticization and the modernization discourses—at times in the same text—produce the Mizrahi family as a site of deviance from an implicit cultural norm. Therefore, the Orientalist emphasis on the Mizrahi extended family structure (the ḥamula) in both disciplines is unable to contain the devastation experienced by these families through the kidnappings performed with the complicity of certain sectors of the establishment. Both narratives have also kidnapped Mizrahi subjectivity by eliding the perspective of Jews from Muslim countries, who in their worst imaginings could have never predicted an act of kidnapping in—and indirectly sanctioned by—the "Jewish state."

Deploying the framework of either modernizing sociology or romanticizing ethnography to write about Jews within Israel while at the same time applying political historiography to write about Jews within Islam produces a selective tale of kidnapping contingent on a political geography. This dichotomous narrativization frames the act of kidnapping in one space as paradigmatic and defamatory, while in the other the *same* act is either ignored or seen as an aberration from the norm. Every negative experience in the Arab world is amplified, allegorized, made synecdochic; it becomes the center of the historical narrative. Every negative experience in Israel, meanwhile, is downplayed within an exoticizing ethnographic account. At a time when both activism and academic research on the issue have entered the public sphere,[28] the structuring absence of the kidnapping case produces the scholarly equivalent of kidnapping—that is, the sequestering of Mizrahi intellectual agency in its own self-historicizing.

The ideological rupture characteristic of Zionist discourse, then, is reflected in much of hegemonic scholarship, even at times when written by Mizrahim. The rupture is reproduced not only in the themes but also in the analytical modes, resulting in a kind of a methodological schizophrenia. Moshe Gat's *A Jewish Community in Crisis: The Exodus from Iraq, 1948–1951*, for example, analyzes the Iraqi political and economic interests in at first refusing and then permitting Iraqi Jews to leave (only on giving up their citizenship).[29] The book also characterizes the active opposition to Zionism on the part of the Iraqi Jewish leadership of Baghdad, depicting hakham Sasson Khdhuri as simply fearing the loss of his status and position to the Zionists.[30] Yet this dissection of motives, interest, and power is abandoned once the author moves to examine the activities of the Zionist movement in Iraq as well as the position of the Israeli establishment. Here, the author shifts into a benign and idealistic official discourse to characterize Israel's "concern" for the Iraqi Jews, the very community being uprooted, largely to the benefit of the Israeli state apparatus in terms of its political, demographic, and economic necessities: settling the country with Jews, securing the borders, obtaining cheap labor, and getting useful military personnel. As with any historiography, it is not simply the issue of "facts" that is at stake, but also the questions of narrative, tropes, characterizations, and points of view. The texts about Arab-Jews tend to be organized around the agency of the Zionist movement and the State of Israel; the reader is sutured into a privileged point of view as well as into implicit "norms of the text."[31] Thus, despite the methodological and discursive rupture, the historical tale remains coherent through the persistence of a hierarchical narrative structure, in which the Zionist idea provides the discursive "glue" that keeps the various elements together.

A rupture of a different nature operates in Amitav Ghosh's *In an Antique Land*, a book that offers a complex picture of Arab-Jewish existence within Muslim space.[32] A hybrid of anthropology and history, the book interweaves ethnographic narratives concerning present-day Egyptian Muslims with historiographical accounts of the lives of Arab-Jews in the twelfth century. Ghosh chronicles a Judeo-Islamic world largely through the travels of a Tunisian Jewish merchant whose existence is conjured up from the shreds of the Geniza archive. The book vividly captures a geocultural Muslim space stretching from the Mediterranean to the Indian Ocean, where Jews lived, traveled, and exchanged goods and ideas. Within this Muslim space, the existence of Jewishness was not perceived in exclusionary terms, as a philosophical and cultural contradiction. Ghosh's anthropology, meanwhile, focuses on his visits in the 1980s to an Egyptian village, exclusively dealing with the lives of contemporary Muslim Egyptians. The book, in other words, produces a fascinating silence about the lives of present-day Egyptian, Tunisian, and other Arab-Jews. In this fashion, *In an Antique Land* splits the geography of identity into two autonomous narrative spaces: ethnography (Muslim Arabs) and historiography (Jewish Arabs). The narrative ends without allowing for a meeting between the subject of historiography and the subject of anthropology within the same text.

In the hegemonic narrative, the continuity of Jewishness means rupture from the Arab Muslim world. At the same time, in the contemporary Arab

Muslim world, the millennia of Jewish existence is at best an unconscious memory, leaving only traces in the footnotes of anti-Zionist ideology. In such discourses, Arab-Jews continue to "travel" in the pages of historical texts as imbricated within a legendary Islamic civilization. Yet, as the post-colonial story begins to unfold over the past decades, Arab-Jews suddenly cease to exist. This split narrative provides a one-way itinerary for Arab-Jews—the State of Israel—where their Arab baggage seems always in excess. Even the more critical narratives, in their unguarded moments, reproduce the fait accompli of violent displacements. In this sense, alliances and conflicts between communities (such as Muslims and Jews) not only have shifted historically but also have produced narratives linked to contemporary ideologies. And as certain strands in a cultural fabric become taboo (for example, the Arabness of Jews), this narrative rests on blurring connections that once existed.

DISCIPLINING: MIZRAHI STUDIES AS A RELATIONAL INQUIRY

While for the purpose of the nationalist telos Mizrahim are detached from the Arab Muslim geography of their belonging, a reattachment to that geography occurs for the purpose of explaining their marginalized position within Israeli society. Hegemonic paradigms in the humanities and social sciences have relied on developmentalist and modernization theories that have produced myriad forms of essentialized Oriental "deviance." This scholarship entails a paradoxical relation to the Arab cultural geography of the Arab-Jews/Mizrahim, manifested within a disciplinary division of labor. On the one hand, Zionist historiography and literary criticism have often exiled Judeo-Arab identity from their texts. On the other, sociology and criminology have placed them at the center, positing Mizrahim as a maladjusted group in Israel. This ruptured discourse extracted Mizrahim from their Arab history only to have it return to explain Mizrahi social pathologies. Mizrahim crowd the pages of Euro-Israeli sociological, criminological, and anthropological texts that provide explanation for the "problem of the gap." Here, the Arab Muslim past looms as deformed vestiges in the lives of Israelis of Asian and African origins. Sociology and anthropology detect traces of underdevelopment, while hegemonic historiography and literary criticism tell the story of the past as a moral tale full of national purpose. The scholarly bifurcation of cultural geography cannot possibly capture the traumatic rupture, the complex transformation of an Arab-Jewish/Mizrahi identity that is at once past and present, here and there—a palimpsestic identity inhabiting the dissonant, interstitial spaces between citizenship, religion, ethnicity, race, nation, and culture.

The hegemonic study of Mizrahim has been neatly parceled out among the disciplines in a narrative whose terminus lies within the territory of Zionism and Israel, as though there were only rupture without continuities within the Arab Muslim world and only wholeness and salvation in Israel. In this sense, geopolitical borders are superimposed on cultural paradigms: Once within the borders of the State of Israel, contemporary Mizrahim are discursively dismembered from the complex Arab cultural space. Performed within the paradigms of development and modernization, the study of Mizrahim has reproduced Eurocentric notions of temporality and spatiality. An Oriental "essence" has also enriched anthropology with an opportunity to study Mizrahim's "exotic" rituals and traditions, often fetishistically detached from their history and politics. The scholarship about the Mizrahim has assumed Israeliness as a telos. Thus, present-day Mizrahi culture and activism tend to be narrated reductively, within the framework of a political geography—the State of Israel—and lacking the wider perspective of a border-crossing analysis.

In this essay, I have critiqued studies of Arab-Jews that employ the Eurocentric and nationalist operations typifying Zionist discourse. A critical Mizrahi scholarship must disengage from the Zionized modes of generating Judaic knowledge, moving beyond ghettoized nationalist discursive spaces. I have argued for a relational understanding of the multiple histories of Jews, histories that stretched over thousands of years, were spread over diverse geographies, and were lived within different ideological regimes. Eurocentric definitions of the history of Jews in the Islamic world cast them into a fixed stereotypical role, playing a millennial role of passive victims lacking any form of agency. Thus, within standard Zionist writing, any ambivalence, or even refusal, of the Zionist gesture of *aliyah* (such as on the part of Communist Arab-Jews) is marginalized in relation to canonical historiography. Recognizing these invisible histories works against the Eurocentric legacies of Zionized Jewish studies to rearticulate the spaces, moments, and subjects of a critical Mizrahi studies.

Charting a beginning for a Mizrahi epistemology requires, as we have seen, examining the terminological paradigms, the conceptual aporias, and the methodological inconsistencies that plague diverse fields of hegemonic scholarship. Producing non-Orientalist and de-Zionized maps of the historical links between the question of Palestine and that of Arab-Jews involves crossing a number of disciplinary assumptions and going against the grain of multiple normative political discourses. Such critical knowledge challenges the socialist as well as the capitalist Zionist narrative of modernization of Palestine and of the Mizrahim; it intervenes in the founding premises of naturalizing one return (Jewish) while repressing another (Palestinian); it deconstructs the folklorization and exoticization of non-European cultures; it demystifies the rescue narrative of the land of Palestine and of Arab-Jews from their Arab Muslim captors; it rearticulates the place of Jews within the Arab Muslim culture as well as within and in relation to Palestine prior to and in the wake of the Zionist movement. Such critical studies interrupt the modernization narrative, whereby anthropology renders Mizrahim as living "allochronically" in another time; in which sociology otherizes Mizrahim as ethnicity in contradistinction to an unmarked Ashkenazi sabra normativity; in which criminology forges an essentialist understanding of Oriental corruption; in which historiography fails to discern the political, economic, and discursive links between the question of Palestine and the Arab-Jewish question in Palestine and in the rest of Arab world; and in which political science assumes Arab-Jewish/Mizrahi and Palestinian struggles as simply an "internal" versus an "external" problem. Critical scholarship, in contrast, deconstructs nationalist paradigms of "inside" and "outside," yet without blurring questions of power and privilege.

Within this transnational mapping, the critique of the Orientalization of Arab-Jews would not entail obscuring the role played by Mizrahim—in their capacity as citizens of the State of Israel—in the continuing occupation and dispossession of Palestinians. This kind of complex positioning recalls other historical situations. In this sense, one might reflect on a useful structural analogy in which Palestinians have replayed the historical role of the dispossessed and occupied Native Americans for Zionism, while Arab-Jews were cast as its displaced and exploited blacks.[33] Or, to put it differently, Mizrahim, like U.S. racialized minorities, suffer at the hands of discriminatory ideology and policies but also have been enlisted in the service of the colonizing nation-state. Yet throughout the modern history of Arab-Jews/Mizrahim, the question of Palestine, like the question of Zionism, is far from being settled, provoking constant dissonance and a maze of contradictions. The transdisciplinary scholarly frame I am proposing here, for its part, hopes to desegregate intellectual spaces and relocates the issues in a much wider and denser geographic imaginary and historical mapping.

This essay synthesizes and reworks ideas, arguments, and methodologies that I have been formulating in numerous scholarly publications over the past two decades. Some of these publications are cited in the notes. This essay appeared in a different version as "Rupture and Return: The Shaping of a Mizrahi Epistemology," *Hagar* 2, no. 1 (2001).

1 My critique of the Zionist anti-diaspora discourse, the displacement of *Ostjuden* onto the Mizrahim, and the menacing heteroglossia is largely taken from Ella Shohat, *Israeli Cinema: East/West and the Politics of Representation* (Austin: University of Texas Press, 1989), esp. 100, 208. For an elaborate critique of the negation of exile, see Amnon Raz-Krarkotzkin, "Exile within Sovereignty: Toward a Critique of the 'Negation of Exile' in Israeli Culture," *Theory and Criticism* 4 (1993): 23–56 and *Theory and Criticism* 5 (1994): 113–32. See also George Steiner, "Our Homeland, the Text," *Salmangudi* 66 (winter–spring 1985): 4–25; Yerach Gover, *Zionism: The Limits of Moral Discourse in Israeli Hebrew Fiction* (Minneapolis: University of Minnesota Press, 1994).

2 On the invention of the Mizrahim, see Ella Shohat, "The Invention of the Mizrahim?" *Journal of Palestine Studies* 29 (fall 1999).

3 For a detailed review of the terms, see the longer version of this essay in *Hagar*.

4 Even subsequent to the foundation of the State of Israel, the Jewish community in Iraq was constructing new schools and founding new enterprises, a fact that hardly indicates an institutionalized intention to leave.

5 This effort is clearly expressed in texts written by Iraqi Zionists. See, for example, Shlomo Hillel, *Ruah Kadim* (Operation Babylon) (Jerusalem: Edanim, 1985), 259–63 (Hebrew).

6 One of the most debated cases concerns the Zionists' placing of bombs in synagogues. See Abbas Shiblak, *The Lure of Zion* (London: Al Saqi, 1986); G. N. Giladi, *Discord in Zion* (London: Scorpion, 1990).

7 See interviews in the following documentary films: David Benchetrit's, *Samir* (Israel, 1997); and Samir's, *Forget Baghdad* (Switzerland, 2002).

8 While the position of Arab-Jews is often used to justify the expulsion of Palestinians, there have been a few attempts to reflect on the position of Arab-Jews vis-à-vis Arab nationalism from a different angle. See Shiblak, *The Lure of Zion*; Ella Shohat, "Sephardim in Israel: Zionism from the Standpoint of Its Jewish Victims," *Social Text*, nos. 19–20 (fall 1988): 1–35; Moshe Behar, "Time to Meet the Mizrahim?" *al-Ahram*, 15–21 October 1998; essays from "Mizrahim and Zionism: History, Political Discourse, Struggle" (special issue), *News from Within* 13, no. 1 (January 1997). See also Tikva Honig-Parnass, "Introduction"; Sami Shalom Chetrit, "The Dream and the Nightmare: Some Remarks on the New Discourse in Mizrahi Politics in Israel, 1980–1996"; Zvi Ben-Dor, "A Short History of the Incredible Mizrahi History"; Moshe Behar, "Is the Mizrahi Question Relevant to the Future of the Entire Middle East?"; and Joseph Massad, "The 'Post-Colonial'

Colony: Time, Space, and Bodies in Palestine/Israel," all in *The Pre-Occupation of Postcolonial Studies*, ed. by Fawzia Afzal-Khan and Kalpana Seshadri-Crooks (Durham, N.C.: Duke University Press, 2000), 311–46; Sami Shalom Chetrit, *Ha-Mahapeikha ha-Ashkenazit Meta* (The Ashkenazi Revolution Is Dead) (Tel Aviv: Bimat Kedem, 1999; Hebrew).

9 For example, Naeim Giladi, a former Zionist activist in Iraq who was imprisoned and tortured but was able to escape one week before execution, gradually came to change his outlook after living in Israel and has become an anti-Zionist activist. He left Israel in the mid-1980s and settled in New York, renouncing his Israeli citizenship. (From my diverse conversations with Giladi in New York during the late 1980s, when we both served as the representatives of the World Organization of Jews from Islamic Countries, an organization member of the United Nations' nongovernmental organization on The Question of Palestine.)

10 I am basing this argument on numerous conversations I have had with Iraqi Jews in Israel over the past two decades. It also forms part of a project that Sasson Somekh and I are currently collaborating on, focusing on the moment of dislocation from Iraq to Israel.

11 For more complex accounts of the histories of Jews, see Maxime Rodinson, *Cult, Ghetto, and State: The Persistence of the Jewish Question* (London: Al Saqi, 1983); Ilan Halevi, *A History of the Jews: Ancient and Modern* (London: Zed, 1987); Ammiel Alcalay, *After Jews and Arabs: Remaking Levantine Culture* (Minneapolis: University of Minnesota Press, 1993); Mark R. Cohen, *Under Crescent and Cross* (Princeton, N.J.: Princeton University Press, 1995); Amnon Raz-Krakotzkin, "Historical Consciousness and Historical Responsibilities," in *From Vision to Revision: A Hundred Years of Historiography of Zionism*, ed. by Yechiam Weitz (Jerusalem: Zalman Shazar Center, 1997); Joel Beinin, *The Dispersion of the Egyptian Jewry: Culture, Politics, and the Formation of a Modern Diaspora* (Berkeley: University of California Press, 1998); and Nissim Rejwan, *Israel in Search of Identity* (Gainesville: University of Florida Press, 1999).

12 On the history of the AIU, see Aron Rodrigue, *Images of Sephardi and Eastern Jewries in Transition: The Teachers of the Alliance Israelite Universelle, 1860–1939* (Seattle: University of Washington Press, 1993).

13 See Zvi Yehuda, "The Jews of Babylon and Cultural Change through the Educational Activities of Alliance Israelite Universelle" (in Hebrew), *Babylonian Jewry*, no. 1 (Fall 1995).

14 *Perah* (Calcutta), 23 September 1885. The translation from the Judeo-Arabic language is mine. A selection from *Perah* is included in the appendix of Yehuda, "The Jews of Babylon and Cultural Change through the Educational Activities of Alliance Israelite Universelle."

15 Herzl's visionary Zionist utopia was the subject of his 1902 German-language book *Altneuland: Old New Land*, trans. by Miriam Kraus (Tel Aviv: Babel, 1997).

16 For other critical approaches to the dominant Israeli sociology, see Shlomo Swirski, *Israel: The Oriental Majority* (London: Zed, 1989); Uri Ram, ed., *Israeli Society: Critical Perspectives* (in Hebrew) (Tel Aviv: Breirot, 1993). Over the years,

Mizrahim have argued against the dominant explanation of the "gap" between Mizrahim and Ashkenazim addressed in such magazines as *Afikim, Ha-Panter ha-Shahor, Apirion, Pa'amon ha-Shkhunut, Ha-Patish, Iton Aher,* and *Hadshot Hila.*

17 Another scholar, Yosef Gross, saw the immigrants as suffering from "mental regression" and a "lack of development of the ego." The quotes from Frankenstein and Gross are taken from Tom Segev, *1949: The First Israelis* (in Hebrew) (Jerusalem: Domino, 1984), 157. The extended symposium concerning the "Sephardi problem" was framed as a debate about the "essence of primitivism." Only a strong infusion of European cultural values, the scholars concluded, would rescue the Oriental Jews from their "backwardness."

18 Kalman Katznelson, *Ha-Mahapeikha Ha-Ashkenazit* (The Ashkenazi Revolution) (Tel Aviv: Anach, 1964; Hebrew).

19 The term "allochronic" is borrowed from Johannes Fabian, *Time and the Other: How Anthropology Makes Its Object* (New York: Columbia University Press, 1983).

20 Located in Or Yehuda, the museum was founded by Iraqi Jews who were among the leaders of the Zionist movement.

21 For a more detailed critique of Orientalist modernization and discourse, particularly what I called "the Zionist masternarrative" and its concomitant "rescue fantasies," see Ella Shohat, *Israeli Cinema,* "Sephardim in Israel," and "Masternarrative/Counter Readings," in *Resisting Images: Essays on Cinema and History,* ed. by Robert Sklar and Charles Musser (Philadelphia: Temple University Press, 1990), 251–78. See also Sami Shalom Chetrit, "Castrated Mizrahi Identity," in *The Ashkenazi Revolution Is Dead,* 57–60; Amnon Raz-Krakotzkin, "Orientalism, Jewish Studies, and Israeli Society: A Few Comments," *Jama'a* 3 (1999).

22 See for example, S. D. Goitein, "The Jews of Yemen," in A. J. Arbery, ed., *Religion in the Middle East.* (Cambridge: Cambridge University Press, 1969); and Goitein, *From the Land of Sheba: Tales of the Jews of Yemen* (New York: Schocken Books, 1973).

23 Herbert S. Lewis, *After the Eagles Landed: The Yemenites of Israel* (Prospect Heights, Ill.: Waveland, 1994).

24 Ibid., 212.

25 Ibid., 26.

26 One of the nurses, Rouja Kushinski, was interviewed on the subject for a report on the Israeli television program *Oovda* (Channel 2, 1996), directed by Uri Rozentzweig with research prepared by Shoshana Madmoni. The nurse confirmed the act of taking children away. Ahuva Goldfarb, a state clerk, and Sonia Milstein, a senior nurse in the immigrant camp Ein Shemer, continued to maintain their belief that forcibly removing children from their biological parents was the right thing to do.

27 On 30 June 1986, for example, the Public Committee for the Discovery of the Missing Yemenite Children held a massive protest rally. The rally, like many Mizrahi protests and demonstrations, was completely ignored by the dominant media. A few months later, however, Israeli television produced a documentary on the subject, blaming the bureaucratic chaos of the period for unfortunate "rumors" and perpetuating the myth of Oriental parents as careless breeders with little sense of responsibility toward their own children. The same discourse was replayed in the mid-1990s, when a forceful protest led by Rabbi Uzi Meshulam overwhelmed the country. Meshulam was delegitimized and portrayed in the media as another David Koresh. Meshulam, who published various documents consisting of firsthand and first-person accounts by Yemeni mothers about the kidnapped babies, is still serving prison time for his campaign demanding access to government files of the case. The Mizrahi struggle to shed light on what exactly took place during those years and, most important, to give the families a chance to meet their kidnapped children is still a major rallying factor for Mizrahim of diverse persuasions.

28 See Dov Levitan, *The Aliyah of the "Magic Carpet" as a Historical Continuation of the Earlier Yemenite Aliyahs* (in Hebrew) (M.A. thesis, Bar-Ilan University, 1983); and investigative articles written by Shosh Madmoni for the magazine *Shishi* and the daily *Yedioth Ahronot* and by Yigal Mashiah for the daily *Ha'aretz* in 1996. See also Shoshana Madmoni, "The Missing Yemenite Children: Sometimes Truth Is Stranger than Fiction," *News from Within* (February 1996).

29 Moshe Gat, *A Jewish Community in Crisis: The Exodus from Iraq, 1948–1951* (Jerusalem: Merkaz Zalman Shazar, 1989; Hebrew).

30 "Hakham" is the Sephardic equivalent of "Rabbi."

31 The term "norms of the text" is borrowed from Boris Uspensky, *A Poetics of Composition* (Berkeley: University of California Press, 1973).

32 Amitav Ghosh, *In an Antique Land* (New York: Alfred A. Knopf, 1993).

33 I insist on the words "structural analogy" since I certainly am not trying to argue for an equation. For further exploration of this point, see Ella Shohat, "Taboo Memories, Diasporic Visions: Columbus, Palestine, and Arab-Jews," in *Performing Hybridity*, ed. by May Joseph and Jennifer Fink (Minneapolis: University of Minnesota Press, 1999).

THE "POSTCOLONIAL" IN TRANSLATION

Reading Edward Said between English and Hebrew

One achieves at most a provisional satisfaction, which is quickly ambushed by doubt, and a need to rewrite and redo that renders the text uninhabitable. Better that, however, than the sleep of self-satisfaction and the finality of death.—Edward Said, "Between Worlds," *London Review of Books*, May 7, 1998

Although Edward Said's ideas have traveled through many worlds, writing about his work as a "traveling theory" requires a sense of cross-border mediation and translation as ideas are hybridized, resisted, contained, and recontextualized. Here I will focus on one form of such "travel," that between the United States and Israel, a situation where the receiving space for Said's ideas is a nation-state whose very foundation engendered this specific intellectual's exile. When Said invokes the right of return to that same place—where a state possesses the power not only to authorize or deny his return but also to oversee the circulation of his texts about displacement—then the question of that intellectual's "out-of-placeness" becomes even more fraught.

While my hope in this essay would have been to tell a purely celebratory tale of Said's pervasive influence on Israeli intellectual life, the highly charged space of Zionism and Israel, and my own intricate positioning, makes that task rather complicated. Beginning in the 1980s, my work initiated a conversation with Said's critique of Orientalism by examining the politics of representation in Zionist historiographical discourse and Israeli cultural practices.[1] The hostile reception of that work in Israel, I think, was partly related to its association with Said's work and even to my own closeness to Said. In those pre-Oslo days, dialogue between Israelis and Palestinians was literally and legally taboo, declared out of bounds by the "only democracy in the Middle East." I want to clarify at the outset, then, that I write as one personally involved in the "translation" of Said's thought into Hebrew. One leftist reviewer of my work compared both Said and myself, in our supposedly naive admiration of the Western "intellectual apparatus," to the "miserable nigger, the victim of colonization, who licks his lips in excitement at the gold buttons and colorful glass beads offered by the cunning white merchant."[2] This rather amusing reproach of our "inauthenticity" as "spokepersons for the Third World" appeals to the old colonial trope of mimicry while projecting the East–West dichotomy onto intellectuals whose biography and analysis clearly refuse that dichotomy. What interests me is the shuttling back and forth of Said's work between one institutional zone and political semantics and another. Here I will consider some symptomatic moments and issues in this cross-border movement, asking when and which of Said's texts have been stamped with an entry visa to Israel, which were permitted to settle, and which have had to be smuggled in or even forced to wander in a *laissez passer* "no-man's land."

POSTCOLONIAL STUDIES GOES TO WASHINGTON

For well over a decade, "postcolonial studies" has been highly visible even beyond the Anglo-American academy. Said's preeminence in the postcolonial field, however, seemed disconnected from the Israel/Palestine debates, where Said's name was also prominent. The animosity generated in the wake of Said's "trilogy," *Orientalism, The Question of Palestine,* and *Covering Islam,* reached its paroxysm with the panicked hyperbole of "professor of terror." In the post–September 11 landscape, subsequently members of the Orientalist right found the time opportune to reconquer what had earlier been "their" ivory towers. They could now enjoy a powerful observation post as self-anointed monarchs surveying these "un-American" activities. A highly visible coalition of (anti-Semitic) Christian fundamentalists, neoconservative Zionists, and culturalist Orientalists all united to bring the academy, allegedly taken hostage by "tenured radicals," back into the warm embrace of Western values. In the June 2003 congressional hearings on Title VI, Stanley Kurtz of the *National Review* denounced many of the leading critical Middle East studies scholars, Said most prominently.[3] What was most striking, however, was the new focus on a different academic discipline—postcolonial studies. Postcolonial theory, which emerged as a prestigious field of inquiry in the late 1980s and which had generally escaped the institutional backlash directed at the revisionist historians and radical multiculturalists, for the first time began to "scan" on the neocon radar.

I do not mean to imply, of course, that the neocons have suddenly become devout exegetes of postcolonial texts. These critics are not in the least conversant with the anticolonial writings and poststructuralist theories— intellectual currents at the very heart of Said's contribution—that shaped what came to be called "postcolonial studies." There *Orientalism* has constituted a key text, opening up the intellectual horizons of English literature studies. Said's intervention, to my mind, also forms part of a larger epochal shift in the academy that began in the late 1960s, the time of the first establishment of ethnic studies and women's studies programs and the academic emergence of diverse critical fields of inquiry: Marxism, Third Worldism, semiotics, feminism. During the same period, area studies programs began to bypass or reject the post–World War Two vision of scholarship promoted by the U.S. Defense Department in the service of Cold War geopolitics. Latin American studies since the 1970s had produced an impressive corpus of work critical of neocolonial policies and imperial discourses. Here the writings of figures such as Fanon, Galeano, Frank, Dorfman, Schiller, and Mattelart played a crucial role, becoming a kind of lingua franca in progressive circles. In Middle East studies, meanwhile, critical scholars—many of whom contributed to *Middle East Report* and *Journal of Palestine Studies*—were politically and intellectually allied with Said's critique of Orientalism, which helped transform the field of Middle East studies itself. Over the past two decades the critical scholars who have been challenging the essentialist and Manichean thesis of "Islam and the West," promoted by Bernard Lewis and more recently by

Samuel Huntington, gradually came to occupy center-stage at the Middle East Studies Association. Although the paradigm shift in Middle East studies came relatively late, it was more visibly contested in the public sphere, especially as a battery of well-oiled foundations and institutes began to take aim at the entire field.

In his exposé, Kurtz accuses postcolonial studies in general of "undermining America's security," yet all the scholars that he denounces from within this vast field "happen" to work on the Middle East.[4] Moreover, his claim that "postcolonial theory" forms the ruling intellectual paradigm in academic area studies (especially Middle East studies) is simply mistaken,[5] for while poststructuralist methodologies are widely practiced in literature departments, they form only a minor presence in Middle Eastern studies departments. The singling out of Middle East studies, then, points to the targeting of both the territory and the author, revealing the missing link that turned postcolonial studies into the public enemy of the day. At last the new guardian angels could meaningfully tie together the two strands of "Said's double career," to cite a 1989 article in *Commentary*, "as literary scholar and ideologue of terrorism," whose "spilling of ink" was deemed akin to "the spilling of blood."[6]

This long and winding road to postcolonial studies passes partly via Jerusalem or, better, Tel Aviv. Said's reception in Israel has varied over the years, in some ways allegorizing the shifting state of the debates about the conflict. Said's entry into media visibility during the first Intifada came in the form of virulent attacks. Israel's largest daily, *Yedi'ot Aharonot*, accused U.S.-based Palestinian professors like Said of "taking control" of the TV screen, luring naive, image-obsessed Americans through a new trompe l'oeil. In a new twist on the old anti-Semitic motif of the Jewish chameleon hiding his innate outsiderness by impersonating "normal" Europeans, the critics charged Said with hiding terroristic intent behind a Western-style mask.[7] The recent attempts by right-wing ideological patrols to intimidate those on campus who challenge the Israeli official line can be traced to this earlier anxiety that new Palestinian "public relations techniques" might provoke a shift in American views. With a direct pipeline to the White House, however, well-endowed research institutes could now threaten to teach straying academics a lesson.

In a verbatim Hebrew recycling of the Kurtz tirade, the *Ma'ariv* journalist Ben-Dror Yemini, who opposes the occupation, praised Campus Watch and called for a withdrawal of government subsidies for anti-Israeli academics in Israel itself.[8] Yemini proclaimed that the recognition by the

Middle East Studies Association (MESA) of the "guru" Said was "one of the biggest hoaxes of Middle Eastern studies" and linked it to Arab funding, further blaming Said for the "silencing of alternative voices" such as those of Fouad Ajami and Bernard Lewis.[9] Acquiring the aura of a prophet in the wake of the second Intifada and September 11, Lewis was said to have predicted the unfolding culture clash and thus the collapse of Said's thesis in *Orientalism*. Asked by the newspaper *Ha'aretz* whether he would recommend *Orientalism* to the Hebrew student, Lewis responded, "Only if the student is interested in the pathology of American campus life"; otherwise, the "book lacks value."[10] Meanwhile, Tel Aviv University Professor Shimon Shamir suggested in his review of Martin Kramer's *Ivory Towers on Sand* that Orientalists from Lewis's school had been "completely marginalized by Saidism . . . haunted by the orientalist label, treated with a mixture of condemnation and disdain." Shamir praises Kramer for addressing the "damage" caused by the Saidian "take-over" of U.S. Middle East studies. He also raises the issue of whether Israeli Middle East studies are guilty of the same charge made by Kramer against their U.S. counterparts, but quickly reassures readers that in Israel these departments are "well anchored in scientific disciplines," without "the same militant slide toward anti-orientalism." Shamir does, however, criticize Kramer for ignoring the positive Saidian contribution to the rejection of essentialism.[11]

Emmanuel Sivan, meanwhile, argues that *Orientalism* lent credence to the "all-embracing smear of the West" and to the "glorification of the East," attributing to Said the very East–West dichotomy that he had so painstakingly disassembled.[12] Sivan further accuses Said of essentialism, even as he himself demonstrates epidermic essentialism by enlisting the Arab identity of Said's critics as proof against Said. Another scholar, Avi Bareli, dismisses the Saidian "analytical method" as offering only a "moralizing approach," whose main objective is to "catch" and categorically condemn "the crook" rather than understand "the historical processes."[13] Such critics evoke Said's name in tandem with their critique of post-Zionist historians and sociologists. The reception of Said's work in Israel, then, has taken place within an institutional context largely shaped by Orientalist–Zionist ideologies. As in the United States, it was not so much Said's study of French and British Orientalism of the colonial past (albeit relevant to the present) that has provoked the backlash; rather, it was the book's implications for a critique of Zionist discourse, especially when mobilized to defend Israel's current policies.

Israeli Orientalists had assailed *Orientalism* long before the Hebrew translation saw the light of day in August 2000, a full twenty-two years after the
original English version.[14] Despite this legacy of hostility, by the time it was
published by the establishment press Am Oved, *Orientalism* could engender quite a few celebratory media interviews with Said.[15] The book is
now being taught in various Israeli university departments, largely by
self-designated leftist professors, some identifying with the label "post-
Zionism," some with "Zionism," and a few with "non-" or "anti-Zionism."[16] More recently, the translation of Said's memoir *Out of Place* generated both accusatory and favorable reviews.[17] Yet what remains unacknowl-
edged is that Said's *The Question of Palestine* had already been published in
Hebrew in 1981, soon after its appearance in English, and that earlier that
same year the literary quarterly *Siman Kri'a* published Said's essay "Zionism from the Standpoint of its Victims."[18]

Defining Said's essay as "controversial," *Siman Kri'a*'s editors, many of
whom were associated with Peace Now, included within the same issue a
response titled, "Zionism, Its Palestinian Victim and the Western World,"
by the historian of Zionism Yigal Elam. Whereas the response to the same
Said essay in *Social Text*, where it had originally been published in English,
highlighted the Holocaust, Elam privileged the putative responsibility of
Palestinians themselves for their own dislocation. "The Palestinian nationalist movement," he wrote, "made a severe mistake, when it initiated
violent confrontation with Zionism," because it was "not ready to pay the
price of diplomatic compromise." Like many liberal Zionists in the wake of
1977, Elam acknowledged that "occupation corrupts" but denied any colonial dimension to Zionism. He concluded with a rush to defend "the
West":

> "Nationalism," "state," "democracy," "self-definition," "citizenship," "equal
> rights," "secular culture," "sovereignty"—all are rooted in a Western con-
> text. . . . It is the West that supplies the only terminological context to solve the
> Israeli–Palestinian conflict, since even the PLO formula of a "democratic
> secular state" comes out of the political philosophy of the West.[19]

This unthinking equation of the West and democracy was made four decades after the advent, in the very heart of Europe, not only of the Holocaust but also of the fascism of Hitler, Mussolini, Franco, and Petain, and
just two decades after French colonialism's brutal war in Algeria. Further-

more, such historians do not take on board the critique of the Eurocentric premises of Zionist discourse itself as shaping its practices in Palestine. In fact, the investment in the Enlightenment narrative of the "West" is fundamental for the Israeli peace camp's vision of itself, constituting at once an ontological apologia and an identity marker and consequently has played a pivotal role in the reception of Said's work.[20]

The Question of Palestine, meanwhile, was published by the now defunct nonprofit press Mifras, some of whose associates were linked to the anti-Zionist group Matzpen.[21] Mifras published a few critical Hebrew writers,[22] and translated a number of works by Arab and other Third World writers, including Ghassan Kanafani's *Men in the Sun*, Paulo Freire's *Pedagogy of the Oppressed*, Henri Curiel's *On the Altar of Peace*, Ali Mazrui's *The African Condition*, Abu Iyad's *My Home My Land*, and Emile Habiby's *The Secret Life of Saeed: The Pessoptimist*. "Despite the daily focus on the complications of the Israeli-Arab conflict," the mission statement declared, "there hardly exists in Hebrew, literatures that open a window to a deep and critical understanding of Arab society and individuals."

Mifras enlisted the peace-camp artist and intellectual Yigal Tumarkin to write the preface, titled, "My Dream Zionism." Yet in defiance of the generic protocols of prefaces, which usually offer a hospitable prelude to the text in question, Tumarkin's introduction deploys the hegemonic narratives against Said. Resurrecting the Promethean making-the-desert-bloom trope, for example, he complains that Said speaks as if "swamps and malaria never existed and are merely part of the Zionist publicity machine." For Tumarkin, Said's book "is a manifesto of frustration," offering a "black and white picture" in contrast to his own "dream Zionism" where "there is light." He thus concludes:

> It is hard to negotiate when one positions himself as a victim of the other side. What occurred was miserable and fated, a tragedy that victimized both sides, and now we need to seek a way to understanding based on logic and not on a division between the righteous and wicked. We have to think about the future and not remain captive to the burdens of the past and its lugubrious memories.

The preface, in dissonance with Mifras's own mission statement, failed to create an intertextual environment that might have placed Said's argument within the larger frame of anticolonial discourse. Tumarkin's preface could not be farther from comparable prefaces within the anticolonialist tradition—for example, Sartre's passionate endorsement of Fanon at the very height of the French–Algerian war in his preface to *The Wretched of the Earth*.

Said's work on literature, meanwhile, did not surface as a real presence in the work of his most likely "interpretative community"—literary theorists within the emerging field of poststructuralism in Israel. A 1988 Hebrew translation of a book by the poststructuralist Christopher Norris, which praised both *Orientalism* and *The World, the Text, and the Critic*, transliterated Said's name wrongly as "Sed"[23] when it could have been easily rendered correctly in Hebrew, a language that possesses almost the exact equivalent letters to the Arabic. The name "Sa'eed" in its Arabic pronunciation perhaps was hard to "hear" or digest within a deconstructionist academic ambiance. In a context where the imagined inferiority of Arabic and Arabs usually goes hand in hand with the valorization of anything English, Edward Said's very name condenses an oxymoronic tension. The miswriting—or better, misreading—of his last name betrays the disconnect between the worlds of anticolonial literature and Israeli literary studies. It betokens both the desire for the new theory of deconstruction and the lack of familiarity with one of the major poststructuralist scholars, whose book *Orientalism* had been foregrounded by Norris himself as an exemplar of interweaving text and context. Thus, at a time when Said's writing was broadening the scope of literary studies in the Anglo-American academy, Israeli literary theory hardly engaged his literary scholarship.

The translated *The Question of Palestine*, by now long out of print, did not leave a visible imprint in liberal-leftist publications. Yet by the late 1990s, *Ha'aretz*'s translations of several of Said's pieces on current events eased its readers into a celebratory reception of *Orientalism*. The shift from the marginal publication of *The Question of Palestine* to the mainstream publication of *Orientalism* reflects shifting trends in the Israeli academy. By legalizing Israeli-Palestinian dialogue, the Rabin-Arafat handshake rendered such academic engagements less taboo-ridden. In the following years, a small but influential group of largely post-Zionist academics helped make Said a legitimate intellectual interlocutor. *Orientalism*'s more recent "travel" into Israel was also facilitated by Said's prestigious status in the Anglo-American academy, just as the elite aura of the term "postcolonial" enabled its current absorption into Israeli academic discourse. The time lapse between the translations, however, suggests a more complex genealogy for critical thinking in Israel and for the trajectory of Said's reception prior to the post-Zionist debate. Mifras's impressive earlier efforts to bring Said to the Hebrew reader should not be deemed irrelevant to the history of the debates. Similarly, over the past two decades, Said's "travel" into Israel was also supported by the Alternative Information Center and its publications,[24] which explicitly articulated Zionism's relation to colonialism.[25]

By now, the impact of Said's work has been felt in various fields in critical writings about Zionist discourses and Israeli practices. Even when Said's writing is not foregrounded, its influence is felt and acknowledged in such texts as Smadar Lavie's ironic look at Israeli anthropology of the bedouins; Ammiel Alcalay's historical reflection on Mizrahi writers as intimately embedded in Arab culture; Yerach Gover's critique of the images of Arabs in Hebrew literature and of Zionist literary assumptions; Azmi Bishara's invocation of Orientalism to address racist discourses about "educated Arabs" within Israel in a context where Bishara's very writing in Hebrew challenges the limits of Israeli citizenship; Sami Shalom Chetrit's historical account of Mizrahi struggle within anti-Zionist paradigms; Simona Sharoni's discussion of the gendered militarism of Israeli society; Sarah Chinski's look at the Orientalist underpinning of Israeli art history; Gabriel Piterberg's examination of the Orientalist foundations of Israeli history books; Henriette Dahan-Kalev's discussion of the Mizrahi as an Orientalized "other"; Irit Rogoff's exploration of the imaging of boundaries in Israeli visual culture; Yosefa Loshitzky's invocation of Said's reading of Camus to critique similar representations of the Arab in Israeli cinema; Dan Rabinowitz's overview of Israeli anthropological texts on the Palestinians; Shoshana Madmoni's account of racist media representation of the kidnapping of Yemeni/Mizrahi babies in Israel; and Oren Yiftachel's discussion of ethnocracy in land development and Palestinian dislocation within Israel.[26]

Amnon Raz-Krakotzkin makes significant use of Said's critique of Orientalism to address the Zionist negation of Jewish exile, highlighting what he calls "religious colonial nationalism." He discusses the dialectics of messianism and redemption as constituting the Orientalist framework of Zionist nationalism and the place of theological debate within it. He also answers *Orientalism*'s critics who faulted the book for ignoring German forms of Orientalism. Instead, Raz-Krakotzkin looks at the Zionist shaping of Jewish history scholarship as itself emerging out of German Orientalist views about Jews in modern Europe. The possibilities offered by *Orientalism* have been extended to other domains within Jewish studies, where the easy East/West dichotomy has also proven problematic in relation to Arab Jews. Ruth Tsoffar offers an anti-Orientalist reading of the interpretations and practices of the Egyptian Karaites in their San Francisco diaspora. Gil Anidjar, meanwhile, suggests that Kabbalah scholarship, especially Gershom Scholem's valorization of mysticism over rationalism, neglected to see the Kabbalah's embeddedness in the Islamic world and Arabic writing.[27]

"POST-ZIONISM"—WHOSE "POST" IS IT, ANYWAY?

The changing discourses of the Anglo-American academy, energized by multiculturalism and the diverse "posts" (postmodernism, poststructuralism, postnationalism, and postcolonialism), facilitated Said's "voyage" to Israel and made possible the marriage of still another "post-" with another "-ism": "post-Zionism." The scholars known as "post-Zionists" did not all identify with the label, constituting a heterogeneous group vis-à-vis the concept of "Zionism."[28] Revisionist historians such as Tom Segev, Avi Shlaim, Benny Morris, and Ilan Pappé performed invaluable scholarly work by challenging the hegemonic account of the partition and of the 1948 exodus, thus provoking the rage of mainstream Zionists. The post-Zionists' rather ambiguous positions on "Zionism," however, were challenged under the impact of the second Intifada. While some explicitly announced themselves devout Zionists (Morris), endorsing the "Barak-offered-them-everything-but-I'm-disappointed-in-the-Palestinians" narrative, a few others became more radicalized, breaking away from "post-Zionism" (Pappé).

The visibility of the post-Zionists was in many ways a product of the Oslo Accords. That these historians could be consulted and help shape *Tekuma* —the TV history series produced for the fiftieth anniversary of the State of Israel—speaks volumes about their positioning as legitimate scholars in the public sphere. It is important to appreciate, however, the identity politics that permitted a favorable reception of post-Zionist scholars in and outside Israel. It is as though Palestinian history could be better heard if mouthed by (largely Ashkenazi) Israeli men. Many of the celebratory articles about post-Zionism treated the work as sui generis, marginalizing the contribution of Palestinian research on the same issues. The revisionist historians, as pointed out by such scholars as Nur Masalha, Rashid Khalidi, and Joseph Massad, basically put an Israeli imprimatur on earlier arguments made by Palestinian scholars.[29] The reception of post-Zionism in this sense has also reflected an Israeli-centric approach to the representation of scholarship, where Palestinian scholars tend to be written out as subjects of intellectual history.

Said himself noted the "schizophrenia" that informed post-Zionist texts. While some establish beyond any doubt that the forced exodus of Palestinians was a result of a specific transfer policy adopted and approved by David Ben-Gurion, they refuse to acknowledge any Zionist plan to empty Palestine of its inhabitants.[30] "Morris's meticulous work," writes Said,

> showed that in district after district commanders had been ordered to drive out Palestinians, burn villages, systematically take over their homeland property. Yet strangely enough, by the end of the book Morris seems reluctant to draw the inevitable conclusions from his own evidence. Instead of saying outright that the Palestinians were, in fact, driven out he says that they were partially driven out by Zionist forces, and partially "left" as a result of war. It is as if he was still enough of a Zionist to believe the ideological version—that Palestinians left on their own without Israeli eviction—rather than completely to accept his own evidence, which is that Zionist policy dictated Palestinian Exodus.[31]

The bifurcated discourse that characterizes even relatively critical circles can in my view be traced to the very origins of Zionism. Elsewhere, I have argued that Zionism as an ideology, and Israel as a nation-state, form an *anomalous* project, narrating itself as liberatory vis-à-vis Europe even as it carries the same banner of the "civilizing mission" that the European powers proclaimed during their thrust into "found lands." Zionist discourse itself thus embodies schizophrenic masternarratives: a redemptive nationalist narrative vis-à-vis Europe and anti-Semitism and a colonialist narrative vis-à-vis the Arab people who "happened" to reside in the place designated the Jewish homeland. Yet unlike colonialism, Zionism also constituted a response to millennial oppression, and in contradistinction to the classical colonial paradigm, it had no "mother country." Metropole and colony, in this case, were conceived as located in the self-same place. Zionist discourse concerning a "return to the mother land" suggests a double relation to that land, where the "East" is simultaneously the place of Judaic origins and the locus for implementing the "West." Thus, the "East," associated, on the one hand, with backwardness and underdevelopment, is associated, on the other, with oasis and solace—a return to geographical origins and reunification with the biblical past. The West, meanwhile, is also viewed ambivalently, both as the historic crime scene of anti-

Semitism and as an object of desire, an authoritative norm to be emulated in the East.[32]

Within a post-Zionist perspective, Zionism ceases to constitute a relevant category, since the Israeli state has presumably reached a post-nationalist stage. The relative legitimacy of "post-Zionism" has derived precisely from a sense of opting out or bypassing the question of Zionism's relation to colonialism. Emerging in the 1990s, the term "post-Zionism" suggested a premature eagerness to claim to have "gone beyond" Zionism even while Zionist ideology exerted more power than ever, both in Jerusalem and in Washington. Echoing various critical-theoretical "posts," "post-Zionism" was also a product of a certain postmodernist euphoria, a time when "posts" were proliferating with abandon. The "post" in "post-Zionism" paralleled Francis Fukuyama's rather precipitous announcement of the "end of history" or Jean-François Lyotard's annunciation of "the death of metanarratives." The similarly euphoric "post-Zionism" pointed to a rather ambiguous conceptual project that promised to carry us beyond the tiresome Zionism versus anti-Zionism debate. Yet what this "beyondness" has meant is a question unto itself—since the implied haven of the "post" remains haunted by Zionism's kinship with both the "national" and the "colonial."

"Post-Zionism" also carries the traces of the term "post-colonial," then at the height of its aura of prestige in the Anglo-American academy, exactly at the time when the prefix "post-" was attached to "Zionism." The questions I have proposed elsewhere with regard to the "postcolonial" in terms of its spatio-temporal ambiguity might equally be posed with regard to the term "post-Zionism"—that is, "post" in relation to what, to where, to when, and to whom? When exactly does the "post" in "post-Zionism" begin? And what kind of location and perspective does the term reflect?[33] And what discourse does "post-Zionism" go beyond? The "beyond" of the "post" in "post-Zionism," unlike in "post-colonialism," takes us into a more complicated realm precisely because the parallelism between Zionism and colonialism remains sublimated. In the term "post-colonial," it is the prefix "post-" that carries an ambiguous spatio-temporality, while the substantive suffix "colonial," despite debates about historical and geographical variations, remains a more or less agreed upon signifier and frame of reference. In the term "post-Zionism," in contrast, it is both the prefix "post-" and the substantive suffix "Zionism" that are contested. It is especially the valence of what follows the hyphen in "post-colonialism" and "post-Zionism," then, that in many ways distinguishes the two fields of inquiry.

Postcolonial theory has recently traveled via the Anglo-American academy into a certain post-Zionist world, where the "colonial" itself has hardly been thought through in any depth. It is in this context that one must understand a rather striking phenomenon central to the emergent post-Zionist–postcolonial discourse. Academic and journalistic texts have fashioned a kind of folk wisdom that posits Homi Bhabha as having surpassed Said. Immediately after Said's death, the leftist columnist Nir Baram wrote what he called a "sober obituary":

> For many years, Said's hegemony has remained dominant, unopposed, despite the unexpected biting from Homi K. Bhabha, a brilliant scholar, who unlike Said redeemed the orient from the ultimate role of the victim and the slave, understanding that the imagination is not one-way but two-way: in other words, the orient also imagines the west and imitates it. Bhabha, speaking about two creatures that move in a constantly changing dynamic space, perfected Said's frozen thesis, and led the way into a much more fascinating discourse."[34]

This vision, which shows Said outclassed by the more sophisticated Bhabha, now constitutes a kind of topos in numerous Hebrew publications. Without engaging in any depth Said's oeuvre or the varied debates around postcolonial studies, the facile recital of the Bhabha-beyond-Said mantra has come to be an entrance requirement for "doing the postcolonial" in Israel, a gate-keeping exercise in terms of which dimensions of the Anglo-American postcolonial corpus merit discussion.

This narrativizing of the English-language postcolonial field seems to date back to the 1994 translation of Bhabha's "The Other Question" in the post-Zionist journal *Teoryah u-vikoret* (Theory and Criticism: An Israeli Forum). The editorial preface to the translation, written by philosopher Adi Ophir and literary critic Hannan Hever, presented the Bhabha-over-Said topos as a way out of Orientalism's fixity with regard to the stereotype.[35] While the editors' efforts to bring Bhabha's text to the Hebrew reader deserve strong praise, the politics of translation and the framing of the debate raise serious questions about the journal's positioning of Said and implicitly of Israeli postcolonials themselves.

By selecting this specific Bhabha piece, and by writing a preface highlighting Bhabha's transcendence of Said, the editors cast Bhabha as the subverter of Said's hegemony. Yet at the time of the translation of Bhabha's essay, the bulk of Said's work was (and still is) largely untranslated—including *Orientalism* and, for that matter, all of Said's literary and postcolonial theoretical work. Although it had translated Foucault, Deleuze, de Certeau, and Spivak,[36] *Teorya u-vikoret* itself never translated any of Said's articles, yet its readers were urged to go "beyond" Said. To really "go beyond" Said, however, the Hebrew reader would first have had to have "gone through" Said's major texts. I am obviously not suggesting that one should not critique Said's work. The problem is that the journal's implicit call to "go beyond" Said—or, better, its suggestion that we are all already beyond Said—was not accompanied by an exploration of the broad theoretical intertext and historical context that inform his work and thus hardly does justice to the intellectual debate.

Postcolonial theory consequently was introduced to the Hebrew reader within an intellectual and political vacuum, not only in relation to the huge body of postcolonial work, but more important, in relation to anticolonial history and writings. In Israel, the anticolonial antecedents of postcolonial writings—for example, texts by W. E. B. DuBois, C. L. R. James, Amilcar Cabral, Aimé Césaire, Frantz Fanon, Léopold Senghor, Roberto Fernandez Retamar, and Maxime Rodinson—have never been translated into Hebrew. Albert Memmi's books on Jewish-related questions, meanwhile, were translated in the 1960s and 1970s, but not his classic anticolonialist texts. In his preface to the recent (1999) Hebrew translation of his 1982 *Racism*, Memmi writes:

> We cannot boast of having created morality and simultaneously dominate another people. For this reason I always regretted that no Israeli publisher agreed to publish any of my writing on these issues, and especially the *Portrait of the Colonized*. . . . I am waiting hopefully for [it] also . . . [to] be published in Hebrew. It will mean that the Israeli public will see itself finally as deserving to cope with the difficulties of its national existence.[37]

The "going-beyond-Said" move, in other words, comes in a general context of little engagement with the foundational anticolonial texts. Bhabha's essay, astonishingly, came into Hebrew existence not only before Said's *Orientalism*, but also before the books of the major figure that both Said and Bhabha assumed as a significant influence and interlocutor: Frantz Fanon. For Israeli postcolonials who discover and ventriloquize Fanon only via Bhabha, the intellectual "jump" into the "post" becomes a magic carpet flying into the land of erasure.

It is the silence about Said's profound and very diverse contribution, the caricaturing or "fixing" of his oeuvre into a few sentences about his putative fixity, that raises doubts about this postcolonial reception of Said in Hebrew. Like a few poststructuralist critics in the Anglo-American academy, these Hebrew writers seem to displace Said's deconstruction of the binarism of colonial discourse onto Said's own text, as if Said, and not colonialism and racism, were binarist. The editors and their followers, furthermore, have filtered Said's oeuvre only through Bhabha's comments on Said in one section of an essay, concerning the fixity of the stereotype, an issue now misleadingly placed at the core of the whole Anglo-American postcolonial field.[38] The very complex and multifaceted field of postcolonial studies—which explores such varied issues as the intersection of race and gender in anticolonial thought, the narrated and constructed nature of the nation, the imperial substratum of texts and institutions, the tropes of Orientalist discourse, the role of the diasporic intellectual in the metropole —gets reduced to a stagist narrative of Bhabhaesque mobility superceding Saidian stasis. Bhabha's own dialogue with and incorporations of Said's writings in other essays such as "On Mimicry and Man," "Signs Taken for Wonder," and "Dissemination," meanwhile, went unmentioned by the editors and the budding postcolonials who were seemingly eager to liberate the Hebrew reader from the Palestinian intellectual Said.[39] This rather tendentious framing of Said's vast corpus elides the common intertexts—specifically, poststructuralist theory and anticolonialist discourse— engaged by both Said and Bhabha. Thus, in the name of going beyond binarism, *Teorya u-vikoret* introduced its own binarism for the postcolonial field, limiting it to a brawling arena where two intellectual wrestlers, one supposedly fixed and static and the other fluid and mobile, fight it out. Their shared (albeit differently accented) poststructuralist concerns with antiessentialism and anti-Manicheanism are here pushed out of the ring.

The scholars who apparently endorse Bhabha's Derridian-Lacanian-inflected discourse, furthermore, do not actually themselves go on to perform that discursive analysis through deconstructionist-psychoanalytical readings.[40] The current editor of *Teorya u-vikoret*, the sociologist Yehouda Shenhav, for example, also repeats the Bhabha-over-Said mantra, associating the latter with phrases like "dichotomous," "static," and "rigid," in contrast with Bhabha's "fluidity," "third space," and "hybridity." Yet in the same text that endorses this destabilizing mode of analysis, the author, oblivious to the methodological inconsistency, also invokes the almost antithetical disciplinary grid of "social psychology,"[41] as though the highly theoretical discourses of Lacanian psychoanalysis and the basically positivist domain of social psychology could be regarded as one and the same thing. The endorsement of the Bhabha style of discourse seems especially curious, then, since most of the texts that claim to go beyond Said do not themselves move in the direction in which Bhabha's Lacanian discourse points. Thus, one has the impression that it is not so much a question of moving into psychoanalytic-postcolonial discourse but, rather, of staging a narrative in which Bhabha ends up delegitimizing Said. A more serious Hebrew account of the English debates, moreover, would have at least acknowledged, if not necessarily embraced, the diverse critiques not only of psychoanalytic theory but also of Bhabha's writings—for example, by Benita Parry, who sees his work as depoliticizing the critique of colonialism through a hyperdiscursive turn. Nor do such postcolonial Hebrew texts actually explore how psychoanalysis might help illuminate a contested history where the fundamental debate, despite an undeniable psychoanalytical dimension, is shaped by the very material issue of land, and where the psychic economy of the conflict is caught up in unequal power relations "on the ground."

Other texts in this Hebrew postcolonial corpus form an amalgam of errors and imprecisions concerning intellectual and political genealogies. In *Teorya u-vikoret*'s recent special issue "The Postcolonial Gaze," the authors of the introductory essay, Shehav and Hever—who once again reduce Said to rigid binarism—seem to suggest that Fanon, the quintessential anticolonial writer, historically belongs to postcolonial thought.[42] They attribute to the "postcolonial" the "effort toward liberation from colonialist discursive modes" while somehow dropping from the equation the anticolonial discourse that had already attempted to do precisely that. In a case of the missing "anti," the reader moves from the "colonial" to the "postcolonial" without passing through the "anticolonial." (I am not proposing here a stagist understanding of history but, rather, a careful sequencing of debates.) In another text, Shenhav writes, in a curiously anachronistic account, that the postcolonial movement developed in the Third World in the 1960s.[43] According to the author's discursive sequencing,

> The multi-cultural movement began in the post-colonial stream that developed in the Third World. . . . This movement was joined by other important struggles of the last thirty years: the feminist, the racial, the sexual, and the generational. . . . To the help of these struggles came the post-modern tradition, which tried to formulate the epistemological basis of new forms of cognition.[44]

Disentangling these scrambled intellectual histories would require more effort than it deserves, but suffice it to say that neither "multiculturalism" nor "postcolonialism" began in the Third World; that the "feminist, racial, and sexual" struggles shaped postmodernism as much as postmodernism "helped" these struggles; and that there never was a postcolonial movement per se, even in the late 1980s. There was only a postcolonial theory, which emerged from diasporic "Third World" intellectuals operating in "First World" academe. Within the Israeli public arena, such authors, in other words, seem to speak confidently of oppositional intellectual history —situated in between the "First World" and the "Third World"—even while demonstrating a shallow understanding of that history. Said's work is thus received in a problematic intellectual environment, giving the impression of a faddish recycling of trends from the Anglo-American academy without a thoroughgoing engagement of the historical trajectories that shaped those trends.

A "POST" WITHOUT ITS PAST

In the U.S. context, the terrain for Said's *Orientalism* in 1978 had been prepared, on the left, by a long series of struggles over civil rights, decolonization, Third Worldism, Black Power, and anti-imperialism. In Israel, intellectuals lived these moments quite differently. With a few exceptions, such as the small Matzpen group and the left wing of the Mizrahi Black Panthers, Israeli intellectuals did not engage in the debates about decolonization–Black Power–Third Worldism. Thus, the arrival of the "postcolonial" in the Anglo-American academy in the late 1980s, unlike its subsequent arrival in Israel, formed part of a distinct trajectory. In the U.S. academy, postcolonial discourse emerged in the late 1980s after ethnic studies had already challenged the Western canon and in the wake of substantial (albeit insufficient) institutional reforms and corrective measures like affirmative action—themselves the result of various antiracist and anti-imperialist revolts dating back to the 1960s and 1970s. While more radical U.S. students were supporting America's "own" indigenous people (as represented in the American Indian Movement, for example), Israeli students were celebrating their state's victory over "their" indigenous people—the Palestinian Arabs.

Postcolonial theory in the Anglo-American academy also emerged out of the anticolonialist moment and Third Worldist perspective; that is at least partly what makes it "post." But in Israel, one finds a "post" without its past. Post-Zionist–postcolonial writing in Israel—and this is another reason why the analogy between the two terms is problematic—comes out of an academic context largely untouched by the anticolonialist debates. In the Third World, anticolonial nationalism gave way to some "course corrections" and a measure of disillusionment, partly due to the return of neocolonialism. This disillusionment with the aftermath of decolonization and with Third Worldism, which provides the affective backdrop for postcolonial theory, had no equivalent in the Israeli context.

The question of exactly when the "post" in the "postcolonial" begins already provoked a debate in English. But to suggest a moving beyond "the colonial" in a nation-state and in an academic space historically untouched by anticolonialist Third Worldist debates requires that we ask this question with even more vigor. In the first instance, anticolonial discourse gives way to postcolonial discourse, but in the second, it is not anti-Zionist discourse that gives way to post-Zionist discourse but, rather, Zionist discourse that gives way to post-Zionist discourse. It is a case, again, of the missing "anti."

Reading Zionism through the prism of colonialism has been a taboo in the Israeli academe. Given this context, one would think that the scholarly embrace of "the postcolonial" would foreground the discussion of Zionism's relation to colonialism. But instead one sometimes finds a kind of upside-down camera obscura discourse, even when in political terms these same writers oppose the occupation. Hannan Hever, for example, criticizes Said for viewing the Law of Return as racist and for not recognizing that the Law of Return, like American affirmative action, was legislated as positive discrimination in favor of refugees and the persecuted.[45] But this analogy is ultimately fallacious. Affirmative action in the United States was intended to compensate those the nation-state had itself oppressed, those on whose backs the nation-state had been created, especially Native Americans, African Americans, and Chicanos/as. In Israel, in contrast, the Law of Return compensated the very people generating the dispossession, those who come to constitute the nation.

To ask Said to accept the Law of Return as a form of affirmative action for Jews misses the basic point: that for Palestinians, the Law of Return simply continues a history of dispossession. The Law of Return–affirmative-action analogy, furthermore, is made in an Israeli context where affirmative action for Palestinians and other minorities has never been institutionalized and where it has often been caricatured, including in so-called liberal-left publications, in terms borrowed from the U.S. right, as a kind of obnoxious "political correctness." Although post-Zionist postcolonials

have certainly made a contribution by challenging certain Zionist ortho-
doxies, one wonders how post this "post" is when a term borrowed from
the alternative American lexicon ("affirmative action") surfaces in the Israeli context in the defense of the dominant ideology; when the Palestinian
desire for a right of return is repressed from the discussion; and when the
relevance of the critique of the "colonial" to the account of the "Law of
Return," "affirmative action," and the "right of return" is circumvented.
As with the term "postcolonialism," the prefix "post-" in "post-Zionism"
erases both colonial lineages and anticolonial intellectual history with a
magical stroke of the "post."

While Hebrew texts on "the postcolonial gaze" may denounce the abuses
of the military occupation, they hardly articulate the links between that
political stance and the Bhabhaesque theoretical model of "third space,"
resulting in an unthinking celebration of the "in-between" in the land of
partitions and walls. Although Said's work engaged the question of flows
between cultures—his notion of "traveling theory" is a case in point—most
Israeli postcolonial texts reject his work in the name of "hybridity," where
presumably "not only the colonized but also the colonizer engages in
mimicry." Under the sign of "hybridity," Nir Baram is thus able to contrast
Said unfavorably with Ajami, praising the latter for his "deep research into
the orient itself" and for his courage for daring to criticize the politics of the
Arab world.[46] This comparison overlooks Said's own criticism of the Palestinian Authority and the Arab regimes while ignoring Ajami's binarist
discourse that essentializes the Western-versus-Eastern clash. Here "fluidity" is mobilized against Said but ends up proposing Ajami, often viewed as
an opportunist who flatters the Orientalist illusions of the right, as the new
model of sly civility.

"Hybridity," an invaluable instrument for cultural analysis—and, indeed, a very old trope in Latin America and the Caribbean—has been
useful both in transcending the myth of racial purity central to colonial
discourse and in challenging a Third Worldist discourse that projected the
nation as culturally homogenous. But "hybridity" must be seen as always
already power-laden. Too often "hybridity" becomes a catch-all term, without any serious probing of its different modalities. In a copy-and-paste
approach to a certain postcolonial discourse in English, the postcolonial
in its Hebrew translation offers an undifferentiated valorization of "hybridity." How can we think through the relation between a postcolonial discourse that reads resistance into the fact of hybridities, on the one hand,
and the current apartheid-like and literally fenced-in reality of Israel/

Palestine, on the other? Think about the cruel hybridity imposed, for example, in construction sites of the Separation Wall, where the linguistic frontiers of Hebrew and Arabic are indeed traversed but where Palestinians are obliged to build the very wall that tears their lives apart. What is gained, then, when the asymmetries of hybridity are bracketed or even elided and encoded as resistant?

In fact, such Hebrew texts lack an in-depth engagement with the English-language postcolonial debate that a decade earlier probed the potentially depoliticizing effects of "hybridity." Notions of "oppression" and "resistance" are too easily dismissed as binarist simplifications, while "collaboration" and "cooptation" happily find their way to an all-embracing space where the colonizer and the colonized perform mutual mimicry. Passing off "hybridity" as always already "resistant" appears to sanctify the fait accompli of colonial violence. Such a "postcolonial gaze" turns a blind eye to Said's gesture of opening a conceptual space for Zionism's victimization in a context that had previously permitted the narration exclusively of Jewish victimization and Zionist redemption. Flattening Said's argument, these texts overlook other productive Saidian categories, such as the critique of "origins" in *Beginnings*; the concentration on power-knowledge "affiliations"; the notion of the "worldly" adversarial intellectual; the idea of "mutually haunting" histories; and the privileging of spatial categories in *Culture and Imperialism*—all of which are highly relevant to the engagement of Israel/Palestine. Instead, Said's function is only to be gone beyond, a point to be immediately departed from and transcended. This current Israeli postcolonial narrative thus relegates Said, and the people he stands for, to what I have elsewhere termed the realm of the "pre-postcolonial" within what Joseph Massad has called the "post-colonial colony."[47] By applying it to Said's influential work, such authors abuse the term "hegemony" while ignoring the centrality of that Gramscian concept to Said's own work, all part of a rush to perform a rather hegemonic burial of Said's oppositional texts.

In the context of U.S.-Israel traveling debates, then, Said occupies a paradoxical site in relation to the "postcolonial." He represents at once a disempowered, displaced Palestinian and an empowered American intellectual. As a Palestinian, Said evokes colonized and dominated people; as an American literary scholar, he evokes the prestigious field of postcolonial theory. Said's own Janus-faced position is part and parcel of the contradictory passing of his work through diverse checkpoints in Israel. Reading Said in Hebrew condenses an oxymoronic friction between the imagined geographies of Arabic (as East) and English (as West): In the former, he is a haunting exile from Palestine, while in the latter, he holds the powerful wand of academic America. That Said's final resting place is in Broummana, Lebanon, not Jerusalem, where he was born, not Cairo, which he left, and not New York, where he lived for decades, provides a suitably troubled and inconclusive allegory to the equally ruptured voyages of his ideas across national borders.

NOTES

I thank Robert Stam, Yigal Nizri, Bashir Abu-Manneh, and Joseph Massad for their comments. Throughout, the translations from the Hebrew are my own.

1 My early dialogue with Said's work includes "The Trouble with Hanna," *Film Quarterly* 38, no. 2 (winter 1984–85) (co-authored with Richard Porton); "Sephardim in Israel: Zionism from the Standpoint of Its Jewish Victims," *Social Text* 19–20 (fall 1988); and *Israeli Cinema: East/West and the Politics of Representation* (Austin: University of Texas Press, 1989). Said's endorsement on the cover of *Israeli Cinema* further pointed to our affiliation, seen as negative in the Israeli public sphere.

2 Igal Bursztyn, a professor at Tel Aviv University, suggested that Said and I, unlike Fanon, are products of Western academe and therefore inauthentic Third Worlders, forgetting that Fanon himself was educated in the French academy: Bursztyn, "The Bad Ashkenazis Are Riding Again," *Ma'ariv*, 7 February 1992 (Hebrew).

3 "Statement of Stanley Kurtz: Testimony before the Subcommittee on Select Education, Committee on Education and the Workforce, U.S. House of Representatives," 19 June 2003.

4 Kurtz, "Anti-Americanism in the Classroom: The Scandal of Title VI," *National Review*, 15 July 2002.

5 "Statement of Stanley Kurtz."

6 Edward Alexander, "Professor of Terror," *Commentary*, vol. 88, no. 2, August 1989. See also "Professor of Terror: An Exchange—Edward Alexander and Critics," *Commentary*, vol. 88, no. 6, December 1989.

7 Arel Ginai, Tzadok Yehezkeli, and Roni Shaked, "The Media Experts," *Yedi'ot Aharonot*, 17 February 1989 (Hebrew). For a more complete critique, see Ella Shohat, "Antinomies of Exile," in *Edward Said: A Critical Reader*, ed. by Michael Sprinker (Oxford: Blackwell, 1992).

8 Ben-Dror Yemini, "Academia under Investigation," *Ma'ariv*, 4 July 2003 (Hebrew). Although Yemini's article was written in Hebrew, the *National Review*'s website provides a link to the article—English and Hebrew seem to reinforce each other's legitimacy. On the links between right-wing Israeli and U.S. policy, see Joel Beinin, "The Israelization of American Middle East Policy Discourse," *Social Text*, no. 75 (summer 2003).

9 Ben-Dror Yemini, "The Faculties for the Hate of Israel," *Ma'ariv*, 17 December 2002 (Hebrew).

10 Uria Shavit, "Peace? Forget about It," *Ha'aretz*, 22 March 2001 (Hebrew).

11 Shimon Shamir, "The Argument That the Anti-Orientalists Love to Hate," *Ha'aretz*, 12 December 2001 (Hebrew).

12 Emmanuel Sivan, *Interpretations of Islam* (Princeton, N.J.: Darwin Press, 1985), 141. For a critique of Sivan's essentialist usage of Arab identity against Said, see Barbara Harlow, "The Palestinian Intellectual and the Liberation of the Academy," in *Edward Said: A Critical Reader*, ed. by Michael Sprinker (Oxford: Blackwell, 1993). Yitzhak Laor suggested with irony that these Arab critics would presumably also have something to say about Israeli Orientalism in "Pam-pram-pam-pam—Post-Zionism," *Ha'aretz*, 15 August 1997; Haim Gerber of Hebrew University, meanwhile, called for a change in attitude toward Orientalism on the part of his Orientalist colleagues, "More on the Orientalism Debate," *Teorya u-vikoret* 14 (summer 1999; Hebrew).

13 Avi Bareli, "The Status of Zionist and Israel Histories in Israeli Universities," in *Israeli Historical Revisionism: From Left to Right*, ed. by Anita Shapira and Derek J. Penslar (London: Frank Cass, 2003), 103.

14 Gabriel Piterberg, teaching at the time at Be'er Sheva University, facilitated *Orientalism*'s publication by Am Oved (translated by Atalia Zilberg) with the support of the Hayeem Herzog Center for the Study of the Middle East and Diplomacy.

15 Ari Shavit, "My Right of Return," *Ha'aretz*, 8 August 2000 (Hebrew). Kobby Meidan, "Nightly Meeting," October 2002, interviewed Said for Israeli TV's Channel 2.

16 In the early 1990s, at the invitation of Mizrahi leftist activists and writers Sami Shalom Chetrit and Tikva Levi, I began translating the introduction and the first chapter of *Orientalism* for a Hebrew anthology of translated anticolonial writings, but the project came to an end for lack of funds from alternative presses and for lack of interest from mainstream publishers.

17 *Out of Place* was published by Yedi'ot Aharonot Books and Chemed Books in 2001. *Ha'aretz* (8 September 1999) translated Said's response to Justus Weiner's accusation that Said manipulated his biography (" 'My Beautiful Old House' and Other Fabrications by Edward Said" in *Commentary*). Dan Rabinowitz ("Politically Contested Childhood," *Ha'aretz*, 26 August 1999) was among those writing in defense of Said. (At the invitation of Rabinowitz, Said delivered the keynote address at the Israeli Anthropological Association meeting in 1998.) Similarly, Amnon Yuval reviewed *Orientalism* positively in *Ma'ariv* (1 September 2000), as did Tuvia Blumenthal of Said's *The End of the Peace Process*, in *Ha'aretz* (2 December 2001), which has not been translated.

18 *Siman Kri'a*, a quarterly sponsored by Tel Aviv University in conjunction with the establishment press ha'Kibutz haMeuhad, translated Said's essay (no. 14 [June 1981]) from *Social Text*'s first issue in 1979.

19 Yigal Elam, "Zionism, Its Palestinian Victim and the Western World," *Siman Kri'a*, no. 14 (June 1981): 367. The author puts his faith in the West's ending the conflict, but he does so on the basis of the West's "political culture" of "equilibrium." On page 368, he writes, "In the Israeli side there is little sensitivity and

understanding of these Western criteria; while on the Palestinian side I doubt it if there is any sensitivity and understanding at all. Even Edward Said still does not improve the picture on the Palestinian side, to judge by his article on Zionism." Elam's word "even" seems to suggest that one expects more from a modern educated Arab living in the West.

20 In his review of *Orientalism*, the leftist Yoram Bronovsky invokes Athenian democracy versus Persian tyranny to criticize Said's critical invocation of Aeschylus: Yoram Bronovsky, "The West Is Right, Sometimes," *Ha'aretz*, 10 March 1995. Bronovsky's argument is premised on the idea that democracy is a Greek inheritance and that Athens was indeed a democracy. In fact, there are many sources of democratic social organizing—for example, in diverse African and indigenous American contexts. Also, Athenian democracy was based on slavery.

21 Ronit Lentin and Yahali Amit translated *The Question of Palestine* (*She'elat Falestin*) (Haifa: Mifras, 1981). I am grateful to Lentin for sharing with me the details concerning its Hebrew publication.

22 Among the original Hebrew books published were Shlomo Swirski's *Campus, Society and State* (Jerusalem: Mifras House, 1982); Ronit Lentin's *Conversations with Palestinian Women* (Jerusalem: Mifras House, 1982); and Yemini's *A Political Punch* (Jerusalem: Mifras House, 1986), recounting his political transformation from rightist to leftist.

23 Christopher Norris, *Decontructzia* (Tel Aviv: Sifriat Poalim, 1988), 88 (in the 1993 edition).

24 *News from Within* dedicated its October 2003 (19, no. 8) issue to Said's memory. Said joined the board at the invitation of Tikva Parnass, then the publication's editor.

25 The previous director of the Alternative Information Center, Michael Warshawski, wrote an anti-Zionist criticism of the post-Zionist historians. The current director, Moshe Behar, intervened in the *Al-Ahram Weekly* debate, in which Fawzi Mansour critiqued Said's articles (published between April 9 and June 25) in an essay titled "Culture and Conflict" (no. 386, 16–22 July), concerning Arab Jews, offering an anti-Zionist reading: Moshe Behar, "Time to Meet the Mizrahim?" *Al-Ahram Weekly*, 15–21 October 1998.

26 The writings include Smadar Lavie, *The Poetics of Military Occupation* (Berkeley: University of California Press, 1990); Ammiel Alcalay, *After Jews and Arabs* (Minneapolis: University of Minnesota Press, 1993); Yerach Gover, *Zionism: The Limits of Moral Discourse in Israeli Hebrew Fiction* (Minneapolis: University of Minnesota Press, 1994); Azmi Bishara, "On the Question of the Palestinian Minority in Israel," *Teorya u-vikoret* 3 (winter 1993); Sami Shalom Chetrit, *The Mizrahi Struggle in Israel, 1948–2003* (Tel Aviv: Am Oved, 2004); Simona Sharoni, *Gender and the Israeli–Palestinian Conflict* (Syracuse, N.Y.: Syracuse University Press, 1995); Sarah Chinski, "Silence of the Fish," *Teorya u-vikoret* 4 (autumn 1993); Gabriel Piterberg, "Domestic Orientalism," *British Journal of Middle Eastern Studies* 23 (1996); Henriette Dahan-Kalev, "Ethnicity in Israel," in Ilan Gur-Ze'ev, *Modernism, Post-Modernity and Education* (Tel Aviv: Ramot Press, 1999); Irit Rogoff, *Terra Infirma* (London: Routledge, 2000); Yosefa Loshitzky, *Identity Politics of* *the Israeli Screen* (Austin: University of Texas Press, 2001); Dan Rabinowitz, *Anthropology and the Palestinians* (Jerusalem: Institute for Israeli Arab Studies, 1998); Shoshana Madmoni, "Media Construction of the Kidnapped Babies Affair" (Ph.D. diss., University of Massachusetts, Amherst, 2003); Oren Yiftachel, "Nation-Building and the Division of Space," *Nationalism and Ethnic Politics* 4, no. 2 (1998). (At the invitation of Yiftachel, Said served on the board of the English-language Israeli journal *Hagar: International Social Science Review*.)

27 Amnon Raz-Krakotzkin, "Orientalism, Jewish Studies and Israeli Society," *Jama'a* 3 (1999); Ruth Tsoffar, *The Stains of Culture: An Ethno-Reading of Karaite Jewish Women* (Detroit: Wayne State University Press, 2006, forthcoming); Gil Anidjar, "Jewish Mysticism Alterable and Unalterable," *Jewish Social Studies* 3, no. 1 (1996).

28 The revisionist sociologist Uri Ram was one of the first to use the term "post-Zionism" in his introduction to his Hebrew edited volume *Israeli Society: Critical Perspectives* (Tel Aviv: Breirot, 1993), where post-Zionism was proposed as a hope for a new social agenda. In the same volume, Gershon Shafir, whose work, unusually, examines the relationship between Zionism and colonialism, also invoked the term to offer a "new universalist tendency" in contrast to the "rise of Neo-Zionism."

29 Nur Masalha, "Debate on the 1948 Exodus," *Journal of Palestine Studies* 21, no. 1 (fall 1991): 90–97; Rashid Khalidi in Jonathan Mahler, "Uprooting the Past," *Lingua Franca* (August 1997): 32; Joseph Massad in a conversation with Benny Morris, "History on the Line: No Common Ground," *History Workshop Journal* 53, no. 1 (spring 2002): 205–16. While some of the revisionist history books refer to Arab and Palestinian sources such as memoirs, diaries, or correspondence, the centerpiece of the argument relies on the declassified Israeli State Archives. Masalha implies that Morris seems hardly aware of the growing body of Palestinian history writing.

30 Edward Said, "New History, Old Ideas," *Al-Ahram Weekly*, vol. 378, 21–27 May 1998. Nur Masalha also had asked how some revisionist historians such as Morris can argue that there was no Israeli expulsion policy when their work rests on "carefully released partial documentation and when much of the Israeli files and documents relating to the subject are still classified and remain closed to researchers?": Masalha, "Debate on the 1948 Exodus."

31 Said, "New History, Old Ideas." Said singled out Ilan Pappé as the only Israeli revisionist historian who showed consistency at the 1998 Paris meeting with Palestinian historians such as Elias Sanbar. Such tensions, I should add, also exist vis-à-vis the question of the Mizrahim. Tom Segev's book *1949: The First Israelis* (New York: Free Press, 1986) was received positively among leftist Mizrahi activists and intellectuals in the mid-1980s. We were thrilled that a book, based on the Israeli State Archives, indeed indicated an intentionally discriminatory policy, yet Segev reproached this reading of his book.

32 I elaborated on this schizophrenic discourse in such texts as "Master Narrative/Counter Readings," in *Resisting Images: Essays on Cinema and History*, ed. by

Robert Sklar and Charles Musser (Philadelphia: Temple University Press, 1990); "Taboo Memories, Diasporic Visions: Columbus, Palestine and Arab-Jews," in *Performing Hybridity*, ed. by May Joseph and Jennifer Fink (Minneapolis: University of Minnesota Press, 1999).

33 Ella Shohat, "Notes on the 'Post-Colonial,'" *Social Text* 31–32 (spring 1992).

34 Nir Baram, "The Crown of the East," *Ma'ariv*, 3 October 2003.

35 Hannan Hever and Adi Ofir, "Homi K. Bhabha: Theory on a Tight Rope," *Teorya u-vikoret* 5 (fall 1994), published by the Van Leer Institute. The translation of Bhabha's subtitle into Hebrew has an interesting and perhaps symptomatic slippage. Instead of the original, "Difference, Discrimination, and the Discourse of Colonialism," the Hebrew subtitle reads, "Difference, Discrimination, and Post-Colonial Discourse."

36 Spivak ("Can the Subaltern Speak?") is the only other postcolonial author to have been translated by the journal, published in an issue that did not generate a reflexive discussion on the journal's own politics of representation—for example, the absence or the very limited presence of local critical "Third World" women (Palestinian or Mizrahi) on its board. *Gramsci*, another major Saidian intertext not translated by the journal, is forthcoming from Resling Press.

37 Albert Memmi's books appeared in Hebrew in the following order: *Pillar of Salt* (Tel Aviv: Am Oved, 1960); *Jews and Arabs* (Tel Aviv: Sifriat HaPoalim, 1975); *The Liberation of the Jew* (Tel Aviv: Am Oved, 1976); and *Racism* (Jerusalem: Karmel, 1999).

38 In fact, the *Teorya u-vikoret* editors selected the 1990 version of Bhabha's "The Other Question," which contained his comment that Said's "suggestion that colonial power and discourse is possessed entirely by the colonizer" is a "historical and theoretical simplification." These words were removed in Bhabha's later version of the same essay in *The Location of Culture. Teorya u-vikoret's* editors were aware of the later version, as they indicate that Bhabha's last paragraph in Hebrew is modified according to it. Yet they frame Said through the prism of the word "simplification," which was omitted in Bhabha's later version but has now become the focal point of Israeli postcolonial studies. For a comparison of the two versions, see Homi Bhabha, "The Other Question," in *Out There: Marginalization and Contemporary Cultures*, ed. by Russell Ferguson, Martha Gever, Trinh T. Minh-ha, and Cornel West (Cambridge, Mass.: MIT Press, 1990), 77; and idem, *The Location of Culture* (London: Routledge, 1994), 72.

39 Bhabha's texts acknowledged Said's work as pioneering, while Said endorsed Bhabha's *The Location of Culture*.

40 Of the few exceptions to systematically deploy a psychoanalytic-postcolonial framework are Raz Yosef, *Beyond Flesh: Queer Masculinities and Nationalism in Israeli Cinema* (Piscataway, N.J.: Rutgers University Press, 2004); and Orly Lubin, who partially incorporates this method in *Woman Reading Woman* (Haifa: Haifa University Press, 2003).

41 On the Bhabha-over-Said argument, see Yehouda Shenhav, "Jews of Arab Countries in Israel," in *Mizrahim in Israel*, ed. Hannan Hever, Yehouda Shenhav, and Pnina Motzafi-Haller (Jerusalem: Van Leer Institute and Hakibbutz Hameu-chad, 2002), 147–48, and throughout his *The Arab-Jews* (Tel Aviv: Am Oved, 2003). On the "social psychology" reference, see Shenhav, *The Arab-Jews*, 115 (Hebrew).

42 See Shenhav's and Hever's theoretical preface in *Teorya u-vikoret* 20 (spring 2002): 11.

43 Shenhav, *The Arab-Jews*, 149.

44 Shenhav, "Precious Culture," in *The Israeli Experience*, ed. Sami Michael (Tel Aviv: Ma'ariv Book Guild, 2001), 87 (Hebrew).

45 Hever briefly contrasts Said with Anton Shammas in an essay on *Arabesques*: Hannan Hever, "Hebrew from an Arab Pen," *Teorya u-vikoret* 1 (summer 1991): 30 (Hebrew).

46 Baram, "The Crown of the East." He also applied this skewed version of postcolonial theory to the Mizrahi question, which was met by a critical response by Sami Shalom Chetrit, "Fed Up with the Askenazized," *Ma'ariv*, 4 April 2003.

47 Joseph Massad, "The 'Post-Colonial' Colony," in *The Pre-Occupation of Post-Colonial Studies*, ed. Fawzia Afzal-Khan and Kalpana Seshadri Crooks (Durham, N.C.: Duke University Press, 2000). On the "pre-postcolonial" and "hybridity," see Ella Shohat, "Notes on the 'Post-Colonial.'"

Index

Page numbers in italics refer to illustrations.

Algerian women: body of, 267–68, 271; cross-racial desire and, 266–70; empowerment of, 266, 272–73; in nationalist representations, 282, 300–302; in revolutionary movements, 56, 266, 269–73, 300–302; sexuality of, 269–70; veiling of, 269–70, 272, 287n52, 300

al-Hakim, Tawfik, 39, 82

al-Imam, Hassan, 82

Allah Tantou, 299

Allen, Woody, 116, 123, 137n21

Alloula, Malek, 64n36, 68n86

Al-Seba'a, Youssef, 82

Alternative Information Center, 367, 381n25; Michael Warshawsk and, 381n25

al-Tukhi, Ahmad, 86

Amator (Kieslowski), 117

America: American Adam and, 19–20, 221; American studies and, 5; Columbus in, 13, 27, 208, 209, 220; discovery of, 19–21, 26–27, 31, 35, 221–22; dissemination of American cultural forms and, 128–29, 137n29; English language and, 128–29; hero imagery and, 19–20, 31, 35, 221; images of wilderness and, 18, 221; postcolonial studies in, 4; Promethean masternarrative and, 20, 22; sabra as, 217–18, *219*, 220, 221, 331, 354; schizophrenic masternarrative and, 221; women's studies and, 4–7; Zionist discourse and, 220–21

Amin, Samir, 198n16, 235

Amir, Aziza, 291, *292*

Anderson, Michael, 125

Anidjar, Gil, 368

Annie Hall (Allen), 116

Anthropology, 9, 24, 96, 279–80, 349–50; cinema and, 24, 96; colonialism and, 134; of Enlightenment thinkers, 279–80; on first human being, 197n15

Anticolonialism: in Algeria, 56, 266, 269–73, 300–302; in diasporic film, 306–7; Fanon on, 266; Hebrew texts of, 372; Israeli literary studies and, 366; Israeli revisionist historians and, 368–74, 382n29, n30, n31, 383n38; postcolonialism and, 242, 374–76; schizophrenic masternarrative and, 221; Third worldism and, 8–9; tropes of, 268–69; women and, 12–13, 56, 266, 269–73, 300–302. *See also* Postcolonialism

Anti-Semitism: anti-Arabism and, 259; blackness in, 259, 262; Diaspora Jew and, 217; feminization of the Jewish male and, 285n27; geographies of, 264; Holocaust and, 213, 216, 217, 259; of Nazism, 213, 216, 261–62; physiognomy of Jews and, 181, 261; Reconquista and, 209–11; Sartre on, 253, 254, 260–61

Antonioni, Michelangelo, 124

Appadurai, Arjun, 297, 328n13

Arab-Jews: Algerian Jews, 24, 49, 76, 107, 129, 131, 252, 254, 264–65, 273, 284n5, 286n39, 372–73, 383n37; aliyah of, 339, 346, 347–48; Arabness of, 77–78, 200n44, 201–5, 215, 224–28, 236n39, 331, 334–37; dislocations of, 205, 222–23, 331, 333–35, 337–40, 355n4; Egyptian Jewish community and, 201–5, 227; Euro-Israeli identity challenged by, 213–16, 224–25, 342; hyphenated identity of, 213–15, 225, 227, 333–45; Israeli identity of, 217, 226–28, 333–36, 340, 341–42, 347; Israeli-Palestinian conflict and, 205, 216, 220–21; Jewish Arabic language and, 231nn33, 34; Moroccan Jews, 226; Muslim Arab culture and, 222–23, 224, 226–28, 335, 342–44, 352–53; Palestinians and, 217, 222, 229, 354; racism and, 217, 219, 222–23, 357nn17, 26, 27; Yemeni Jews, *215*, *218*, 224, 338, 348–50, 357n26, n27, 367; Zionism and, 213–15, 339, 356n9. *See also* Iraqi Jews; Israel; Mizrahim; Palestine, Palestinians; Sephardim; Zionist discourse

Arabs: crosscultural identification of,

286n40; in cultural hierarchies, 263–
64; films of, 83, 85, 86–87; in Hollywood orientalist films, 24, 25, 31,
50–51, 56, 57–60, 64n35, 130; Jewish
identity and, 220–21, 263, 339–44;
language and, 53, 102n12, 120, 130,
208, 223, 239, 257, 309–10, 366; literature of, 77–78, 192–95, 200n50;
Martinicans, 263–64; music of, 226,
257–58, 303–5; racism and, 33, 39,
41–43, 209–10, 213, 215–16, 220,
261–63; Spanish expulsion of, 13,
209–10, 212–13; in Tunisia, 301,
302–5; Western imaginings of, 53, 56,
67n71, 130. *See also* Algeria; Egypt;
Islam; Palestine, Palestinians
Archaeology: as body metaphor, 154–55;
in Egypt, 33–39, 194–95; in Israel,
220, 347; in Palestine, 220, 347; psychoanalysis as, 32–33, 154; in rescue
narratives, 33–35, 65n53, 193
Area studies, 3, 4, 5, 6, 7
Around the World in 80 Days (Verne), 29,
30, 56, 63n30, 125
Art: arabesques, 80, 81; calligraphy, 72,
75, 76–77; cartoons, 141, 142, 146;
discovery narratives in, 20; graven
images, 72, 75–77, 82, 101n1; history
of, 78; mimesis in, 78, 79; Orientalist painting, 49, 53; verism in, 78–80;
Western modernity in, 78–80,
103n17, n18, 199n25, 288n83
Ashkenazim, 204, 206, 216, 224–26,
343–44
Auerbach, Erich, 80, 103n20
Azoulay, Jacques, 257, 258

Baccar, Selma, 293
Bacon, Francis, 25–26, 154, 155
Baker, Josephine, 47, *48*
Bakhtin, Mikhail, 107, 116, 128, 134,
135n1, 251–52
Balanchine, George, 199n25
Balazs, Bela, 111
Ballas, Shimon, 231n32; *Vehu Aher*,
231n32
Banzer, Hugo, 149

Bara, Theda, 183, *184*, 195
Barakat, Henri, 82
Baram, Nir, 371, 377
Bareli, Avi, 363
Baring, E., 197n12
Barthes, Roland, 9, 42, 120, 252
Battle of Algiers, The (La Battaglia di
Algeri), 56, 68n86, 300, 301, *302*, 320
Bautis, Marta N.: *Home is the Struggle*,
306
Bayt Allah al-Haram, 86
Bazin, André, 31, 64n34, 96, 113
Be Good My Children (Chang), 306
Bellocchio, Marco, 124
Bellow, Saul, 198n24
Belly dancing, 49–50, 103n18, 311
Benga, Ota, 312
Ben-Gurion, David, 216, 369
Benjamin, Walter, 100, 276
Ben Lyazid, Farida: *Bab Ila Sma Maf-
touh*, 321–22; *Door to the Sky*, 321–22
Ben-Yiju, Abraham, 202, 227, 228
Bergman, Ingmar: *Persona*, 116
Berkeley, Busby, 55, 68n83
Bernal, Martin, 62n17, 171, 172, 176
Bhabha, Homi, 371–74, 383nn35, 38, 39,
41
Bible, 84–86, 90–91, 93–95, 96, 98–
99
Bilal, Mu'adhin al-Rasul, 86
Billop, Camille, 317
Bishara, Azmi, 367
Black is Beautiful movement, 188, 319
Black Narcissus (Powell and Press-
burger), 24, 41
Blackness: Afrocentrism and, 62n17,
168–69, 171–72, 175–78, 197n15;
Arabness and, 286n40; Arab racism
and, 263; Black Power movement
and, 188, 190; of Cleopatra, 168–69,
171–74, 176, 189; construction of,
258–63, 320, 329n34; Fanon on, 253–
55, 286n40; geographies of, 171–72,
255–56; Jews and, 200n44, 222,
231n28, 253–54, 259, 262–64,
286n40; language and, 262; Mizrahim and, 111, 222, 375; Negritude and,

Charar, Baha Eddine, 86

Chase-Riboud, Barbara, 190

Cheang, Shu Lea, 317

Chenzira, Ayoka, 317, 319–20

Chetrit, Sami Shalom, 367, 380n16

Chicanos/as, 5, 211–12

Chinski, Sarah, 367

Chion, Michel, 98

Christ images, 74, 90, 91, 92, 93–94, 95, 104n33, 180, *186*

Cildo Meireles, 127

Cinema: actantial slot in, 100; anthropological role of, 24, 96; Arab films and, 83, 85, 86–87; Arabs in Hollywood films and, 24, 25, 31, 50–51, 56, 57–60, 64n35, 130; aural effects in, 108–9; Bible in, 84–86, 98–99; cartography of, 26–28; censorship of, 43–45, 47, 91, 137n21, 182; colonialism and, 23–24, 40–41, 50–51, 62n9, 62n17, 118, 300, 301, 302–7; dialogue of, 12, 111–13, 116, 119–20, 122–29, 315, 317; dubbing (post-synchronization) and, 122–27, 315, 317; graven images and, 71, 72; Islam in, 83–90; of Japan, 36, 117, 136n10; location shooting in Third World and, 29; map imagery in, 26–27, 63n31; New Wave films and, 120, 128; non-Western images in, 23, *23*, 24, 31, 46; novels adapted for, 19, 20, 24–25, 29, *30*, 56, 63n30, 71, 82, 125; post–Third Worldist feminist film and video and, 291–96, 326n2; subtitles, 113, 119–23, 136n20, 137n25; translations of film titles and, 114, 115–18, 137n19. *See also* Hollywood; individual movie titles

Cléo de 5 á 7 (Varda), 120

Cleopatra: actresses cast as, 182, 183, *184*, 186; blood of, 171, 178, 186; *Cleopatra* (DeMille), 23, 33, 185, 186; *Cleopatra* (Mankiewicz), 183, 186, *187*, 188, 189–90, *191*; cosmetic industry ads and, 183, 185, 199n38; Egypt represented by, 185–86, 190–91, 195–96, 200n44; in Eurocentric discourse, 176–78; feminist readings of, 185,

190; film images of, 23, 33, 185–91; nose of, 179–81, 185; racial identity of, 168–76, 178, 182–83, 185, 189–90; in Shakespeare, 195, 200n50

Cleopatra Jones, 189, *191*

Coffee Coloured Children (Onwurah), 317, 320

Colbert, Claudette, 183, 189

Colonialism: Africa in discourse of, 176–77, 197n15, 198n24; Algerian women and, 268–69; American hero and, 19–20, 29, 31, 35; Arab-Jewish culture and, 206; assimilation and, 56, 133–34, 231n33, 273–74, 331, 333–35, 342–43; barbarism and, 130, 229n9, 276, 279, 283; biological determinism and, 174; caricatures of, 133; cinema and, 23–24, 29–39, 40–41, 50–51, 62n9, 62n17, 300, 301, 302–7; construction of identity and, 254–55; exhibitionism and, 33–38, 49–50, 312–15, 329n25, 342–43, 347; of France, 280; genocide and, 134, 211, 259; globalization and, 13–14, 297–98, 327nn9, 10; good–bad binaries of identity and, 265, 324; historical norms of, 175–76; homoeroticism, 56–57, *58*, 68n86; Israel and, 216–17, 222, 370, 376; language and, 107–8, 128–34, 216, 223–24, 257, 337–38; literature of, 236–37; maps and mapping of, 26–30, 63nn30, 31; naming in narratives of, 13, 19, 26–27, *28*, 197n15, 210, 221, 333–35; novels and, 19, *20*, 24–25, 56; partitions and, 207, 215; Prospero complex and, 14, 19, 134, 256, 271; rape narratives of, 261, 268–72; sexuality and, 13, 32, 39–40, 42–43; slavery, 42–43, 67n64, 240, 243–44, 276, 279–80, 288n79; therapeutic norms of, 256–58, 282; virginity imagery and, 19–21, 42–43, 154, 221–22; whiteness as beauty and, 182–83, 185. *See also* Anthropology; Anticolonialism; Diaspora; Dislocations; Eurocentrism; Hybridity; Orientalism; Postcolonialism; Rescue narratives

337, 340, 369; problematic terminology of, 337; right of return and, 331, 332, 335, 340, 376–80; of Spanish Expulsion (1492), 13, 21, 208, 209–10, 212–14. *See also* Rescue narratives

Djebar, Assia:, 306

Doane, Mary Ann, 119

Dobson, Tamara, 189, 190, *191*

Dogma (Smith), 93

Donner, Clive, 128

Dorfman, Ariel, 361

Dr. Strangelove (Kubrick), 108

Du Bois, W. E. B., 372

Du Camp, Maxime, 194

Edison, Thomas, 194

Egypt: archaeology in, 33–39, 194–95; Camp David Accords and, 239, 248n8; censorship in, 130, 133; cinema in, 31, 33–38, 35–37, 38, 64n34, 66n63, 83, 85–86, 321; feminization of, 186, *187*; Freud on, 33; Greek influence in, 169–70, 177, 178; hieroglyphics of, 72, 96; *In an Antique Land* (Ghosh) and, 202, 223, 226–28, 351–52; Jewish community in, 201–5, 227; music in, 37, 303–5; national identity in, 35–39, 66n63, 133, 171–72, 192–96; as point of origin of history, 175–76, 197n15; Western appropriation of antiquities of, 33–38, 201–5, 227. *See also* Cleopatra

Eikhenbaum, Boris Mikhailovich, 109, 111–12

Eisenstein, Sergei, 96, 112

El-Abnoudi, Atteyat, 293, 321; *Ahlam Mumkina* (Permissable Dreams), 321

Elam, Yigal, 364–65

El-Saadawi, Nawal, 297, 321

English language, 107–8, 125, 127–32, 366

Enlightenment: aesthetics of, 179; anthropology and, 279–80; barbarism and, 130, 229n9, 276, 279, 283; black enlightenment and, 278; Cairo Geniza as project of, 201–5, 226–27; Caribbean revolutionary discourse and, 278; colonialism and, 275–76, 278–80; dialogue of, 12; Eurocentrism of, 179, 278–81, 288n79, 365; Fanon on, 278–81; Haskalah and, 220; humanism of, 275–78; philosophers of, 279–80; race and, 179, 279–80, 288n79; Zionist discourse and, 219, 365

Espinosa, Julio Garcia, 296

Essentialism, 10, 12, 244–45, 258, 282, 354, 361–62, 373, 389n12

Ethnic studies, 3, 4, 6, 7, 258–61, 361

Eurocentrism: aesthetics of, 317–18; Afrocentrism and, 62n17, 168–69, 171–72, 175–78, 197n15; beauty and, 179–81, 188; biological racism and, 173–74; blackness and, 255–56; Cairo Geniza project and, 201–5, 226–27; classical Greek influences on, 175–78, 281; cultural syncretism in, 177–78; discovery narratives and, 18–20, 24–26, 62n17; Egypt and, 194; Enlightenment and, 179, 278–81, 288n79, 365; Eurocentric historiography and, 208; Euro-Israeli discourse and, 205–6, 213, 216, 222, 227; feminism and, 8, 10, 11, 291–94; forced migrations framed by, 209; of Jewish studies, 206; in medical practice, 257–58; narrative and, 78–79, 103nn16, 17; national identity and, 208; non-Western influences on Western art and, 78–80, 103n17, n18, 199n25, 281, 288n83; norms of beauty and, 319–20; Orientalist ideology and, 53, 67n17, 74; physical anthropology and, 197n15; racial identity in, 172–75, 176, 197n13; representations of Arabic language and, 130; rise of the State of Israel and, 349; of theory, 11; women in film and, 40–41; of Zionism, 213–16, 332

Europe: Britain, 221–22, 238, 240; colonization by, 210; Euro-Israeli nationalism and, 213; European Christianity and Sephardim and, 211–14; dispossession and, 35–37, 38, 66n63;

Fanon on, 252; female sexuality and, 32; on femininity, 32–33, 64n37; on Jewish identity, 102n4; metaphor used by, 110; on psychoanalysis-archaeology analogy, 32–33, 154; on rape, 33, 271; on translation, 120; Fräulein Elisabeth Von R. and, 32
From Manger to the Cross (Olcott), 84, 94, 95, 104n33
Fukayama, Francis, 290, 370
Fusco, Coco, 312–13, *314*; *The Couple in the Cage: A Gautinaui Odyssey*, 312–13, *314*; Heredia and, 312–13; *Two Undiscovered Amerindians, 314*

Galeano, Eduardo, 276
Gang's All Here, The, 46, 47
Garcia, Anna Maria, 149, 293
Gat, Moshe, 350
Gee, Deborah, 317, *318*
Gender: American family and, 144; bias in illness diagnosis, 141; cartographic images and, 29, *30*, 63n31; cinematic portrayal of God and, 93, 97; colonial encounters and, 19, *20*, 21–24, 62n9; cross-gender identification and, 54, 68n86, 269–70, 300; discovery narratives and, 24–25, 35, 62n17, 62n22, 63n21; heroic status and, 25; labor divisions by, 144; language differences and, 137n31; in nationalist representations, 300–302; sexual violence and, 271–72; social mobility and, 267; Spectacle of difference and, 46–50, 103n18, 185, 311; Third World nationalist revolution and, 299; title translations and, 116, 117–18; transsexuality and, 51, 57–58; tropes of, 19, 21, 51, 57–59, 268
Genette, Gérard, 41
George, Margaret, 171
Getino, Octavio, 111, 296
Ghosh, Amitav, 202, 223, 226–28, 351–52
Gibson, Mel, 94
Gilbert, John, 119
Gilliam, Angela, 149

Glissant, Edouard, 274–75
Globalization, 13–14, 297–98, 327nn9, 10
God: Arab Muslim cultural practices and, 82–83; casting actors as, 91–93; Christian representations of, 91; English as language of, 92, 108; invisibility of, 73, 90, 94, 97; monotheism and, 71–74, 102n4; visual representations of, 74–75, 77, 82, 93–94, 104n33; voice representations of, 97–98
God, the Devil and Bob, 92
Godard, Jean-Luc, 94, 108, 136n20, 137n23; *Breathless*, 120; *Contempt*, 128, 136n20; *Deux ou trois choses que je sais d'elle*, 120, *121*; *Hail Mary*, 94; *Masculin, Féminin*, 119–20; *Sauve qui peut (la vie)*, 137n23; *Tout va bien*, 124
Goitein, S. D., 227, 348; *Mediterranean Society*, 205
Golan, Menahem, 27, 57, 285n35
Gomez, Sara, 293; *De cierta manera*, 295–96, 299
Gomez-Peña, Guillermo, 313, *314*; *Two Undiscovered Amerindians, 314*
Gone With the Wind, 42, 69n90
Gonzales, Leilia, 297
Gorillas in the Mist, 40, 42
Gover, Yerach, 367
Grant, Lila, 317
Grant, Michael, 169–70, 171
Greece: classical statuary of, 179; Cleopatra and, 169–72; Eurocentrism and, 175–78, 281; Greek-Egyptian miscegenation and, 169–70; Greek mimesis and Islamic arabesque and, 80; Hellenism of, 80, 103n20; as point of origin of history, 175; racism in, 172, 197n12
Green, Renee, 313–15
Green Pastures, The (Connelly and Keighley), 92, *93*
Grewal, Inderpal, 8, 297
Griffiths, D. W.: *The Birth of a Nation, 42, 43, 44*; *Intolerance, 23, 24, 31, 33, 185–86*

cinema and, 17, 24, 26, 29–31, 29–
32; Cleopatra and, 195; in Egypt, 36–
39, 239; globalization and, 13–14,
297–98, 327nn9, 10; mestiza as personification of, 301; science and, 29–
31; of scientific discovery, 29–30; verism and, 79

In an Antique Land (Ghosh), 202, 223,
226–28, 351–52

India, 42, 207, 237, 240–42

Indiana Jones, 25, 26, 27, 31, 33–35

Indigenous peoples: colonialism and,
209–11, 221–22; European encounters with, 21–22, 25, 37, 62n9, 62n14,
209–11; *How Tasty Was My Frenchman* and, 21–22, 25, 37, 62nn9, 14;
Inquisition compared to genocide of,
211; minority communities and, 265–
66; whitening of, 21–22. *See also*
Native Americans

Ingram, Rex, 92

Interdisciplinary studies, 6

International Monetary Fund, 242, 299,
327n10

Iraqi Jews: AIU (Alliance Israelite Universelle) and, 343–44; citizenship of,
335, 340; communal identities of, 333–
36; displacement of, 337–40, 355n4;
forced migration of, 337–38; Jewish
identity of, 334–35; Zionism and, 337–
38, 339, 346–47, 350–51

Ishtar, 55, 56

Islam: architecture of, 77, 78; art in, 72,
74, 76–77, 79–81; calligraphy and,
76–77; feminism and, 7, 272, 321–22;
in film, 83–90; graven images and,
77; *Intisar al-Islam*, 86; *al-Jahiliyah*
and, 74; Judeo-Islamic space in, 224–
25; polygamy and, 39; Prophet Muhammad and, 74, 83–84, 86–90;
Qur'an and, 74, 76–77, 82–84, 86–
88, 130. *See also* Arab-Jews; Arabs;
Palestine, Palestinians

Israel: academia in, 363–69, 372, 376,
380n12, 380n19, 381n20, 382nn29,
30, 31; aliyah and, 338–41, 346, 347–
48; Am Oved (press) and, 364; Arab-

Jewish identity in, 225–27, 333–35,
338, 340–42; archaeology in, 220,
347; changing national identities in,
205–6; citizenship in, 229; colonialism of, 216–18, 222, 370, 376; film in,
84–85, 116, 333; ingathering of exiles
(*Kibbutz Galuiot*) by, 215, 216, 328n19,
331–33; Israeli-Palestinian conflict
and, 205, 216, 220–21, 239, 363, 368;
Law of Return and, 331, 332, 376–78;
Mifras (press) and, 365, 366–67;
Mizrahi cultural production in, 224–
26, 231n33, 333–34; modernization
narrative in, 345–46; *Nikui Rosh* and,
84, 85; peace process and, 238, 239,
248n8, 368; political activism of
Sephardim in, 228–29; Promised
Land imagery and, 217, 221; revisionist historians in, 368–74, 382n29,
382n30, 382n31, 383n38; Said's reception in, 362–68; Sephardi cultural
identity in, 224–26; *Siman Kri'a* and,
364; *Tekuma* (TV series) and, 338, 368;
Teoriyah u-vikoret and, 371, 372, 373,
374, 383n38; Westernness of, 216,
225, 346; Yemeni Jews in, 349–50,
357n26, 357n27, 367. *See also* Palestine, Palestinians; Zionist discourse

Iyad, Abu, 365

Jabès, Edmond, 76, 102n11, 231n27

Jabor, Arnaldo, 131

Jackson, Michael, 320

Jacobs, Harriet, 67n64

James, C. L. R., 278, 372

Jameson, Frederic, 46, 52, 67n70

Jamila, 300, 302

Jayawardena, Kumari, 297

Jesus of Nazareth (Zeffirelli), 93–94

Jewish identity: Arab-Jewish identity in
Israel, 225–27, 333–35, 338, 340–42;
Arab-Jews as challenge to, 213–15;
Arabness of Arab-Jews, 201–5, 215,
224–28, 236n39; of Ashkenazim,
204, 206, 224–26; blackness and,
200n44, 222, 231n28, 253–54, 262–
64, 286n40; Chicanos (Crypto-Jews)

Jewish identity (*continued*)
and, 211–12; construction of, 253–54,
258–61; diaspora and, 201–6, 217–
18, 227, 331; Frantz Fanon on, 264–
65; geography in, 333, 336, 340;
hyphenations of, 213–15, 225, 227,
334–35, 339, 341–42, 344; inferiority
complex of, 217, 219; ingathering of
exiles (*Kibbutz Galuiot*) by, 215, 216,
328n19, 331–33; language and, 216;
Middle Easternness of Jews, 224, 225,
226, 229; Muslim Arab culture and,
215, 342–44; Ostjuden and, 225–26,
331; pogroms and, 213, 341–42; problems with terminology of, 334–36;
sabra and, 217–18, *219*, 220, 221, 331,
354; as white, 260, 262, 263, 361. *See
also* Anti-Semitism; Arab-Jews; Israel;
Sephardim; Zionist discourse
Johnson-Odim, Cheryl, 149
Jones, Terry, 94
Judaism: graven images proscribed by,
72, 75, 77, 101n1; Hebraism v. Hellenism, 80; Judaic studies and, 206;
Judeo-Islamic space in, 224; language
and, 72–73, 76, 80, 103n20, 223–24;
as national identity, 335; racial identity
of, 175; *Raiders of the Lost Ark* and, 35,
65n48, 96–97; religious images of, in
film, 84–85; textuality in, 76; universalism of, 277, 288n72
Julien, Isaac, 306

Kanafani, Ghassan, 365
Kant, Immanuel, 71, 101n1, 279, 288n79
Kaplan, Caren, 8, 297, 308
Karanth, Prema, 293
Katterjohn, Monic, 59
Katznelson, Kalman, 346
Key Largo, 112
Khalidi, Rashid, 368
Khalifeh, Sahar, 239
Khdhuri, Sasson, Hakham, 337, 350
Khush (Parmar), 306
Kieslowski, Krzysztof, 117
King and I, The, 24, 40
King Kong, 182

King Solomon's Mines, 27, *28*
Kismet, 31, 52, 186
Kly, Y. N., 279
Knowing Her Place (Krishnan), 306
Kracauer, Siegfried, 24
Kramer, Martin, 363
Krishnan, Indu, 306
Kubrick, Stanley, 108
Kulthum, Umm, 303–5
Kurtz, Stanley, 361, 362

Lacan, Jacques, 252, 373–74
Lady in the Lake, 88
Laing, R. D, 257
Lan, Meri, 141–42
Land, land ownership: images of wilderness and, 18, 221; "make the desert
bloom" imagery and, 221, 347; maps
and mapping and, 26–30, 63nn30, 31;
Palestine as empty land, 217, 331; population transfer of Palestinians and,
369; possession and, 32; Promised
Land imagery and, 217, 221; virginity
imagery and, 19–21, 217, 221–22, 347
Landeta, Matilda, 291
Lang, Fritz, 108
Language: accents and, 130–31; Americanization of, 131, 133; calligraphy and,
72, 75, 76–77; colonialism and, 107–
8, 128–34, 216, 223–24, 257, 377–78;
defined, 106–8; dialects of, 123–24,
128–29, 137n30; dialogue and, 12,
111–13, 116, 119–20, 122–29, 315, 317;
dissemination of American cultural
forms and, 128–29, 137n29; dubbing
(post-synchronization) and, 122–27,
315, 317; English, 107–8, 125, 127–32,
366; exile and, 309–10; hierarchies
of, 107–8; intonations of words and,
134; linguistic reciprocity and, 127–
28, 129, 134; metaphors and, 109–10;
multilingual films and, 121; physical
gestures and, 125–27; as sign of civilization, 129–30; silence and, 96, 110–
13, 118–19, 136n11; social class and,
128; song lyrics and, 108; subtitles
and, 113, 119–23, 136n20, 137n25;

translations of, 113–14, 257–58; transnational communication and, 309–10

Last Temptation of Christ, The (Scorsese), 94

Latin America, 2; Anglo-American intervention in, 130, 239; cinema and, 46–47, *48*, 118; eroticized images of, 47–49; Good Neighbor Policy and, 46; hybridity and, 243, 246, 377–78; Latin American studies and, 361; modernisms in, 243, 246; nationhood in, 246; sterilization policies in, 149; syncretism and, 243; tropicalist movement and, 244, 246; Westernness and, 47, *48*; white heterosexual desire and, 57; women in film and, 291. *See also* Brazil

Latin Lovers, 130

Latinos, 57, 130–31

Lawrence, T. E., 56, 69n88

Leaden Time, The (von Trotta), 117

Lean, David, 56, 130; *Lawrence of Arabia*, 24, 25, 31, 55, 56, *58*, 64n35, 130

Leclerc, Georges-Louie, 179

Lee, Helen, 317

Lefkowitz, Mary, 171, 172

Leigh, Vivian, 183

Le Moine, Yvan, 92

Leo Africanus, 177

Leonviola, Antonio, 92; *Ballerina e buon dio*, 91–92

LeRoy, Mervyn, 130

Levinas, Emmanuel, 277

Lévi-Strauss, Claude, 9

Lévy-Valensi, Eliane Amado, 277

Lewis, Bernard, 361–62, 363

Lewis, Herbert S., 348

Lewis, R. W. B., 19

Leyda, Jay, 123

Life and Passion of Jesus Christ, The (Zecca), 94, 104n33

Liminano, Eva, 291

Lindsay, Jack, 169

Lloyd, F. P., 147

Locke, John, 279

Loshitzky, Yosefa, 367

L'Ouverture, Touissaint, 278, 279

Lubiano, Wahneema, 8

Lubitsch, Ernst, 125

Lumière brothers, 29, 194

Lyotard, Jean-Françoise, 290, 326n1, 370

Macey, David, 32–33

Madmoni, Shoshana, 367

Maginn, William, 179–80

Maids and Madams (Hamermesh), 40

Maimonides, Moses, 75

Malcolm X, 68n86, 287n49

Maldoror, Sarah, 293, 295; *Monongambe*, 294; *Sambizanga*, 294

Mankiewicz, Joseph L., 183, 186, *187*, 188, 189–90

Mannoni, Octave, 19, 256, 271

Marable, Manning, 276

Martin, Emily, 142

Marx, Karl, 252–53, 276

Masalha, Nur, 368, 382nn29, 30

Masculinity: of black men, 260–61, 268, 270; control fantasies and, 25, 29, 30, 32, 55, 57, 59; cross-gender identification and, 54, 68n86, 269–70, 300; eroticism and, 56–57, 186; feminizations of, 56–57, 61n2, 185–86, *187*, 285n27; homoeroticism and, 56–57, 68n86; macho culture in film and, 295–96; mythologies of, 21–22, 142, 150; penis and, 261–62; phallus and, 29–30, 47, 260, 261, 262, 287n27; rescue narratives and, 31, 33, 51–52, 56–60, 68n86; revolutionary masculinist discourse and, 267–69; science and, 152; Third World nationalist revolution and, 299; transgressions of male space and, 57, 59, 60

Maspero, Gaston, 35–36

Massad, Joseph, 368, 378

Mattelart, Armand, 298, 361

Matzpen, 365, 375

Mazrui, Ali, 365

Mazumdar, Vina, 297

McClintock, Anne, 27, 301

Measures of Distance (Hatoum), 306, 308, 309–12

Medical discourses: cultural norms in therapeutic practice and, 257–58, 282; of endometriosis, 142, 145, 150, 156; hysterectomy and, 146; limitations of, 155; pathologizing menstruation in, 145, 150; prejudiced diagnoses of, 145; psychoanalysis and, 32–33, 154, 252, 255–58, 373–74, 383n40; reproductive medicine and, 144, 146–49, 293; sterilization policies and, 148, 149, 293; women's agency in, 151–52, 153–60

Melford, George, 41

Méliès, George, 63n32; *Le Voyage dans la lune*, 29, *30*

Memmi, Albert, 49, 129, 131, 254, 284n5, 372, 383n37

Mercer, Kobena, 319–20

Merleau-Ponty, Maurice, 107

Mernissi, Fatima, 297

Metz, Christian, 108, 109, 112, 135n3

Michael, Sammy, 338–39

Middle East Studies Association (MESA), 362–63

Milagros Lopez, Maria, 149

Millner, Sherry, 152

Mills, Charles W., 279

Mimesis, 77–84, 103nn17, 18

Miranda, Carmen, 47, *48*, 130–31

Mizrahi, Moshe, 121

Mizrahi, Togo, 82

Mizrahim: in academic scholarship, 338, 352–54; allochronic discourse about, 346, 354, 357n19; Arab Muslim culture and, 352–53; Ashkenazim and, 204, 206, 224–26; blackness and, 111, 222, 375; cultural production of, 226, 333–34; dislocations of identity of, 333–36; Euro-Israeli self-image challenged by, 225; as exotics, 348, 353; family structure of, 350; historiography of, 352–54; identity in Israel, 340–41; migrations of, 223, 226, 231n32; North African Jews and, 285n35; Palestinians and, 229; political activism of, 228–29; population transfer of, 332, 333–34; racism

toward, 222, 339, 346–49; self-definition of, 334–35; in Zionist discourse, 215–16, 332–33, 336, 355n1

Moffatt, Tracey, 25, 63n20, 322–24, 329n36

Moi, Toril, 32

Monty Python's Life of Brian (Jones) 94

Morris, Benny, 368, 369

Moses, 73, 74, 84–85, 91, 102n4

Mountains of the Moon, 56

Mudimbe, V. Y., 198n19

Muhammad, Prophet, 74, 83–84, 86–90

Mujeria (Osa/de la Riviera), 306

Mukerjee, Bharati, 231n34

Mulatto/a, 267, 268, 270, 286n43

Mulvey, Laura, 255

Murnau, F. W, 117

Museological projects, 33–38, 342–43, 347

Naldi, Nita, 183

Naqash, Samir, 227

Nasser, Gamal Abdel, 85, 268, 286n45, 305

National Geographic, 51, 80

National identity: of Arab-Jews, 215, 222–23, 334–36, 342–43, 347; of Cleopatra, 185–86, 190–91, 195–96, 200n44; in Egypt, 35–39, 66n63, 133, 171–72, 192–96; in film, 96, 109–13, 118–19, 120, 136n11, 137n25, 306–7, 308–12; geographical belonging and, 207–8; language as, 53, 102n12, 120, 127, 130, 208, 216, 223–24, 231n33, 231n34, 239, 257, 309–10, 366; of minority communities, 265–66; race and racism and, 255, 263–64; in Third World, 7, 13–14, 239, 243, 297–99, 306–8. *See also* Israel

Nationalism: in Algeria, 282, 286n39, 300–302; In America, 7; of Arab-Jews, 214–15, 222–23, 342–43, 347; of Arabs, 181, 193, 282, 335; blackness and, 273–74; of Euro-Israelis, 213–19; gender in nationalist representations and, 300–302; national culture and,

Parry, Benita, 374

Pasolini, Pier Paolo, 124; *The Gospel According to Matthew*, 94

Passage to India, A, 42

Passion of the Christ, The (Gibson), 94

Passion of Remembrance, The (Julien), 306

Pépé le Moko, 130

Peries, Sumitra, 293

Perper, Maria Menna, 156

Persona (Quando as Mulheres Pecam), 116

Peterson, Nancy, 141

Pickford, Mary, 183

Pied Noir, 262, 265, 273

Pieterse, Jan, 229n9, 288n84

Pinky, 44

Piterberg, Gabriel, 367

Pomeroy, Sarah B., 170

Pontecorvo, Gillo, 127, 328n15

Portillo, Lourdes, 306

Postcolonialism: Bhabha and, 371–74, 378, 383nn35, 38, 39, 41; chronologies and, 238–39, 241; development of, 374–75; geographies of, 237–38, 243–44; hybridity and, 244–47, 377–78; independence movements and, 239–40, 246–47; Israeli revisionist historians and, 368–74, 382n28, 382n29, 382n30, 382n31, 383n38; literature of, 236–38; neocolonialism and, 39, 131, 239–43, 240–43, 246, 249n14, 327n10; postcolonial studies and, 3, 4–6, 207–8, 360–62; psychoanalytic theory and, 373–74, 383n40; Third World and, 32n2, 234–36, 238–40, 243, 247, 249n14, 326n2, 375–76; use of term of, 234–39. *See also* Post-Zionism

Postcolonial studies, 4–6, 207–8, 360–62

Poststructuralism, 5, 7, 373

Post–Third Worldist feminism, 291–96, 299–300, 326n2

Post-Zionism: meaning of "post" in, 370–71, 376–77; Oslo Accords and, 368; postcolonial and, 370–71; postmodernism and, 370; revisionist

historians and, 368–74, 382n28, 382n29, 382n30, 382n31, 383n38; Said and, 366–67, 369–70, 382n30

Powell, Michael, 41; Emeric Pressburger and, 24, 41

Powell, Robert, 93–94

Presley, Elvis, 51–52

Privilege (Rainer), 150

Psychoanalysis, 32–33, 154, 252, 255–56, 373–74, 383n40

Queer studies, 3, 6, 7, 10

Question of Color, A (Sandler), 317, 318–19

Quincentennial of the Spanish Expulsion (1492), 21, 213, 214, 223–24, 241

Rabinowitz, Dan, 367

Race, racism: African inferiority, 177, 198n24; in American academia, 3–6; Arabs and, 33, 39, 41–43, 209–10, 213, 215–16, 220, 262, 263, 335; beauty in, 179–80, 182–83, 188, 199n38, 312, 315, 318–20; biological racism, 173–74, 261; blood and, 142, 173–75, 178, 182, 186, 210, 261–62, 273; in cinema, 117, 315, 317; Cleopatra and, 168–76, 178, 182–83, 185, 189–90; community relationalities and, 263–65; construction of identity and, 253–54, 263–64; cross-racial desire and, 41–42, 56–57, 58, 183, 266–68, 270, 300; Enlightenment philosophers on, 279–80, 288n79; exceptionalism and, 3–4; exhibitionism and, 49, 312–15, 329n25; geographies of, 171–72, 255–56, 264, 265; in Greco-Roman world, 172, 197n12; in Hollywood casting, 182–83; infidelism and, 210–11, 230nn11, 12; interracial homoeroticism and, 56–57, 58, 68n86; in Israel, 285n35, 339, 346, 349–50, 357n17, 357n26, 357n27, 367; Jews and, 200n44, 217, 219, 222–23, 262–63, 270, 285n35, 339, 346–50, 357nn17, 26, 27; miscegenation and, 42–46, 67n64, 169–70, 182, 261,

266–67, 270, 273, 285n35; Mizrahim and, 222, 339, 346–47; mulatto/a and, 267, 268, 270, 286n43; national identity and, 255, 263–64; Negritude and, 252, 253, 255, 277; passing and, 189, 260, 261, 270, 317; physiognomy in, 179–81, 185, 186, 261, 262; postcolonial studies and, 5–6; in representations of God, 92–94; in reproductive medicine, 144, 147–49, 293; scientific racism, 173–74, 179, 261–62; skin color and, 174–75, 179, 183, 319, 320; slavery and, 42–43, 67n64, 240, 244, 276, 279–80, 288n79; Spanish immigration policies and, 213; stereotypes of good and evil and, 189–90, 265, 293–94, 324. *See also* Anti-Semitism; Blackness; Rape narratives; Whiteness

Raiders of the Lost Ark, 26, 27, 31, 33–36, 64n35, 65n48, 96–97

Rainer, Yvonne, 150

Rape narratives: Algerian women and, 271; in *The Birth of a Nation,* 42, 43, 44; colonialism and, 261, 268–72; female sexuality in, 42–43; in film, 42, 43, 44, 305; Freud and, 33, 271; gender hierarchies and, 271–72; man-on-man rape, 272; racism in, 42–43, 260; rescue narratives as, 42–44, 57, 59, 85

Rapp, Rayna, 148

Raz-Krakotzkin, Amnon, 367–68

Reiner, Carl, 91

Relationality: of blackness, 258; colonialism and, 40, 207–8; defined, 9–10; ethnic relational studies and, 258–61, 259; Fanon's situational diagnosis and, 251, 255, 264; feminism and, 2; identity and, 255; relational analysis and, 7–8, 10, 11, 251, 259; of Third World with postcolonial, 246–47

Renan, Ernst, 130

Rescue narratives: Arab Jewish migration to Israel, 217; Arabs in, 60; in archaeology, 33–35, 65n53, 193; Cairo Geniza, 201–5, 226–27; European

colonization in, 276; in films, 35, 44, 57–59, 65n48; gender identity in, 68n86; ingathering of exiles (*Kibbutz Galuiot*) in, 215, 216, 328n19, 331–33; land reclamation as, 217, 331, 347; masculinity and, 31, 33, 51–52, 56–60, 68n86; in *The Mummy,* 35–37, 38, 66n63; naming authority in, 19, 333–36; Orientalist discourse and, 51–52; in *Raiders of the Lost Ark,* 26, 27, 31, 33–36, 64n35, 65n48, 96–97; rape narratives and, 42–44, 57, 59, 85; transfer of cultural artifacts as, 33–38, 201–5, 227; veiling and, 272, 292; in Zionist discourse, 369–70

Resnais, Alain, 117

Retamar, Roberto Fernandez, 372

Return of the Jedi, 29, 31

Richards, Nelly, 8

Road to Morocco, 44, 45, 47

Robinson Crusoe, 19, 20, 24–25, 56

Rocha, Glauber, 296, 301; *The Lion Has Seven Heads,* 134

Rocky Horror Picture Show, The, 112, 123

Rodinson, Maxime, 372

Rodney, Walter, 276

Rodriguez, Marta, 293

Rogoff, Irit, 367

Rondon, Candida Beltran, 291

Roots, 190

Rosi, Francesco, 124

Rouch, Jean, 198n19

Ruiz, Raoul, 134

Rushdi, Fatima, 291

Rushdie, Salman, 82–83

Russell, Bertrand, 107

Sabra, 217–18, 219, 220, 221, 331, 354

Sadat, Anwar, 239

Sadji, Abdoulaye, 267

Sahara, 51, 56, 57–58, 60

Said, Edward: *Beginnings,* 378; Bhabha and, 371–74, 383nn35, 38, 39, 41; criticism of, 362–63, 364–66, 371, 372, 374, 376, 378, 380n19; *Covering Islam,* 360; *Culture and Imperialism,* 378; Hebrew translations of, 364–67,

59; veiling and, 32, 47, 49–50. *See also* Body; Cinema; Masculinity; Rape narratives; Women

Shadyac, Tom, 92

Shakespeare, William, 195, 200n50, 271

Shamir, Moshe, 219

Shamir, Shimon, 363

Shammas, Anton, 384n45

Sharif, Omar, 56

Sharoni, Simona, 367

Shawqi, Ahmad, 193, 194–96; *Masra' Klyubatra* (Shawqi), 195

Sheik, The, 41, 44, 49, 55, 56, 57, 60

Shelley, Percy Bysshe, 194

Shenhav, Yehouda, 373, 374

Shields, Brooke, 51, 55, 57–59

Shlaim, Avi, 368

Silences of the Palace (Tlatli), 301, 302–5

Silent movies, 96, 109–13, 118–19, 136n11, 137n25

Simple histoire, Une (Harnoun), 124

Singin' in the Rain, 315–16

Sivan, Emmanuel, 363

Slavery, 42–43, 67n64, 240, 244, 276, 279–80, 288n79

Slaying the Dragon (Gee), 317, *318*

Slechta, Josef, 118

Smith, Kevin, 93

Smith, Mona, 306

Snow, Michael, 115

Social class: of Arab Jews in Israel, 217, *218*; blood as marker of, 175; cosmetic industry advertisements and, 183, 199n38; dialect and, 128–29, 137n30; medical discourse and, 144, 147, 148; racial identity and, 173; repression of women and, 54, 68n78; in Third Worldist film, 296–97, 301, 302–5

Social Text, 364

Solanas, Fernando, 111, 296

Solberg-Ladd, Helena, 293, 295; *Nicaragua up from the Ashes*, 295, 299

Somech, Roni, 200n44

Son of the Sheik, 49, 55, 56

Soyinka, Wole, 195, 200n50

Spanish Expulsion (1492), 21, 208, 209,

212–14, 223–24, 241; *El Santo Oficio* and, 211, 213

Spielberg, Steven, 35, 65n48, 96

Srour, Heiny, 293, 295; *Hour of Liberation* (Sa'at al Tahrir), 295; *Leila wal-dhiab*, 295

Stam, Robert, 14, 103n16, 207, 279

St. Denis, Ruth, 79, 103n18

Steiner, George, 76, 114, 127–28

Strauss, E., 227

Streicher, Julius, 262

Sulieman, Elia, 308–9, 310

Sweet Sweetback's Baad Asssss Song (Van Peebles), 129

Swirski, Shlomo, 381n22

Syncretism: in art, 78; cultural syncretism, 175–78, 212; of Greek mimesis and Islamic arabesque, 80; hybridity and, 212, 244, 245–46, 348; Jewish identity and, 177–78, 210, 214–24; in Latin America, 243; in Mediterranean culture, 78; mestizo and, 174, 244, 274, 301; modern Arabic literature as site of, 77–78; in monotheism, 71; multiculturalism of Moorish Spain and, 210; novels and, 78, 103nn15, 16; in postcolonial studies, 244; of Sephardi-Jewish and Muslim cultures, 214

Taine, Hippolyte, 32

Tarzan, 51, 67n72

Tati, Jacques, 109

Taylor, Elizabeth, 183, 186, *187*, 188, 189–90, *191*

Ten Commandments, The, 31, 35, 72–73, 84, *85*

They Met in Argentina, 44

Thief of Bagdad, The, 31, 55

Third World: anticolonialism and, 8–9; cultural exports from, 298, 328n12; diasporas of, 246; diasporic films of, 306–10, 326n6; exoticism of women, 47–51, 321; film industry in, 29, 118, 131, 291–98, 299–300, 326n2, 326n5, 326n6, 327nn9, 10; First World in, 8–9, 24–25, 131, 297–98,

and, 57, 59; sideshows as, 312–13; spectacle of difference and, 46–50, 185; surveillance of women and, 27, 51, 52, 55, 80, 185–87

Voz do Brasil, 124–25

Vygotsky, Lev, 112

Wahbi, Youssef, 82, 83

Wallerstein, Immanuel, 235

Wavelength (Snow), 115

Weekend in Havana, 46

Welles, Orson, 123; *Touch of Evil*, 128

Wenders, Wim: *Der Amerikanische Freund*, 128; *Im Lauf der Zeit*, 117; *Kings of the Road*, 128

White, Charles, 179

Whiteness: as beauty, 179, 182–83, 185; in *The Birth of a Nation*, 42, 43, 44; Christ images and, 92, 93–94, 186; of Cleopatra, 169, 171–73; cosmetic changes and, 175, 183, 315; in Enlightenment aesthetics, 179; homoeroticism and, 56–57, 58, 68n86; of Jews, 260, 262, 263, 361; miscegenation and, 42–46, 67n64, 169–70, 182, 266–67, 270, 273, 285n35; Negritude Movement and, 252, 253, 255, 277; passing as, 260, 261; racial stereotypes of good and evil and, 189–90, 265, 324; as universalism, 254; whitening of indigenous peoples and, 21–22

Willemen, Paul, 112

Wittgenstein, Ludwig, 107

Women: Aborigine women, 25, 63n20, 322–23, 329n36; African American women, 42–48, 67n64, 147, 267, 271; agency in medical treatment of, 147, 151–52, 153–60; American women's studies and, 4–7; cross-gender identification and, 54, 55–59, 68n86, 269–70, 300; in discovery narratives, 25, 63n21; feminine imagery on maps and, 27, 63nn30, 31; fertility of, 47, 48, 143–44, 148–49, 268, 286n43; gendering of colonial encounters and,

20, 21, 62n9; God portrayed as, 93; harems and, 47–48, 52–55, 67n73, 68n77, 68n78, 186, 311, 321; Hottentot Venus (Saartjie Baartman), 313–15, 329n25; hysteria and, 141–42; miscegenation and, 42–46, 67n64, 169–70, 182, 266–67, 270, 273, 285n35; mulatta, 267, 268, 270, 286n43; as national allegory, 300–302; nudity and, 21–22, 26, 32, 62n14; Palestinian women, 295, 308–12; penetration metaphors and, 29, 30, 32–33, 35; post–Third Worldist feminist film and video, 291–96, 326n2; prostitution and, 303; in revolutionary movements, 269–73, 295–96, 300–302; Third World oppression of, 272–73; veiling of, 32, 47, 49–50, 80, 267–70, 272, 287n52, 300, 321. *See also* Algerian women; Body; Cleopatra; Feminism; Gender; Race, racism; Rape narratives; Rescue narratives; Sexuality

World Organization of Jews from Islamic Countries, 229

Yawar mallku, 149

Yemini, Ben-Dror, 362–63

Yiftachel, Oren, 367

Zecca, Ferdinand, 94, 104n33

Zeffirelli, Franco, 93–94

Zionist discourse: aliyah and, 337, 338–41, 346, 347–48, 353; Arab-Jewish identity in, 65n46, 205–6, 215–18, 224–25, 339–45; common Jewish nationality and, 214–15, 225–26, 336, 342; discovery narratives in, 220–21; East/West dichotomy in, 216, 217, 364–65, 369–70; Eurocentricity of, 213–17, 365; Geniza used in, 227; Hebrew language revival in, 216; ingathering of exiles (*Kibbutz Galuiot*) in, 215, 216, 328n19, 331–33; Islamic-Jewish history in, 213–14, 342; Jewish Holocaust in, 213, 216, 217; *Jugend-*

Zionist discourse (*continued*)
kultur and, 217–18; "make the desert bloom" imagery in, 221, 347; Palestine in, 217, 369, 376–77; pogroms in, 213, 341–42; Promised Land imagery in, 217, 221; rescue narrative in, 369–70; of revisionist historians, 368–74, 382n28, 382n29, 382n30, 382n31, 383n38; sabra in, 217–18, *219*, 220, 221, 331, 354; Said's *Orientalism* and, 363, 364, 366–68; victimization narratives in, 214, 215–16

Al-Zouhour-al-Qatela, 83, 130

ACKNOWLEDGMENTS AND CREDITS

Acknowledgments for Previously Printed Articles

"Gendered Cartographies of Knowledge: Area Studies, Ethnic Studies, and Post-colonial Studies" was published as "Area Studies, Gender Studies, and the Cartographies of Knowledge," *Social Text* 72 (fall 2002): 67–78 (special issue, "911 —A Public Emergency?" ed. by Brent Edwards, Stefano Harney, Randy Martin, Timothy Mitchell, Fred Moten, and Ella Shohat).

"Gender and the Culture of Empire: Toward a Feminist Ethnography of the Cinema" was published under the same title in *Quarterly Review of Film and Video* 131, nos. 1–2 (spring 1991): 45–84 (special issue, "Discourse of the Other: Postcoloniality, Positionality, and Subjectivity," ed. by Hamid Naficy and Teshome H. Gabriel). It appears here with the permission of Harwood Academic Publishers GmbH. Copyright © 1991 Harwood Academic Publishers GmbH.

"Sacred Word, Profane Image: Theologies of Adaptation" was published under the same title in Robert Stam and Alexandra Raengo, eds., *A Companion to Film and Literature* (Malden, Mass.: Blackwell, 2004).

"The Cinema after Babel: Language, Difference, Power" (co-authored with Robert Stam) was published under the same title in *Screen* 26, nos. 3–4 (May–August 1985): 35–58 (special issue, "Other Cinemas, Other Criticisms").

" 'Lasers for Ladies': Endo Discourse and the Inscriptions of Science" was published under the same title in *Camera Obscura* 29 (fall 1993): 56–89 (special issue, "Imaging Technologies, Inscribing Science," ed. by Paula A. Treichler and Lisa Cartwright).

"Disorienting Cleopatra: A Modern Trope of Identity" was published under the same title in *Cleopatra Reassessed*, ed. by Susan Walker and Sally-Ann Ashton (London: British Museum, 2003), 127–38.

"Taboo Memories, Diasporic Visions: Columbus, Palestine and Arab-Jews" was published under the same title in May Joseph and Jennifer Fink, eds., *Performing Hybridity* (Minneapolis: University of Minnesota Press, 1999), 131–56.

"Notes on the 'Post-Colonial' " was published under the same title in *Social Text* 31–32 (spring 1992): 99–113 (special issue, "Third World and Post-Colonial," ed. by John McClure and Aamir Mufti).

"Post–Third Worldist Culture: Gender, Nation, and the Cinema" was published under the same title in *Feminist Genealogies, Colonial Legacies, Democratic Futures*, ed. by M. Jacqui Alexander and Chandra Mohanty (New York: Routledge, 1996), 183–209.

"Rupture and Return: Zionist Discourse and the Study of Arab-Jews" was published under the same title in *Social Text* 75 (spring 2003): 49–74 (special issue, "Palestine in a Transnational Context," ed. by Timothy Mitchell, Gyan Prakash, and Ella Shohat).

"The 'Postcolonial' in Translation: Reading Edward Said between English and Hebrew" was originally published under the title "The 'Postcolonial' in Translation: Reading Said in Hebrew," *Journal of Palestine Studies* 33, no. 3 (spring 2004): 55–75 (special issue, "Essays in Honor of Edward W. Said," ed. Rashid Khalidi).

Credits for Illustrations

Figure 32. Photograph by Lynne Jackson, courtesy of the photographer; Figure 40. Courtesy of Inigo Manglano-Ovalle; Figure 43. Photograph from the author's collection, courtesy of Nathan Axelrod; Figure 44. Photograph by Shimshon Wigoder, courtesy of the photographer; Figure 46. Courtesy of Meir Gal; Figure 53. Courtesy of Women Make Movies, New York; Figure 54. Top, courtesy of Women Make Movies, New York; bottom, courtesy of Elia Suleiman; Figure 55. Courtesy of Coco Fusco; Figure 56. Courtesy of Renee Green; Figures 57–59. Courtesy of Women Make Movies, New York; Figure 60. Courtesy of Arab Film Distribution.

ELLA SHOHAT is professor of cultural studies at
New York University. Translated into many languages,
her publications include *Israel Cinema: East/West and
the Politics of Representation, Unthinking Eurocentrism*
(coauthored with Robert Stam), and *Talking Visions:
Multicultural Feminism in a Transnational Age.*

Library of Congress Cataloging-in-Publication Data
Shohat, Ella
Taboo memories, diasporic voices / Ella Shohat.
p. cm. — (Next wave)
Includes bibliographical references and index.
ISBN 0-8223-3758-4 (cloth : alk. paper)
ISBN 0-8223-3771-1 (pbk. : alk. paper)
1. Feminist theory. 2. Feminist criticism.
3. Postcolonialism. 4. Identity (Psychology) 5. Zionism.
I. Title. II. Series.
HQ1190.S3498 2006
305.4201—dc22   2006001671